D1497999

Flashpoint
Poland
(Pergamon Policy Studies—52)

Pergamon Policy Studies on the Soviet Union and Eastern Europe

Related Titles

 PERGAMON POLICY STUDIES ON THE SOVIET UNION AND EASTERN EUROPE

Flashpoint Poland

George Blazynski

Pergamon Press
NEW YORK • OXFORD • TORONTO • SYDNEY • FRANKFURT • PARIS

Pergamon Press Offices:

U.S.A.   Pergamon Press Inc., Maxwell House, Fairview Park, Elmsford, New York 10523, U.S.A.

U.K.   Pergamon Press Ltd., Headington Hill Hall, Oxford OX3 0BW, England

CANADA   Pergamon of Canada, Ltd., 150 Consumers Road, Willowdale, Ontario M2J, 1P9, Canada

AUSTRALIA   Pergamon Press (Aust) Pty. Ltd., P O Box 544, Potts Point, NSW 2011, Australia

FRANCE   Pergamon Press SARL, 24 rue des Ecoles, 75240 Paris, Cedex 05, France

FEDERAL REPUBLIC OF GERMANY   Pergamon Press GmbH, 6242 Kronberg/Taunus, Pferdstrasse 1, Federal Republic of Germany

Library of Congress Cataloging in Publication Data

Blazynski, George, 1914-
  Flashpoint Poland.

  (Pergamon policy studies)
  Bibliography: p.
  Includes index.
  1. Poland—History—1945-   I. Title.
DK4440.B57 1979   943.8'05   79-15320
ISBN 0-08-024638-9

Printed in the United States of America

To Teresa, my wife,
and to Tali, my granddaughter

Contents

Acknowledgments

This book tries to analyze the position of contemporary Poland between the years 1970 and 1979, the situation inside the country and to look into its future. Poland is the key country in the Soviet bloc and developments there are bound to have repercussions in other "socialist" countries of Eastern Europe. This book is in some respects an unusual one. It is based on extensive research in Poland and in the West - including Britain, United States, Germany, France, Italy, Belgium - and on my long-standing experience of broadcasting to Poland. But, perhaps foremost, it is based on many hundreds of conversations I have had in Poland during my ten visits there between 1964 and 1979 with scores of individuals from all walks of life - from the establishment and with ordinary people, both churchmen and laymen. In a sense it is therefore a collective effort, with contributions from many people.

My acknowledgments thus are rather long. I am grateful to Sir Hugh Greene both for his comments on the draft manuscript and his encouragement. I greatly benefited from conversations with Noel Clark, Maurice Latey, Gregory Macdonald, Konrad Syrop and other former BBC colleagues, from their comments and publications; from conversations with fellow broadcasters in Munich and in Paris; with fellow journalists Chris Cviic of the Economist, Nicholas Carroll of the London Sunday Times, Richard Davy of the Times, David Lascelles of the Financial Times, Victor Zorza formerly of the Manchester Guardian, and many others. I owe much to the many recorded discussions I have held with journalists and experts like Brian Beedham of the Economist, Bernard Nossiter of the Washington Post, André Fontaine and Michel Tatu of Le Monde, Flora Lewis of New York Times, Dr. Leopold Labedz of Survey, Dr. Roger Morgan, formerly of the Royal Institute for Foreign Affairs in London, Philip Windsor of the London School of Economics,

Erwin Duncker of <u>Die Welt</u>, Dieter Schröder of Süddeutsche Zeitung, and Michael Scammel, editor of the London <u>Index</u>.

I am most grateful for the assistance given me <u>by the</u> BBC Central European Service in making available the necessary files; the BBC Monitoring Service for their excellent summaries of world broadcasts; to Radio Free Europe Research Department in Munich and particularly James F. Brown whose help was invaluable.

This book could not have been what it is without many contributions from scores of people in Poland who were most willing to talk openly to me and express their honest and firmly held views and opinions. My heartfelt thanks to all of them from whatever segments of society they come.

My special grateful thanks to Christopher Nowakowski whose "corrective" reading, comments and substantial editorial work contributed greatly to the book in its present form. Thank you also to Carol Bartlett who had the unenviable task of transcribing several tapes, typing the manuscript, and helping in preparing the index.

However none of those whose suggestions or views I have sought are responsible for the book's contents or errors. This responsibility is mine alone.

Introduction:
A Look Back
in Anger

A terrible beauty is born.

W.B. Yeats in "Easter 1916"

Poland, the most Latin country east of the Oder River, has for over ten centuries been an integral part of Western European civilization and heritage in Christian, social, cultural and political terms. Ever since embracing Christianity in 966 Poland has regarded herself as a legendary bastion of Christendom, holding out against the East, or as the only country which could extend eastward the very frontiers of Western civilization, or both. In the process foreign armies have raced across Poland's frontiers, killed her people and burned her cities. The Germans and the Russians have throughout history been the principal offenders, their excesses in modern times dwarfing in horror anything attempted before. Yet more than once Poland has saved the West from an Eastern deluge of one kind or another and suffered in consequence. The Poles' long record of suppression, revolt and, on occasion, of conquest, include countless examples of suicidal bravery, and very few of calculated prudence.(1)
  Whatever history held in store for them the Poles always relied on the West. They still do in more modern and qualified terms - despite the bitter disappointments in the aftermath of World War II. A thousand years of history cannot be erased from people's minds at one stroke by any political and social system. Polish idealism and romanticism have however gone: they lie buried beneath the ruins of somber wartime memories. A cold political realism, often tainted by cynicism, has come into being instead. The Poles have become much more politically mature and sophisticated than before - often, indeed, to

the overripeness of skepticism. The nation's modern awareness has been shaped in this manner after it has been sys-
tematically deceived by its own rulers, and sometimes by
others.(2)

Years of Nazi occupation followed by years of Stalinist
terror firmly established antiauthoritarian feelings linked with
patriotic nationalism more obviously than perhaps anywhere
else in Europe. The Poles are adept at frustrating the objectives of any authority and particularly of one which they do
not easily accept.(3) They have remained strongly in-
dividualistic, with an abhorrence of uniformity, a sense of
humor, a pride in national history and in their own achievements. Like quicksilver, the nation eludes all firm pressures
to conform while, at the same time, accepts grudgingly the
reality of unavoidable geopolitical limitations, and tries to
secure maximum advantage from them.

Particular wartime and postwar events have contributed
greatly toward the pronounced formation of the nation's attitudes and toward the present situation in Gierek's Poland,
which this book attempts to analyze. If the Poles now look
back in anger they have every reason to do so. However, it
is not my intention in this book to go into historical details
which have been interpreted thoroughly in many other publications. But certain facts remain unalterable, and must be
considered. The Poland of 1939 lost the war. After the war
the completely alien ideology and political system of communism
were imposed on the people, not by a national revolution, but
by the advancing Soviet armies.

During the years of German occupation, an underground
state, unique in Nazi-ruled Europe, was born in Poland - a
state with its own Home Army (380,000 strong), its own underground parliament, courts, press, vast provincial administrative network and the largest intelligence organization
anywhere in Europe, which supplied the Allies with vital
information. The London-based Polish government in exile was
represented in the country by a minister plenipotentiary.

The communists (who had before the war existed illegally
as a small and politically insignificant party) appeared on the
underground scene only after the German invasion of Russia,
except for Gomulka and a handful of so-called "native" communists who had remained in the country after the German
invasion against the orders of the Comintern. One of the first
actions of the communists was to accuse the Home Army of
being anti-Soviet, which was true in so far as the overwhelming majority of the nation was anticommunist.

It became clear that Poland, because of its geographical
position, was the primary objective of Stalin's policy in Eastern
Europe. A noncommunist Poland would have excluded the
Soviet Union from Eastern Europe. Poland thus became in
many respects both the crux of the British-American-Soviet

alliance and its bone of contention.(4)   Stalin's long-term plan of expansion, the helplessness of the Western powers in what was a sphere of Soviet military operations, the rejection of Churchill's idea of a second front along the "soft underbelly of Europe," all prejudged the fate of Poland.

The first Soviet step in September 1939 was the annexation of over a third of Poland's prewar eastern territories in full agreement with Hitler.   After the German invasion of Russia, Stalin established diplomatic relations with the London Polish government, and agreed to "amnesty" thousands of imprisoned Poles and to form a 75,000-strong Polish army on Soviet soil, which he soon forced out of Russia by cutting off its vital supplies.

The second step was the mass murder of Polish officers in the Katyn forest.   The American House of Representatives select committee has declared unanimously that the Soviet NKVD was responsible for this deed.   Simultaneously a Soviet-sponsored political group of Polish communists was formed in Moscow, while a Soviet-led division was also organized. Trained activists were parachuted to Poland to re-create the Communist party (under the seemingly innocent name of the Polish Workers' party), to infiltrate the Polish underground state, set up cells for an eventual seizure of power and to denounce members of the Polish national resistance to the Gestapo.   Cooperation with the Gestapo in this particular task also became the top assignment for the Soviet intelligence network in Poland.

In January 1944, the Soviet army crossed the prewar Polish-Soviet frontier and enjoyed the local help of Home Army detachments acting on orders from London.   Very quickly, however, the Home Army units were arrested and their officers shot.   And finally in August 1944 when the massive uprising started in Warsaw, the Soviet armies stood calmly on the east bank of the Vistula River, quietly watching the city for over two months while the Nazis suppressed the uprising and burned Warsaw to the ground.

Together with their own puppet "provisional government" the sheer force of the Red Army managed to brutally eliminate any national, independent groups in the country.   The way was cleared for a complete sovietization of Poland.   While the country was shifted westward all the opponents of the regime were eliminated, forced to flee or imprisoned.   Step-by-step the country was transformed into a perfect satellite state, obedient to Moscow's orders, ruled by secret police and exploited by the Soviet Union as few colonies have ever been.(5)   For every 1,000 citizens in prewar Poland, 220 perished - a much higher percentage than in the Soviet Union. Thus in the shadow of foreign tanks, and from out of the ruins of Warsaw and other cities, from the ashes of their recent past, the disillusioned and exhausted Poles began the tremendous job of reconstructing and rebuilding their country.

In 1951 Gomulka, the general secretary of the Communist party, was arrested. His "sins" were "Titoism" and "bourgeois nationalism," one of the periodical aberrations of the communist system. Until the summer of 1948 he had served Soviet purposes in Poland well. In the difficult task of imposing an alien communist regime on his country he had acted both as a driving force and as a lubricant.(6) But for all that, Gomulka has realized that he would never be able to impose communism in Poland if the Party were to remain exclusively the guardian of Soviet interests. His nationalism was thus a form of compromise between communism and the people.

During the war, Gomulka had tried to organize anti-German resistance even before Hitler attacked Russia and then condemned the communists' cooperation with the Gestapo. Later he strongly opposed the dismantling and looting of German property by Soviet troops on Western territories assigned to Poland and clashed on this issue with Marshal Rokossovsky, commander of Soviet armies.(7) Then he opposed the blind imitation of Soviet "socialist" experiences and quickly came into conflict with his Stalinist colleagues and with Stalin himself. Gomulka argued against agricultural collectivization, maintained that there was no need for a single Party dictatorship and that the pace of industrialization ought to be adjusted to Poland's needs. He thus advocated a "Polish road to socialism."

In contrast with the practice in neighboring countries Gomulka was not brought to trial for fear of what he could say about the past misdeeds of his Polish comrades, but was quietly exiled in a security police villa near Warsaw instead. This way he was available in October 1956 to rescue the Party from complete disintegration.

Gomulka was arrested by Lieutenant Colonel Swiatlo, deputy director of "Department 10" of the Polish Ministry of Public Security, who defected to the West in December 1953 and disclosed all the intimate details of the Party leaders' crimes and intrigues over several years. Department 10 was responsible for the ideological and political purity of the Party leadership: a counterintelligence service against all sorts of "deviations" - actual, imaginary or simply fabricated for specific purposes. Swiatlo was in charge of all the operations and files, and in emergencies could contact Beria directly. The picture he presented of personal relations between top communists and their attitude to many innocent victims of their terror was particularly nauseating. The overwhelming impression was one of a group of utterly ruthless and dishonest men who stopped at nothing in order to obey the orders of their Soviet masters and to foster their own private interests.(8)

Swiatlo was interviewed by this author for several weeks in Washington and his revelations were beamed to Poland, from

September 1954 onward, in over 150 broadcasts by Radio Free
Europe. Never, save in wartime, did any broadcasts have
such a massive and captive audience. The Party was shaken
to its very roots, the secret police apparatus completely de-
stabilized.

Even with the milder climate in Moscow, Swiatlo's broadcasts sparked off a specific Polish popular movement for
democratization and for greater liberalization of political life,
in which the leading roles were played by the intelligentsia
and the students, by the young workers and some young
Party activists. Fear of the security police was quickly disappearing. Writers and journalists who had been hitherto
afraid to write the truth now began to do so. Censorship was
eased. People questioned everything publicly and loudly and
came near to questioning the communist system itself. The
thaw in Poland in 1955-1956 went further than anywhere else
in Eastern Europe.

In the specific Polish conditions then prevailing the very
opening of political safety valves brought about the explosion
it was intended to prevent. This was preceded by
Khrushchev's denounciation of Stalin at the twentieth Soviet
Party congress and the mysterious death of Bierut ("muscovite"
Polish Communist party leader) in Moscow during the congress.
Straining under appalling living conditions, thousands of
workers took to the streets in Poznan on June 28, 1956 demanding "bread," "freedom," and "the end of Soviet domination." They attacked prisons, Party buildings and the police
headquarters. The security police opened fire and the army
intervened, but the soldiers fraternized with the demonstrators. Crack troops restored order - though with clear
restraint. For the Party itself, bitterly divided internally, the
Poznan revolt was a political disaster; 53 were dead, over 300
injured. The riots showed that the workers were bitter and
ready to fight, that people were solidly against the regime,
that the Party organization was bankrupt, and that the army
and the uniformed militia were wholly unreliable.

Poznan also helped to bring home the fundamental contradiction of communism. If a modern society is to be run
efficiently, its people must be given freedom and initiative.
But when this happens they may take a view of their rights
and interests which is quite different from that of the ruling
party. Poznan, in fact, was the clearest demonstration that
the communist's mythical "leading" role in a single-party
system was out of date.

Except for this last imperative of the system, events in
Poland had gone too far by then to reverse the course toward
more humane change, even if the Party initially tried to blame
"imperialist agents" for the revolt. Bowing before dangerously
growing pressure from below, the new leaders called desperately on Gomulka for help and reinstated him as a top Party

authority at the eighth Central Committee plenum on October 19, 1956. A truly revolutionary atmosphere reigned in the country with workers and students standing by waiting to be armed. Soviet troops began moving toward the capital. Polish officers disobeyed orders from their minister of defense, Soviet Marshal Rokossovsky, himself of Polish origin. Then four members of the Soviet politburo led by Khrushchev descended unexpectedly on Warsaw. But heavily armed units of the Internal Security Corps loyal to Gomulka took over Warsaw and deployed along positions commanding all approaches to the capital with strict orders not to allow any army formations to enter the city. In the Belveder Palace the Soviet leaders became virtual prisoners of the Poles and on at least one occasion there was an exchange of fire between Polish army units and advancing Soviet troops.

Gomulka became first secretary of the Party and outlined the specific "Polish road to socialism." He purged the Party and the army of Soviet advisers and officers, and convinced the Russians that the domestic concessions were designed to both strengthen socialism in the country and to improve Soviet-Polish relations once Soviet economic exploitation of the country ceased. He also released the leader of the Catholic Church, which had been the mainstay of Polish resistance, Cardinal Wyszynski, from internment.

Gomulka was not the architect of the "Polish October." He was thrust into power on the crest of events and the party managed to effect the transfer of leadership simply because he had been available. His strength rested largely on noncommunist foundations. The support given him by the people was essentially anti-Soviet and anticommunist even though the illusory hopes for a better democratic form of communist government and for the sovereignty of Poland were fairly strong both within and without the Party. Meanwhile, Cardinal Wyszynski sensed the Polish mood with perfect accuracy, recognizing in Gomulka the man of the hour, and used his tremendous authority in the cause of realism and moderation. The result was that the October revolution remained a guided one. And as far as Khrushchev was concerned the Soviet leader faced uncomfortable alternatives given the mood of the Polish people and the uprising in Hungary, catalyzed by events in Poland.

The tragedy of the "Polish October" has always been that people wanted to see in it seeds of further evolution toward a more comprehensive freedom, albeit within the geopolitical requirements. Hopes were running too high and proved to be entirely unjustified, but not because the leaders betrayed the "spirit of October." They betrayed the people's trust, but they did not betray themselves. In Gomulka's "Polish road" program there were two categories of changes: those changes in which he himself had always believed, and other changes forced on him by strong pressure from below. In time the first category of changes was essentially retained although somewhat curtailed. The changes in the second category were all drastically withdrawn.

October was not the beginning of a new era, but the beginning of the end, of the reversal. It resulted in the restabilization of the power system shattered by popular pressure. And Gomulka spent the remainder of his 14 years in office chipping steadily away at the pedestal his countrymen had built for him in 1956.(9) Yet with all these qualifications it would be unrealistic to minimize the significance of these events. The Poles had demonstrated that no power is omnipotent, that even a highly oppressive system can be attacked and compelled to retreat, and that, even in a country whose independence was limisted by geopolitical realities, successful pressure could be exerted without provoking Soviet military intervention.

Poland's "autumn" in March 1968 marked another sad milestone in its history. It was compounded of three elements; massive student demonstrations fully supported by intellectuals, a deep leadership crisis with Gomulka on the brink of downfall, and the threat of a "Czechoslovak infection." And for the first time in Polish history, antisemitism became the official policy of the government when Gomulka, after the six-day Arab-Israeli war warned against "a Zionist fifth column." In the climate of regression from October 1956 thousands of students demonstrated peacefully in Warsaw and other cities demanding freedom of expression, abolition of censorship, and shouting for "a Polish Dubcek." Warsaw writers publicly denounced Party interference in cultural activity and creative endeavors. Massive and brutal reprisals by the security police under General Moczar (minister of the interior) followed and some order was restored after several days. Almost 3,000 students were arrested.

Moczar controlled not only the security forces, but also the militia and mass media. A man of strong nationalist leanings, and leader of the Partisans (a veterans association) he opposed Moscow-imported communist leaders of Jewish origin and made his bid for power, supported by some hard-liners in the Party. To his repertoire he added the deplorable campaign to investigate and purge the Jews. They were made the scapegoats for what was a rebellion of the young thinking generation against double-think and double-talk, opportunism and downright lies.(10) The students had flown in the face of what they had been taught. They had demanded the right to think for themselves and had grown sick of sterile conformity.

It was touch and go for Gomulka who pursued two lines of attack to save himself. First, he went along with Moczar to an extent, maintaining the Partisans in their already strong positions and introducing his own loyal supporters into other posts. Secondly, he managed to convince some ambitious younger Party members that they had nothing to gain with Moczar but had a real chance with the present leadership. Finally at the November 1968 Party congress politboro (PB) member Gierek's support saved Gomulka and most of his associates from defeat.

But the real clue to Gomulka's rescue was the invasion of Czechoslovakia and the Brezhnev doctrine. Gomulka was a persistent and pressing advocate of Soviet armed intervention, arguing that if the rot were not stopped in Prague he could not guarantee what would happen in Poland. After the intervention and once Brezhnev launched his doctrine of limited sovereignty, Gomulka was safe for a while. The more so since Moczar and his views were unacceptable in Moscow. Unwittingly, perhaps, Gomulka had contributed to Moscow's policy formation by his pressure to invade Czechoslovakia.

And so the scene was set for what was known as Gomulka's "little stabilization" - a euphemism for economic stagnation, internal political inertia and uniformity. Isolated in his crumbling tower of power, surrounded by two or three trusted associates, suspicious of "counterrevolution" everywhere, Gomulka completely lost touch with the situation in Poland.

List of Abbreviations

AFP	Agence France Presse
AND	Augemeine Deutsche Nachrichter
ANSA	Name of the Italian Press Agency
AP	Associated Press
BBC	British Broadcasting Corporation
BPO	Basic Party Organization
CC	Central Committee of the Polish United Workers Party (Communist)
CCTU	Central Council of Trade Unions
CDU	Christian Democratic Union (West Germany)
CDW	Committee for the Defense of Workers
CIC	Catholic Intelligentsia Club
CSCE	Conference on Security and Cooperation in Europe (Helsinki)
CSU	Christian Social Union (West Germany)
DPA	Deutsche Press Agentur
FNU	Front of National Unity
MBFR	Mutual Balanced Forces Reduction (conference in Vienna)
PAP	Polish Press Agency
PB	Political Buro of the Central Committee of the United Workers Party
PCIC	Polish Catholic Intelligentsia Club
PUWP	Polish United Workers Party (Communist)
RFE	Radio Free Europe
SCC	Secretariat of the Central Committee of the Polish United Workers Party
SPD	Socialist Party of Germany (Socialistische Partei Deutschland)
SWB	Summary of World Broadcasts
UPI	United Press International
VPC	Voivodship (provincial) Party Committee

I

Gierek's Miracle: December 1970- June 1976

1 Gomulka's Legacy

> Resolved to die in the last
> dyke of prevarication.
>
> W. Burke

"The Polish economy is at a sharp turning point and all the wheels are grinding to a halt," an economist summarized the situation to me in Warsaw in 1969, and nobody seemed to know what to do. Since 1969, the leadership decided on a transition from an extensive to an intensive economy, with emphasis on profitability, wages related to productivity, limited measures of decentralization, and efficiency in production for export. Priority was given to "selective development" - to industries essential for modernizing the economy and those with the best prospects for competing on world markets.(1)

An industry disorganized by sporadic reforms and conflicting directives was unable to adapt its output to the changing patterns of industrial and consumer demands. Much of Poland's substantially expanding output ended up as unwanted stock gathering dust in the nation's warehouses, and by the end of 1970 their total value reached roughly half the estimated 1970 gross national product.(2) The basic fault, much older than 1969, was overinvestment in heavy industry at the expense of consumer industries and, in particular, a marked underinvestment in agriculture. All criticisms for the intelligentsia and signals of popular discontent were either ignored or provoked the angry retort from Gomulka that the country was already living beyond its means and there was no scope for improvement.(3)

Grave errors in agrarian policy and two consecutive years of bad harvest combined to produce a major food crisis.

3

Gomulka, finding himself in a weak position within the Party, and pressed by an ideologically motivated dislike in some Party circles of the growing prosperity of the country's essentially private peasantry and by the dogmatic goal of achieving self-sufficiency in grain, began to increase the prices charged to the peasants for fodder, while holding meat procurement payments steady. By thus eliminating or reducing the peasant's profit margin, this policy decreased incentives in animal husbandry. Poland was suddenly faced with severe shortages of meat and dairy products.(4)

The country also faced the specter of mass unemployment. A PB decree of 1970 ordered industry to lay off 200,000 surplus workers and specified how many people each enterprise was to dismiss. Since no alternative employment was provided, the number of jobless began to rise, and the 1971-1975 economic plan envisaged half a million unemployed.(5) Poland had the lowest rate of increase in real wages of all the countries in Eastern Europe, only 1.7 percent in 1970. Moreover, in economic reform and technology it was clearly lagging behind all the East European countries.

The mood of impatience and the sense of resignation felt by many Poles as a result of the regime's "do-nothing" policies, were chiefly responsible for the decline in national morale, which reached its lowest ebb since Gomulka's return to power in 1956.(6) While the leadership was not unaware of the implications of these developments, there were very few indications that it possessed the ability or the credibility to initiate the comprehensive reforms so obviously required.

Plans for starting a new system of economic management were to be introduced on January 1, 1971. In January, too, for the first time, investment funds would be allocated according to financial criteria rather than by decree. Although in May 1970 the Central Committee (CC) had approved a new system of material incentives based on the principle that workers' earnings should reflect the economic performance of individual enterprises, Gomulka decided that there should be no wage increases until the middle of 1972 because of the unexpected food shortages and the perennial shortage of other consumer goods. To the workers the new system was tantamount to a two-year wage freeze and in many cases a decline in real earnings.(7)

The trouble was that these botched reforms, however necessary, involved price increases. A wholesale price system which has not changed in ten years was bound to be put out of line with production costs, and so was the retail price system. The extraordinarily inept handling of the announcement of the steep price increases would have been enough to arouse the anger of the people at any time. Coming as it did just before Christmas, the government's announcement proved to be too much to bear. This was the drop which made the brimming cup of mistrust overflow. Any government which could act thus, especially in Poland, seemed to be possessed by a death wish.

The motives of the economic reform program of 1969-1970 pointed to a certain irony in the course of events that led to Gomulka's fall. The reform program was inspired, at least in general outline, by the younger technocrats in the Party leadership who were taken into key Party positions by Gomulka himself in 1968 when, with their help, he defeated Moczar's bid for power. These were younger, better educated men largely uninvolved in the factional battles of the late 1950s and early 1960s. In 1969 they demanded repayment of the debt Gomulka had incurred in 1968. They began to move ahead politically on their own and during 1969 appeared to have an important voice in determining major policy shifts in Poland. But these were the same innovations which Gomulka had stubbornly rejected throughout the sixties and some aspects of which he had fiercely denounced as revisionism. Now he had submitted to the influence of new forces within the Party leadership. In the end Gomulka was made a scapegoat for his colleagues.

Economic problems apart, there was another factor which led to the December eruption: the enduring and mutual lack of confidence between the Polish people and their leaders. Besides, a new class was making itself felt: the workers. Praised to the skies and exploited to the bone under Stalinism, they were beginning to feel that they were coming into their own.(8) The self-perpetuating Party bureaucracy was still remote from the class whose "vanguard" it was supposed to be, but economic reform programs changed the workers' situation. The rusty but somehow cozy factories, those "indoor-relief" houses in which enormous work forces enjoyed total job security, in which there was no point in excessive effort and no bother about whether the product was wanted or not - all that was to vanish. Some factories would have to shut. Some workers would become underpaid. Shop prices would begin to rise, as the old socialist subsidies were taken off, and this terrifying prospect of insecurity faced men and women whose trade unions were merely a transmission belt for whatever changes the Party machine was decreeing from above.

The tragic December events were, therefore, preceded by years of bitterness and discontent with social and economic policy and with the way of managing the Party and the state.

2 One Week That Shook the Communist World: December 1970

They rose in dark and evil days
To right their native land,
They kindled here a living blaze
That nothing shall withstand.

J.K. Ingram in " Memory of the Dead"

The chronicle of events given below is an attempt to show the day-by-day and even hourly changes which took place in Poland during one week in December 1970. In trying to reconstruct the events as they occurred, I have relied on media coverage, both Polish and Western, as well as eye-witness accounts by people I have spoken to in Poland who were either themselves participants in the events or, who, working as journalists, had a grandstand view of history in the making. Other sources include conversations I have had with members and chairmen of various strike committees which sprang up as well as with various Party officials and ordinary people. Not the least of my sources was Gomulka's own un-witting contribution in the form of a secret memorandum in which he presented his version of December events and circulated it to trusted Party activists in 1971.

GDANSK AND WARSAW

Wednesday, December 9
Warsaw
    The politburo of the Party decides on wide-ranging in-creases in prices of consumer goods, to be partially offset by

reductions in the prices of consumer durables. This decision is taken by Gomulka, Kliszko and Jaszczuk, and is fully supported by Moczar. Gierek leads the opposition to the price package. He bangs the table and declares that he cannot associate himself with a decision which would be so unfair to the working people. Gierek votes against the increases and then leaves the meeting.

Saturday, December 12

A letter from the politburo justifying the decision is read out at meetings of Party activists throughout the country. Some of the Party secretaries read out what they were told to read and then admit that they are depressed, and have completely lost faith.

Deputy Premier Kociolek, who had been first Party secretary in Gdansk, December 1967 - June 1970, arrives in Gdansk and at the Voivodship (Provincal) Party Committee (VPC) meeting explains the reasons for the increases in food prices. The increases are rejected as "madness" by the meeting. A worried Kociolek telephones Gomulka in Warsaw, but is told that there will be no going back on the decision.

Late in the evening, Radio Warsaw announces that the changes in the retail prices of several consumer commodities and manufactured products, as approved by the government, will come into force the following day, Sunday, December 13. Increases in food prices will range between 3.9 percent and 36.8 percent. Durable consumer goods are to go up between 6.7 percent and 69 percent and this is to include such substantial items as building materials, coke, lignite, textiles, footwear, shirts, knitwear, clothing etc. The prices of some other consumer durables are, however, to be reduced by 8.6 percent to 40.5 percent. Families with the lowest incomes are promised an additional family allowance in 1971. At the same time prices paid to peasants for their products are to be increased but they will also have to pay 22.4 percent more for fodder.

According to official sources the price changes will reduce the real incomes of the families in the lower income brackets by two percent(1), but in fact it is nearer seven percent. The main burden of these price changes will fall on the urban population.

Monday, December 14

Gdansk - 0730 hours

Three thousand workers from two departments of the Gdansk shipyards march to the administration building and ask to talk with the authorities.

1100 hours

A well-disciplined column of about 1,000 shipyard workers has marched on the Party provincial committee building. A junior secretary of the VPC, Jundzill, tries to speak to the gathering crowd...his words were greeted with whistles and

drowned out in the uproar. No other Party official is willing
to negotiate with the workers. They are ordered instead to go
back to work and to behave themselves; then talks could
begin. "In our workers' democracy," the workers are told,
"there is a time and a place and there are legally established
forms of discussion between representatives of society and the
authorities elected by society."(2) This hypocrisy heightens
feelings among the crowds. Fist fights erupt. The demonstrators seize a militia patrol car.

The workers' column, now swollen by workers from other
shipyard departments and factories, proceeds to the Gdansk
Polytechnic calling on the students to join the demonstration.
The students refuse.(3) Another group of workers tries
unsuccessfully to persuade the personnel on duty at the radio
station to broadcast an appeal to all workers in the country.
1600 hours
        The first clash between the demonstrators and the militia
occurs: a column of motorized militia patrols is too weak to
hold back a crowd of over 3,000. The vanguard of the crowd
pushes ahead, throwing paving stones at the militia and
security police. The crowd marches on the Party headquarters
once more. They shout: "We want bread!" and "The press
lies!" Young men hurl rocks through the windows of the
press house, a theatre and the investment bank.(4)
1815 hours
        Another attack is staged by the crowd on the Party
headquarters. They manage to burn the printing plant located
in the cellar. Security police and militia go into action, using
tear gas, but this has little effect. Appeals to disperse fail
and the clashes outside the building as well as in front of the
main railroad station and in some other parts of the city continue until 2200 hours. Buses, cars, newsstands, shops, and
fire engines are burning all over the city.
Monday, December 14
Warsaw - 0900 hours
        The sixth plenum of the CC assembles to discuss the
crucial tasks facing economy in 1971. Gomulka mentions that
the PB has sent a special letter about price increases to the
Party organizations, but dismisses the question of public
reaction as of no real consequence.

The news of the disturbances in Gdansk reaches Warsaw
at 1300 hours when the CC is still in session. The meeting is
not informed of the events. Radio, television and press are
silent on what has been happening on the coast. However,
the news does infiltrate into the Party headquarters and, in
fact, two simultaneous plenary sessions seem to be taking
place: one, official, in the conference hall, under the watchful
eyes of Gomulka, the other with members gathered in the
lobbies seeking some links with the bitter, tragic reality of the
emotions bursting on the streets of Gdansk and rolling on with

terrible momentum. Immediately after the plenum, the Gdansk VPC first secretary, Karkoszka, and PB member Deputy Premier Kociolek return to Gdansk. A "local general staff" is formed to take charge of the situation.

Foreign Minister Jedrychowski flies to Moscow and returns later in the evening.

Tuesday, December 15
Warsaw - 0000-0100

In the Party headquarters Gomulka denounces the disturbances as counterrevolutionary attacks on the Party and the state by antisocialist elements. He asks Brezhnev for "brotherly Party" help to squash the counterrevolution. He also sends his closest associate, PB member Kliszko, to the coast to take command of operations. He takes with him the chairman of the trade unions, PB member Loga-Sowinski.

In his subsequent secret memorandum Gomulka maintains that Kliszko misinterpreted his theory of counterrevolution. What he told Kliszko was that each open protest against the people's power served the interests of counterrevolution, regardless of the motives of those who protest and thus became hostile to the people's power. He never suggested to Kliszko that the security forces should open fire, but ordered him instead to act "energetically" and to ensure that peace and order prevailed. Gomulka admitted however: "My basic error was that I, myself, did not go to the coast."

Tuesday, December 15
Gdansk - 0100 hours

Shipyard night-shift workers refuse to go to work and announce a general strike for 0700 hours.

Later Kliszko arrives with Loga-Sowinski and immediately goes into hiding in the headquarters of the provincial trade unions, where he establishes his "operational command." According to his own version he was not sent by Gomulka but went on his own initiative in full consultation with Moczar who was in charge of security forces. A Yugoslav journalist on the spot reports that Kliszko immediately assumed supreme command.(5) He was the one who ordered the proclamation of a state of emergency. It was Kliszko who gave the order to fire on the workers, and who sent the messages to Warsaw about the real outbreak of a counterrevolution. He interfered with all the decisions of the "local operational staff" (Kociolek and Karkoszka) and faithfully maintained the counterrevolution theory.

0700 hours

Over 1,500 workers gather in front of the administration building of the Lenin shipyards. The first secretary of the local Party committee tries to speak but he is met with cries of "Out! Get rid of him!"

A column of over 3,000 marches towards the city and is joined by many others. The marchers shout: "Hang Gomulka!

Gomulka out! Cyrankiewicz out! Kliszko, Kociolek, Moczar, out! Out! Out!" The head of the column approaches the militia headquarters and the presidium of the Municipal National Council, and is joined, according to subsequent local media reports by a crowd of rowdies and hooligans. The militia headquarters and the prison are attacked by the crowd, shouting, "Free the arrested." A cloud of tear gas hangs over the area, as the militia using their truncheons try to stop the attack. The crowds, armed with iron bars, break into the building and set the ground floor on fire.

A pitched battle between security police and demonstrators rages in front of the Municipal National Council buildings, and another struggle develops at the main railway station. A column of black smoke rises near the station. Several militia and security forces cars and trucks are burning.

0800 hours

Security police helicopters circle above the Lenin shipyards, transmitting accurate reports to armed units of the militia on the ground. Groups of workers leaving the shipyard to join the demonstration in town are now suddenly fired upon by the militia shooting from hiding places at street corners. The Lenin shipyards are in an uproar. Another column is forming. The management warns the people not to go out into the streets, but the workers do not listen. They move toward the gate but find that the shipyards are surrounded by security police. Shots are fired again. The workers turn back and stay in a tight, silent crowd in front of the management building. Two of them are dead, 11 injured. At 0900 hours the Lenin shipyard workers proclaim a sit-down strike. In other plants and factories throughout the coast the strike spreads and rallies are in progress.

0930 hours

The crowd of demonstrators, now over 10,000 strong, shaken by the first victims, attack the Party building with redoubled fury. "The silent passivity of the crowd of adults, their indifferent or aggressive attitudes, making it impossible to save the people inside the Party building, is horrifying," reports the Party daily, Glos Wybrzeza. The workers set the provincial Party building on fire using various incendiary devices. The security police inside fire into the air from the fifth floor but the salvo brings a roar of laughter from the crowd in the streets.

Evacuation of the building is ordered. People try to slide down from the windows on ripped-up stair carpets. The security forces in the courtyard are surrounded by the aggressive crowd. Faces are grim. Party employees fleeing from the burning building are beaten up.

Two militia officers are trapped inside the Party building. The crowd pronounces a death sentence on them. The fire

department appliance coming to the rescue is stopped and set on fire. Attempts to evacuate the officers by helicopter come to nothing... the wind keeps blowing away the rescue line.
1445 hours
With some difficulty the security police manages to push the crowd away from the Party building. The two trapped men manage to leave the burning building wrapped in wet rags after running along the flaming corridors.
1500 hours
Elsewhere in the city the battle is still raging, exploding tear-gas canisters are heard, and gas gets into peoples' eyes. A column of coast guard unit carriers, summoned to protect public utilities, is moving up. Outside the main railroad station young men jump on the armored cars and force the guards to leave three vehicles. One of the young men falls under the treads of the armored car. People carry the victim into the hall of the station. Flowers are showered on him. The excited crowd set fire to a plundered newsstand and a neighboring kiosk. The flames spread to the baggage and mail rooms of the station.
1800 hours
A curfew is introduced throughout the triple city of Gdansk, Sopot, and Gdynia. It is decided to call out the army into the city. Fire brigades and militia are patrolling the streets.
The outcome of the day's riots is grim. The headquarters of the provincial Party committee, of the Municipal National Council, and the railway station are burned down. Many shops have been looted and demolished. Six people were killed and 300 injured according to official announcements. The militia arrested 120 persons for plundering shops.
Deputy Premier Kociolek appears on Gdansk television and says: "The demonstrations and riots have been exploited by hooligans and social scum. Forces safeguarding public order used firearms in self-defense and the authorities are determined to do everything within their power to restore order."(6)
Late evening
At the hastily summoned meeting of the VPC is attended by only half the members (the rest were on strike). Kliszko is visibly shocked, and infuriated. He shouts: "Do you realize, comrades, what is happening? The Party building is on fire. This is counterrevolution. If need be I will go out and speak to the workers." There are loud voices from the back of the hall: "Why don't you?" A worker shouts: "I took part in burning down the Party building. I am not ashamed but proud of it. This was the symbol of our misery and injustice." Kliszko rings Gomulka and declares: "This is a counterrevolution." A journalist attending the meeting later said that Kliszko did not care about workers being shot dead.

He is only shocked by the destruction of a myth - "the infallible Party." Kliszko accuses the Gdansk Party organization, numbering some 3,000 activists, of having all but ceased
to exist, and maintains that if no proper measures are taken
the shipyards in Gdansk and Gdynia will be destroyed by the
workers. The theory of "threatened sabotage" is born.

Tuesday, December 15
Warsaw - morning

Deputy Premier Jaroszewicz flies to Moscow to attend the
executive committee meeting of Comecon.

Wednesday, December 16
Gdansk - 0400 hours

Army detachments enter the city. Tanks and troop
carriers are protecting public buildings and utilities and
standing by the shipyards to be on hand in case of sabotage
there. The whole coast is cordoned off from the rest of the
country. Telecommunications are interrupted, and flights
stopped.

0700-1530 hours

At the shipyard a crowd of almost 5,000 gathered outside
the administration building demands an answer to grievances
contained in a resolution voted on the previous day. The
authorities appeal to people not to leave the shipyards and
point out what happened the day before, when workers' demonstrations resulted in rowdies and hooligans running wild in
the city. The warning is repeated that the army will use
force to prevent disturbances in the streets.

All over the shipyards and docks the strike is complete.
At separate meetings thousands of workers elect workers'
committees which draw the lists of their demands: pay raises
up to 30 percent, reduction in taxes, freezing of prices,
punishment of those responsible for the state of the national
economy, withdrawal of the army. Workers' own militia maintain order and discipline in the shipyards.

Evening

Deputy Premier Kociolek on Gdansk television speaks of
the decision of the authorities of the shipbuilding industry to
stop work in the Gdansk and Gdynia shipyards at the end of
the second shift. He concludes: "I want to say in all frankness - there are, in the majority, demands incapable of fulfillment, just as it is impossible to reverse decisions already
taken. Once more I repeat the call addressed to you, shipyard workers - resume your normal work."

Thursday, December 17
Gdansk - 0200 hours

Three thousand shipyard workers go home and the remainder of the work force leaves at 0600 hours. Work stops in
several other plants in the Gdansk area.

Thursday, December 17
Warsaw - 0700 hours
     Three days after the beginning of the riots on the coast,
the Warsaw media - the main Party paper, Trybuna Ludu, in
particular - reports in vague and general terms about the
disturbances. Trybuna Ludu admits that for at least two days
Gdansk "became the scene of tragic happenings." The paper
describes these events as "street incidents." "Unrestrained
adventurers" are blamed by the paper, together with loosely
defined "instigators," who took advantage of the fact that
part of the personnel of the Gdansk shipyards, having quit
work, went out into the streets in the morning. Only through
the use of force and the establishment of a curfew was "a
great wave of adventurism and robbery curbed."
1930 hours
     The resolution of the Council of Ministers introduces a
state of nationwide emergency for the first time in postwar
Polish history. The second paragraph of the resolution reads:
"The militia and other authorities responsible for maintaining
public order and security will take all legal steps, including
the use of arms, to restore order...."
2000 hours
     In a nationwide radio and TV broadcast(7) Prime Minister
Cyrankiewicz refers to the "tragic events in Gdansk and on
the coast," but stresses that as a representative of the
people's power, he has to guard superior state interests.
Everybody will understand this, Cyrankiewicz says, including
those who "have today been carried away by different
emotions, which have been made use of, as usual, on the one
hand by anarchistic hooligan and criminal elements, and on the
other hand by enemies of socialism, and of Poland." He
accuses the strikers of displaying a lack of prudence and
responsibility. The prime minister admits that there are
problems which might be disturbing the working class, but,
"there are no problems which could not become the object of a
matter-of-fact discussion and necessary clarification."
     He warns that matters of "basic importance for the state
and for the existence of the nation" had been raised by these
latest events. The consequences, he says, could undermine
Poland's position achieved in alliance with the Soviet Union.
The wording of his reference to the Soviet Union is intended
to suggest to Poles that if the trouble should become more
serious the Kremlin might feel its own interest threatened and
might perhaps even feel it necessary to intervene.
     This is not the government's estimate of the existing
situation. It is a threat designed to calm the nation. The
manner and the content of the premier's address suggests that
the government is afraid about the situation in the country
as a whole, and not just about the coastal towns. But his
view of the Russian bogey is designed to exploit the lesson of

Czechoslovakia.   This is the pistol which Cyrankiewicz now places on the card table.(8)
Evening
     At a villa near Warsaw, following his return from Katowice where he had spent the previous day, Gierek discusses with "some people" possible changes in leadership.
Friday, December 18
Warsaw - evening
     Two trends are clear in all official comments on the "tragic events" in the coastal cities: 1) price changes are an economic necessity but they were badly timed and 2) it was not only the hooligans who had taken to the streets.   There is a "deep grievance" of the working people, Warsaw Radio says, which had been exploited by "extremist or anarchist elements."
Saturday, December 19
     The Party daily, Glos Wybrzeza, reports that: "All industrial plants of the three cities (Gdansk, Sopot, Gdynia) are operating without disturbance."   But in the same edition the paper writes about a strike in the foundry.   In the Zamech factory, meetings are still being held in many departments.   In the afternoon, demonstrating workers march through the streets.   Various elected workers' committees prepare long lists of demands and grievances.
     Radio Warsaw reports that life in the coastal cities of Gdansk, Sopot, and Gdynia is almost normal and the shipyards are preparing to start working "at full swing" once more. Additional stations for blood donors are also opened.
     The chairman of the Provincial National Council, reports that in the area of Gdansk, Gdynia and Elblag, court proceedings have been instituted against 201 persons charged with looting, robbery and arson, 179 of whom are at present held in custody.   During the demonstrations, the health services aided 346 persons, 265 of whom were militia men and soldiers, 81 civilians.   Twenty-seven persons died as a result of injuries.   The funerals took place during curfew hours and only the immediate family attended, with priests present.(9)
     At the session of the Gdansk VPC, first secretary Karkoszka states: "We were confronted here with a genuine demonstration by the working class, caused by discontent with the economic situation.   The immediate cause of these demonstrations was the increase in the prices of food."   But he also stresses that demonstrations were exploited by dissident elements, often outright hostile to the Polish society.

                              GDYNIA

Tuesday, December 15 - 0700 hours
     One thousand workers leave their jobs in the Paris Commune shipyards.

<u>0900 hours</u>
After a rally in the shipyards 1,500 workers arrive at the Municipal National Council. The chairman, Marianski, asks the plants' representatives to come into the building and talk calmly. The strike committee, elected in the shipyards, goes in. Marianski talks with them at length and promises that many matters would be settled at once and others would be forwarded to higher authorities. They leave calmly.

<u>1500 hours</u>
Crowds begin to disperse homeward, some return to the shipyards and start a sit-in strike.

<u>Evening</u>
Another meeting of the Municipal National Council takes place attended by the chairman and about 30 delegates from various plants. Later, on Kliszko's orders, the chairman, Marianski, is arrested together with all members of the local Party committee because he was talking to "counterrevolutionaries." Rumors circulate that three of the workers' delegates who negotiated with Marianski are also in prison.

<u>Wednesday, December 16</u>
From early morning leaflets are distributed throughout the shipyards calling for a strike and demanding the release of those arrested. A crowd of demonstrators gives the management a deadline: "By 1330 hours the three shipyard workers arrested yesterday are to be back with us." The workers also demand that the army be removed from the shipyard gates. This is refused, but the management promises to continue trying to obtain the release of the three men arrested. The atmosphere becomes less tense. People begin to disperse to their homes.

But, as <u>Glos Wybrzeza</u>, the Party paper, reports, "...the aggressive elements take over." Some shipyard management members are beaten up. Others are taken as hostages. A delegation of strikers is received by the secretary of the Party municipal committee and presents an ultimatum: the strikers delegation is to be accepted as the only authority in the shipyard. Moreover it insists on the release of the arrested members of the "interplant strike committee" and the acceptance of a number of economic demands.

The fires in Gdansk hang like a heavy pall over Gdynia. Here too, according to <u>Glos Wybrzeza</u>, threats of arson and destruction of harbor shipyards and communal facilities grow constantly. In the evening army units enter the shipyard.

In fact no damage is done or threatened by shipyard workers to any shipyard equipment, the ships or any other facilities in their places of work. The shipyards are entered mainly by militia and security police units dressed in army uniforms, escorted by armored vehicles and tanks.

In the evening, Deputy Premier Kociolek ends his speech on coastal television channels with an ardent appeal: "Once more, I repeat the call addressed to you, shipyard workers - resume normal work." (See Wednesday, December 16, Gdansk - evening.)

2000 hours

The association of the shipbuilding industry sends a telephone message to the Paris Commune shipyards in Gdynia to stop work on December 17. None of the shipyards are working anyway. This information is published after Kociolek has appealed on television to workers to resume work next morning on December 17.

Thursday, December 17

0550 hours

At the intersection of three streets, by the shipyards railway station, an armored cordon of militia, security police and the army is posted and ordered not to admit workers to the shipyards. The electric commuter trains stop near this intersection. A Polish reporter describes the scene:

> Near the kiosk, the army places a huge loud-speaker. When the people start to pour out of the trains, a hoarse voice calls on them to go back, not to approach the army and the tanks, but the crowd grows and presses closer and closer to the cordon. Shots are fired by security forces. There are paving stones beneath the crowd's feet. The bullets ricochet off the pavement. Then the bridge above the tracks begins to burn. Tear gas cannisters are thrown from militia helicopters into the crowd."(10)

0630 hours

On the square in front of the main railway station, the crowd attacks the building which houses the prosecutor's offices. People surround the tanks and try to climb on top of them. Warnings are ignored. The security police uses fire-arms.

0730 hours

At the shipyard railway station about 5,000 people are fighting with militia, security police and the soldiers. The cordon can hardly withstand the attack of the crowds. Oil is taken from a locomotive and the station is set on fire. Four consecutive columns move forward. The last column carries the dead bodies of those shot at the shipyard railway station, using railway carriage doors torn off their hinges as im-provised stretchers. Shots still reverberate in the vicinity of the shipyard station. The crossbridge over the railroad line is still on fire. Tear-gas shells are still being thrown into the crowds by the militia.

Outside the presidium of the Municipal National Council the militia units retreat behind military tanks and armored cars

under pressure of the crowd. The army commanders call out
to the people to halt, warning them that they will be forced to
resort to arms.

0900 hours

Ambulances take the wounded to the hospital. The
security police shoot into the hard pavement at the feet of the
crowd. Ricochets hit the oncoming people who are determined
at all costs to set fire to the presidium of the Municipal
National Council. Another four are killed. The situation is
steadily growing more ominous. The attacking crowd tries to
push the soldiers and the militia back into the side streets.
They storm the presidium of the council seven times in all.
The military and the militia repulse the attackers with difficulty each time.

In another city station three trains are halted by the
people. The appeals to disperse coming through the loudspeakers are drowned out by the whistles of the steam
locomotives seized by the crowds. On the railway tracks near
the stopped trains, rioters start a fire.

It is only by early afternoon that the security forces
manage to get the situation under control. So ends Gdynia's
"bloody Thursday." According to official estimates 13 people
are dead, 75 severely wounded. In the background remains
the tragic figure of Deputy Premier Kociolek, seen by many as
a dreadful "agent provocateur."

The previous evening he had so ardently appealed on
coastal television screens to all shipyard workers to go back to
work. And when, early in the morning, they indeed alighted
from their trains at the Gdynia shipyard railway station, they
were faced by an armored cordon and the massacre followed.
According to the reports in the Krakow weekly, Zycie
Literackie, the management of the Gdynia shipyards had
asked the "staff" (this was the code name for PB member
Kliszko and his operational headquarters) to announce
repeatedly over radio and television that work in the
shipyards had been suspended until further notice, so that
people should not come to work in the morning. But the
"staff" refused permission for the broadcast.

Kociolek was aware, judging from his speech on December
16, that there was a possibility of work stopping in the shipyards for the time being. But at the time of his appeal on
television he did not know that even as he was speaking
Kliszko was giving orders to special security headquarters to
establish a "special command unit" to occupy the Gdynia shipyards. He did not know that the security police and the army
would occupy the shipyards during the night and that the
armored cordon around the shipyards would be given orders to
shoot on sight anyone who tried to enter the shipyards.

Nowhere during the riots, in the shipyards and other
plants along the coast, was any damage done to the equipment

or ships by the workers. On the contrary, great pains were taken to ensure that the equipment was well guarded and maintained even during the sit-in and general strikes. Kliszko was supposed to be in complete charge of the security operations along the coast and logically he was the man to give orders to shoot or to deploy forces within the shipyards. He himself launched the theory of "threatened sabotage" as soon as he arrived on the coast. This could justify a "deterrent operation" no matter what the cost in terms of lives.

In conversations with me, many journalists and strike leaders frankly blamed Kliszko for Gdynia's "bloody Thursday." One more version of the events in Gdynia came from Gomulka's secret memorandum. According to him the Gdynia massacre was a provocation. Provocation by whom? Gomulka did not give a clear answer. But in his memorandum he emphasized more than once that a sharp political and personal conflict existed between himself and Moczar who had been in charge of security forces for a considerable time. Somebody who was interested in provoking the shooting has provoked somebody else, wrote Gomulka.

SZCZECIN

Thursday, December 17
        The workers in the Warski shipyards are on strike, shaken by the news from Gdynia and Gdansk, by the price increases and the refusal of Party and trade union organizations to discuss workers' demands and grievances. A huge column of shipyard workers marches out into the city, joined on the way by workers from other plants as well as by hooligans and some hell-bent teenagers. The demonstrators shout: "Gomulka out! Moczar out! Cyrankiewicz out! Kliszko out! Jedrychowski and Jaszczuk out!" The intensity of the violence is much greater here than in Gdansk. The Party headquarters are burned down. The militia headquarters and prison are attacked twice, and the first shots are fired by the militia and the security police. Several other public buildings are also on fire. Militia and security police go into action. The demonstrators hurl Molotov cocktails. The city is cut off from the rest of the world.

        The first secretary of the VPC, Walaszek, and his closest associates refuse to speak to the workers. They are taken from the Party building by the army in armored cars and placed under house arrest in the divisional army headquarters.

        Frantic appeals are broadcast by Party, municipal and trade union authorities. The local station broadcasts a warning to parents and teachers not to let young people and children go out into the streets. A special broadcast appeals to the workers to "stand guard in defense of the socialist system." It says that hiding behind the backs of the workers and honest but misled people are hostile and unruly elements, including common bandits.(11)

A curfew is imposed from 1800 hours until 0600 hours. According to a doctor from the general city hospital, 250 militia officers, some of them severely wounded, are treated.

Friday, December 18

The full strike continues in the shipyards and many other factories. Further clashes with security forces and shootings occur in the city. The Provincial National Council introduces summary court proceedings throughout the whole Szczecin area.(12) The strikers are accused of irresponsibility. The local Party paper states that the demonstrations are a thoughtless move by only a part of the employees of the shipyards, their reasons are political and the consequences of their action tragic for the city. The overwhelming majority of the VPC members are on strike.

At 1915 hours the chairman of the Provincial National Council, Lempicki, broadcasts an appeal to all citizens to help check "the bank of youngsters looting and demolishing our city."(13) According to official estimates 16 people are dead and 117 seriously injured but reliable unofficial sources put the number of dead at 35.

Saturday, December 19

A general strike begins in the whole city and will end on December 22. The workers occupy the shipyards. On the gate to the shipyard, a huge sign proclaims: "This is an economic strike, not a political one." Other signs, some even scrawled on planks, explain: "We are workers, not hooligans."

The freely elected workers' self-government and workers' strike committee takes over not only the shipyards but also the whole city and the army has to negotiate with them as to what can be done to help maintain peace and order. The committee organizes the distribution of bread and milk for the people, and allows some shops to open under their own control. The streets are patrolled not only by the army units but also by the workers' shipyard militia with red and white arm bands (Polish national colors). The people are feeding soldiers on duty during the cold days and, according to all the participants, the army behaves "very well." Not only in Szczecin, but also in Gdansk and Gdynia all the Party activists with the exception of three or four secretaries are on strike.

All the shipyards and other plants are now in the hands of the workers. They are talking to reporters of the local radio station and the interviews are faithfully broadcast. The whole shipyard area is patrolled by the workers' own militia. Shipyard radio broadcasts communiques on matters of general interest and informs the strikers in the shipyards about the situation in the city. They are indignant about some hooligan excesses in the streets.

The employees of the printing plant stop work in sym-
pathy with the demands of the shipyard workers, but, being
aware of the importance of the printed word, decide to print
the current issues of the popular daily paper, Kurier
Szczecinski, but not the official Party paper. The Kurier
faithfully reports what is happening in the city. According to
eye-witnesses and journalists I have met this is the hey-day
of the press and radio in Szczecin. For the first time since
the war they are free of any censorship. No contact exists
with any authorities. The Party is in complete disarray.
Broadcasters act on their own, impose their own self-
discipline. Reporters all over the city give news and information as it comes in without any distortions or bias.

The workers' self-government elects its own authorities
who negotiate as equals with some provincial Party and
municipal leaders. In a controversial but calm discussion,
problems of wages and prices are thrashed out as well as the
causes and the course of events.

The Kurier Szczecinski reports that Saturday passes
calmly in the city but that the situation remains tense. Work
is not resumed.

At 1445 hours the local radio station reports that everything is calm, but several further plants are now on strike.

THE COUNTRY AT LARGE

December 16-19

Strikes in several factories are reported from Katowice,
Poznan, Wroclaw, Slupsk and Elblag.

Clashes between demonstrators and the militia occur in
Krakow, Lodz, Slupsk and Elblag, where one worker is killed
and three wounded.

In Warsaw several of the biggest plants have been on
strike since the beginning of the week. Militia units secure
the factories. Fire engines are stationed in the huge courtyard of the Party CC headquarters. New strike committees
spring up like mushrooms in Warsaw and many factories all
over the country. Although the coast is cut off from the rest
of the country, most of the strike committees' leaders remain
in contact through emmissaries and occasionally by telegrams
and telephone. Special units of strike emmissaries are organized in Warsaw and it already becomes clear on December 19
that if there is no change in leadership and policies a well-
organized and fully supported general strike will begin on
Monday, December 21. There is a lull before the storm. A
much more ominous and dangerous confrontation, paralyzing
the whole country, could take place on Monday, December 21.

The night of December 17-18
Warsaw

Gomulka asks Defense Minister, General Jaruzelski, what the army will do in case of a serious conflict. The minister replies, vaguely, that "the army will do its duty." It becomes clear that the army does not and will not support Gomulka's counterrevolution theory and will only maintain order if the danger is too great. In his secret memorandum, Gomulka explains that at this very moment he felt completely isolated and came to the conclusion that the army would not back him. It was clear, writes Gomulka, that the situation could not be defused without the use of force. What he planned to do was to withdraw the militia and security police units and to introduce the army which would obey him and not "that gang of provocateurs."

When he received a noncommittal reply from Jaruzelski, Gomulka says that he came to the conclusion that he himself was no longer in charge of the situation and "I fully realized that there was nothing else for me to do but to ask our Soviet comrades for help."

Gomulka sends a message to Brezhnev requesting military assistance in putting down "the counterrevolution in the country." In his memorandum he argues that this would not have led to further bloodshed. The Soviet units, he wrote, would not have necessarily had to intervene in the streets. The announcement itself that Gomulka had Soviet divisions at his disposal would, according to him, be enough to stabilize the situation within the Party and government apparatus, to eliminate the "provocateurs," and to reestablish order.

Early in the morning of December 18 Gomulka receives a message from Brezhnev refusing the military aid requested by the Polish leader and advising him to seek a political solution to the conflict. If Gomulka fails and goes down, the field is open for a free election of a new Party first secretary except that Moczar must be out of the running. In his secret memorandum Gomulka admits that the Soviet answer was a devastating blow. "I did not expect such an answer from our Soviet comrades. I did not show this message to anybody since this would have been a death sentence on me. It was more than my nervous condition could bear."

Jaroszewicz returns to Warsaw after three days in Moscow and informally conveys to the politburo members the gist of the Soviet message sent to Gomulka.
Friday December 18

Gomulka is asked to summon a politburo meeting by a group of members opposed to pure repression of the strikes. At first Gomulka opposes the suggestion and argues that he considers his policy of repression to be absolutely correct until order is restored. Kliszko points out that the strong-arm policy has been successful since street demonstrations in

Gdansk-Gdvnia had ceased and the Szczecin outbreak had changed into a peaceful occupation strike. On the other hand, Gomulka's opponents are aware of the widespread work stoppages throughout the country and know that mass workers' meetings are planned for Monday in the whole country. Gomulka finally agrees to call the PB meeting.

Saturday December 19

Politburo of the CC meets under Cyrankiewicz's chairmanship and lasts for over seven hours. Gomulka, already seriously ill, argues his case, although he knows that he cannot rely on Brezhnev's help. He accuses others of supporting counterrevolutionaries. Minister of Defense, General Jaruzelski again refuses his request to throw the army behind the Party leader and supports Gierek instead, but he accepts that the army must play a part in maintaining order. Moczar boasts that the situation has been stabilized by himself and his security forces.

The Gomulka group holds out for several hours before the decision to ask Gomulka for his resignation in favor of Gierek is reached. Loga-Sowinski finally breaks the deadlock by switching his vote to Gierek. It is decided to call a session of the Central Committee for the next day, Sunday, 20 December. Moczar assures Gierek that he would bring the members of the CC to Warsaw by air "under his protection." But he refuses to leave the intelligence network of the security police at Gierek's disposal and Gierek, therefore, has to rely on the army intelligence.

Sunday December 20

Gomulka suffers a minor stroke, temporarily losing his eyesight. At three a.m. he is forcibly taken on a stretcher out of the conference room and then by an armored car to a clinic. The politburo meeting is now chaired by Gierek. Cyrankiewicz and Kliszko are asked to call on Gomulka in hospital and obtain his resignation. It is given in writing and the matter is reported back to the politburo, which proceeds to reconstitute itself and the secretariat.

The slightly depleted seventh plenum of the CC assembles not in the Party headquarters in Warsaw but outside Warsaw in the Natolin Castle, for the first time in postwar history. The CC members are brought by planes from outside Warsaw. Gierek is elected first secretary of the CC with only a few abstentions.

1945 hours

Radio Warsaw broadcasts a Polish Press Agency (PAP) communique announcing the far-reaching changes in the leadership of the Party. An earthquake hits the top Party leadership.

During this crucial week 45 people were killed, according to official sources, and 1,165 seriously injured – about 300 according to unofficial estimates. Over 3,000 people were arrested.   "In politics, what begins in fear usually ends in folly" (Samuel Taylor Coleridge).

A cruel joke was circulating in Poland immediately after the December riots: "The first aim of socialism is the worker and that is why, when the Party orders the shooting - they aim at the workers first."

2000 hours

In his first radio and television appeal to the nation, Gierek says: "A quarter of a century ago, our nation entered upon the road to socialism.   No hostile forces are in any condition either to lead us astray from this road or to turn us back."(14)   He urges the people to remain calm and to return to work, but he is frank about the background of the demonstrations.   Gierek acknowledges that workers had taken part in the disturbances and that people had been killed.   "The working class was provoked beyond endurance."   He admits that the country survived the disaster, that it faces great danger and he implies that chaos still reigns supreme.   But at the same time he raises three important questions: What led to the catastrophe?   Why did it come to a social conflict?   Why could the problem not have been solved in any other way? These are questions obviously addressed to the Party and to his predecessor, particularly when he says that the events had recalled "in a painful manner the fundamental truth that the Party must maintain a lasting link with the nation, that it must retain its common language with the working people."

Again blaming the older leadership of the Party, Gierek promises an immediate inquiry into the special needs of low-income families and announces the revision of the economic plan not only for 1971, but for 1971-1975, admitting that there had been "badly thought-out conceptions" in economic policy, as well as "real difficulties."   Serious problems had grown, but, as Gierek says, the motives of the workers' protests were honest, although some of them were driven by emotions and went on strike.   The danger in this otherwise honest reaction was that it had been exploited by the "enemies of socialism." The new leader is unable to avoid, however marginally, this accusation which is both unnecessary and unrealistic.   Nevertheless, he does not blame the workers for the riots, but responds directly to their demands by promising higher wages.

The Party, stresses Gierek, must give the nation a full answer to all these questions.   It will be a difficult but self-critical, clear and truthful answer.   He strongly insists that the leadership must make it an "iron rule" to consult fully the working class and the intelligentsia in solving the problems facing the nation.   Political and organizational conditions for such a consultation and cooperation will be created.

In foreign policy, Gierek is at pains to reaffirm that Poland intends to consolidate her alliance with the Soviet Union, and continue to march alongside the "entire socialist

commonwealth," but he also envisages the cooperation with all
states irrespective of their social and political systems and
normalization of relations with West Germany.

After the announcement of the changes in the leadership
and Gierek's speech, a Gdansk shipyard worker defined the
situation with a working man's brisk lucidity over the local
radio station: "We, the workers, know precisely what the
government should give us and what we should request from
the government. Our duty is to work. But, in exchange for
our work we ask for the fulfillment of our demands. We also
became convinced during these December days, that the power
lies with the people."(15)

EARTHQUAKE AT THE TOP

The only difference, after all their rout,
is that the one is in, the other out.

Charles Churchill

Gomulka's reckless handling of the riots on the coast and
the possibility of further outbreaks of this sort was the major
reason why the Soviet leaders deserted him in December 1970.
Before they did so, however, they had to make sure that his
successor did not have any dangerous ideas. They also had
to be certain that the new politburo included men they knew
well and could trust, and that these new people would possess
sufficient influence. Gierek was the only man acceptable both
to his Polish comrades and to the Soviet leaders, but he had
spent his formative years in France and in Belgium and had
not been in close relations with the Russians after his postwar
return to Poland. If he were to be the first secretary then
the prime minister had to be someone the Soviet leaders knew
better than Gierek. Jaroszewicz fitted the bill rather well.(16)
During the war he had served as a political officer in the
Polish army in the Soviet Union. He had been deputy premier
and Poland's representative on the Comecon executive committee under Gomulka and had had close contacts with Soviet
leaders. His responsibilities kept him in Moscow much of the
time and by a stroke of fortune he found himself there between 15 and 18 December. It was rather significant that
there was a curious delay between Pravda's announcement of
the new politburo and secretariat on December 21 and the
publication of Brezhnev's warm congratulations to Gierek on
December 22. During the intervening days, secret talks had
taken place between the two leaders and some of their colleagues which fully satisfied the Russians. Jaroszewicz became
the prime minister on December 23.

Five top Party leaders lost their politburo and Central Committee secretariat posts: Gomulka, Kliszko, Strzelecki, Jaszczuk, and Spychalski. Out of these five only Gomulka had "resigned." The other four were "discharged" from their duties. Gomulka's "resignation" was explained by "his severe illness." The plenum even sent him "best wishes for a speedy recovery."

It was one of the ironies of history that the workers who brought Gomulka back to power only 14 years ago had themselves thrown him out. His career - which seemed to have been crowned with success just a few days before, when the treaty with Bonn which in effect recognized the Oder-Neisse frontier was signed - had ended with the bitterness of failure. It also ended with his repudiation, not only by his Party (with only a few loyal exceptions), but perhaps even more important to him by the Polish working class, of which he always honestly considered himself a part and which, according to his own lights, he sought devotedly to serve.(17) He had failed not only the working class but the whole nation. Gomulka was a fundamental communist, passionately subscribing to those few tenets of Leninism which his limited but tenacious mind could grasp. He was molded in the era of the underground, out of touch with, and distrustful of, modern life, modern ideas and modern people. He learned his Marxism-Leninism reading a pamphlet while walking from one wall of the prison cell to another in prewar Poland. Besides, he was highly authoritarian in temperament, and accepted no argument once his mind was made up.

Gomulka could not be entirely blamed for all the failures that led Poland to the December crisis, although deficiencies, his shortsightedness in some fields and his attitude of mind certainly contributed considerably to them. According to Gomulka in his memorandum, he had been convinced by Jaszczuk that only a most comprehensive price increase would produce new means for the improvement of the economy. Even if the increase needed to be as comprehensive as it was, Gomulka wrote in his memorandum, it should not have been introduced at one stroke but by stages and certainly not in the pre-Christmas period. "This was a great mistake for which I feel I am responsible, although I am not the only one to be blamed for it."

Yet Gomulka had done quite a lot for the country. He will be remembered not only for the 1970 Polish-West German treaty. Although his relations with the Catholic Church were highlighted by certain periods of crisis and even confrontations, he was sufficiently clever never to attempt a mass offensive against the church. Nor did he make any move to recollectivize Polish agriculture. Moreover, he was a man who personally disliked terror and brutality as an instrument of power. But he did allow the security apparatus, shattered by

Swiatlo's revelations (see Introduction) broadcast to Poland, to reconstruct itself after 1956 until, under the orders of General Moczar, it became a powerful factor in Polish politics and a threat to Gomulka himself.

Gomulka was a half-measure man. He restrained those who sought to put Poland back into a sullen dark-age while simultaneously cooperating with them and trying, as he wrote himself in his memorandum, to persuade them. At the same time, he also restrained those who sought to bring Poland into the modern world.

In a most telling epitaph on Gomulka, Milovan Djilas, once Tito's comrade-in-arms and his second closest associate, then a dissenter, imprisoned and sentenced more than once, wrote:

> Poland and the whole world changed, but Gomulka did not. His modesty and conciliatoriness, Party-mindedness and patriotism thus were transformed into obstinacy and a peremptory manner, into bureaucratism and pedantry. There are few historical figures who began so courageously and ended so disgracefully. Gomulka cannot complain that history did not give him a chance.

Along with Gomulka his oldest comrades who had followed him into disgrace in 1948 and were brought back to power with him in 1956, joined him in political oblivion. Kliszko, Gomulka's closest associate, was responsible for the ideological, propaganda, cultural front for the cadre policy, but was also in charge of the security operations on the coast. Spychalski was a former minister of defense and lately the head of state. Jaszczuk, the economist scapegoat for the eruptions after the price increases, was also the architect of the ill-conceived and extremely difficult-to-understand scheme of incentives to be introduced on January 1, 1971. He was the chief exponent of a rather timid economic reform the regime has been hesitantly trying to apply since the end of 1968. Strzelecki, a sinister figure, a hard-line champion of diverse interests of the older apparatchiks, stood for the status quo reaction in Polish communist politics. Widely linked with General Moczar and the Partisan group, he played a rather dubious and cynical role throughout the sixties.

THE NEW TEAM

In the new eleven-member politburo there were five newcomers: Babiuch, Jaroszewicz, Moczar, Szydlak and Olszowski. Among the candidate members of the new Politburo only Jagielski remained in his former position, while the other three members were entirely new: Jablonski, Jaruzelski, and Kepa. Four newcomers joined the seven-member Party CC secretariat: Gierek, of course, together with Babiuch, Barcikowski and Kociolek.

Most of the new leaders came mainly from the Stalinist Association of Polish Youth, which disappeared after October 1956. (For more on Gierek, see section, "The Man and the Leader" in Chapter 4.) Some of them (Babiuch, Szydlak) had worked with Gierek in Silesia where he was first secretary of VPC for many years. Jablonski, a historian by education, and a prewar member of the Polish Socialist party which was taken over by the Communist party, in 1948, spent the war with the Polish army in the West and returned to Poland in 1945. General Jaruzelski, the minister of defense, came from an intellectual family. In 1943 he joined General Berling's Polish army in the Soviet Union and served during the whole campaign of the Polish First Army. He was appointed minister of defense in April 1968.

Jozef Kepa's background was almost typical of the new generation of Party "apparatchiks" rising to power in the last few years. Promoted to first secretary of the Warsaw Party organization in December 1967, he distinguished himself particularly in March 1968 as a hard-liner, an orthodox communist, who readily dismissed all "liberal" nonsense. Kociolek was a typical modern Party "apparatchik" with a university education. Efficient and ruthless, Kociolek was originally thought to be Gomulka's personal choice as his successor.

Olszowski, born in 1931, could claim a most brilliant political career in a Party not enthusiastic in its support of youthful talent. Actively engaged in the student and youth organizations, particularly in the Polish Student Association, he took over the organization in October 1956. Later, as head of the CC press bureau, he was responsible, in 1968, together with Moczar, for what was described by the mass media as anti-Zionist propaganda.

Moczar, born as Mikolaj Demko, was one of the most controversial figures in the new politburo. A communist since 1937, he was active during the war in the communist resistance movement. Since the war he served mostly in security services, became at one time the minister of the interior, and brutally suppressed the students' demonstrations in March 1968. As CC secretary since July 1968 he remained in charge of security services within the Party, yielding the interior ministry to Switala who acted under his direct orders during the December events. Moczar had ambitions and formidable power, based covertly on his control of the security apparatus and overtly on his presidency of ZBOWiD, the ex-combatants association. He became a recognized leader of the Partisan group in the Party, relying on a network of branches of this association all over the country. The Partisan group led by

Moczar was strongly nationalistic and "anti-Zionist," in other words, antisemitic (see Introduction). Playing too strongly on Polish nationalism, Moczar did not at times conceal his suspicions of the Soviet Union. Always bidding for supreme power in the Party he was not trusted by the Soviet leaders and became unacceptable both to them and to his Polish comrades.

In 1970, though Gierek and Moczar seemed to have very little in common, a coalition for power had been arrived at between those two with neither being able to do without the other for the time being. Moczar had been thwarted once again in his bid for supreme power, but seemed to have achieved the next best thing, full politburo membership. His position was rather a curious one in terms of communist politics. On the one hand, as a strong nationalist he must have been watched very suspiciously by the Soviet leaders. This sort of approach could not please the Kremlin. On the other hand Moczar, as a man who was for many years in charge of the secret police, intelligence and security services in Poland he must have had close links with the KGB. His career, therefore, depended very much on the state of play between the Party and the security services within the Soviet Union itself.

The most significant retention from the old politburo was that of Cyrankiewicz, the longest serving prime minister whose political survival had for a long time been the subject of many Polish political jokes. In the tumultuous situation he also represented a symbol of governmental continuity and stability. The departure of Jaszczuk was not accompanied by a complete elimination of the reformist-technocrat group inside the politburo. Kociolek and Tejchma still remained, and Olszowski had now joined them.

The accent in the PB was on youth. Not only was Gierek himself, at 59, eight years younger than Gomulka, but he formed a conspicuously young leadership team. The average age of full politburo of the Central Committee members was reduced from 57 years in 1968, to 51 in 1971 and in the Secretariat of the Central Committee to only 45. This made Gierek's new team one of the youngest not only in the communist bloc, but also in Europe a a whole.

Many of the new members at the top of the Party hierarchy had relatively short experience in the communist ranks. Only two out of the 19 top Party leaders participated in the communist movement before World War II. The rest joined the Party after the war, several of them not until the early fifties, and therefore had no links whatsoever with either Comintern or Cominform.(18) The new team's claim to rule therefore, unlike Gomulka's, was not based on long-standing participation in the revolutionary struggle, but rather on educational achievements and administrative experience, acquired through a gradual rising from the ranks in the Party to high positions.

These new people were not professional revolutionaries but administrators and as such they were less ideological and more pragmatic than their predecessors. These were the communists of a new vintage, less concerned with a distant vision of a proletarian paradise than with everyday practical issues. As products of an industrial society, they understood its functioning well; of proletarian background, they were genuinely concerned about improving the workers' lot. Their exposure to Western influences, including German, which remained strong in Silesia, had impressed upon them that the path to improving living standards was through improved economic performance. Their first priority was the development and modernization of the Polish economy. Naturally, they were bound by Marxism-Leninism and their attitude did not imply criticism of the political system, but rather reflected their desire to increase its efficiency. Similarly, their attitudes toward the Soviet Union were marked less by the quasi-religious zealotry of early communists, than by the sound recognition of political realities.(19)

In this first shake-up in the top leadership of the Party, Gierek had to play cautiously and skillfully. He had to maintain the appearance of at least some continuity in the government and within the Party. It was necessary to show Moscow that he was not severing all the ties with the past; he therefore retained some of the pro-Soviet "reliables." It was expedient to include as many as possible of his close associates on whom he could rely; and to get rid of disloyal people. So as not to frighten the Soviet comrades too much, Gierek retained in the politburo such old Stalinists as Kruczek, as well as some survivors of the Gomulka team like Jedrychowski, Loga-Sowinski, and Cyrankiewicz. On the other hand, Babiuch, Szydlak, Barcikowski and Jaruzelski were certainly Gierek's men. But even the survivors of Gomulka's team after the disastrous December events could be relied upon to follow the new leader. Moczar, on the other hand, could certainly count, at least for the time being, on Kepa and perhaps on Olszowski who had cooperated with him in the past. But Olszowski was too clever not to see that the situation had been changing.

Gierek's "inner cabinet" consisted of three fellow "Silesians": Babiuch, Szlachcic, and Szydlak. The immediate future of Party politics depended at the end of December 1970 on the interplay of three forces: Gierek and his associates, Moczar and his influence within the country, and the younger reformer-technocrats. The Soviet estimate of the performance of the new leadership was, of course, decisive.

FIRST DAYS AFTER ...

The new leaders, echoed by the media, appealed to the
nation to "bring order back into our house." The workers
began gradually to resume their normal work, although only
"provisionally" in Szczecin. After a short communique on
December 21 about Gomulka's health the former leader became a
"nonperson," although he continued to write letters to
Brezhnev.

At the Sejm session on December 23, Marshal Spychalski
resigned as head of state and was replaced by Cyrankiewicz
who, in turn, resigned his premiership with the words: "In
view of recent events, which I was not in a position to
prevent, I consider that I should not continue to fulfill the
function of chief executive." The new Prime Minister
Jaroszewicz promised to streamline the economic planning and
to "aim at a full normalization of relations between state and
church." Gierek announced the distribution of 7,000 million
zlotys, in consultation with the workers, to help low-income
families and the freezing for two years of food prices as raised
by Gomulka. The trade unions chairman Loga-Sowinski admitted that the December events revealed the most severe
dissatisfaction of the workers with the trade unions activities.

Answering the leadership's appeals Cardinal Wyszynski(20)
described on December 24 the recent events as "unprecedented
in our history" and said, "We beg of you, do not accuse.
Show understanding, forgive, feel compassion, put your hands
to the plough, so that there can be more bread in our fatherland, and justly distributed ... first of all to the children of
the nation." Not without a projection in the future, which
might be rightly understood by the new Party leaders, he
added: "Perhaps I have not tried enough, I have not ad-
monished enough, perhaps not warned and begged enough -
although it is known that my voice was not always listened
to...."

THE SIGNIFICANCE OF DECEMBER EVENTS

Never in the postwar history of communism have the
myths and the imperatives of the system been stripped so
naked. Never has the Party which is supposed to represent
the interests of the workers been forced so dramatically to a
humiliating, unconditional surrender at the hands of the
workers themselves.

According to three CC members I spoke to in Warsaw, the
workers' revolt produced an earthquake of historical dimensions
which shook the whole socialist bloc including the Soviet Union.

It was, they said - and their view was shared by most journalists - the most important event in the communist movement since the war, if one discards Stalin's death as a natural phenomenon. The reason was simple, as everybody I spoke to agreed. The working class in a communist state had rejected and changed the leadership of the Party and forced the new leadership to change the policies. The upheaval was the more chilling because the workers discovered the power they had even under the communist system and imposed their will. At the same time the people at large realized that without pressure from the workers, who had stood alone, nothing could be done. Only the workers can change the situation.

The Party leadership was totally unprepared. They did not want to accept the reality because they lived in a ficticious atmosphere of infallibility and righteousness. Once it had happened everything burst at the seams and the chaos was complete. There would have been, I was told, a genuine danger of Soviet military intervention in December if the riots had spread on a massive scale to the rest of the country, and if Gierek had proved unable to control the situation when he took over. As it happened, the Soviet comrades were the happiest of people once they realized that there would be no need for military intervention. They were fully aware, as one journalist put it rather colorfully, that "the pork meat is much cheaper than the gun meat," and that an armed intervention would have meant a bloody and costly fight.

3 A Year of Agonizing Reappraisals: 1971

> When shall the softer, saner, politics
> whereof we dream, have play in each
> proud land?
>
> Thomas Hardy in "Departure"

In an atmosphere of high tension and expectation major pronouncements coming from two centers of power outlined both the consequences of the upheaval and prospects for the future.

In his New Year's message, Gierek(1) promised the nation that the latest tragic lesson would not be wasted. "There are no such issues among us Poles," he believed, "which, united, we are unable to solve in conformity with the interests of the nation and the raison d'etat of a socialist state." He assured the people that, although many lessons in the past history of Poland had gone unheeded, from this last lesson "we will draw indispensable and realistic conclusions."

The Episcopate in its New Year's message called on people to avoid further violence.(2) It implicitly condemned the methods used by the state to quell the disorders. The pastoral letter was interpreted as a positive response to the prime minister's assertion in the Sejm that he would aim at a full normalization of relations between church and state.

It expressed the trust that pronouncements by the authorities would be put into effect and addressed itself with a feeling of fraternal respect and community to all countrymen: "After these terrible losses, we raise only one appeal - do not add further suffering. Everything must be done so that everyone feels safe and respected."

It then listed rights which, the Episcopate thought, it was the duty of the authorities to respect: the right of freedom of conscience and freedom of religious life with full normalization of relations between church and state; the right of freely shaping the culture of one's own nation, in accordance with the spirit of Christian principles of the coexistence of people; the right to social justice expressed in fulfilling just demands; the right to truth in social life, to truthful information, and of free expression of one's views and demands; the right to material conditions ensuring decent life for the family and each citizen; the citizen's right not to be insulted, harmed, or persecuted. Respect for these rights was the condition for peace in social life.

Comparison of Party and church pronouncements showed that there were areas of agreement and that some of the demands put forward by the church were parallel to the promises made by Gierek in his two speeches. On the surface, it would appear from what Gierek said that the era of imposing decisions from above without reference to the people, and based on the principle that the Party knows best and knows all, was over. But the question remained whether a change of people would be enough, or whether the institutional forms of consultation had to be modernized or new mechanisms created; in other words, a fundamental transformation in the relationship between rulers and ruled.

In trying to introduce such basic changes the leadership had to find a common language with the whole nation. The church, in its two pronouncements suggested that, within strictly defined conditions, such a possibility existed. On the other hand the Party leader qualified the changes by saying that they had to conform to the raison d'etat, in other words, to the realities of Poland's geopolitical position and her alliance with the Soviet Union. But within these limitations a lot could be done once the principle had been accepted that really democratic institutional forms have a key importance even in a socialist system, and that only through these institutional forms could the people in top positions contribute toward a free development of the country, to the solutions of political crises, and to the establishment of a real contact with the nation.

There were no guarantees in the existing system that a true dialogue would be conducted with the population, neither were there any guarantees preventing a return to arbitrary methods. Four dramatic upheavals in postwar Polish history had forced the Party to indulge in soul-searching and self-criticism, after which the situation invariably solidified into the status quo once more after a few years. The conditions were now different, but Gierek nevertheless faced an unenviable situation.

The country which the new leader inherited from Gomulka was, as one Polish commentator told me "like a volcano that might erupt at any moment." Gierek's freedom of maneuver was complicated by fourteen years of Gomulka's mismanagement. Badly needed reforms of the economic system had been delayed so long that by 1970 only drastic measures could be introduced with all the consequent hardships on the population.(3) The Poles, however, after two decades of intensive industrialization and limited consumption, were in no mood to accept further deprivations. They demanded instead to have their sacrifices tangibly rewarded by an improved standard of living.

Notwithstanding the economic dilemma the credibility of the communist system had also been shattered. Poles who had supported Gomulka in 1956 only to become thoroughly disillusioned with him, were not disposed to place much trust in the promises of his successor.(4) After such a letdown people demanded action rather than more promises and the new leadership could no longer count on their unlimited patience.

In addition to his other problems, Gierek lacked an effective political instrument with which to carry out new policies. The Party, torn by internal dissensions, was in complete disarray. He himself was faced with the challenge from some other leaders and, particularly, from the middle echelons of the Party apparatus in the provinces, who were afraid of or simply opposed to any change.

Last, but not least, Gierek had to carry out his policies with an eye on Moscow. The Soviet Union had acted with unusual restraint during the December crisis. Yet, he could not ignore the heightened Soviet sensitivity to political changes in Eastern Europe after 1968. After all, Moscow had already shown that it would abandon overnight any ally unable to maintain order at home. Yet, despite its support for Gierek, the Soviet leadership could hardly have been pleased about some aspects of the Polish scene, including the legitimization of workers' spontaneous action, the use of aid from Moscow to subsidize a higher standard for the Poles rather than that of Soviet workers, and the continued pressure by the people and the Party elite to make Poland more self-assertive internationally. There was a clear emphasis on Poland being an equal partner of the Soviet Union and also on Poland's special ties with Western Europe.

And yet, within little more than a year, Gierek managed to bring the situation under control, acting energetically and with great political skill, and moving on a broad front to attack the most urgent problems first, while not ignoring the others.

DEFUSING THE SITUATION: PHASE ONE

By any standards December 1970 was a constitutional and political tinderbox. At the root of most of the trouble was the arrogance of Party power which rode roughshod over the aspirations of the people. In contrast to Gomulka in October 1956, Gierek had no ready-made program of economic, social and political reforms. He had to react to events as they happened. His first priority was to try to put out the most dangerous fires and to make as many economic concessions as was possible within existing limitations.

The day after he had taken over, Gierek revoked all the emergency measures and abrogated the order of the Council of Ministers on ensuring security and public order. His aim was to prevent further rioting, to defuse the explosive situation on the coast and to gain a measure of popular confidence. He immediately reversed the Party's initial condemnation of the riots which had earlier been called "irresponsible actions" fomented by "hostile, anarchist and criminal elements," and declared, instead, that they were in the main, a manifestation of legitimate working-class grievances. The government then announced that it would undertake a fundamental reappraisal of the former economic development strategy, with the intention of ensuring a more harmonious economic course which would take into account the needs of the working people and avoid the past error of production for production's sake. Among specific improvements it promised better market supplies, more housing, and a revision of the bonus scheme.(5)

Gomulka's price increases were maintained and described as necessary: "There is no possibility of a return to the former abnormal state in the prices system," said Radio Warsaw.(6) But the government had frozen these increased prices as well as working norms for two years, suspended the controversial wage freeze, and lifted all employment restrictions such as a ban on overtime. To cushion the price increases, measures designed to compensate lower paid workers and low-income families were introduced. The statutory minimum wage was increased by 17.6 percent, family allowances by 25 percent and minimum pensions and disability payments were raised. About ten million people would benefit from these tax-free and back-dated increases.(7) At the beginning of 1971 the average monthly wage of an industrial worker was 2,537 zlotys(8) The shipyard workers, who spearheaded the December riots, earned between 2,800 and 3,400 zlotys. Massive sales of stocks of consumer goods at prices reduced to $7\frac{1}{2}$ percent of their previous level were introduced and the prices of some more industrial consumer goods reduced. An equality in holiday periods between white and blue collar workers was announced.

These measures were designed as a stopgap to ease some of the economic burden on the community. In an unprecedented letter to the chairmen of the workers' self-governments and to the managing directors of industrial enterprises the SCC impressed on them in very strong terms that all the just demands of the workers must be satisfied within the limitations of the financial resources.(9)

But at least as important were several immediate local measures in the coastal towns and in the textile center of Lodz. Wage raises between 5 percent and 25 percent and many other improvements were immediately granted to textile and shipyard workers, merchant seamen, dockers and some others in these danger areas as well as in Wroclaw. It appeared, therefore, as some workers told me, that despite previous Party lies there were financial reserves available. In an effort to avoid chain reactions elsewhere in the country, the mass media remained silent about these local measures.

With the aim of establishing a closer link with the working class and the entire nation, Gierek launched a dialogue with the workers by organizing a series of consultations with workers' representatives to discuss the implementation of the regime's concessions. In all his meetings and official speeches, Gierek's emphasis was on Polish patriotism and nationalism, on the unity of all the people, both believers and nonbelievers, which, he said, was absolutely necessary in the critical days through which the country was living and also for the future progress and development of the nation.

On December 29, the first-ever report on a politburo meeting appeared in the press - in accordance with Gierek's promise to make the government more open and to inform the people more fully than before. A Polish-Soviet economic five-year agreement signed at the end of 1970 provided for an increase of mutual trade by 67 percent and for the supply of two million tons of Soviet grain.(10)

Between January 5 and 16, in 11 days, Gierek and Jaroszewicz went to Moscow, Prague and East Berlin. The most important of these visits was to Moscow to plead Poland's stability and loyalty and to request further economic assistance, at the same time showing that the new leadership was in control of the situation at home. Other PB and SCC members went to East Berlin, Prague, Sofia, Budapest, Bucharest, and Belgrade. While PB member Tejchma discussed ways and means of reforming socialist democracy in Poland with Tito, other Party leaders tried in other socialist capitals to reassure the frightened leaders of the Communist parties that the situation in Poland would not get out of hand.

But they also pressed for immediate economic assistance. Within a few weeks imports of consumer goods from some of these countries liquidated all the surpluses in balance of payments which had been in favor of Poland.

The Voice of the Media

Truth, fact is the life of all things;
falsity, "fiction" or whatever it may
call itself, is certain to be the death.

Carlyle in Latter Day Pamphlets

At the time when Gierek and the Episcopate were outlining
their respective attitudes, Warsaw papers suggested to the new
Polish leadership that the recent changes had opened new
opportunities but that these would not be fulfilled automatically
and required much effort on the part of the leadership if they
were not to be wasted. Though the message was carefully
wrapped up, the contents suggested that the country was
witnessing the slow rebirth of a new spirit of some independence in the media, although it was still a far cry from the
daring outbursts of October 1956.
   Several issues were raised. First of all, the main Party
paper, Trybuna Ludu, warned that a full assessment of what
had happened and what could be done had to wait until the CC
undertook this task. Immediately, the popular daily Zycie
Warszawy, stressing that there can be "no responsibility
without independence" wrote: "Anyone who says he knows
best, automatically makes it unnecessary for others to think."
There is public opinion which should express its own views
and work out its own analysis of events. This might only be
helpful to the Party, which had committed many grave errors,
for it did not take into account the feelings, the attitudes and
the demands of the people. No other newspaper went as far
and as deeply into the causes and consequences of December
than did the well-known sociopolitical weekly, Polityka, whose
editor, Rakowski, was reputed for a long time to have been
one of the few journalists to hold Gomulka's confidence.
"Although there are various degrees of responsibility,"
Polityka said, "the Party was responsible for the causes which
gave rise to the tragic events.... The picture presented by
propaganda was far from reality." It went on to admit the gap
between propaganda and what people really thought: "Such
practices, sanctioned the very dangerous social phenomenon of
double-thinking, having one standard for public consumption
and another reserved for private use." The riots were an
alarm signal indicating that serious disease still existed in the
political organism, all the more disconcerting since it has been
heard for a second time in Poland's quarter century of socialism, wrote Polityka.
   The tragic week in December created a very tricky
problem for the Party propaganda machine which, in any case,
was in complete disarray: how to justify and reestablish the

"leading role" of the Party, one of the imperatives of the
system, and one which looked decidedly sick at the moment.
At first the main Party paper, Trybuna Ludu, kept quiet
about the "leading role" of the Party, but only wrote about
the "leading role of the working class."

However, soon Trybuna Ludu proudly stated that "Our
Party through its own strength and courage of decision,
showed the way out of the crisis. It thus confirmed its right
to perform the leading role in the nation's life at the moment
of such a difficult trial." These were obviously, by any
standard, ridiculous statements after what had happened in the
crucial weeks in December when, in the coastal towns the
Party apparatus to all intents and purposes disappeared from
the surface of the earth. Some of those who "led" just fled,
and went into hiding. Others went on strike themselves and
the remaining few did not even try to do anything at all.
Besides, if, as some papers asserted, the Party had once
again found within itself forces which led the country out of
the crisis, why was a tragic upheaval and massive workers'
protest necessary to force the Party to enter the road of basic
political and economic reforms? Why were these forces, which
had now surfaced, unable or unwilling to act independently
much earlier? Why, if one accepts the Party jargon, was the
breakdown of "Leninist norms," whatever they mean, tolerated
for so many years?

In an answer to all these questions Trybuna Ludu simply
stated: that "the best pages of history were written by the
nation under the leadership of the working class and its
leading force, the Party." The paradox of this statement was
even then quite obvious. The "best pages" of the postwar
history, however tragic in its immediate consequences, at a
given time, were written by the nation itself, against the
express will and policies of the "leading" Party. This was the
case in June and in October 1956, in March 1968 and in the
most tragic way in December 1970. There were several
achievements, but there was also no doubt that the industrialization of the country could have been achieved without the
tremendous sacrifices which people had to suffer over so many
years. Other countries have been transformed into industrial
powers without a "leading" role of any party, far less a Communist party, and within a modern capitalist system. This did
not mean that in December the workers rebelled against socialism in Poland but what they proved was that socialism as
implemented over the past several years was not the kind of
socialism which the nation wanted and which the leading Party
was trying to enforce.

Another problem arose: Was the change of leaders enough
or would more widespread and really democratic institutional
forms of dialogue and consultations with the people be necessary? Here the weekly Polityka was quite emphatic in calling

for "new mechanisms" of consultation which would eliminate atrophy and the possibility of conflicts between authority and the people. But some other Party newspapers stubbornly maintained that the existing forms were quite good, and only the links with the masses within these forms should be re-established. The same papers in the same articles also wrote that well-intentioned people had seen the faults in the economic mechanism for a long time past. Why, therefore, if the existing forms were satisfactory, had all these people failed or were unable to do anything?

The real issue boiled down to what the independent Krakow Catholic weekly, Tygodnik Powszechny termed as a definitive attitude of the leadership towards the citizen and a strictly defined method of ruling. The people were manipulated, said the weekly, and the nation rejected this sort of governing. There were no institutional ways and forms to express justified opposition, even within an industrial enterprise.

Criticism of the previous leadership was initially mainly anonymous. It concentrated on phenomena rather than on persons, and names were usually implied rather than stated. Only in January did provincial Party papers(11), for the first time, charge the former Party leadership by name, with many original sins such as conservatism, despotism, arrogance, self-righteousness and with the most damning "violation of Leninist norms" of Party life. History repeated itself. In October 1956 Gomulka had said: "The Party must strongly adhere to the Leninist norms of Party life and in the past these norms have been broken." After December 1970 Gomulka was accused of the same sin although only a few months earlier he received the Order of Lenin and was praised by the Soviet leaders as a most consistent and distinguished Leninist.

At the same time warnings against over optimistic hopes were apparent much earlier on than after October 1956. Already in January the local Party daily, Glos Szczecinski, warned workers against those "political gamblers" who wanted to set Poland on the path Czechoslovakia took in 1968. Some Warsaw papers left no doubt that any group(12), or force outside the Party could possibly hope to influence the process of "renewal." The Party and only the Party, can steer this development, wrote Trybuna Ludu.

The problem of the raison d'etat appeared once more on the horizon. The argument had been very much abused in the past, but it did appear this time in a more sensible and more realistic way. Rakowski, in Polityka, admitted that there were forces which would like to see People's Poland in a still more difficult situation than it was already in. There were people, he said, who felt that "the worse things are, the better for them." The warning not to overstep the more sensible limits of raison d'etat sounded rather clear. On the whole there was

an expression of satisfaction that during the December events
there were no apparent anti-Soviet demonstrations but there
was also a warning that there existed a limit to anything that
could be done and that the Soviet alliance remained one of the
taboos which must be preserved as such.

The People Speak Out

Truth is bitter and disagreeable to fools;
but falsehood is sweet and acceptable.

St.   Chrysostom

The first economic and some political concessions forced by the
workers in the danger areas, notwithstanding their importance,
did not manage to restore complete normality. Spontaneous
mass workers' meetings discussing the events and their consequences, the demands of the workers and their complaints
were stormy, controversial and, in most cases, had all the
aspects of an uncompromising confrontation. The strikes and
stoppages continued, and tension began growing again, for
reasons which were understandable.
      In the first few weeks of January 1971, the leadership
was clearly playing for time. Many meetings in the provinces
were reported in a dour, dry language stressing only that all
the main problems had been discussed. There was, for instance, no mention about the demands of workers, who at VPC
meetings in Gdansk and Szczecin asked for the punishment of
those responsible for the suppression of riots, and for the
workers' councils to be recognized as the most important
channel for workers' participation in decision making in industrial establishments. While the leadership allowed the
people to speak their minds only some local media along the
coast reported in more detail what was actually said and what
was discussed. Everything, on the insistence of the leadership had to be left to the plenary session of the CC which
would tell the people the whole truth and nothing but the
truth. But the people demanded full information now - the
details of those killed and injured, and disclosure of the
actions of the security forces in December. By sealing off
information originating from the coastal towns, the Party hoped
to avoid the contagious effects of various demands in the
country as a whole. An Italian communist journalist reported
in January from Warsaw(13) that the whole of Poland was like
one vast speaker's corner in Hyde Park. The Polish press
called this a return to the dialogue between the nation and the
Party. That this dialogue gradually degenerated into new
ferment, into new interruptions of work, was withheld from the

public.   The readers of <u>Trybuna Ludu</u> were only informed about a new enthusiasm for production pledges.

The continued workers' grievances fell by now into two categories. The overriding economic factors played their part, but strong political demands also appeared on the surface. The initial economic concessions offered nothing to skilled industrial workers who already earned more than 3,000 zlotys a month. They continued, therefore, to press for either adequate wage increases on a national scale or for a complete abolition of Gomulka's price-increase package. At the same time the workers insisted, in over 2,000 demands and in an open letter to Gierek, on the punishment of those who had given orders to shoot in December 1970, on economic and social reforms; on reshaping the Party; and on free elections to their local workers' Party organizations. Free elections had already been forced on local authorities both in the coastal towns and to some extent in Lodz. In numerous statements and leaflets the workers' demands also included the release of all demonstrators still under arrest and a moratorium on further sanctions against strikers, the improvement of public information on state policies, and the transformation of the trade unions and workers' councils into genuine channels for the institutionalized expression of workers' interests.

The local Party organizations maintained, quite rightly, that these demands did not challenge the existing system. The workers did not raise the question of the validity of socialism or of Communist party rule itself. Yet, the workers' protests in January represented a devastating criticism of the whole post-1956 system. Continuing mass action made the workers the most dynamic element on the Polish political scene at the beginning of 1971. The strength of their movement was the more remarkable because of the absence of what could be termed in communist jargon "revisionist forces."(14) The link between such elements of the elite and the workers had accounted for the major eruptions of unrest in 1953 and 1956 in Eastern Europe. The assertiveness of the workers, standing alone, without any support from either intellectuals or students, represented not merely a new factor on the Polish political scene but a unique phenomenon in the communist world.

One of the main subjects raised at the workers' meetings was the role and activities, or rather the lack of them, of the trade unions. They were accused of acting for many years in an atmosphere of formalism and bureaucracy without paying any attention to the defense of workers' rights and to satisfying the workers' just demands, of complete isolation from the everyday life of the worker, and of disregarding the workers' councils - one of the links in the workers' self-government.(15) In Szczecin, Gdansk, and Lodz the workers demanded that the trade unions would have to cease to be a mere transmission belt for directives of the Party and economic administration.

But in January there was still no official answer as to whether the revitalization of the existing forms, which had failed miserably over so many years, would be enough or whether new mechanisms of dialogue and participation would have to be created. Partial answers were given to this question at various meetings by the people at large. In Szczecin the students insisted that the analysis of the December events should be undertaken straight away by the VPC which must disclose all the details without waiting for the plenary session of the Central Committee.(16) The mass media did not disclose the crucial facts of what was happening in the country, claimed workers in Szczecin. The Party continued to live in isolation, away from the people, and did not enter into a dialogue with the nation, accused the workers in Gdansk and Oliwa on the Baltic coast. The Party was overcentralized and people without any qualification in Warsaw still decided everything, complained workers in Lodz. In Gdansk one of the workers stood up and said: "If we have to work hard we want to know now what the prospects are of improving our standard of living."

The leadership made it possible for everybody to speak their minds. The political pressure from below was probably reinforced by the impact of the Polish-West German treaty, which had hopefully deflated Polish fears of German "revanchism." For many years the Party had justified its rule to the nation with the argument that it was the only political force acceptable to the Soviet Union as a partner in an anti-West German alliance guaranteeing Poland's territorial integrity. Now that the German factor disappeared, the Czechoslovak bogey was put forward as an alternative argument. But all the evidence so far proved that the Soviet leaders would have been most unhappy, and, therefore, were unwilling to intervene. Since, however, few Poles could conceive of adopting the relatively bloodless acceptance of Soviet intervention displayed by the Czechs, the threat of Russian military involvement was a high card in the hands of the leadership. When Gomulka pulled that emergency brake handle labeled "Soviet Help" nothing happened. But, the implied threat ran, if things got badly out of hand, Gierek might not even be given the chance to reach for that brake.

Toward Another Confrontation

In the first two months of 1971 the question was: Would Gierek be able to remain in control of the situation which showed all the signs of explosive ingredients and of a new confrontation?

January 5

On the very day when in Moscow Gierek and Jaroszewicz are discussing with the Soviet leaders the situation in Poland,

3,000 shipyard workers in Gdansk are on strike for the third day. They demand that 200 workers arrested after the December revolt be released from prison and ask Gierek to come to Gdansk and listen to their complaints face to face.

One worker says: "Many of us firmly believed that things had changed and were improving after all that has happened during December. But there is really no change. We complain about further deceptions being perpetrated by the leadership."(17) Another worker maintains that the personnel changes are not enough - the system has to be changed within the existing limits: "The strikers must be very cautious because of the surveillance by police acting under Warsaw orders is very strict. The workers prefer to go to their workshops. But once there, they just sit on the floor and do nothing."

January 11

A total strike at the Warski shipyards in Szczecin is averted at the last moment by the personal intervention of PB member Szydlak, and the dismissal of the VPC secretary, Walaszek.

January 14

Demonstrations by workers in Elblag.

Radio Gdansk announces that in Gdynia shipyards 21 meetings of workers discussed the problems and the discussions were very harsh and controversial.

January 15

The chairman of the Central Council of Trade Unions (CCTU), Gomulka's former close associate Loga-Sowinski, resigns and admits that the trade unions failed to perform their duty in December in defending workers' interests. He is replaced by PB member Kruczek, a hard-line Stalinist who had survived the internal party purges when Gomulka took over and after the March upheaval in 1968 was promoted to full membership of the politburo. Workers on the coast protest against this new appointment.

January 18

The strike at the Lenin shipyards in Gdansk is almost complete by morning, but later the workers, some of whom have been on strike eight days, go back to work when the management announces that a joint delegation will go to Warsaw.

The list of demands is very comprehensive: the publication of a complete list of those who were killed and injured during the December riots; permission for the families of the dead to organize the funerals; removal of Head of State Cyrankiewicz, and of Minister for Foreign Affairs Jedrychowski; expulsion from the PB and other Party authority of Loga-Sowinski, of Deputy Premier Kociolek, and of General Moczar who is blamed for the bloody repression of the riots; punishment of all the others who were responsible for the repression; Gierek and Jaroszewicz coming to the Gdansk shipyards to face

the workers; a general increase in wages and an improvement
in conditions of work; free elections to workers' councils and
local trade union organizations; abolition of unrealistically high
working norms; release of workers arrested before Christmas
and reinstatement of those dismissed from their jobs; and
finally, freedom of the press, and abolition of censorship.
January 19
        In Warsaw Gierek and Jaroszewicz receive the so-called
joint delegation-representatives of port and ship repair yard
employees from Gdansk and Szczecin-who present them with a
list of 2,000 various demands and grievances. But no representatives of the Gdansk and Szczecin shipyards are included
in the delegation.
        While the strikes in the shipyards on the coast continue,
the transport workers in Gdansk go on strike asking for an
increase in wages.
January 22
        In a gesture to defuse the growing tension, several
leaders of local Party organizations in Gdansk and Elblag are
dismissed.
January 22-24
        The atmosphere in the Szczecin shipyards is extremely
tense and volatile because, as workers themselves told me, the
tactics which the leaders choose to form the so-called delegation which went to Warsaw to see Gierek, indicated that they
had drawn no proper conclusions from the December lessons.
Besides, those responsible for the bloody events have not been
punished.
        On January 23 there is a general strike in Szczecin.
This time another strike committee takes over, maintaining
order in the city, assuring the distribution of food. The man
in charge is a non-Party worker. For three days the strike
committee administers not only the shipyards but the whole
city of Szczecin.
        The situation becomes explosive, and, according to what I
was told in Warsaw, could have had incalculable consequences
if it were not for the personal intervention of Gierek.
January 24
        Gierek and Jaroszewicz together with PB member, Minister
of Defense, Jaruzelski, and the recently appointed acting
Minister of the Interior Szlachcic, arrive in the Szczecin shipyards. But the gates are closed and guarded by the strike
committee members. The limousines in which the leaders arrive
are stopped and Gierek has to ask permission to enter the
shipyards. The strike committee representatives refuse, at
first, to admit the new Minister of Interior Szlachcic, but later
allow him to enter. The leaders go on foot to a mass meeting
with the workers but first meet their new freely elected representatives. The confrontation between Gierek and the shipyard workers lasts nine hours - the whole night - and the dis-

cussion is transmitted over public-address loudspeakers across
the shipyards.

Gierek Faces the Workers in Szczecin

This crucial confrontation was recorded and a transcript
of the tape became available in the West.   Gierek and his
colleagues were introduced by the chairman of the strike
committee, Baluta, who presented them with a list of demands
including: the Gomulka price increases to be completely withdrawn; immediate legal democratic elections to trade unions,
workers' councils, Party and youth organizations; workers to
receive their full pay for the period of the strike; the authorities to give guarantees of full personal security to the
strikers and members of the strike committee, and no reprisals
to be taken against them; direct and permanent dialogue with
the workers' representatives on the strike committee; and
security services to stop arresting workers taking part in the
strike.

Gierek replied to the demands:

> I would like to ask you comrades for a little
> patience and understanding. I was aware that the
> situation in Szczecin was intolerable.   Comrade
> Gomulka in whom we had unlimited confidence for so
> long, made wrong decisions. There was an op-
> position. But we could not do anything, and the
> little that we did was immediately wrecked by the
> bureaucracy....
> We are at the end of the line....Everything is
> very bad. The worst of it is that we don't know
> how to get out of it....The only solution is that you
> work still harder so that our economy produces its
> maximum....
> I say to you: help us, help me....When it was
> proposed that I take over the leadership of the
> Party, at first I thought I would refuse....I am
> only a worker like you....But if I had done that,
> there would have been a bloodbath.
> You will tell me that a bloodbath took place
> anyway, that there were many deaths. That is
> true, and I pay homage to those who fell. But now,
> and I tell you this in all solemnity, as a Pole and as
> a communist - the fate of our nation and the cause
> of socialism are in the balance. I promise to grant
> your demands to the maximum, but I ask certain
> things of you: for example, to cease the attacks
> against the Soviet Union....The Party will be re-
> novated. We will get rid of the incompetent people.
> As to lowering the price of foodstuffs, there is no
> possible way of going back to pre-December
> prices....But all elected bodies will be open to all,

both Party members and non-Party people, even to
members of the strike committee, why not?...

   Don't demand from us a democracy for all, for
friends and enemies alike.   The erroneous reports
will be corrected but it is out of the question, at
this time, to encourage agitation among the workers
by publishing your demands....If anyone has been
arrested for a strike action, he has to be released
immediately....I know that it cannot satisfy you
completely, but you must understand that that's the
limit....

After Gierek's speech, various workers' representatives
spoke.

A delegate from department K-1:

   Does Comrade Gierek know that we can no
longer count the number of corpses here in this city
and in these yards, because it is hard to calculate
how many have been picked up in the street?
People were falling, bullets were whistling and those
bullets were bought with money earned by our
sweat.   That's really too hard to bear.   How is it
possible that the working class can be turned
against the working class?   Comrade Gierek tells us:
there won't be any sanctions against the strikers.
Official sanctions perhaps.   But how about other
sanctions?   Actually they catch the shipyard workers
like rats.   They jump on them noiselessly in a
corner, behind trees, they beat them up.   These
militia methods have to be changed.   And the leaders
have to be changed - the new aristocracy that is
going to steal everything....(ovation in the hall)

A delegate from department K-2:

   So many young people have been killed, shot
from behind, in the back, in the head.   There is
proof.   I am an eye-witness.   And then those killed
in the streets have been wrapped up in nylon bags
and buried in secret like cattle.   But the people will
not let this go by.   But Comrade Edward is the
right kind of man.   Let's give him at least a year or
two and we will see the results.(applause)

A delegate from department K-5 attacked the overblown
bureaucracy in the shipyards:

   We are working for ten people in cozy offices.
What use are all these gentlemen?   Sometimes a week
goes by without me seeing one of them do a hand's
turn....

A delegate from department W-2:

I ask for a frank answer from the first secretary. Must blood flow to change the Central Committee of the Party and the government? Shouldn't we consider limiting the duration of office to avoid events like 1956 and 1970?....

A member of the strike committee:

Our best weapon is the truth. Lies are useless to us. Everyone knows that two opposing tendencies have taken shape in the leadership and that they are at each others' throats. If the tendency behind the old policy comes up on top, those of us who started the strike will end up in the nick....

A delegate from the local Party organization:

Comrade Gierek tells us that we have to save money which is precious to our country. We know that, but we can take some money back from those who are living too well on our labor. Our society is divided into classes. There are people who no longer know what to do with their socialism and they are already looking for something better."

A delegate from the transport department:

Comrade Gierek, do you know what a change is? It is here among us workers and strikers, in our shipyards, so it is with us that you should hold discussions instead of sending the militia after us as if we were bandits....

A delegate from shipyards repair department:

Do we punish criminals in our country or do we pay them? Someone answer me. We Poles chastise the Germans for their crimes, for shooting at us. Let the first secretary of the Central Committee give me the answer: Are crimes punished or rewarded?

Finally at the end of this 9-hour session in the early morning hours Gierek took the floor again and said, among other things:

You have told me here that 14 years of Gomulka was too long....I will do my utmost to make sure that my period will not be too long....

During those 14 years things generally happened something like this: There were staff meetings
of a group of two or three persons and this staff
would take the decisions under Comrade Gomulka....
Many of the government's decrees, while this ex-
ceptional autocracy of Gomulka's held sway, were
decided in his office, and the government only
learned about certain decisions by reading the
papers.

You could ask: Yes, but what about the Political Bureau? There wasn't much of the bureau, one
could say. If some members brought up something
they were either isolated or discriminated against....
I could have resigned. Only other comrades explained to me, "Don't do it, because if there are
incidents, no matter what it is, they will say you
caused them. They are going to say you were the
motive force behind the incidents...." I would not
like people to think I wished to blame others and
whitewash myself. I am no angel. If I look at some
matters with the benefit of hindsight, I can see that
in certain cases I was wrong....I solemnly promise
you that we will do our utmost to make the house-
cleaning genuinely thorough....(18)

By any communist standards this was the most unusual
confrontation between the communist party leader and
thousands of workers.

Gierek had to go to Szczecin in a critical situation which
could have easily gotten out of control. But this confrontation
with the workers was also the most telling evidence, so far, of
the new style of approach to people at large which Gierek
introduced. He certainly made some firm promises and blamed
the autocratic Gomulka's rule for much of what had happened,
but he also admitted that others, including himself, were not
blameless. And he provided a very vivid illustration of the
struggles and methods applied in the top Party hierarchy.
The leader was always right and whoever opposed him must
take the blame if the leader's decision brings on tragic consequences.

But above all, from the human point of view, Gierek was
talking to the workers as equals. And seldom, if ever, has
the leader of the ruling Communist party pleaded so persistently and humbly for help, assistance, understanding and
patience. At the same time Gierek very strongly implied that
if there was no stabilization based on hard work, if the
demands went too far and were too widely publicized, there
would be dangers for the country as a whole. This appeal
should be related to Gierek's pleading with the workers not to
attack the Soviet Union, which, by implication showed how

strong anti-Soviet feelings prevailed among the workers on the coast. The warning was clear enough. As a result he managed to appease the workers and to win most of them over because his intervention was not just a simple gesture.

As reported by local radio stations in Gdansk and Szczecin the workers at various meetings confirmed over and over again that Gierek came to the shipyards because they had insisted on it.(19)

One of the workers told me some months later: "We wanted him to come because we wanted him to give us, face to face, some undertakings which, if the need arose we could remind him of." Another shipyard worker said: "We gave him the credit of confidence for a limited period of time to make it possible for the leadership to achieve what they want and what we approve."

In a vivid metaphor the Krakow weekly, Zycie Literackie, described the change in the atmosphere, which was just beginning to take shape, as "an end of the dialogue of the deaf." But the Szczecin meeting was not yet the end of confrontation.

January 25

Gierek and Jaroszewicz, with Szlachcic, and this time another PB member, Babiuch, appear in the Gdansk shipyards and hold discussions with the striking workers there.

The authorities announce abandonment of the controversial incentives system worked out by Jaszczuk which sparked off, among other things, the riots in December.

In the Szczecin shipyards the situation begins to return to normal and work is resumed. The strike committee elected the preceding week transforms itself into a workers' committee, representing the whole of the workforce in the shipyards. Among the 38 members of the workers' committee, only seven belong to the Party.

At the end of January and the beginning of February, free elections to all the workers' and local Party organizations on the coast took place.

January 27

In his confrontation with the shipyard workers in Szczecin, and Gdansk, Gierek appeals for calm, order, and patience.

The Episcopate issues a communique in which it emphasizes the courage of workers who struggled for their rights in December.(20) But the Episcopate warns that the difficulties in the country should not be underestimated. It appeals to the nation for order and calm as being the best guarantees of independence. The Episcopate welcomes the Party's announced intention of improving relations with the church, but makes clear that its interest was in a church-state reconciliation which respects the church's interests and not one dictated by the Party.

February 6-7
    The long-awaited and often postponed eighth plenary
session of the CC assembles in Warsaw to analyze and assess
the situation both in the December and post-December periods
and to draw conclusions from the lessons learned. (See the
next section of this chapter, "The Party Diagnosis and
Remedies".)
February 12
    In Lodz, Poland's textile center, seven textile mills are on
strike. Initially the number of workers on strike amounts to
10,000 and they demand an increase in wages of between 20
percent and 25 percent. Soon all the workers from other
factories join in the strike, which is well organized. The
production lines are safeguarded by the workers, and there
are no clashes with hooligans. Earnings in textile mills are
much lower than average for the country.
    Workers in the Ursus tractor factory in Warsaw and in
the railway works in Wroclaw in southwest Poland are on
strike.
February 13
    While the strikes are continuing the prime minister
responds with pleas for restraint and cooperation in maintaining market equilibrium. To exceed the existing financial
limits under pressure, he says, would be disastrous and would
harm the economy.
February 14
    With a general strike on in Lodz the situation becomes
explosive once again and Jaroszewicz decides to go to the city.
A meeting is arranged in the Grand Theatre and Jaroszewicz
begins his speech arguing that the strikes should be only an
ultimate weapon when all other procedures had been exhausted. The audience appears to be extremely polite and
deferential to the prime minister, applauding all the right
passages in his speech. Jaroszewicz becomes suspicious and
asks the Party leader sitting on the platform beside him: "Are
these really the workers?" "Oh, yes!" the local Party leader
answers. "But, are these the strikers?" asks the prime
minister. "Well....in fact....no..." admits the local Party
leader. It transpires that the local Party organization was still
living in the times of Gomulka and had filled the whole theater
with Party members, carefully selected for the occasion. The
prime minister is not happy and asks again: "Where are the
strikers?" He learns that the strikers are holding their
meetings in the textile mills.
    Jaroszewicz goes to the Marchlewski plant and then to
another enterprise. It is already 11 p.m. and the two
meetings last the whole night. Petitions, grievances, and
demands are presented to Jaroszewicz in writing and shouted
at him by the audience. He tries hard to make himself heard
and understood. And then comes a most revealing moment:

"Do you support us?" shouts the prime minister.

"Yes!" answer the workers.

"Are you going to help us?" asks Jaroszewicz, echoing Gierek's by now famous slogan.

"No!" answer the workers, "You have to help us first!"

One of the women workers approaches the platform, turns her back on Jaroszewicz, displays her pants and says: "Look at my pants, they are torn and dirty but I cannot afford anything else." Jaroszewicz promises some help but refuses to agree to an immediate raise of wages by 20 to 25 percent.

February 15

Exhausted by the acrimonious and controversial all-night session in Lodz, Jaroszewicz returns to Warsaw.

In Szczecin an important shipyard workers' conference lasting 26 hours strongly criticizes the trade union organization which, as they say, has no idea of what is going on in the shipyards and has no contacts whatsoever with the shop floor.

While the general strike in Lodz continues and the workers refuse to budge from their demands, the authorities are forced to capitulate. In the evening Radio Warsaw(21) broadcasts the following announcement: "Thanks to the credits obtained during the last few days from the Soviet Union, and also taking into consideration a possible increase in our own meat production in the second part of the current year it has been decided to lower prices of food, including meat and meat products, to their former levels which existed before December 13, 1970." In other words, under strong pressure from the workers, Gomulka's price increases package is completely withdrawn, although only three weeks ago Gierek in Szczecin described the return to pre-December prices as absolutely impossible.

Jaroszewicz gives an improvised speech on television and retracts the arguments put forward only two days earlier in the Sejm and in his discussions in Lodz.(22) He declares that the direct cause of the workers' dissatisfaction has thus been eliminated and he pleads for the workers' support and help.

Moscow grants 100 million dollars cash credit in hard currency. It also arranged for Warsaw to make special use of Poland's credit balance at the Comecon International Bank for Economic Cooperation. The main purpose of these measures is to enable the Polish leadership to import large quantities of food and consumer goods from both capitalist and socialist countries. On top of the two million tons of grain promised by the Soviet Union in the five-year Polish-Soviet agreement signed at the end of December, more grain is to come from the West, and the American government grants 25 million dollars credit for the purchase of agricultural products. Some 100,000 tons of meat and meat products are to be imported by Poland during 1971 - mainly from Denmark and the countries of the European Economic Community (EEC). Imports of consumer goods from socialist countries are to rise by 28 percent.

February 16
    The minister of light industry goes to Lodz to help in discussions with the delegates of the strikers. Several local Party leaders and activists are dismissed.(23) The situation in the textile mills begins to return to normal.
February 24-25
    At the plenary session of the Central Council of Trade Unions, the activity or rather passivity of the organization in December is severely criticized. However, the principle of state syndicalism is not blamed, only the application of these principles in the past at various trade union levels. The new union leadership, struggling to maintain Party control over the organization, issues a resolution promising to satisfy some of the workers' demands.(24) Yet the CCTU is criticized in Szczecin for devoting "too little attention" to workers' complaints.

The Party Diagnosis and Remedies

When Gierek took the chair at the long awaited eighth plenum of the Central Committee (February 6-7, 1971) the Party was debating crucial issues in an atmosphere of new and continuing confrontations between the leadership and the workers, and he himself was faced with several dilemmas.
    In coastal towns Gierek warned the workers that insistence on "unrealistic demands" would be playing into the hands of those who had brought upon Poland the present catastrophic situation, in other words, those within the Party who were still opposing his leadership and policies. The crucial question was: How far could the Party go in blaming the previous leadership for the present crisis without undermining the official thesis that the system was sound and only the leaders were at fault? When I asked the question, Must fundamental changes come about only as a result of tragic and disastrous events?, a CC member answered, "I cannot see any institutional changes and guarantees at present in our system against such upheavals." Another journalist, a Party member said, "The Party has always been a tiny minority group. There must, therefore, be harsh discipline and full support for the leaders which necessarily leads to autocracy. The people who know that the 'old men' such as Gomulka are wrong, and either unable or unwilling to assess the situation realistically, will not budge. They are afraid of internal and external consequences since they know that they represent a tiny minority of the people."
    Another dilemma for Gierek was: How far could he go in purging the Party of Gomulka's followers? His own Silesian Party paper warned that there would be no repression, no witch hunting within the Party. But, as the paper reminded

its readers, one group within the Party was calling for a
continuation of that wholesale purge which was "unfortunately"
interrupted after the student demonstrations in Warsaw in
1968.

Finally, as quoted by coastal radio stations, the workers
had complained that the "process of renewal" was continuing
among the people, but within the Party itself, the bureaucracy
remained supreme. We give Gierek, said one of them, the
credit of confidence for as long as he applies in practice
policies which we approve of. The workers had realized that
they are not as powerless as it was once thought. The dilemma was how to reconcile the leading role of the Party, which
had broken so many promises in the past, with the pressure of
the people who wanted at last, to be co-rulers in a country
ruled in their name.

At the CC plenum, from which Gomulka was absent, the
leadership submitted a detailed assessment of the December
events for discussion and approval by the Central Committee.
The criticisms of Gomulka and his leadership expressed in the
PB document and during the debate could be grouped under
three headings: 1) the mishandling of unrest in the Baltic
cities; 2) the responsibility for incorrect policies which had
caused or contributed to the crisis; 3) an exercise of power
and style of leadership contrary to the correct Leninist
principles. The faulty policies which led to the December
crisis and for which Gomulka was blamed were both political
and economic, spelled out many times before the plenum.

In a first-ever television and radio report on the
proceedings of the first day of the CC plenum, PB member
Olszowski stressed that the new program of the Party and a
new approach based on the principle of broad consultation with
workers and with Party and non-Party people, would help to
reconstruct ties between the Party and society. But Olszowski
left no doubt that there must be an absolute monopoly by the
Party in shaping the nation's future. After what had happened in December this statement was, to say the least, very
much out of touch with reality.

Gomulka was accused of wielding authority contrary to the
principles of collective leadership and internal Party democracy.
His behavior during the December events illustrated a tendency toward concentrating increasingly autocratic power in
his hands. He was moreover criticized for forming, within the
PB, an inner leadership of a few chosen men who had freer
access to him and who supported him whenever necessary.
Only two of these people were explicitly named and singled
out for severe censure: Kliszko and Jaszczuk.

Gomulka was also accused of neglecting ideological
problems, appointing revisionist elements into the higher
echelons of the Party and the government, of passivity toward
reactionary subversion inspired by imperialist circles in liter-

ature and science, and of failure to entrust the running of the country more to the Party activists who had participated in the underground struggle against the Germans.

The new leadership felt it had to find a scapegoat for the tremendous upheaval of December and for the disastrous situation in which the Party found itself. The scapegoats were, not unexpectedly, Gomulka and his two principal associates. The new leaders had, of course, been Gomulka's colleagues but their excuse was that though they had seen Gomulka's faults and mistakes, they were powerless to prevent them, still less to remove him from office. This, by the way, was not so much an indictment of Gomulka himself but mainly of the system and its structure. It proved once again that there were no mechanisms which could efficiently change policies and oppose errors and grave mistakes.

Some of the speeches at the plenum offered a fascinating additional insight into the contrasting attitudes and currents of thought among the Polish communist hierarchy.

Wincenty Krasko, head of the Central Committee Cultural Department said:

> The brain of the Party suffered from serious disorders. There was a sharp contradiction between the intellectual and educational achievements of the people, and the anachronistic working style of the leaders. Every leader can make mistakes but he should admit them and if he considers that he did not commit any mistakes he should have the courage to defend his attitude and his decisions. There must never be a conflict between the Party and the working class, but if it comes to that, as it did in December, one has to face it even at the price of losing face.

PB member Moczar accused Gomulka of being unable to stand having independent people around him. But he also said:

> The old leadership was thinking in terms of methods of the nineteenth century, while there were continuing changes all around us...did not realize that the people did not believe the Party and that the peak of our weakness came on December 12.

The secretary of the Warsaw VPC, Szafranski confessed that:

> For a long time one could sense that there was something terribly wrong with the Party. We got entangled in the mechanism of power which we ourselves had created. Authority became transformed into autocracy.(25)

Personnel changes had been carried out by the second day of the plenum. The plenum resolution recognized Gomulka's previous merits and services to the Party and the country, but also found that he was guilty of "serious mistakes in the management of the Party in recent years," which resulted in a weakening of its links with society, the emergence of irregularities in economic development, and finally in an open and political crisis in which wrong methods were used. In view of this the plenum suspended him as a CC member. Kliszko and Jaszczuk were removed from the CC, the former because "he displayed a lack of realistic thinking and acted in an irresponsible manner aggravating the conflict with the working class." This confirmed earlier reports that he was responsible for the Party's handling of the riots, including the order to shoot at the demonstrators in the coastal cities. Jaszczuk was removed because he directly interfered with the activity of the government and contributed to the forcing through of a number of erroneous economic decisions which led to the December events. Kociolek and Loga-Sowinski "resigned" from the PB. Four new members of the CC included General Urbanowicz, deputy minister of defense and the chief of the army political administration.

Finally, on the second day of the plenum came Gierek's long-awaited speech, broadcast for the first time in full to the nation. The new Party leader sounded at times like a great statesman, but he also appeared like a good country teacher trying to explain the most elementary rules of good conduct and commendable behavior:

> We have turned back a dangerous trend of events. Social tensions which existed in December, and grew up not only on the coast but also in other parts of the country and threatened incalculable consequences have been defused. Late in the day, but not too late, our Party found courage enough to face reality eye-to-eye and power enough to lead the country out of its crisis.

Understandably enough Gierek did not mention the fact that the Party had no other way except to change its leadership and policies under the overwhelming pressure from the people and because it was threatened by a general strike in the whole country as of December 21.

According to Gierek, the initially peaceful character of the workers' protests changed because no effort was made to defuse tension, or to start sincere talks with the workers. As a result the workers took to the streets and the demonstration transformed itself very quickly into elemental, unrestrained force which the workers did not want, but were unable to stop. Dangerous riots were a natural consequence of such a situation, and antisocial elements appeared on the streets, destroying buildings, looting and plundering shops. According to Gierek, the real tragedy was that no political means were applied, only force. The use of force as the only answer to workers' demands and protests had hardened, deepened and spread the demonstrations and the violence. A real catastrophe was just around the corner, said Gierek. "Unfortunately," Gierek went on, "the previous leadership did not understand the character of the events and their real causes. This attitude was mistaken and catastrophic in its results."

This was an open admission that whatever had changed so far, had been due to the people pressing for change in a most violent way. Gierek turned upside down the first official version of the events, and rightly so. This had happened before in Polish postwar history. The Poznan events in June 1956 were described as the work of hooligans and adventurists, to be "corrected" only a month later at the Party plenum and presented as genuine workers' protest. The same happened in October 1956. And on all these occasions, the new leadership tried to maintain that the general Party line was right, that the Party as such was not really at fault, and had led the people out of the crisis. For political purposes, such interpretations might appear to be necessary, but obviously this had nothing to do with the real situation and with the events as they happened.

According to Gierek, the workers' demonstrations were not directed against the socialist system and its basic principles. This was certainly true to a great extent, but Gierek did not mention that the demonstrations were directed against socialism, its structure, and its methods, as practiced in Poland in recent years. He admitted that the Party found itself in an extremely difficult situation and, like Gomulka in October 1956, so Gierek in February 1971 appealed for a hard struggle against both revisionist and dogmatist tendencies within the Party. The trouble with the description "revisionism" and dogmatism" is that the meaning of these words changes in the communist jargon depending on circumstances and political requirements. Something condemned as revisionist one day appeared to be a creative Marxist thought of the leading Party the next day and vice versa.

Another grave error of the previous leadership, Gierek emphasized, was the taking over by the Party leadership of functions which should belong to the government. More and more social and economic reality was misunderstood. But he also stressed that to put all the responsibility on the old leaders would be too simple: "Each of us bears part of the responsibility for what happened, although this responsibility is not distributed in equal shares."

Gierek also tried to answer the question: What guarantees are there that, in the future, social problems and conflicts would be solved by correct methods? His only answer was that the Party must exercise its functions as the leading force according to Marxist-Leninist ideology. This was not saying very much since the Party was supposed to be doing just that over the last 30 years, and had not managed to avoid riots and upheavals. Yes, ran the argument, but these only broke out when the Party, or rather a leader, deviated from the "Leninist norms." A truer answer would be that Leninist norms or no Leninist norms, the people were convinced that the existing system could function much more efficiently and democratically, and should undergo an evolution in which the people and their truly representative organs could really participate in decision making.

Now, Gierek promised consultations. The Party, relying on experiences and views of the workers, peasants and intelligentsia, would shape political thought, would outline the direction of implementation of policies, and would become the main center of mobilization and activation of all the forces of the nation. Besides, there had to be more discussion before decisions were taken and more discipline in implementing them. In short, guarantees, said Gierek, that in the future no mistakes would be repeated, should be sought not in miraculous formulae but in a deep and real "renewal," mainly within the Party.

As if not to leave any doubt about his loyalties, Gierek said: "Poland may only develop as a socialist state, inseparably allied with the Soviet Union, with her neighbors and allies. Secondly, the historically tried leading force of the Polish nation is, and remains, our Party." Gierek very strongly emphasized, therefore, the two imperatives of the system he had inherited and at the same time he defined the limits of his own scope for political maneuver which he could not overstep. He concluded his speech by appealing, almost desperately, to the nation as a whole for "the most noble proofs of patriotism."

For the first time, after almost two months since the December events, Gierek disclosed the official figures showing the extent of losses, both in human lives and in property. He announced that a special commission would further investigate the December incidents. The plenum also decided to convene the Party congress at an earlier date.

There were several passages in Gierek's speech which must have been welcomed by the country at large: the honest assessment of what and why really happened in December, although he did not say whether in the opinion of the Party the security forces overreacted; the personnel changes in the leadership demanded for at least two months by the workers and which were now partly implemented; the drastic reorientation in economic policies with an emphasis on consumer goods and on a raising of living standards which was undertaken; the promise of consultation before crucial decisions were taken; the strong condemnation of the previous leadership for both the erroneous methods and mistaken political concepts; the accent on the importance of the role of youth and on the fact that young people had to have a real vision of the future which would spur them to work harder; and, finally, the unqualified condemnation of the use of force in December.

But, at the same time, Gierek was very careful in talking about greater liberalization, any political reforms, any re-structuring of mechanisms of consultation. He glossed over the role of trade unions and of the press. He did not mention the demands of the workers for autonomous trade unions and for the strengthening of workers' councils. Nor did he mention anything about the punishment of those responsible for the December events, as demanded by the workers. And when he talked about dialogue and consultation he emphasized, perhaps more strongly than ever, that this dialogue and con-sultation must be real and widespread within the Party. But his remarks about consultations contained a typically Gierek accent on Polish nationalism and patriotism.

Much of what Gierek said and promised had earlier been voiced by Gomulka, after October 1956. But perhaps the point was that this was Gierek who was doing the promising and he was certainly a different man than any other Polish communist leader. Even so, Warsaw humor had it doubts and the fol-lowing joke was soon in circulation:

Question: What is the difference between Gomulka and Gierek?
Answer: None - only Gierek does not know it yet!

There was no doubt that Gierek was at that time, both for internal and external reasons, in an extremely delicate position. He had yet to consolidate his power within the country and, at the same time, he had to prove how far he would be prepared to go in reviving the country and the economy in the light of events in Czechoslovakia in 1968. The average reaction of people to the plenum could be summarized in one short sentence: "Let's see whether Gierek will pass the test, whether he will be able and prepared to introduce the maximum of changes within allowable limits." As for the re-action of the workers, two examples seemed to be particularly significant. In Szczecin, the member of the CC who spoke at the Plenum emphasized at the meeting with the workers that it was difficult at that stage to say to what extent the workers' demands had been satisfied. In another instance, the local Gdansk radio station(26) quoted a worker who complained, "Those who are ruling want always to know how we work and what we achieve, but they will never even permit us to ask them how they work and what they have achieved."

The next day, after the plenum, at a press conference for foreign journalists in Warsaw, the interpress agency editor announced the new composition of the Party leadership and for the first time ever, outlined how the secretariat's work would be redistributed:(27) Gierek - general responsibility for all matters; Babiuch - personnel matters; Barcikowski - agriculture; Moczar - army, security, administration, and the health service; Olszowski - the press, culture front, and youth questions; Starewicz - the politburo secretariat; Szydlak - propaganda and ideology; Tejchma - foreign affairs, science and the Sejm. The correspondents did not receive an answer to their question about who was to be responsible for economic matters.

A few days later in the Sejm two deputy premiers, Majewski and Kulesza, were relieved of their positions. Krasko was appointed deputy premier in charge of culture, science, education and youth, and the Office for Religious Denominations, i.e., the negotiations between the state and the church. There was no surprise at the dismissal of the minister of the interior, Kazimierz Switala, who had "resigned" for health reasons some time ago; neither was there any surprise in the appointment of General Szlachcic as minister of the interior. He was regarded by some highly placed Party members as Gierek's "undercover agent" in the Ministry of Internal Affairs when it was headed by Moczar. The new foreign trade minister was Kazimierz Olszewski. Perhaps the most interesting development was the major shake-up in the Planning Commission where three deputy chairmen were relieved of their duties as well as the chairman, Majewski, who was thus made the scapegoat in the government, as Jaszczuk had been earlier in the Party for the former regime's much-criticized economic policies and concepts.

DEFUSING THE SITUATION: PHASE TWO

After the Lodz general strike and the eighth CC plenum, Gierek's further measures had managed to disarm the forces of popular discontent even though sporadic stoppages and strikes lasted until the summer.

In an unprecedented "dialogue with the masses" he went out of his way to sell to the people, over the heads of the Party activists, the leadership's new image and working style. In over 200 meetings he confronted ordinary people in every region, listening to complaints, explaining, asking for help from believers and nonbelievers alike. His solicitous approach to the workers, his personal contact with them, and his adeptness in distancing himself personally from Gomulka's policies did a great deal to improve a still uncertain situation.

His style was complemented by his policies. A major redirection of the economy, with vague promises of comprehensive economic reforms, emphasized all the elements of consumerism.(28)   He promised a dynamic economic development, modernization of industrial production and at the same time a significant rise in the standard of living. As his close associate, PB member Babiuch, said: "Our policy is based on the fundamental idea that the highest goal of socialism lies in the constant satisfaction of the material and spiritual needs of the people, on the basis of dynamic economic development." Another PB member, Szydlak, defined the essence of the evolving economic model in these terms:(29) "Increased consumption is an important and necessary factor in the process of economic growth, a factor which stimulates production and technological progress, improves organization and results in greater labor productivity." Here was, in a nutshell, the whole rationale behind the new economic policy. Hard work properly rewarded was to be the mainspring of economic progress.

This pragmatic, consumer-oriented approach had the distinct personal imprint of the new leader. While Gomulka's opening to the West was strictly limited, Gierek was ready to entertain any possibility of getting credits from abroad, of extending industrial cooperation with the West and of getting the most modern technological know-how from Western countries. The new socioeconomic policy was based on the assumption that it was already possible for the present generation to benefit from the economic progress of Poland. The crux of the problem was how, without ignoring economic growth, to attain the maximum possible standard of living. In fact, the new leadership accepted the unlikely concept that, for a socialist state, increased consumption was an important and necessary factor in economic growth, as Szydlak wrote in the Party paper, Trybuna Ludu.(30)

Over 160 major industrial enterprises were singled out for special attention and enjoyed what could be called a hot line with the secretariat of the CC and with Gierek himself. Because, as he himself stressed, the elite of workers in leading industrial plants must become "the principal fortress of socialism."(31)   Regular channels of information about the activities of the Party and government leaders had also been established; short communiques were now issued after each PB meeting.   A government spokesman was appointed in March 1971 to act as a regular liaison officer between the Council of Ministers and the press.   A journalist from the weekly Polityka was invited to sit in on three cabinet meetings with a view to stripping away the unnecessary veil of secrecy and unapproachability.   A highly successful phone-in television program called "The Citizens' Tribune" was launched.   In this program top Party leaders answered questions coming in from all over the country. Gierek rescinded a 1970 law restricting the release of information to the press by local officials and enterprise managers. Several sensitive and pressing problems were now thrashed out in public.

Gierek also promised to promote greater participation in the government by the people from outside the ranks of the Party. In February 1971, an independent deputy, Halina Skibniewska, was elected a deputy speaker of the Sejm. And at the same time, PB member Tejchma declared the strengthening of all representative bodies, particularly the Sejm, to be a major Party goal.(32) In June 1971 the presidium of the National Unity Front (FNU), an umbrella organization through which the Party supervised political participation of the two so-called allied parties (the United Peasants' party and the Democratic party), as well as of other organized groups, was restructured to provide for stronger representation of non-Party people. Breaking with the tradition that a communist should hold the post, the Front elected a non-Party man, Professor Groszkowski, to be chairman of the presidium and two other non-Party figures to be deputy chairmen.

In three major areas, Gierek showed a willingness to compromise and very shortly pragmatism had become the hallmark of his leadership.(33) He offered tolerance, reconciliation and even cooperation to the church. He introduced a new agricultural policy emphasizing the role of individual peasants and improving their lot. To the workers, whose newfound militancy was at once a major threat and, if it could be harnessed, a primary source of social momentum, Gierek provided an immediate improvement in the standard of living.

A special commission for the modernization of the functioning of the system of the economy and the state under the chairmanship of PB member Szydlak, was created. It included representatives of the political leadership, academics, economists and administrators. Its task was to be the drafting of principles for the reform of the administration, of a new economic-financial system, and an examination of ways of making use of science to stimulate the country's modernization and development. Another committee of experts was formed to report on the state of education in the country and to suggest ways and means of modernizing the whole educational system.

Gierek's first hundred days were perhaps without precedent in the history of the communist system. There was never, during such a short period, so much done in innumerable meetings and discussions at all levels with all groups of the population to sort out the problems. Once the most immediate material demands had been satisfied, further reforms were undertaken, though much more cautiously and slowly. The Sejm was supposed to be the supreme organ in the land, but only provided that all the deputies were absolutely unanimous about the basic principles of building socialism.

Within these limits the activities and the functioning of the Sejm could be enlarged. But, as Professor Zawadzki, a law expert stressed, the people's power must be secured against, what he called, internal forces remaining on antisocialist positions, which required the prohibition of political parties opposing the socialist system, and of antisocialist propaganda.(34)

In the trade unions, the leading role of the Party had to be strengthened in the sense that the unions would be, as Trybuna Ludu said, not only a transmission belt of decisions from above, but also a transmission belt of demands from below. But the basic reconstruction of the CCTU was shelved for consideration by a special commission.

Another problem was the workers' self-government which, as everyone agreed, did not play any real part. But the basic role of the workers' council within the workers' self-government was not emphasized any more. The Party tried to reactivate the existing, and for many years passive, "conference of workers' self-government" in which the workers' councils were only a part. The leading role of the Party had to be strengthened by eliminating some spontaneous organizations which grew up in and after December such as strike committees or, as in some provinces, the workers' consultative committees advising the Provincial National Councils (local government).

The separation of functions between the Party and the government was outlined by Gierek when he said that the Party would work out the general line of the policy for the government and the government would have the initiative and responsibility for the methods, ways and means of implementing this line in solving particular problems.

Although there was in the middle of 1971 an unmistakable decrease in tensions in the country, difficult unsolved problems remained in the triangle of relations between Gierek, the Party and the people. And it was the question of how to revitalize and change the Party which presented a serious dilemma.

While strenuously avoiding confrontations, Gierek moved with dispatch and determination to consolidate the Party's comprehensive political control. Describing his leadership's attachment to an unbending interpretation of the leading role of the Party, Gierek told the CC in April that:(35) "The Soviet comrades are motivated by the correct principle that for a Leninist party, anarchist loosening of social discipline which amounts to a parody of democracy is just as harmful as bureaucratic centralization which paralyzes the development of Party organizations, and of initiative and activity among communists." Here, of course, was his dilemma: how to re-establish and then to reconcile the comprehensive leading role of the Party and its overall political hegemony with promises of consultation and participation of the people in decision making.

His pragmatic approach to problems of socioeconomic development had been accompanied by comprehensive efforts to invigorate ideology in the nation's life. And there was never any doubt that the ultimate aim of the leadership was the socialization of Polish society. The question remained: What sort of socialist society, and by what methods was it to be achieved?

At the end of February, Gierek unexpectedly cancelled his meeting with one of the leaders of the West German Social Democratic party, Herbert Wehner, and rushed from Warsaw to the provinces where he called several meetings, both with the Party activists and workers' organizations. The suddenness of this tour was remarkable, particularly after the cancellation of price increases, and the removal of eight of the 19 first secretaries of provincial Party committees. Observers in Warsaw suggested two explanations. There were many people in the Party apparatus who opposed the present leadership because they felt endangered in their comfortable positions, and in the struggle between the new and the old they strongly rejected the "renewal." They were still treating the people with disdain and were fully convinced that the Party had to govern itself and not accept any consultations with outsiders. Moreover, Gierek's opponents in the Party were fomenting trouble by suggesting to the workers in certain big enterprises that they should ask for huge wage increases straight away. This brought up another difficulty. From the economic point of view, the leadership was unable to make further concessions which could bring immediate financial improvements. But, at the same time, Gierek had to take into account the pressure and the influence of his opponents in the Party hierarchy.

It was rather interesting that the cancellation of price increases which, by definition, strengthened Gierek's position was exploited by the propaganda as a direct result of special Soviet credits. Politically, by taking this line, Gierek tried to show to his opponents that his present policy had the full support of the Soviet party. Moreover, this line had put a form of obligation on the Soviet leaders to help Poland further if need be. Gierek was, therefore, strengthening his position against the pressure of his opponents and, at the same time, he seemed to be telling the people that he was able to secure the limits within which he is going to undertake certain economic maneuvers.

All the Party leaders underlined the necessity to fully implement the promises of the eighth plenum because as the secretary of the CC, Starewicz, who later became Poland's ambassador to Britain said: "The people are watching us every day, every hour. They watch what we are doing and they watch our everyday practice." Various statements made in March 1971 could be regarded as a reaction to workers' demands which were mostly of an economic nature, sensible,

and did not overstep the limits of political reality. The socioeconomic weekly, <u>Zycie Literackie</u>, quoted a worker from
Krakow who said quite clearly that there was no reason whatsoever to accord the new leadership full confidence immediately: "Let us wait and see what will be done in concrete
terms for the whole nation." In a discussion on the Gdansk
radio station, a well-known journalist was convinced that in the
present situation if any of the newly appointed Party leaders
in the provinces was inclined toward dictatorial tendencies, his
comrades would have thrown him out immediately, without
waiting for a new upheaval. According to a participant in
another discussion broadcast by Radio Warsaw(36), the most
important fact of the post-December months was that not only
were the errors of the previous leadership disclosed, but that
the people were clearly told that it was their task to ensure
that the new leadership would not commit new errors and new
mistakes.

The political and economic measures run on two parallel
tracks - one to galvanize the Party demoralized by the methods
and policies of past years; the second to link the Party closer
with the people, not in the form of directives imposed from
above, but in the form of consultations. Whether one liked or
not, the Party was the only instrument of power, and therefore some difficult decisions had to be taken. On the one
hand the Party had to create an atmosphere of confidence in
what it was doing; on the other hand, given the new style of
government, resistance to changes had to be eliminated at all
levels and simultaneously an effort had to be made to satisfy
the material and political demands which the leadership regarded as realistic in the present situation.

Regular rotation of cadres was advocated by some Party
leaders and by the press. This would serve a dual purpose:
it would prevent incompetents from performing responsible
functions and being shielded from social criticism, and it would
prevent meritorious persons who did not commit serious errors
from being given a change of job. The idea was finally
abandoned because, as one journalist explained to me, "In our
present situation rotation of cadres is useless. It is like a
barrel of herrings and the result of any statutory rotation
would be that a herring from the bottom of the barrel would
appear suddenly at the top and vice versa; but they are all
still the same herrings." Gierek himself maintained that
stabilization of cadres who passed the test was of tremendous
importance.(37)

While several personnel changes were made at lower and
provincial levels, many Party "apparatchiks" were still living
in an atmosphere of old ideas and methods, firmly entrenched
in their own positions. Even if the local Party bosses could
not decisively influence the policy of the top leadership, they
could always wreck the progress of reforms. Gierek(38)

admitted that there were people in the Party who in critical
situations broke down, were ideologically mixed-up and had
lost their faith in the creative possibilities of socialism.

Similarly, at the top of the Party, there were people who
wanted to solve the problems by applying hard discipline and
by strengthening the position of the Party, not by dialogue,
but by enforcing solutions from above. This was the period
when new tensions, unrealistic and exaggerated demands would
have played into the hands of the old-type Party "apparatchiks," who could then say with a smile, "We told you so."

The Party reaction could be explained to a great extent
by the fact that, in December and during the subsequent
growing tension, the workers had forced the Party to introduce progressive changes, and had become a dominant
factor in the country. By satisfying workers' demands the
leadership in fact rewarded them for the protests in December
and later. What the leadership was trying to do now was to
maintain, within acceptable and realistic limits, the spontaneously growing consequences of the workers' December triumph.
The post-December developments in Poland provided other
communist leaderships with an excellent lesson. They proved
that there were certain changes acceptable to the Soviet
leaders, who had certainly come to the conclusion that any
alternative would have had much more dangerous consequences.
What was more, the economic guidelines for the twenty-fourth
congress of the Soviet Communist party resembled to a very
great extent the revisions of economic priorities already envisaged by the new Polish leadership in December 1970.

By May 1971, Gierek was in a strong position, not only
thanks to Soviet support, but also because there was no
personal alternative to his leadership within the Polish party.
One of his difficulties was that after a series of immediate and
important economic concessions his long-term economic plans,
while positive in themselves, could not produce immediate
spectacular results. His other problem was that while Moscow
was ready to make several concessions it became equally clear
that there were limits which could not be overstepped.
Gierek himself confirmed this indirectly when he said that by
"solving the December crisis within our own means and by
ourselves we managed to avoid dangers threatening the country.(39)

The Party appealed to the people not to exacerbate the
"December wounds." But the memory of December lived on.
On May 1 a most unusual parade was held in Szczecin. At the
head of the parade marched a group of women in black, then a
man carrying a large cross and another man in black with a
clenched fist in a black glove, and then a group of men in
black. All these people were relatives of workers killed in
December. They stopped for one minute's silence in front of
the platform where Party and government dignitaries, including

the secretary of the CC, Barcikowski, watched the parade. "It was the longest minute in their lives and Barcikowski looked terrified," I was later told by a journalist who watched the parade. On the next day the man with the clenched fist was arrested. Shipyard workers protested. A delegation went to Warsaw to intervene and in July there was a two-day protest strike in some of the departments of the shipyard. The arrested man was then released.

Gierek, a realist and a pragmatist, had to remain within certain limits. That is why, in the atmosphere of drastic economic changes, the political reforms had to be very limited and slow. But in the middle of 1971 there still remained the question of whether (and if so when), after material demands had been satisfied and the economic development gained its momentum, the political demands would begin to come to the surface in an ever-stronger form.(40) Thoughtful people were analyzing in depth and changing their opinions of the postwar methods and structures which had been, until December, accepted as an unavoidable deficiency. In 1971, Gierek presented the nation a vision of "another Poland - a house- and car-owning democracy," a vision which, based on hard work and gradual gains rather than improbable leaps, earned for itself a certain credibility. Skepticism remained slightly muted rather than defeated. Gierek inherited a situation in which the country had turned into violent frustration and imposed on it a new political stability which found expression in acquiescence and in the hope that progressive change had replaced the downward spiral of stagnation, drift and mistaken decisions.

First Six Months: Reactions to Change

When, in July 1971, I talked to prominent journalists, intellectuals, officials, economists, and ordinary people, all agreed that there was a new, more humane style of government and a new refreshing atmosphere at least at the top. Gierek was trying to face squarely and directly the most painful and accumulated human problems and firmly believed in direct contact with ordinary people. For these reasons and also because he had taken some immediate economic and social remedial measures, however limited, Gierek had a "limited credit of confidence." As an economist described the situation to me: Gierek had an overdraft on people's confidence. If he does not pay up by regular installments, if he does not deliver the goods, the overdraft might be withdrawn.

What Gierek had done so far in those six months was summarized for me by a prominent journalist and member of the CC in a well-known Polish story: There was an impoverished Jew living with his wife and three children in one very small room. Then the Rabbi asked him to also accommodate a goat in the room. He had to obey and he did so. All that Gierek had done so far was to throw the goat out of the room.

There were also a number of apprehensions. Faced with accumulated difficulties and with the passive resistance at the Party and local government levels, Gierek might have been tempted to fall back comfortably on old discredited methods. He was, after all, in a position of strength, pushing the country forward. But as in any new team the time would unavoidably come when they would be too exhausted to maintain the pace of dynamic drive and changes. What then? Nothing much could change within the present framework of the system.

Gierek was fully aware that workers remembered what he promised, and that they were waiting and might be ready to take to the streets again. He accepted this situation. After his meeting with the workers on the coast he knew that he had to act quickly and rationally because there was a danger that he would "ruin the Party and the system." The Party remained his top preoccupation since, as one journalist and Party member told me, there were many Party organizations, particularly along the coast, without a single subscribing communist. The prevailing attitude in the Party was still "us and them," meaning workers versus intellectuals, and in the country as a whole, "us and them" meaning the people and the rulers. But the gradual elimination of bureaucratic stupidities and absurdities that prevailed for so many years slightly defused existing tensions if only because at last "somebody was doing something" as one Catholic politician suggested.

Looking at Gierek and the situation from the point of view of ordinary people I met there was certainly no enthusiasm or excitement. People remained skeptical, and most of them had few illusions about their present leaders and system. "We have heard all this before," they said, "but...Gierek is a different man, and certainly better than Gomulka." "Perhaps he will at last do something for us," both a taxi driver and a teacher told me. "He is certainly on probation," a postman explained.

On the whole, a wait-and-see attitude prevailed in the country, and particularly among those shipyard workers and textile workers I met on the shop floor in Baltic cities and in Lodz. There was also an overall feeling of limited militancy and of power. "It was not enough," I was told, "to move those responsible for December to other posts, or to pay them retirement pensions; they should be punished. Justice had to be done and be seen to be done." "We are watching Gierek all the time. If he delivers the goods he is all right, if not we will strike again," workers in Szczecin and Gdansk told me. "After all, the Party has been telling us for many years," said a worker in Gdansk, "that the working class is the leading detachment of the nation. If we are to lead, then we will certainly replace inefficient Party and government leaders by better men, if need be."

Workers seemed, however, to be aware of limits which could not be overstepped since "our great friend" might lose patience and intervene. "Gierek is a 'working man's politician' and he seems to understand our determination," said the workers in the shipyards. "We have to earn additional money because our wages are not enough, so we work privately." When I asked where they were getting raw materials, tools, etc. to work privately, the answer was very simple: "We take them from the shipyards! After all, we are supposed to be, so the Party has been telling us all the time, co-owners of the shipyards, so surely the owner can take from the works whatever he needs in an emergency. This is an emergency." The workers I met seemed to be satisfied with the fact that they were able to have their say, to remove Party, trade union officials and even managers who they felt were not up to standard or not reacting properly to workers' justified demands. There was, at least on the coast and in Lodz, a give-and-take relationship between the management and the workers' organizations.

What impressed me most was the efficiency with which the workers' councils were acting on behalf of the workers. At the same time I came across a most vociferous condemnation of the trade unions. "The unions," the workers told me, "should be defenders of the workers and not institutions to distribute cinema tickets. What good was there in one more rigid administration, in paid activists enmeshed in routine who had long since forgotten what a shop and factory hall looked like? Let the unions defend us against the meanness of large and small petty chieftains," the workers told me. "Let them defend us against ossification, against the underrating of our basic needs."

What was significant beyond this was that the workers felt angry enough, and also free enough, to express their feelings without any real hope of bringing about drastic political changes. They did not believe that riots could get the Russians out of Poland or remove the Communist party from power. Behind their anger they sensed that the Party and government were not sure any more of their course. This was the classic invitation to a revolt, and people detected it in the same way that animals are said to detect fear in their opponents. It meant that change of some sort was unavoidable before very long unless the Polish regime was prepared to rely indefinitely on the barbarous methods - in themselves a sign of fear - that were used against the December protests. The workers I met were a new generation which had grown up since that time when the need for revolutionary struggle could excuse all. What they have shown was that communist governments could no longer base their claim to power on external threats or internal coercion. Nor could they claim that any protests were a threat to the system itself or fomented by outside influences.(41) When I discussed this with two foremen, what mattered to them, apart from the overriding problem of improvement in the standard of living, was a permanent change of political climate and a clearly detectable radical change. But if there was no clearly definable economic progress, primarily in everyday life, and given another "December crisis," the people, and first of all the workers, might well come out against the whole system as such.

When I discussed the problem of the middle and lower Party and government apparatus a warning came from one experienced journalist and Party member: "That's it. That's where Gierek stands or falls in his bid for some reforms and stabilization." The general attitude of this apparatus was one of wait and see. Most of these people were trained during the past several years in the old ways and methods - afraid of taking responsibility and making decisions, always waiting for a directive from above. In many cases these were people without any qualifications, reappointed, in most cases, only because they were absolutely loyal and had some so-called revolutionary achievements in the past. They had much to lose in material terms if they were thrown out. The new style of approach, as represented by Gierek, was for them entirely new, unknown, and impossible to grasp.

Gierek promised that there must be a strictly observed separation of functions between the Party which "leads and inspires the nation" and the government which "governs the country." Local Party and government officials had lived for so many years with the routine that the first secretary of the local Party organization would even decide the appointment of the chairwoman in an office, that they were now unable to adopt another approach. One journalist told me a story from his own experience. He wanted to arrange a simple meeting with somebody and he rang the first secretary of the VPC, who told him that according to the "separation of functions" the decision in this particular case belonged to the chairman of the National Council. The chairman, however, argued that he could not commit himself without the approval of the first secretary of the VPC.

So what could be done? Most of my sources suggested that a mass purge would be unthinkable for two reasons: it would lead to complete chaos, and it might prove difficult to find proper people to take over.

An equally difficult problem lay with the government apparatus. First, because people unsuitable for Party jobs were moved to government departments; and second, because many local conservative and dogmatic officials tried to keep strictly to the letter of government executive orders. At one of the meetings Gierek said that if directives and executive orders were in conflict with common sense, then common sense must be used in solving the problems. It was easy enough to say that, but, as I was told, local officials were simply terrified by such a possibility. Laws, executive orders, directives: "It's a complete jungle of frequently conflicting decisions." The Krakow Party paper, Gazeta Krakowska, found that in 1970 there were 18,000 new laws and government executive orders passed in one year alone. This number should be multiplied by the so far unknown number of executive orders issued by local authorities in an effort to instruct officials how the government executive orders should be applied in their particular regions or even in industrial establishments. No human being would ever be able to extricate himself from this jungle, one Party official and journalist told me.

Everyone realized that something had to be done. According to one distinguished journalist, the problem boiled down to three questions: 1) Would Gierek be able to neutralize the middle apparatus for the time being? 2) Would he be able to remove some people cautiously and shift others? 3) Could he change the whole apparatus? A Catholic politician suggested that one of the reasons Gierek was trying so hard to be everywhere and to speak personally to ordinary people, was a brave attempt to establish contact with the people, above the heads of local Party and government authorities, and at the same time impress on local activists that this was the way it should be done in the future. Otherwise little progress would be achieved in stabilizing the situation and then in pushing the country forward on the road to development and progress. A joke circulated in Warsaw at the time:

Question: Why, during one week was there a shortage of milk.

Answer: Because Gierek forgot to attend a meeting with the cows, and the cows therefore, did not produce milk.

GIEREK'S PROGRAM FOR POLAND

At the plenary session of the CC on September 4, 1971, it was disclosed that the Party's sixth congress, the first to be held under Gierek, would open on December 6 with Poland's "further socialist development" and long-term economic planning as the main topics on the agenda.(42) Two days later a document embodying the leadership's "guidelines" for the congress was published and, according to Gierek, these amounted not to a "closed program" awaiting the country's endorsement, but to a "basis for discussion." This was an unusual approach to a Party congress. In what seemed to be an attempt to make the congress a national, rather than a purely

Party affair, Gierek stressed that non-Party people had made
an important contribution to preparing the draft and that
representatives of non-Party groups would take part in the
congress.(43) This was again without precedent.

The guidelines, intended as a program of reform to set
Poland on a new road, offered few concrete proposals. The
impression was given that the key decisions, especially in the
crucial economic field, had not yet been taken. Thus the need
for the trade union reform, a more rational system of administration, and a greater decentralization were mentioned in
the most general terms. Indeed, on these subjects the
document amounted to a directive to the Party-government
commission now examining social and economic policies, rather
than a blueprint for wider discussion.

Public opinion was the main target of the promised development of the authority of the Sejm and the announcement that
a new constitution was in preparation. Gierek hoped that
these proposals would create an atmosphere for the pre-
congress debate which would reveal the strength of his support in the country as a whole and help overcome the inertia
in the middle ranks of the Party from which his regime was
suffering. The guidelines stressed the need to raise the
quality of the average Party member without suggesting how
this was to be done.

Moreover, even the brief CC session indicated that not
everyone in the Party was satisfied by Gierek's present course
or shared his view that the new regime has "solved the social
conflict" in Poland and embarked on improvements with the
"full support of all working people." The Warsaw Party organization secretary warned against the activities of "antisocialist internal forces" and the readiness of "dogmatic and
revisionist elements" to ally themselves with discontented
groups.

One of Gierek's motives in issuing his guidelines at an
early stage was probably to strengthen his hand by appealing
to the country, while the imprecision of some of the proposals
reflected continuing disagreements and Gierek's unwillingness
to give the old guard cause for complaints. Similarly, the
concentration on the economy, including the emphasis on
consumerism, and the brevity of the document's references to
constitutional and other political changes were probably
prompted by the leadership's need to keep Soviet suscep-
tibilities in view. Gierek obviously did not expect Moscow to
permit political as well as economic experiments in Poland.

In the guidelines the former leadership was criticized for
the severity of its economic plans, which had even brought a
decline in real wages in some places, and the people were
assured that the raising of living standards was a permanent
objective, not merely a technical one. However, the leadership
had clearly made all the concessions that it could afford for

the time being and was now concentrating on reforms in
management and planning, accompanied by repeated reminders
that harder work is the key to higher living standards. The
reforms advocated in the guidelines fell short of those being
put into effect in Hungary, however. It was suggested that
they should be introduced as pilot schemes only in 1972 and
then more widely in 1973.

Full economic accounting, i.e., the concept of profitability, would be the watchword in the large industrial enterprises. But, though the elimination of bureaucracy and some
decentralization of decision making were recommended, central
planning would remain. Indeed, it was laid down that the
reforms should be based on the increased effectiveness of
central planning, for instance, through a greater concentration
on general rather than factional interests. Other suggestions
were for a more clear-cut definition of the respective tasks of
the central and local organs, including an end to interference
by higher organs in the affairs of lower ones, and a more
careful selection of "leading personnel," mainly managers, on
the basis of ability. The details of the reforms, however,
were left to the commission of experts, who were instructed to
draw up a comprehensive program for modernizing the administration.

The wider problem of ending the country's apathy and
encouraging workers to contribute more to its emergence from
economic stagnation was tacitly acknowledged in the admissions
of past failures and promises of a better future. But room for
maneuver only three years after the Czechoslovak events was
extremely limited. Thus the trade unions were urged to
continue the detailed analysis of their weaknesses that were
partly responsible for the December crisis, and the importance
of both the unions and the workers' self-government conferences was stressed although the subject was dealt with very
sketchily. Similarly, all the references to developing "socialist
democracy" and enhancing the prestige of the Sejm were
prefaced by reminders of the "leading role" of the Party. Any
free play for "alien" tendencies and activities by "antisocialist
forces" was especially ruled out. In the section on foreign
policy, the greatest stress was laid on the Polish party's unity
with the "fraternal Communist parties," above all that of the
Soviet Union.(44)

The discussion on the guidelines was much wider in the
country than at any time since the war. Gierek went as far
as to write many personal letters to various distinguished
people outside the Party, inviting them to take part in the
discussion. On the other hand, according to a public opinion
poll conducted by the Polish Radio, over 60 percent of
respondents did not read the guidelines at all and just over 16
percent glanced through them.(45)

Gierek himself and many of the top Party leaders took part in the meetings which elected the delegates to the congress. As a result, of just over 1,800 delegates, 308 came from large industrial enterprises and 237 represented the Silesian region. Among those elected, the overwhelming majority were workers and young people who as Gierek expected, would understand and support the new line.

In the mass media and at some meetings, interesting demands were voiced, questions put to the leadership, and suggestions made. The weekly, Polityka, discussing the guidelines said that alternative solutions were possible and that there was no suggestion of the "apostolic infallibility" of the Party.

In its cultural policy, the Party, according to Deputy Premier Krasko(46), now understood that art "cannot be commanded to do this or that" and therefore possibilities for more intellectual freedoms existed. Outlining the new policy he gave an assurance that there was a place for works not directly committed in the ideological sense, but of course works of outstanding ideological and artistic value must have priority. When the journalists discussed the congress guidelines(47), one of Poland's most distinguished commentators suggested that censorship might soon be eased, underlining the importance of such a move if the public's confidence in the press was to be restored. A newspaper could not be edited with an eye on just a narrow section of the Communist party. The guidelines, however, viewed the mass media as instruments for the implementation of Party policy.

One of the main characteristics of the pre-congress debate was the condemnation of the policy of the previous leadership. The new chairman of the Front of National Unity (FNU), a non-Party man, Professor Groszkowski, emphasized that never before in the postwar years had there been conditions for such a full expression of the social and political maturity of the people. Gierek himself said: "Whether anybody is a convinced Marxist should carry less weight than whether he is useful in his work and whether, given a proper chance, he could be more useful still." The weekly, Polityka, took up this problem, writing: "Among the millions of non-Party people there are many superior in intelligence and performance to many Party members. A wise cadre policy must strictly observe the principle of equal opportunity for Party and non-Party people."

Many papers raised the issue of guarantees that the process of renewal would not be reversed. Gierek answered this question at one of the meetings: "There are not, and cannot be, full guarantees. The success of the Party program depends on the attitude of the whole nation, on intense work and study." And he appealed to youth to share in the solutions of all problems, because young people had to know about all the difficulties. At the time of his appeal the students' weekly, <u>ITD</u>, wrote: "We did not show enough confidence in young people and very often we have treated them like children," and reported that views alien to socialist ideology persisted among some young people.

In the pre-congress debate, Gierek also stressed two other points. First, he said that the workers in the big industrial enterprises, "the elite of the working class," are the main political basis of the Party. Second, he said, "We have to assess highly and pay attention to the officers of our industry," and therefore to the technocrats. This last statement clearly related to the existing problem of changes at the middle and lower levels of the Party and economic administrative apparatus.

The weekly, <u>Polityka</u>, suggested that "the psychological barrier" between the rulers and the people had been broken. This barrier had prevented ordinary people from forcing the authorities into making correct and just decisions.

At a meeting with mass media editors, Gierek(48) rejected uniformity, saying: "It would be difficult to expect everybody in Poland to have identical views on the methods of solving socioeconomic problems in the development of the country." But while he was ready to accept discussions of any problem and would take into consideration any views, he would strongly reject any "efforts to revive attitudes and views foreign to socialism." This statement was closely linked with the problem of the continuing dialogue with the people. In the Warsaw newspaper, <u>Zycie Warszawy</u>(49), Professor Szczepanski, a well-known Polish sociologist saw the key to the solution as being in the "partnership" between the people and the authorities instead of enforcing decisions by supposedly infallible directives from above. The power, he said, can be based exclusively on extermination of protest and opposition but then the art of governing becomes the art of repression. The basic factor of full citizenship is to be independent of arbitrary power. The citizen is not subordinate to the power of the state but takes part in it and controls it.

Basic decisions must be shaped in a sort of triangle between the demands of the people on one side, real economic and human possibilities on the other, and a taking into account of the limitations arising from the alliance with the Soviet Union. Gierek's dilemma could therefore be summarized as follows: mitigation of an alienation of the ruled from the rulers was the condition of further progress and development of the country; on the other hand, a fully open and honest dialogue remained limited by unavoidable imperatives of the system.

In contrast to the sketchily formulated political reforms, in the economic sphere a drastic change had certainly taken place. This, to a great extent, reflected Gierek's own approach to solving the problems of the country by giving absolute priority to economic progress, development and modernization. The pragmatic, consumer-orientated approach was unmistakable. One of the first major policy decisions of the new leadership had been to scrub the version of the 1971-1975 five-year plan already worked out under Gomulka. By June 1971, a new draft was ready and reversed the economic priorities which had been regarded as inviolable in economic planning during the 14 years of Gomulka's rule.

The new economic priorities were clear in the key target figures set for 1971-1975. Individual and social consumption was to increase by 38 percent, as against 27 percent achieved in the previous five-year period. Real wages were scheduled to rise by some 17-18 percent, at an average annual rate of 3.4 percent, nearly twice the average growth rate registered during the previous decade, 1961-1970. The housing construction target was increased by 25 percent over that of the previous five-year plan. Finally, an additional 1.8 million work places were to be developed to assure full employment and particularly in the area of light industry and services.

This dramatic change of priorities necessarily involved a considerable reallocation of investments resources. For the first time in postwar Polish history, agriculture, food processing, and consumer goods industries, as well as housing construction, were granted a priority in the allocation of raw materials and investment funds over heavy industry and other sacred cows of Marxist-Leninist economics.

The priority of heavy industry had been reduced. Within an overall increase in industrial investment by 53 percent, outlays on consumer industries were raised by 98 percent, or in effect, doubled. Group B (consumer and light industries) investment would rise in 1971-1975 by 42 percent compared to the 36 percent in the past five years. Output in group A (heavy industry and capital goods) would continue to rise swiftly and should amount to 52 percent. This was determined, Gierek said, by the requirements of modernization in the economy, the raising of export capacity, and by necessity of completing several investment projects already begun. The revised five-year plan provided for an increase of national income by 38-39 percent, (34 percent in the previous plan), based on the planned growth of industrial output by 48-50 percent, on the growth of agricultural production by 18-21 percent and on an expansion of services and thus on a rapid and harmonious, well-balanced development in all fields of the national economy.

In the modified strategy international trade was to become, for the first time, an integral part of the economic life and an effective engine of growth, instead of being simply a measure for removing shortages or surpluses. It was expected to make a significant contribution to the supply of consumer goods and to provide technological means for the modernization and expansion of productive capacities throughout the economy.(50) The plan envisaged the use of foreign credits from nonsocialist countries to supplement the limited foreign-exchange earning power of the export sector.

In tackling the task of increasing food output, particularly meat production, and in raising wages, the leadership was already quite successful. Sizable meat imports and the announcement of a new agricultural policy with incentives for private farmers providing temporary relief (see "Agriculture: Socialized or Private?" in Chapter 4). The real wages rose in 1971 by 5.3 percent. Despite the unprecedented 10 percent increase in purchasing power, the government was able to keep inflationary pressures in check by producing 7 percent more consumer goods than in 1970. A 36.7 percent increase in food imports in 1971 and a 16 percent increase in imports of consumer goods, contributed to a record trade deficit of over 162 million dollars in 1971.(51)

All the target figures in the new five-year plan accepted by the sixth Party congress were revised upward at least three times over the next two years, including the key targets for individual consumption and real earnings. This represented an attempt to ensure the flexibility of the plan according to current needs and possibilities as they emerged. In the conditions in Poland, it seemed to be the only successful way to do the most that could be done. The history of this plan was certainly unique in East European countries.

Gierek's boldness in reappraising economic priorities and introducing drastic changes contrasted with his caution and hesitancy in introducing a comprehensive reform of economic planning and management. At the February 1971(52) plenum of the CC, Gierek said: "The whole system of economic management must be completely overhauled and adapted to the new strategy of social and economic development." The responsibility for devising such a program was given to a special commission chaired by Gierek's closest associate, Szydlak. Despite this promising beginning, evidence soon began to accumulate that the Party was not ready to accept radical changes in the existing economic system. Trybuna Ludu wrote: "The main characteristic of our reform should be a constructive attempt to reconcile the principle of central planning with that of providing greater scope for initiative and independence at a lower level of economic management." But Professor Pajestka, vice-chairman of the Planning Commission, said that the most difficult problem was how, in a socialist system, to reconcile the principle of central planning with the need to decentralize decision making and increase the play of market forces.

Although the CC in September promised to work out and present to the congress the basic principles of the reform of the system of economic management, the Party leaders failed to report on the reform at the congress and instead informed the delegates that the commission was considering several alternative solutions.

At the congress Gierek summarized four conclusions which the Party drew from the December events. First, the problems of the working people always had to be kept in the center of the Party's attention. Social efforts in the construction of socialism should always result in a tangible improvement of the material and cultural conditions of the life of the people. Second, the working class is the main social force of socialism and constant ties with it are a condition of the successful development of the socialist system. Third, construction of socialism required a systematic strengthening and raising of the leading role of the Party to constantly higher standards. Fourth, in the contemporary conditions of the class struggle and rivalry between socialism and capitalism, developments which delay progress and open the door to the activities of opponents to socialism, must be prevented.

Like his predecessor, Gierek reaffirmed that the Party would strongly oppose any phenomena of revisionism and also would overcome dogmatic petrification marked by lack of faith in the strength of the working class, and in the creative powers of the nation. Very much depended on the selection of the new Party leaders. Here Gierek suggested an astonishing approach when he said that it was important to listen to the opinions of non-Party members about candidates for the Party. The Party had to continue to try to activate non-Party people, keep them informed, take their opinions into account, and entrust them with responsible tasks and positions.

Gierek reaffirmed that the Party would try to perfect the system of consultations with the people. While the "division of functions" between the Party and the "independent" government was again emphasized very strongly, the control of its activities had to be much more effective. Control by whom? By the "leading Party" of course. Gierek did not mention the free elections which the workers on the coast and elsewhere in the country demanded from their various organizations, but he only stressed that socioeconomic progress required "increased participation of the working people in government and control of the state apparatus."

Few people had any illusions that Gierek would preside over a Czechoslovak-type liberalization, but expectations did seem justified, mainly because of the short-term economic achievements, that far-reaching, although measured, reforms would be set in motion. That this would not be the case became clear at the Party congress. The supreme Party body formally adopted drastic economic changes, but otherwise either ambiguous or even cautious resolutions were passed on various areas of concern which had been designated earlier as ripe for reform. The period of retrenchment had begun.

The changes in the top leadership carried out by the newly elected Central Committee should be regarded as Gierek's crowning achievement in a steady process of sweeping personnel changes which he initiated in December 1970. The changes went in two directions. With the exception of one or two of "yesterday's men," there was a clean sweep of the old guard; Cyrankiewicz, Jedrychowski and Moczar were removed from the PB. Their gradual demotion with the final blow coming on the last day of the congress proved once again that Gierek was a skillful politician. With a few exceptions new PB members and secretaries of the CC were either technocrats and economic experts, or people from Silesia with whom in one way or another Gierek had been closely associated in the past as first secretary of the Katowice VPC. Among them were Minister of Defense, General Jaruzelski, who in December 1970 refused to support Gomulka; Zdzislaw Grudzien, who replaced Gierek as first secretary of the VPC in Katowice, and Minister of the Interior, General Szlachcic.

The convening of the Party congress almost one year earlier was meant to demonstrate the leadership's confidence in the success of its consolidation policies, a signal directed not only toward the frustrated and paralyzed Party apparatus, but also to Poland's "fraternal allies," particularly to Soviet Union. In a more substantive sense, it was convoked in order to legitimize Gierek's rule, and in more specific terms to preside over the reconstruction of leading Party organs. Gierek emerged from the congress as the unchallenged leader of the Party and as an orthodox but pragmatic communist with a modern outlook, who means to make the present system work.

4 Forward with Gierek: 1971-1975

Much done, and much designed, and more desired.

William Wordsworth in "Evening Walk"

THE MAN AND THE LEADER

"Hard are the ways of truth and hard to walk"

John Milton in Paradise Regained

Edward Gierek is of genuine proletarian origins. Son of a Silesian miner, he was born in January 1913, in the village of Porabka, which at the time was under czarist Russia. Coming from a strongly Catholic family, the young Gierek was a very active member of the Association of Sodalis Marianus, devoted to the cult of the Virgin Mary, the "Queen of Poland." Forced by poverty to emigrate, his family went to France in 1923 where Gierek, at the age of 12, found work as a farmhand and a year later in a coal mine. He soon became a member of the French trade union organization, and in April 1931 joined the French Communist party. In 1934 he got into serious trouble with the French police for helping to organize the first sit-down strike in French history and was deported in August of that year to Poland. Indeed, it was an irony of history that when Gierek came on an official visit to Paris in 1972 as first secretary of the CC, the French minister of the interior had to rush through a special directive cancelling the 1934 order of Gierek's deportation.

In June 1937, Gierek again emigrated, this time to Belgium, where he worked in the mines and joined the Belgian

Communist party. During the German occupation of Belgium he organized Polish underground resistance groups and participated in acts of sabotage in the mines and the communications network. This part of his official biography was, however, contested by Colonal Henri Bernard, an organizer of resistance groups in Belgium and a professor of military history at the Belgian Military Academy. Bernard claims that Gierek "remained discreet and inactive" and was "not recognized as a member of the Belgian resistance." Immediately after the war, Gierek became co-founder of the Polish Workers' party (Communist) and of the Union of Polish Patriots in Belgium.(1)

In 1948 Gierek finally returned to Poland where he joined the Polish Workers' party CC staff as an instructor in the organizational department. In due course Gierek was sent to Silesia to take charge in the VPC first of organizational and then of economic matters. Throughout this period he studied in his spare time and graduated from the Krakow Academy of Mining and Metallurgy in 1954.

Gierek's Party career was checkered. In March 1954, he was elected to the CC and has been a member ever since. In March 1956 he became secretary of the CC and a few months later a PB member, only to lose this last position in the October 1956 upheaval. In March 1957 he was appointed first secretary of the Voivodship (Provincial) Party Committee in Katowice, at the same time retaining his position as CC secretary. In March 1959, he was reelected to the PB and has been a member of that body ever since, but lost his SCC post in 1964. Finally he returned to the CC more than 6 years later when, at the seventh Central Committee plenum, on December 20, 1970, he became its first secretary.

It was in the Silesian town of Katowice that Gierek made his mark and reputation, between the years 1957 and 1970. He had successfully administered Poland's most important industrial and mining area and earned a reputation for orthodoxy in political and ideological matters, and for pragmatism in social and economic policy. He was always at his best discussing concrete problems, particularly economic and administrative ones, and he certainly disliked various ideological arguments and debates. He proved to be not so much a reformer but an extremely efficient manager, and an administrator with a very pragmatic approach to all problems.

He was, moreover, much more approachable than many other communist functionaries. Gierek certainly found a common language not only with the local Silesian miners but also with the people at large. He came back from the West full of illusions and faith in socialism and while in Silesia he was able to avoid the intra-Party struggles and intrigues filling the corridors of power of the CC where, by an accident of history, many unqualified, unprepared and frequently blinkered people were deciding the fate of the country. In Katowice, by contrast, nothing was easier than to see Gierek and present him with the problems and ask for his intervention in Warsaw. On Sundays he took his walks in the park of Chorzow, which was laid out at his insistence, and where ordinary people met him and shook his hand. He regularly went to the local stadium to watch his favorite soccer team, shouting and encouraging the players together with thousands of miners. He was trying all the time not only to win, but to increase his popularity. One could detect an inclination to paternalism in his behavior and Warszawians were often joking about "the good uncle from Silesia, the friend of the workers."(2)

Gierek would not tolerate other opposing leaders and functionaries, nor did he believe in following a multitude of policies. When he first arrived in Katowice as first secretary he humbly asked the full VPC for their "understanding and help" because "I must learn everything from you." Yet just one year later he had thrown out everybody on the committee except one commissionaire. A British correspondent observed him at this time during a big meeting in Katowice.(3) Gomulka was there, quietly leaning on the table, while Gierek, wrote the correspondent, kept in constant motion, making notes, fidgeting with his place card, and arguing with Gomulka. For he was now the powerful king of the Silesian industrial basin, the political boss, radiating pride in his achievements, and enjoying a certain amount of genuine popularity with the miners, who formed the privileged elite of the area and the basis of his support.

Gierek had the advantage of a solid foundation to work from - rich and efficient coal fields, a relatively stable population, and a strong working-class movement. By recruiting able men and showing a not inconsiderable talent as a realistic administrator, he built up on this foundation. Structural economic reforms introduced in his area encouraged enterprises to be more conscious of profits and to cooperate more effectively with one another.

It was said that Gierek took this stand mainly because he was concerned about the well-being of his own Silesian constituency. Certainly his subsequent standing in the country owes a great deal to the reputation he acquired as the working man's politician, one who stood up for what he saw as being in the best interests of the Silesian workers, often to the detriment - so his opponents claimed - of the interests of the rest of the nation. He pressed for increased investments in the coal industry, for instance, at a time when the health and modernization of the economy dictated a switch to oil and gas. His other main demand was for a more favorable treatment of Silesian workers on the grounds that their production was so important to the nation's economic well-being as to merit better rewards than workers in other areas. He had won his

point and Gomulka tried to buy him off by granting Silesia the
concessions Gierek demanded. On the vital question of
reforms in the economic system, Gierek tended to defend his
local reforms while resisting reforms devised in Warsaw. He
quarreled with Gomulka on this and other scores, frequently
ignoring directives from the CC or even Gomulka himself.
Silesia under Gierek was often jokingly referred to as the
"Polish Katanga" while Gierek was dubbed the "Polish
Tschombe."

By and large Gierek disliked the Party setup in Warsaw
and the atmosphere prevailing there. At many meetings in his
home constituency he could raise applause with a local joke
about "those people up there in Warsaw"; he knew how to
foster local pride. The Silesians, under Gierek, came to feel
superior to Warsaw. When he once met a Western diplomat who
said that he had stayed in Warsaw for over three years,
Gierek quipped: "How on earth could you survive for such a
long time among all those people whom one cannot possibly
take seriously?" For Gierek, Warsaw had always been a symbol of traditionally Polish "bagatelle."

Politically, Gierek was, for a long time, a loyal Gomulka
man. But after the students' riot in Warsaw in March 1968 he
delivered a strong speech which, although it paid lip service
to Gomulka, was generally much nearer to the ideas represented by the Partisan group under General Moczar, the
minister of the interior, who was responsible for the repression of the students' riots. Moczar used the riots to step
up his campaign against the Moscow group within the Party
(many of them Jews, who had spent the war years in the
Soviet Union) and to try to overthrow Gomulka. In his key
speech in March 1966, Gierek worried the more liberal of his
supporters by approving the treatment of the student demonstrations and blaming the "posthumous children of various
kinds of the old system: revisionists, Zionists, and servants of
imperialism."

Many observers claimed that Gierek's speech did not
reflect his real views, but that it was dictated by purely
tactical considerations of the kind that often take precedence
over matters of principle in communist power struggles. This
might suggest that Gierek was not a man of principle. He had
certainly trimmed his sails to meet prevailing Party winds on a
number of occasions, but his firm stand against those aspects
of economic reform prepared under Gomulka by Jaszczuk, which
were unjust to the working people, suggested that there were
some principles for which he was prepared to fight.

During the summer and autumn of 1968, Gierek rescued
Gomulka in intra-Party faction struggles, throwing his own
support and that of his many associates behind Gomulka at the
crucial elections to the new CC. But he moved into the background for a while after this, although maintaining his
contacts with the right people in the Party.

At that time Gierek was not regarded as someone interested in democracy and he showed no signs of sharing the Czechoslovak and Hungarian belief that economic reforms, to be effective, required political reforms and greater democratization. On the contrary, Gierek was nearer the East German school, which held that efficient management and material incentive could bring prosperity without political relaxation. He was, however, a realist and open to new ideas if he could be persuaded that they were practicable. Speaking fluent French and Flemish he liked to show interest in literature and modern painting but was never a great friend of literary intellectuals. He valued first of all the managers and technocrats, scientists and skilled workers, and has always been known as the candidate of the technocrats for the leadership of the Party.

A real dilemma faced Gierek when in 1970 he was elevated from his position in the Silesian region to the highest post in the country. Poland as a whole contrasted badly with the prosperous Silesian region. It was poorer, less well organized, more demoralized, and much of the local political power was in rival camps. The problem was how to transplant his realistic approach and pragmatism from a region where he had been very successful to a national scene and on a national scale. His greatest asset was perhaps the fact that, in contrast to all postwar communist leaders, Gierek had spent his crucial formative years in the West and consequently had nothing to do with Moscow's methods of training Party leaders nor with the Soviet approach to "building socialism." However ideologically orthodox Gierek might have been, he cut the ideological tirades in his speeches to the bare minimum. Instead he talked to everybody in down-to-earth terms, showing his pragmatic approach to problems which he was successfully able to solve in Silesia.

When meeting workers, Gierek would frequently embrace them in a fraternal greeting. More than once he was seen to bow and kiss the hand of a woman worker, true to traditional Polish courtesy. Perhaps these were empty gestures designed to win popularity. But such gestures in a communist dictatorship where popular votes count for little, showed he genuinely cared, and the embraces and hand kissing stemmed from an inner conviction that he was at one with the workers. All this generated a kind of admiration for the man. For here was a very different personality with a new and different style! There was an immediate contrast with Gomulka. Gomulka had a different manner altogether. He was an aging autocrat who would never look you straight in the face but would slide past you with his secretiveness and suspicion. But Gierek went up and shook you by the hand, he remembered your name and how many children you had.

When Gierek was installed in Warsaw many of his comrades maintained that a change of personality was not sufficient to initiate a profound evolution. Nevertheless, the new style and the new spirit of his leadership manifested itself straight away.

There was a lot of admiration for what was called the new pragmatism. It was felt that the subsequent boom was achieved not by ideological formulas, but by pragmatic action. "Whenever we had a problem," an economist told me in Gdansk, "we no longer asked ourselves, what is the answer according to Marx or Lenin? We thought out a solution and then asked: Does it work? And if it does not: why not?"

Gierek proved to be a very clever political operator within the Party, when he subtly and cautiously moved people from one position to another after having strongly consolidated his own position. He most certainly tried to maintain a balance between various conflicting forces, to play one against another and to quietly eliminate any potential rivals. But, until 1976 at any rate, he also proved to be a clever tactician in carrying out certain policies. Quite often he acted by surprise, thus disarming in advance any potential opponents. When he undertook to carry out an unpopular political decision he acted swiftly, but once he was faced with the opposition from the people he cleverly delayed the action, went into consultations, asked for opinions and reactions, and then, while maintaining the basic principles of the changes, he toned them down and made them more acceptable to the people.

For a few years after the end of 1971 he established himself before the nation as a sort of "father figure." His strongest weapon continued to be patriotism, and Gierek's repeated public references to the nation and national spirit accounted for much of his continuing acceptance as a national leader. He cleverly played on Polish nationalism. His unprecedented "opening to the West" was certainly dictated by economic necessities and requirements. But it also closely followed traditional historical links between Poland and the Western civilization, and the inherent national feeling that Poland has always been part of the West European heritage.

However, Gierek remained true to his earlier beliefs that what was needed were economic, dynamic and modern development, radical increases in the standard of living, but without any significant institutional political reforms even within the existing system. On balance he has proved to be neither bound by the traces of orthodoxy nor moved by the spirit of liberal reform.

Gierek's ultimate aim remained the "socialization of Polish society" with comprehensive political control of the Party extended as widely as feasible. But what Gierek did was to change the tone of Party leadership from confrontation to cooperation and consultation (within limits); from revolution to evolution. Rather than confronting society with changes through Party directives Gierek has chosen to accelerate the

processes of social change which he hopes will come to the aid
of the Party.

But even so, at the beginning of 1975 people still regarded Gierek as a "good chap" and if anything went wrong
they blamed the Party, not the man – the exact opposite of the
orthodox communist doctrine. This would suggest that, in the
minds of many ordinary people, Gierek could do much more
good for the nation if it were not for the opposition, or to say
the least, unhelpfulness of the Party apparatus.

Gierek is a tough man and he can be very tough in
critical situations, without, however, overstepping the limits of
sometimes necessary toughness. The test for Gierek came
after June 1976 when he faced an overwhelming demand for
"consensus socialism" which, by the way, he tried to some
extent to build up over the previous few years. But this time
he was faced with a strong demand for political reforms, which
went against Gierek's belief that economic progress and
development that satisfied the economic needs of society would
be enough without political relaxation.

Whenever Gierek had difficulties and was faced with a
confrontation between the Party and the people, a widely
known joke was repeated to illustrate his dilemma. When
Gierek took over, his predecessor, Gomulka, gave him three
sealed and numbered envelopes and said: "When you are in
trouble, open these envelopes in sequence and you will know
what to do next." At the sign of the first difficulties Gierek
opened the first envelope and read: "Blame your predecessor
for everything." This he did. Trouble came yet again and in
the second envelope he was advised, "Reorganize things."
("We are facing that now," I was told by a Communist party
member in 1974). Then, when more trouble came, Gierek
opened the third envelope. The message was simple: "Start
preparing three new envelopes."

The obvious cornerstone in Gierek's foreign policy
remained the close alliance with the Soviet Union. But, although he was watched very closely, not only by the Soviet
leaders but also by the leaders of other ruling Communist
parties, he managed to achieve substantial room for maneuver
in his relations with the Western countries. This was because
Gierek made no bones about his absolute loyalty to the Soviet
Union.

I had a chance to observe Gierek at close quarters during
his various official visits in the West. On most occasions he
made an excellent impression on his hosts. A strongly built,
and fairly good-looking man, well dressed, adhering to strict
diplomatic protocol whenever required, and very much relaxed
and joking when the official part of the visit or banquet was
over. There was no inferiority complex in his behavior. He
was as much at ease with presidents Pompidou and Giscard
d'Estaing or with Chancellor Schmidt as with presidents Ford

and Nixon or with the King of the Belgians. When he was
speaking he sounded like a Western businessman or politician,
and certainly not like the leader of a Communist party. His
down-to-earth and pragmatic approach to problems appealed to
some Western leaders, particularly to the West German chancellor and the French president. Full of dignity and courtesy
whenever the occasion required, he was at the same time
feeling as an equal among equals and he clearly enjoyed it.
The Soviet leaders must have been obviously happy that here
was a man who could present the smiling face of detente to
the West certainly more gracefully than the Russians. For this
reason, and most of all for the stabilization inside Poland, he
was allowed by the Russians to do things his own way. How
far Gierek can stretch this margin of freedom, or even wants
to, only time will show. He is a communist, so his constant
declarations of loyalty to Moscow are not entirely fake. But
he is also a Pole. What he was doing was trying to prove in
the face of considerable growing skepticism in the country,
particularly in 1976, was that it is possible to be both at once.

THE PARTY: THE POWER AND THE WEAKNESS

All political parties die at length
of swallowing their own lies.

Dr. John Arbuthnot in Life of Emerson

        On taking power after the initial earthquake in the
leadership in December 1970, Gierek had to tread carefully. A
firm believer in the "leading role" of the Party, he had to
consolidate the Party and reinstate its control, eliminate
factions and opposing groups within the Party and to establish
himself as an undisputed leader. He played his game skillfully
and carefully and proceeded with the job gradually, often
unobtrusively.
        Two basic principles underlined Gierek's actions. First,
he has not courted popular support in a way that might
weaken the foundations on which his position ultimately rests.
At the beginning of 1971 he stated quite clearly that the
nation's guarantees for the future boiled down to: "the Party
fulfilling its function as the guiding force in accordance with
Marxist-Leninist ideology."(4) Despite considerable emphasis
on "socialist democracy" throughout society, the leadership has
countered the argument for institutional guarantees with the
claim that the Party's "correct line" was only distorted by
small cliques in the former regime. The Party as a whole,
whose "activities and members were acting in the best of
faith," was absolved of reponsibility for the past crisis,(5) as
doctrine required that it should be.

Secondly, Gierek claimed that "those who were instructed to restore order were guided...by supreme concern for the highest interests of the country." No official was held publicly responsible for the brutal repression except Kliszko - and even then only in veiled terms - at the Party plenum in February 1971. Moczar, in charge of security in 1970, even became a PB member. The Party leadership had bowed so obviously to the pressure from the nation that many people in Poland might have gained the impression that another push or two could have exacted far greater concessions. At such a time you do not sack the country's chief policeman but you make it clear that he has, if anything, more authority than before to deal with any opposition.(6)

In the first post-December days the significant lack of criticism of the former cadre chief, Strzelecki, reflected Gierek's healthy respect for the strength of the apparatus entrenched in the Party and state system during the Gomulka years. Avoiding the type of wholesale purge that might have led to a confrontation with them, Gierek instead chose to court their favors while simultaneously strengthening his hand through selective dismissals of officials in the central and regional Party organizations. The Gomulka-appointed bureaucrats did not, at that time, constitute a faction group but they were a powerful force for the vested interests that Gierek would have to confront and control if even limited change was not to be undermined at every level.(7) In matters of policy, although a spectrum of attitudes existed among the leaders ranging from the conservative orthodoxy of Kruczek to the more liberal tendency of Tejchma, the members of the leading party bodies exhibited no significant differences in their strategy.

There was, perhaps, one proviso. Gierek's long-range goal of economic modernization and his means of achieving this goal were inspired by an awareness of Poland's needs. He was also perceptive enough to appreciate the "objective conditions" of Poland's present situation and to form his policies around them. This sometimes resulted in decisions which seemed devoid of ideological content, and some of his associates were dissatisfied with the nearly total pragmatism of many of Gierek's moves and were reacting with the frustration that comes from lost illusions.(8)

The Gierek-Moczar alliance proved very quickly to be a marriage of convenience.(9) Gierek moved against Moczar in the spring of 1971. When Gierek returned from Moscow, he quickly relieved Moczar of his SCC duties in charge of security affairs and the army, transferring that responsibility to his close follower, Stanislaw Kania. When, early in 1971, Moczar went to Olsztyn to consult with a small group of his closest Party supporters and to plan a mini-coup d'etat against Gierek, the Party leader interrupted his official visit to the Czechoslovak Party congress in Prague, appeared suddenly in

Olsztyn and put an immediate stop to any behind-the-scenes
maneuvers. Shortly afterward Moczar was demoted to the post
of chairman of the Supreme State Control Chamber with nominal
responsibilities and without political significance, and "resigned" from the SCC. He was sent to Finland to attend the
Finnish Party congress and in his absence, Gierek launched a
wholesale purge of Moczar's supporters in the security apparatus. Deputy Minister of the Interior, General Matejewski
and several other high-ranking officials were arrested, tried
and sentenced to 12 years in prison. Some 200 officials had
been summarily dismissed from the security apparatus. By the
end of 1971, at the sixth Party congress, Moczar was dismissed from the PB and one of his supporters, Warsaw Party
secretary Kepa, was retained as a deputy PB member but was
denied promotion to full membership. Finally, in May 1972
Moczar lost yet another of his power bases when he was removed from the chairmanship of the influential ex-Combatants
Association (ZBOWiD). Thus Moczar faded out of the political
scene, and so to a great extent did the Partisans. (See the
new team in Chapter 2.) And so one potential contender for
power was removed.

Two others were moved to other positions. These
belonged to the group of reformers and pragmatists of a different vintage and of different views. Olszowski was linked
with Moczar and, while retaining his PB membership, lost his
position in the SCC when he became foreign minister. Another, one of the most intelligent, even brilliant young pragmatists, Tejchma, again while retaining his PB membership,
lost his CC secretaryship when he was appointed deputy
premier. In political terms his transfer from the SCC to the
government presidium could hardly be regarded as a promotion.
While Tejchma and Olszowski occupied opposite ends of the
liberal-conservative spectrum represented in the leadership,
they shared a common stature and a following of which Gierek
was undoubtedly well aware.

The top Party bodies, the PB and the secretariat, were
gradually filled with people who had made their Party careers
under Gierek's patronage and those who had been with him
when Gierek was the first secretary in Silesia. The first rule
of communist power politics, as in democratic politics, is that
the leader must be able to count on a reasonably stable
majority. This Gierek achieved within a year in the two top
Party bodies.

Having either removed or neutralized his potential rivals,
Gierek moved to weaken the resistance of the entrenched
bureaucrats in the Party apparatus at the local and middle
levels. Avoiding an outright confrontation with this powerful
group, he gradually secured, in 1971, the replacement of 40
percent of the district and local Party leaders and by the end
of 1972 he had replaced 14 out of 18 provincial Party sec-

retaries.(10)   The "individual talks" conducted in 1971 with
approximately half of the Party's 2,300,000 members, resulted
in a purge from the Party of about 100,000 people, many of
whom were not attuned to the policies of the new leader. He
also sought to increase the number of workers in the Party
and in its major bodies, an act that has been explained in
doctrinal terms, but which really reflected Gierek's opinion
that he could deal with this group much more easily than with
the "apparatchiks."

Despite all these efforts many elements inside the Party
apparatus were either unwilling or unable to accept the new
demands that were placed upon them. They were particularly
afraid of making decisions for themselves without a clear directive from the center. In certain cases, age and talent were
involved, but, on the whole the failure of the "renewal" process to permeate down to the middle and lower echelons of the
Party was due to the determined resistance of the officials,
based either on hard-line philosophies or the defense of vested
interests. Many of them decided to sit back and "outlast"
Gierek. Gierek himself said quite openly in September 1971
that there were people in various positions within the Party
who knew how, but did not want to work. "We must part
company definitely," he said, because "they will never help us
solve the country's difficult problems."

The sixth Party congress in December 1971 sanctioned a
major turnover in the CC membership. Of the 115 full members of the new CC elected in December 1971, only 49 had
been members of the previous body. Even more strikingly, 68
of the 93 candidate CC members were elected for the first
time. In political terms the main result was the replacement
of representatives of the Gomulka era with individuals more acceptable to the new Party leadership. In terms of profession,
the number of workers had increased, but this group continued
to be underrepresented in comparison with their members in
the Party as a whole, while the Party and government apparatus was still considerably overrepresented.

To galvanize and revitalize the Party, Gierek convened
the National Party Conference in October 1973, an interim
event between the official Party congresses. The conference
was a forum not only for emphasizing the economic successes
recorded thus far, but also for the political message, that this
success had vindicated the entire Gierek approach. The conference was also called for the purpose of stimulating a consensus on Gierek's objectives, and to associate the Party as
a whole with the major decisions taken by the leadership. The
discussions themselves did show some departure from the well--
rehearsed uniformity which normally characterized such an
event. There were some criticisms and questions were asked,
but all of them were dealt with in a very pragmatic way by the
leaders. This revealed a conscious effort to imply that the

consultative role of lower echelon officials and interest groups
within the Party has been expanded.(11)

At the same time, however, Gierek announced that Party
membership cards were to be renewed between then and 1976.
By this device Communist parties periodically reviewed their
membership in accordance with criteria laid down by the current leadership. In this particular case, although ideological
consideration were obviously playing an important part, nevertheless Gierek's leadership tended to lay greater emphasis on
professional competence and personal initiative.

The reorganization of the local government in 1973 and
1975 provided Gierek with another chance to shake the Party
apparatus to its very roots (see section, "Administrative Reform, in this chapter"). Sixty-eight thousand Party officials
became redundant and had to take up other jobs.(12) This
made it possible for Gierek to inject some new blood into the
bureaucratic apparatus, but at the same time the move caused
severe irritation, frustration and disappointment among the entrenched bureaucrats and created more ground for feeding
anti-Gierek attitudes. As long as he had support from Moscow
and as long as his policies brought the expected results, the
apparatus, while locally sabotaging the general policies, and
committing sins of omission, did not try, for the most part, to
present any anti-Gierek front.

There were three factors involved: 1) The bureaucratic
machine, partly shaken up, was entrenching itself again by
the end of 1974 and the tougher careerists were often proving
the most skillful at advancing themselves. 2) Since 1973,
Moscow's pressure to tighten ideological and political control
gave a handle to those who wanted to further their careers by
doing Moscow's work. 3) The new men in power at local levels
were members of the former Stalinist Pre-October 1956 Polish
Youth Association, - tough, hard-liners for the most part -
and in the newly elected CC of the Party at the congress in
December 1975 the entrenched Party apparatus increased their
membership quite considerably. The local apparatus had regained more and more control in the regions, while Gierek
could not entirely count on them as a reliable information
channel, nor as a conveyor belt of people's reactions in their
own area. Local activists have always tried their best to
please the leaders, whatever the real situation. On December
15, 1970 two local Party committees unanimously passed a resolution stating that all the people fully accepted the price increases, vigorously condemned the excesses of "adventurers"
on the coast and enthusiastically supported Gomulka. Six days
later the same two committees unanimously accused Gomulka of
brutal repression of the workers' justified protests on the
coast and enthusiastically supported Gierek.

In 1974 Gierek faced another crisis in the top leadership.
In June Szlachcic was removed from the SCC and the PB and

was appointed a deputy premier instead. For almost four years Szlachcic had been one of Gierek's closest associates in his "inner cabinet" and was regarded as number two in the Party. His dismissal opened a major crack in the semblance of unity which the Communist party had maintained during the previous three years. In the secretariat Szlachcic had been responsible for security forces, intelligence services, contacts with foreign Communist parties, and some cadre appointments. Most of my sources in Poland described him as being very intelligent and building a power base for himself among the intelligentsia and among people who at one time or another were closer to the nationalist (while not antisemitic) attitude of the Partisan group. He certainly had great influence over the day-to-day running of Party affairs and was accessible to anybody who wanted to "adjust" Party policies. The overall opinion was that the main reason for his fall was to remove a potential contender for power.

Needless to say, not all the members of the top Party leadership at the end of 1975 shared identical views on tactical approaches to problems of socioeconomic development and political rule. By then Gierek's leadership was by no means a homogeneous group, but his personal preeminence was sufficient to impose a working unity and to forestall any challenges either in the form of the enhanced personal status of rivals or of alternative platforms.

Gierek has chosen to foster a long-term transformation of Polish society with the double goal of modernizing the economy and of socialization of the country as a whole. To revitalize and reassert the Party's authority, Gierek has done several things. There were many more CC meetings than at any time in postwar history, involving discussion of the policies, but in fact just reaffirming the documents which had been prepared by the PB and the SCC. This was one aspect of centralization within the Party. The loudly proclaimed division of functions between the Party and the government was steadily disappearing, except perhaps in one area.

Gierek took over as a leader of technocrats and pragmatists, who were pushing forward and trying to create the new expert managerial class. Strict Party control, I was told in Poland, was being eroded and reduced by some managers. This growth of managerial strength and influence was strongly opposed by various people at the top levels of the Party. Most of them fully realized that the system as "we have known it for years, is outdated"; but the question, still unanswered in 1976 remained: How far would this erosion of Party control and this strictly economic approach go? This was, as one journalist emphasized to me, a political and ideological problem.

The "leading" role of the Party was, in fact, being eroded in practical terms by life itself, but also, by the people at large who, while accepting that this was one of the unavoidable, however unfortunate, imperatives of the system, were rather clever in quietly outflanking this principle in their various personal activities, not only in the economy, but also in culture and sometimes on political issues.

The principle itself has undergone several interpretations, none of them practicable or useful. Basically the "leading" role of the Communist party has nothing to do with Marx. It could be argued that it is even anti-Marxist. It was Lenin's idea and his creation: an elitist oligarchy with supreme, unrestrained and uncontrolled power. The Stalinist interpretation; "the Party is responsible for everything" went even further, meaning that the Party not only determined policies but also interfered with their implementation by the government, thus duplicating their work. This brought the upheaval of 1956. The next interpretation - that the Party "recommends" and the government governs, basing its decisions on Party recommendations - brought, in effect, the upheaval in December 1970. Since then it was being stressed that the leading role of the Party limits itself to educating people and inspiring policies, but the government which implements them is independent. This was a contradiction in terms. How on earth could the government or parliament be independent if they had to implement the policies "inspired" by the Party.

Gierek's experiment in the daring interpretation of this imperative of the system, in which he firmly believes, failed because the principle as such is self-defeating. It does not admit varying and different views on basic issues affecting the country. Relying on expert opinions of various groups in society certainly helped to lessen the impact of this overriding principle, but the consultations were possible only within limits and as long as the opinions expressed did not undermine the principle itself. The principle has to be adhered to since it maintains in power a "leading" small minority group, as some communists admitted to me themselves. The net result is that the "leading" role glides helplessly over the surface of society and has to reassert itself every now and then in a forceful manner which, in turn, hampers real progress, damages the relationship between rulers and ruled, and quite often results in tragic upheavals. In other words, it is one of the imperatives of the system that makes the system itself almost unworkable.

THE CHURCH: A KEY FORCE IN THE COUNTRY

He is to be feared who fears the gods.

Aeschylus in "Septem Duces"

Every year hundreds of thousands of Poles make their annual pilgrimage - some on foot, others by bus, by truck, or by horsecart. Their destination is the centuries-old Pauline monastery and church on the Jasna Gora hill just outside Czestochowa, with its miraculous image of the Black Madonna, the most revered shrine in Poland. On one occasion over one million pilgrims assembled there - to attend masses, and to listen to the sermons of Cardinal Stefan Wyszynski, the primate of Poland. At six in the morning thousands of people, young and old, women and workers in their overalls, attend the first mass.

In 1973, 10,000 pilgrims marched from Warsaw to Czestochowa, 80 percent of them young people. They sang their own kind of songs, played guitars, and recited prayers written by themselves. Their new look was very well received by the older pilgrims, simple people who said: "Well, the young are different. They depart from our customs, but it is good that they are with us - that we are together."(13) Recently a Party official complained to me: "What can we do? Most of our activists attend church services, marry in church, and go to Czestochowa often on foot. But who could possibly expect them to walk even a few yards to buy a copy of Trybuna Ludu." "We don't care how many thousands go to Czestochowa," another official told me, "but we do care very much what is said in sermons." The Party is apprehensive, yet what can they do? When I spoke to Kakol, the minister in charge of the Office of Religious Denominations, and asked him about censorship in the country, his reply was: "There is, of course, censorship, except for 18,000 pulpits where the priests say what they like and it is really nobody's business what they can say on occasions."

June 1971
Corpus Christi Day in Warsaw
The center of the city was closed to traffic and militia patrols were diverting traffic from the main streets, because an estimated crowd of 400,000 was descending on the center, to take part in the Corpus Christi procession led by the primate of Poland from one altar to another erected in the streets. They heard the voice of Cardinal Wyszynski over the loudspeakers. Young girls threw rose petals before the proceeding cardinal who was accompanied by the bishops. And for the first time Warsaw television news bulletins widely covered these processions in Warsaw and other cities in filmed

newsreels. Small wonder that some journalists from "brotherly
socialist" countries were amazed and shocked at this spectacle.
July 1974
Sopot
          This is a famous resort on the Baltic Sea coast, filled at
that time of the year with thousands of tourists from all over
Poland, mostly young people, basking in the sun and swimming
in the sea.   But at six in the afternoon in the town's two
churches, masses were held.   Not only the churches themselves, but the courtyards and adjoining streets were overflowing with mainly young people, in jeans and T-shirts, in
miniskirts and hot pants.   There were old women and old men,
the workers in Sunday suits, soldiers in uniform and even
some militia officers.   The mass was heard by those outside
over loudspeakers.
May 1975
Warsaw
          In a newly built housing development, a modern cement
jungle with all "mod-con" consumer facilities, a nearby bus
depot has a huge placard which proclaims in red letters: "Long
Live the Working Class - the Leading Force of the Nation!"
Just three meters away, surrounded by a beautiful fence,
stands a recently erected wooden cross, four meters high.   In
this banal decor of a workers' housing settlement where the
apartment blocks, like so many cubes of cement, seemed to
stretch as far as the horizon, this little corner had something
unreal about it.   How could a slogan and a symbol of two
supposedly opposed faiths so openly coexist and confront each
other?
          Poland is a country with a strongly ingrained Marian cult.
Every year in May, in all the churches late afternoon and
evening masses are held in homage to St. Mary.
May 1973
Krakow
          This is a city of churches and once the home of Polish
kings.   From six in the afternoon onward all the churches are
full and the courtyards overflow with people, both young and
old, singing hymns.   As one Party official told me, in some
districts they had to change the time of the Party executive
committee meetings during May, from late afternoon to very
early in the morning, because otherwise the attendance in the
evening would be reduced to two or three members including
the first secretary of the committee...the others would all be
attending Marian masses in the churches.
May 15, 1977
Nowa Huta
          Named after Lenin, this giant complex of foundries and
steel works, the first new "socialist" town, was built years ago
just outside Krakow.   Thousands of Catholics - workers,
soldiers, women and girls - stood in the rain as the first new

church in this postwar industrial town was consecrated 17 years after earlier religious clashes.(14) It was here in 1960, that hundreds of believers, including old women, moved in to protect a wooden cross which had served as a center of open-air worship. When police proposed to remove it, the crowd stoned them. The police replied with tear gas, but the cross remained. For several years between four and six thousand workers from this "socialist" town attended 12 masses every Sunday - masses said in the open air below the cross - kneeling in the rain, sometimes in the snow, very often in the mud. Now, I was told, there were two new plants in Nowa Huta: a new steel works and a new "factory of the Holy Ghost" - in other words, the new church, the Notre Dame, the Queen of Poland. It was fascinating and, at the same time, unusual to look at this highly modern church built on three levels - and reminiscent of the style of the famous churches of the French architect Le Corbusier - against the background of huge steel structures in the foundry complex. The church itself was built by thousands of volunteers and amateurs helped by 30 specialists and qualified workers. The granite facade, for instance, was built using two thousand stones which could only be found in one river in the countryside. The stones were brought across and polished by young people. Near the church stands a massive steel cross, 70 meters high, a gift from Austria. Within the church itself, in the crypt, in the chapel of reconciliation, there are a series of moving Pieta, entitled "Christ in Oswiecim [Auschwitz]," executed by a well-known Polish sculptor. The consecration of the church was attended by 50,000 people.

The Catholic Church insists that many more places of worship must be built than the authorities will give permission for. In some cases the people have built a makeshift chapel without planning permission. On at least three occasions these chapels were torn down and razed to the ground by the militia. That in turn provoked some local riots and strong condemnation from the primate. On the other hand, in one of the southeast Polish dioceses, the local bishop managed over the years to build clandestinely 20 new chapels or small churches in the countryside with the help of peasants and ... local Party members.

The church represents not only a spiritual, but also a historical and patriotic force much stronger than the Party itself. In any dangerous situation, such as during upheavals and riots, the church has always stood on the side of peace, order and the interests of the nation. And on these occasions its policy has not only helped the Party leadership, but also saved the system from complete disintegration, a course which might have incalculable consequences in the present geopolitical situation.

There is hardly a village in Poland where the priest is not the dominant personality of his parish. Once I was driving in the foothills of the Tatra Mountains in southern Poland, passing through a very small, charming village. My young Polish companion, who had asked for a lift, showed me a quite imposing building near the local church. You find there, he said, the office of the local Party secretary, a tiny local militia station, a fire brigade and...a large parish office of the local priest. All together but "obviously the priest is very much in charge." To wipe out the influence of the priesthood in Poland would be a moral as well as a physical impossibility. And no Polish government, unless it wished to divorce itself entirely from the will of the nation could afford to ignore the wishes or the will of the church.

The head of the church in 1976, 75-year-old Cardinal Wyszynski, has proved a very hard bargainer. Uncompromising when the interests of the nation and the church were threatened, but at the same time a subtle diplomat who always knew when to cooperate, what to support, and what to oppose and when. Wyszynski fought always on his own territory, never forgetting his principal weapon: the immense prestige of the church and of its primate. Nor did he forget that traditionally, over the centuries, between the death of one king and the enthronement of his successor, the primate of Poland always assumed the supreme functions of the interrex. As a noncommunist journalist told me jokingly, Moscow would probably be happiest if the primate could be installed as the regent of Poland. The knowledge that the nation had been in the church's hands for a thousand years before the communists arrived has sustained the self-confidence of the church in the country. When one goes into the cellars of Poznan cathedral and looks at the uncovered and faithfully preserved parts of the foundations of the original church built there a thousand years ago, and compares these with the foundations of the communist system which have a history of but 30 years, the church's attitude becomes clear.

In the year 966 Prince Mieszko the First was baptized into the Christian faith. His son founded the archbishopric of Gniezno and gave Poland both religious and political independence. Since then Polish Catholicism has become a mystical, political formula for the self-realization of the nation as being distinct from Germans and Russians, from the orthodox and protestant churches, from all rationalist, reformist and revolutionary movements on the Euro-Asian continent.(15) The strong identification of the Catholic Church with Polish nationalism from the tenth century onward is a key factor in Polish history. Poland, that Eastern outpost of Western Christianity, defended itself against incursions from the East and thereby defended, at the same time, the whole of Christian Western Europe. The traditional identification of

Poles with Catholicism in post-reformation Europe was enhanced after the partitions of Poland at the end of the eighteenth century when the Catholic Church did much to preserve the national identity by direct participation, or at least by serving as a national rallying point. During the last war and the German occupation, the church and its hierarchy took an active part in the resistance movement. Thousands of priests were imprisoned and about one-third of them were killed or perished in concentration camps. The church then emerged from the war with an enhanced prestige. And when the communists took over, with the past in ruins, with the old social order destroyed and old ideas discredited, religion was the one unchanging and unchanged beacon for a nation sailing in the turbulent and hostile waters of the Stalinist postwar period.

The political role of the Catholic Church after the last war has been shaped by its history. Traditionally, the church and its hierarchy were not inclined to participate directly in the exercise of power. They learned from history about the instability of political regimes. They understood that institutions deeply rooted in society, in its feelings and traditions, were in fact, better fitted to survive. Instead of fighting for political power, the church concentrated its efforts on strengthening itself institutionally and on defending the interests of the nation as a whole against any measures by the communist leadership which the church regarded as endangering both the traditional and Christian values in the country.(16)

From the communist point of view the influence of the church is a danger and a challenge to the whole Marxist concept. It is the only mass organization outside Party control and it is engaged in the fight for the soul of Poland. In spite of all the administrative harassments of the church and Episcopate's protests, the church in Poland now has not only more followers, but more churches, parish priests, bishops, and seminaries than ever before. It has the only Catholic university in the communist world, and there are even Catholic deputies in the Sejm. The church is the greatest power in communist Poland and in this lies both its strength and its weakness - strength because the communists know that they cannot destroy the church and they dare not challenge it in a head-on clash; weakness, because, by presenting a danger to communism, by speaking on behalf of the nation as a whole, the rulers of Poland are faced with the unenviable dilemma of either surrendering or embarking on the long and perhaps hopeless task of working for the slow and gradual erosion of the church so that future generations might perhaps give their loyalty to Marx and his doctrine.

As Cardinal Wyszynski has said, almost in so many words, the communist regime is fighting the church because the church is so strong. In no other communist country is

the church either so strong or so identified with national
aspirations as to be the natural rallying point for all the
forces opposed to communism and in no communist-ruled country is communism itself as weak as it is in Poland. There is a
joke often heard in Poland: In one of the churches in Warsaw
three rabbis are seen attending mass. One of the congregation asks the rabbis, "What are you doing here? You are not
Christians?" One rabbi replies, "No, but neither am I a
Marxist!"

The fundamental conflict comes down to the simple fact
that there is a struggle for the allegiance of the nation, of
which both the church and the Party are determined to be the
sole guarantor and sole spokesman. The church knows that
nothing is less stable or more historically transient than a
political regime, and therefore what matters for the church is
to see that religion and church are as firmly and deeply rooted
in the masses of the nation as possible. And without doubt,
the church can claim that it is certainly more deeply rooted
than the Communist party. The Communist system is still
regarded by very many Poles as a foreign, imposed, and
imported product even if many of the communist leaders are
regarded as Polish patriots who are trying to do the best they
can in the existing circumstances. But the nation is an
entity, global and indivisible. Who, therefore, has the right
to speak in the name of the nation, to express its aspirations
and to defend its interests? The primate or the first secretary? It is not only a question of ideologies. There are
also two powerful forces confronting each other. One, the
Party, a small minority, is kept in power by virtue of Poland's
geopolitical position. The other, the church, is relying on its
thousand-year-old tradition, on its mass following (over 90
percent of Poles including most Party members, are Catholics),
and on its immense prestige built up over the centuries. Both
sides, while determined not to surrender their positions, know
that an open confrontation can only lead to deadlock or disaster. They also realize that it is in the interest of each of
them to keep the temperature of the conflict as low as
possible.

The church-state battles of the last years of the Gomulka
era have been, with the coming to power of Gierek, replaced
by a more subtle interplay of forces. In his typical pragmatic
approach, Gierek straight away launched an initiative aiming at
full normalization of relations between the state and the
church. Immediately after December, Gierek realized that the
church was there to stay permanently, and that the unity of
the nation and the mobilization of all its creative forces were
impossible to achieve without the support of the church. The
Episcopate welcomed the Party's announced intention of improving relations with the church and joined Gierek, just as it
had joined Gomulka in 1956, in appealing for calm to avoid

outside intervention. But the Episcopate also raised its own institutional demands, while simultaneously making more directly political appeals for full respect of human rights which the Episcopate listed in detail (see Chapter 3). This statement of principles may have represented a maximum set of demands, but there was no evidence that the Episcopate was prepared to modify them substantially.

Various church grievances, if not so frequently and not so blatantly raised, still awaited settlement. These included: the ownership of church property in the western territories which were regarded by the government as war booty and rents were collected from the church for use of monasteries and church buildings; the taxation of the clergy, church institutions, and the Catholic University in Lublin; the policy of issuing permits for building new churches; the state's demand that a full inventory of church property be made and always kept ready for state inspection; the state's interference in religious instruction outside schools in 18,000 "catechetic points"; and the conscription of clergy and seminarians for military service as well as attempts to close some theological seminaries.

The concrete measures promised by the leadership were not immediately forthcoming. On January 25, 1971, Radio Warsaw reported that the government had authorized the appropriate agencies to prepare the necessary legal documents for the transfer to the Catholic Church of property titles to churches and other ecclesiastical buildings in the western and northern territories (former German territories). Here was a sign of the government's good will for all to see at home and abroad, which certainly signified a form of recognition of the permanent nature of organized religion in Poland. In response to this announcement, the bishops issued a communique "accepting with satisfaction the Premier's December normalization declaration" and viewing his January 25 property transfer decision as "indicative of further acts seeking to establish normal relations between the Church and the State."(17) In a show of goodwill and in the atmosphere of another confrontation between the Party and the workers (January-February 1971) a pastoral letter came down strongly on the side of law and order and justice for all, so that the new leaders "might find the right way to tranquillity and sound development, faithful to their promises to respect the citizen's basic human rights."

But no concrete steps have yet been undertaken. The Episcopate, for instance, complained that "the attitude of the education authorities to religious instruction, not only has remained unchanged, but has even, in many cases and in certain respects, become worse." Under-Secretary of State Skarzynski, of the Office of Religious Denominations, told the Episcopate that the government would begin talks only after unquestioning recognition by the church of the "socialist system."(18) This clearly indicated that the state expected the church to make a formal declaration of something that would be at the very least, an expression of gratitude. But then the Party, seriously misjudging the situation within the Polish hierarchy, was apparently counting on differences of opinion which might have existed within the Episcopate. They were still thinking in terms of Cardinal Wojtyla of Krakow and other "moderate" bishops opposing the more conservative and uncompromising primate. In the forthcoming years, Cardinal Wojtyla became closer to the primate than anybody else and in some respects proved to be even more uncompromising than the cardinal himself.

The leadership quite quickly realized that there was complete unanimity within the Episcopate and on March 3, 1971, the primate and the prime minister met in the first summit between the two leaders in eight years, and negotiated for three hours. According to both Party officials and the ecclesiastical sources I spoke to in Warsaw, both men were satisfied with the talks. At a meeting of the government presidium, Jaroszewicz stressed that the primate was certainly correct in some of his strictures, particularly when he complained about the attitude of the Party apparatus at the lower level and the situation of clerics in the armed forces. Those responsible, said Jaroszewicz, should be convinced that there was a new climate in the church-state relations and he described Cardinal Wyszynski as a reasonable man and a political realist.

A new framework for contacts between state and church was established. This discussion of general policies involved: Krasko, deputy premier and a secretary of the CC; Kania, representing the authorities; and Bishop Dabrowski the secretary of the Episcopate, speaking on behalf of the church. Under Secretary of State Skarzynski, the head of the Office for Religious Denominations, was in charge of everyday contacts and negotiations. The government bill on church property in the western and northern territories had been agreed on between the church and the government.

The government was quite explicit about the quid pro quo of its normalization program. In June 1971, PB member Szydlak asserted that full normalization depended on the church's "full recognition of the socialist character of the state and its socialist perspectives." In October 1971 Skarzynski said: "The church authority must recognize the socialist order in our country. The people's state for its part will acknowledge the social value of the church's educational function in relation to believers."

But behind the facade of all official statements the contacts between the church and the state were maintained continuously and several concessions were made. Over the period of two and one-half years, the state transferred the legal rights of the church properties in the western and northern territories to the church. Not only were the rents paid by the church annulled, but certain rebates for sums already paid were made by the government. In 1972 the church had been relieved of its obligation to keep detailed inventories of all its property and was exempted from paying income tax on part of it. The second step meant, in effect, that many rural priests whose income came from small church lands could now enjoy a guaranteed standard of living. The first step removed the church's lingering fear that the government might confiscate its sacred property. The income tax overdue by the Catholic University in Lublin, amounting to about 64 million zlotys, was cancelled. In 1971 alone, government permission was given for the building of 30 new churches, while in the preceeding few years, before December 1970, only one such license was granted. By the end of 1974, 160 permissions were given by the government, but the primate claimed that in view of social changes, rising population, and the transfer of the population from the countryside to towns about 1,000 new churches were needed.

The need for many more churches than the number of permissions granted had caused a great rush of illegal church building in 1971-1973. The materials for these churches, or rather makeshift chapels, were secretly collected over many months, then the simple structures were built overnight or over the weekend and the loyal people turned out to defy any attempts by the authorities to pull them down. Dozens of such churches were in use over the countryside and quite a few of them had been granted legal authorization after some wrangling. On some occasions the militia intervened to destroy the illegally built makeshift chapels. The most famous example of this was the one in the small village of Zbrosza Duza, about 30 miles south of Warsaw. The tabernacle, containing the consecrated host, was seized by the militia. Three days later the militia returned to the scene in order to prevent children from building an improvised shrine. The primate issued a very strongly worded public protest to the government accusing it of acts contrary to official declarations regarding freedom of worship, and demanded respect for the religious freedoms of Poland's predominantly Catholic population. The militia intervention in Zbrosza he described as a "sacrilege without precedent in Poland."(19) In an unusual move, a Polish government spokesman responded to this attack, justifying the action by the fact that the chapel was built illegally and constituted a health hazard to the faithful; but the spokesman also made it clear that "It must be emphatically stressed that the event has absolutely no bearing on church-state relations."(20) Just over a year later Cardinal Wyszynski was able to consecrate the foundation stone of a new church in the same place.

In another open gesture of accommodation the authorities helped airlift some 1,500 Polish Catholics to Rome for the ceremonies beautifying the Polish martyr, Father Maksymilian Kolbe, who died at Oswiecim [Auschwitz]; they then facilitated travel to Rome for the Holy Year celebrations by about 3,000 pilgrims. Several church dignitaries from Italy, Germany, France, the United States and Austria were given visas to come to Poland, including Cardinal Konig of Vienna. In May 1972 a pilgrimage of some 150,000 Silesian miners took place in Piekary Slaskie, the most venerated shrine in Silesia and one of the most important Marian shrines in Poland. In the course of these celebrations, Cardinal Konig celebrated a festive mass and was overwhelmed by what he called, "the devotion and faithfulness of the miners, engineers, technicians, and students of the Silesian industrial district, who came to Piekary."(21) Needless to say, the Polish primate and the Polish bishops were able to travel abroad and to Rome whenever they wished without any difficulty.

In the first two years when Gierek fervently sought the support and help of the entire nation, the intention to continue to aim at "complete normalization of relations" was re-iterated, as was the Party's "appreciation and recognition" of the quality of work and creative activities of citizen-believers. But even in those days the leadership, although showing a substantial amount of goodwill, was either unprepared or unable to meet all the demands of the church and to solve all the outstanding problems. The clumsy handling, particularly at the lower level of the Party apparatus, of church-state relations, created unnecessary friction and local confrontations.

Church-state relations were also slightly jaundiced by a sudden callup of many student priests for military service. Under a rule introduced by Gierek, no theological seminary students had to undergo military training. Church officials expressed amazement at the scale of the call-up which started in all parts of the country and affected 70 seminarians in Krakow alone. The Episcopate strongly protested to the authorities.

Thus, despite Gierek's unequivocal and rather sensational statement the problem of believers (see section, "Gierek's Program for Poland," in Chapter 3) remained a very tricky one. The Party leader was determined to put into practice his promise about an equal start for believers and nonbelievers, Party and non-Party people, particularly in the economic administration. He did realize that there were tremendous untapped reserves of qualified and able people among the believers. PB member Babiuch, responsible for cadre policy, emphasized once again the need for placing highly qualified non-Party specialists in executive positions (22), but little was done to accomplish this aim. As the leader of the Znak group

of Catholic deputies, Professor Stomma complained in the
spring of 1972, "Efforts to release social energy at the lower
level among believers were still unsatisfactory. This restricted
social activity and adversely affected progress in the
country."(23)

There was strong opposition at the local level of Party
apparatus. Local Party bosses, jealously guarding their influence, continued to discriminate against non-Party specialists.
Some Party members argued that to replace a Party member at
any level by a non-Party expert meant the rejection of the
principle of the leading role of the Party. The editor of
Polityka, Rakowski, regarded the situation as a political
anachronism. It did deprive, according to him, management at
all levels of excellent people and at the same time it ideologically downgraded the composition of the Party itself. Many
believers joined the Party not for ideological reasons, but
because this was the only way for them to make a career, and
if they were honest people, to work efficiently for their
country and leave behind them some real achievements. Other
journalists, and even Party officials I spoke to, maintained
that such an anachronism was bound to deepen the divisions
within society.

Since the beginning of 1971 the church-state dialogue
within the country was closely interwoven with the negotiations
between Warsaw and the Vatican. This historical development
happened only after Gierek came to power. In April 1971 in
Rome and again in November in Warsaw, Skarzynski conferred
with Archbishop Casaroli, secretary of the Vatican's Council
for Public Affairs, in other words an unofficial Vatican foreign
minister.

The main stumbling block was the Vatican's refusal to
recognize the Polish western frontier, and to normalize the
church administration in the newly acquired territories. Both
the government and the Episcopate pressed hard for final
recognition of the frontiers. Following long-established usage
the Roman Curia has refused, since 1945, to install as fully
fledged bishops those Polish nominees who acted only as
apostolic administrators in these territories on the grounds
that the territorial changes have not been finally recognized in
a binding international treaty. What added insult to injury
was the fact that the surviving German former holders of the
sees in question continued to be listed in some Vatican publications with their old titles. As long as Bonn continued to
dispute the legal status of the territories the Vatican had to
regard the situation as provisional and could not appoint
bishops without taking the Polish side in the dispute, and
without damaging its relations with West Germany. At first
there was a hope that the Vatican would take a decisive step
after the West German-Polish treaty was signed in Warsaw in
December 1970. But then Archbishop Casaroli argued that it

could be done only after the ratification of the treaty by the
West German parliament.   This was regarded by the government, the Episcopate and the Polish people as "most unhelp-
ful."

Finally, on June 28, 1972 Pope Paul VI appointed Polish
resident bishops to replace the apostolic administrators in the
western and northern territories.   The announcement, made
by a Vatican spokesman at a press conference in Rome, conferred Vatican recognition of full Polish sovereignty on these
lands.(24)   The decision also involved the delimitation of new
diocesan borders to bring them into line with Poland's present
frontiers.

The issue of recognition of the Oder-Neisse frontier had
been for many years perhaps the only area in which the attitudes of the church and the state coincided, without any
friction.   Such a move on the part of the Holy See was, in the
church's eyes, required in order for the clergy to perform its
normal duties.   On the government's part the issue was seen
primarily as a political one, involving the international
recognition of Poland's postwar borders.   The government
spokesman reiterated this view when, after noting that the
Polish authorities favored the decision, he claimed that the
Vatican had drawn conclusions from the real territorial political
situation which had already existed for 27 years.(25)   An
official of the Polish Episcopate also hailed the pope's action,
adding that "on this issue the Polish Episcopate and the Polish
government are unanimous."(26)

The way seemed to be open now for further negotiations
between Warsaw and the Vatican leading to normalization of
relations at the government level.   But in this new triangle of
church-state-Vatican, new problems relating to conflicting
interests and aims of the negotiations and of the final agreement came to the surface.   An accommodation with the Vatican
at the highest level was certainly in the interests of the Party
and government.   Even the very fact of an agreement would
be viewed by the people as lending the government an aura of
respectability.   At the same time if the government could deal
directly with Rome, the image and prestige of the church
hierarchy were likely to suffer.   The Polish leadership might
have tried to settle the normalization of church-state relations
within the country directly through the Vatican and above the
heads of the Polish Episcopate.   The Episcopate was fully
aware of this danger, particularly since Archbishop Casaroli,
the main architect of the Vatican's Ostpolitik, was very keen
on coming to terms with the Polish government, as he had
done with Yugoslavia and Hungary.   But the primate, fully
supported by all the bishops in his many discussions in the
Vatican, made the point that before any agreement could be
reached his full approval must be sought since the Vatican "is
too far away to understand fully the intricacies of church-state

relations in Poland." He made sure that there could be no Warsaw-Vatican normalization before church-state normalization in the country, although he was prepared to accept the Vatican's help in this area.

In November 1973, Foreign Minister Olszowski was received in audience by the pope, the first such visit to the Vatican by a Polish government minister since the war. Olszowski's visit was immediately followed by the Polish primate's three-week stay at the Holy See during which he was received three times at private audience by the Pope to "report in detail on the current situation of the church in Poland." Immediately after his return to Warsaw, Cardinal Wyszynski spelled out in a series of sermons the conditions under which any normalization could be achieved in relations with the state.(27) In the first place, Poland's 30 million believers had to be granted not only full religious freedom, but also a new role in the country's social, cultural, and business life. This could not happen, the Cardinal said, until at least the following problems were satisfactorily solved: the church had to be free to educate the nation's youth in the spirit of the gospel; the attempts to impose atheism had to be abandoned; and discrimination against Catholic citizens in public and professional life had to cease ("We cannot be pariahs," said the Cardinal, "in the homeland for which we, too, work honestly."). The centuries-old Catholic civilization in Poland had to be given more scope; Catholic writers and artists should have access to mass media; an independent Catholic press should be established; and the problem of the construction and repair of church buildings had to be settled satisfactorily.

In February 1974, Archbishop Casaroli came to Warsaw for the first time as an official guest at the invitation of the Polish foreign minister. This was something new and remarkable in Polish-Vatican relations. He was given a red-carpet treatment and had several talks with top government leaders. In a joint communique the two sides promised to contemplate the establishment of "permanent working contacts," stating that the normalization of church-state relations was the subject of a "particularly thorough discussion." Among other problems Casaroli raised the controversial education reform (see section, "Educational Reform," in this chapter) the permission to erect new churches, and the problem of securing equal rights and opportunities for Catholics.

After three days of official visit Casaroli moved from the government guest house to the primate's palace and spent another few days in long discussions with Cardinal Wyszynski, briefing him about the details of his conversations with the government representatives, and trying to agree how to co-ordinate the Vatican's established Eastern policy with the views and demands of the church hierarchy in Poland. The official

stand of the Polish Episcopate on all questions of church-state
relations released on January 25, 1974, provided a basis for
discussion between the two church dignitaries. According to
this document(28) the Polish hierarchy welcomed the planned
normalization of Polish-Vatican relations as another step toward
improving church-state relations in Poland. The bishops
reiterated their former demands formulated by the cardinal
after his return from Rome.

While some Polish media were accusing the Episcopate of
an uncooperative attitude in Warsaw-Vatican negotiations, it
was disclosed in Rome that only in February 1974, after
Casaroli's visit to Warsaw, had the Polish government for the
first time expressed its will "in official, authoritative and
public terms," to negotiate with the Episcopate. The Vatican-
Polish talks overlapping into this area were also supposed to
work out what was termed a "recognized juridicial basis"
providing an improvement of the overall situation of the church
in Poland. Such a basis could in the future be embodied in
some form of written agreement, but the signing of such a
document and the resumption of diplomatic relations which it
might imply remained at present a far off goal in the Vatican's
view.

Diplomatic relations were thus not established, but, after
another round of talks in Rome, in July 1974, it was agreed to
institute "permanent working contacts" designed to improve
church-state relations in Poland. These contacts implied
regular periodic consultations which would provide an easier
format for a more coordinated, organic approach to pending
church-state problems. The Holy See reiterated that the
Episcopate would, in any case, be consulted on all matters
raised in Polish-Vatican talks and kept informed about their
progress.

Toward the end of 1974, Kazimierz Szablewski, a diplomat
of long standing, was appointed head of a Polish team to
maintain working contacts with the Vatican with the permanent
residence in Rome. Archbishop Luigi Poggi became chief of
the Vatican delegation, a "traveling nuncio," visiting Poland
regularly and having talks both with the government and the
Episcopate. He had had long experience of Polish affairs
which he handled in Rome in the sixties and was on very good
terms not only with the primate, but also with many Polish
officials.

Toward the end of 1973 and more so in 1974, two parallel
developments made an impact on church-state relations in
Poland. Under strong Moscow pressure the reinforcement of
Marxist indoctrination and the tightening of the ideological
screw were in line with similar developments throughout
Eastern Europe as the countries of the bloc prepared to face
the challenge of detente, and of a closer relationship with the
West which was bound to be enlarged by the Helsinki conference.

Some sections of the Party felt that while the Soviet bloc was doing everything to strengthen its ideological unity in the face of detente, it was hardly the moment to be making further major concessions to the church which openly rejected the Party ideology.

But the Polish leadership had also chosen to foster a long-term transformation of Polish society with the double goal of modernizing both the economy and society and thereby undermining the traditional strength of the church. "Socialization" was the ultimate aim. The Episcopate's response had been to be a loyal opposition - loyal to programs designed to improve the material side of life in Poland and to programs which the church regarded as in the interests of the Polish nation as a whole, but to oppose the increasing emphasis on Marxism-Leninism in society. Thus the leadership found itself in a paradoxical situation. On the one hand it desperately needed the church's support in implementing its socioeconomic policies and in securing a form of continuous dialogue and understanding with the nation; on the other, after almost three years of relatively pragmatic rule, it began to place increasing stress on ideology. The leadership seemed to play on two levels. While making minor gestures and continuing the dialogue with the church on minor issues which were solved locally or sometimes even on a national level, the main controversies remained. Meanwhile, new problems appeared on the horizon.

The issue on which church and state came into most serious conflict was that of educational reform (see section "Educational Reform," in this chapter). The church supported the modernization of the educational system, but also had strong objections. From the Episcopate's point of view the proposals would reduce the time available for children to attend religious instruction classes organized in churches or parish buildings in their own villages and would reduce the influence of parents on children's education. The other unacceptable concept in the reforms was to introduce a uniform curriculum and, as the prime minister had said, the socialist state alone would henceforth define educational objectives.

According to the official interpretation accepted by the Sejm: "The cornerstone of the new system is the socialist educational ideas contained in the program of the Communist party, which leads the nation in the building of a socialist society." This meant, stressed the Episcopate's statement on May 7, 1973, that the new system is based purely on atheistic principles which completely excluded any influence by the Catholic Church.(29) The ultimate aim of the government was to unify society on a materialistic basis, with no freedom of conscience or choice. The statement made it clear that the church would defend the rights of parents to bring up their children according to their beliefs, and the state had a duty

to respect this right. An appeal made by Poland's Episcopate
to the nation amounted to a manifesto rejecting the regime's
attempts to introduce atheism and laicism in the life of the
nation - contrary to the constitution - and threw down a
clear challenge to the leadership.(30) On several other
occasions the primate and the Episcopate strongly attacked
various aspects of the educational reform. "We know that
this is not a Polish invention," said Cardinal Wyszynski in
August 1973, "that it does not originate within the spirit of
our people. Importations of this type can only harm the
nation, and must, therefore, be distrusted." In another
pastoral letter, the bishops accused the government of
exerting pressure on students to try to get them to accept
the communist ideology adding that these attempts to involve students against their will in an ideology foreign to
them, deprived the young people of necessary spiritual
qualities.(31)

Under heavy and repeated pressure from the church and
other quarters, the implementation of the education bill was
postponed for two years until 1975 and some of its more controversial clauses were deferred as late as 1978. In his
Christmas message in 1973,(32) Cardinal Wyszinski expressed
satisfaction over the postponement of the educational reform.
He called the planned reform "the greatest threat to the
church of Poland in the last 25 years" and strongly repeated
his contention that education must have a national not a Party
character since "Parties change but the nation remains."
Clearly, an East European church leader could only talk in
such terms if he enjoyed tremendous local support.

It was in 1974 that, for the first time, there was a clear
discrepancy in official presentation of the policy toward the
church. In March, PB member Szydlak(33) described the
church as the only center of rightist social forces that had at
its disposal a coherent philosophical outlook, a strong organizational base, and numerous cadres. He lashed out at the
"reactionary wing of the Episcopate" which was the "main
organized antisocialist group in our country, a veritable center
uniting all the antistate 'currents' while at the same time
representing their last hope." On another occasion
Werblan, secretary of the CC, denounced what he described
as the "organized antisocialist activity of the reactionary
section of the church hierarchy in Poland."

At about the same time, on occasion of his official visit to
the United States, Gierek took up an entirely different attitude
as shown in two interviews published by American papers. In
one of his interviews he said:

> We have never considered the Church a chal-
> lenge to the Communist party or to our system, and,
> in fact, the Church has never tried to endanger the

system or the Party. We, on our part, have never tried to endanger the Church. Neither in our practice today, nor in our endeavours for the future will we attempt to minimize the role of the Church of Poland.(34)

In the other interview, Gierek(35) insisted that the church is "a substantial force in Poland and can help maintain moral values common to all people, regardless of faith."

What appeared to be the two faces of official policy in 1974-1976 became much sharper in profile when the new head of the Office of Religious Denominations, Kakol, was appointed with the rank of full minister in May 1974. An astute and quick-witted man, the Polish Lawyers Association refused to reelect him to its top body because, as recent editor of the association's weekly, Prawo i Zycie, he became a prominent and often vicious spokesman of the antiliberal and antisemitic faction of the Party led by General Moczar in the stormy days following the March 1968 student riots. To a British journalist Kakol(36) said in October 1974: "As a jurist and a citizen, I wish to carry out the constitution, which prescribes respect for the church and for the freedom of religion. But, as a communist, I want to diminish the influence of the church."

In May 1976 he confidently briefed Party activists and in July gave an interview to French and Italian journalists. When meeting Party activists Kakol(37) treated the church as an enemy which should be "annihilated" if possible or at least made "harmless." Religion had to be in the long run totally "extirpated" from human conscience and thought. The current policy of normalization of relations with the church in general and the Vatican in particular, he assured his audience, remained a tactical expedient expertly used by the regime. As if to dispel all of his audience's doubts, Kakol stated in conclusion: "Even though as a minister I am obliged to smile in order to inspire confidence, as a communist I shall fight unyieldingly against religion and the church both from an ideological and from a philosophical viewpoint."

It was this official "smiling" face that the minister displayed to Western journalists interviewing him.(38) He assured them that both the church and the state had succeeded in finding a common basis of understanding on which to cooperate constructively. The Poles, he said, build socialism in factories, and learn honesty in churches. He praised the majority of the Polish bishops for their unquestionable patriotism, and the primate as "a good patriot" and a "loyal opponent" whom he held in "great esteem."

When I talked to Kakol in 1974 he told me that the bishops were inundating him with memoranda on every conceivable subject and on every aspect of government policy. The bishops were all thanked very politely for their interesting communications, but their questions were neither discussed nor answered in detail. Here, of course, the minister was wrong. He might not have answered the memoranda in detail, but they were certainly taken into account and under the church's pressure some government policies were either postponed in implementation, changed or adjusted.

More significant, however, were the apparently contradictory declarations made by top Party leaders. It was rather difficult to assess how much of what was said was intended to calm apprehension and ease pressures both within and without the Party. The policy of driving a wedge between what were termed reactionary elements and progressive factions both within the Polish Episcopate and in the Vatican was an old act, overplayed quite unsuccessfully, many times before by the Party. There was no evidence that, however conservative he might appear at times and however harshly he might press some demands, the primate was not fully and unanimously supported by the Episcopate. Thus when Kakol spoke about the "annihilation of the church" he was being either naive or politically unrealistic or indeed might have been trying to appear more communist than some communists themselves.

In a Catholic country like Poland the Party needs the church if it is to rule without upheavals and disastrous consequences. Gierek wants to "socialize" society but he is pragmatic and realistic enough to understand that he cannot do much without the cooperation of the church and he does realize that he will not be able to go too far, even if he wanted to, against the church's attitude and reactions. Even if Gierek disliked some of the cardinal's strictures, and even if he was unwilling or unable to accept all the demands, according to all the available evidence, the two respect each other. There is even a degree of mutual confidence because in their different ways they both try to have the interests of the nation at heart.

As for the policy of wedge driving advocated by some hard-liners in the Party, on the seventy-fifth birthday of the primate, at an official anniversary celebration in the archepiscopal palace in Warsaw, the under secretary of state representing the prime minister handed to Cardinal Wyszynski, his "distinguished host," a bouquet of flowers sent, along with best wishes, by the premier. The government quietly suggested in the Vatican that the pope should not accept the primate's resignation which, according to the church's rules, he did offer on his seventy-fifth birthday. As a senior churchman in Warsaw told me: "They know Cardinal Wyszynski well. They would rather have a priest they know than a priest they do not know." The primate's resignation was not accepted and the pope asked him to carry on.

Archbishop Luigi Poggi, the traveling nuncio, head of the Vatican's team for permanent working contacts with Warsaw, visited Poland three times in all - in 1975, 1976 and in 1977.

He traveled the length of Poland, visited almost all dioceses
and held several talks with top government leaders. But he
always acted in full consultation with the Polish Episcopate.
During Poggi's first month-long stay in Poland, the primate
made it absolutely clear in a sermon that if the government's
negotiations with the Vatican representative were to lead to
any real agreement, the topics of these discussions should
focus in the future on problems connected with the church and
its believers, rather than concentrate on international
issues.(39)

   Seen in retrospect the papal nuncio's first Polish visit
was a double success. In his handling of talks on Warsaw-
Vatican detente, Poggi proved beyond any doubt an apt and
versatile negotiator. And it clearly appeared that Warsaw
attached great importance to the normalization of its relations
with the Vatican. But far more important was the positive
impact of his visit on the development of church-state affairs.
The last bishops' conference in which Poggi took part noted in
its communique the Episcopate's full satisfaction with the
results achieved during the nuncio's visit, and the hope that
it would contribute to a more adequate assessment in the
Vatican of "those problems of the church in Poland which
should find a satisfactory solution within the framework of a
properly understood normalization of church-state relations."
Poggi stressed on various occasions that there could be no
doubt about the "full and complete understanding in this
matter between the Holy See and the Episcopate." After Poggi
left Poland the primate welcomed the results of his visit, which
he described as a modest beginning to what he called difficult
conversation, but publicly admitted for the first time that the
authorities definitely seemed to be exhibiting "more understanding of the church's problems."(40) And he repeated
demands for full civic freedoms to be granted to all citizens
irrespective of their beliefs as guaranteed by the Polish constitution.

   Archbishop Poggi's second longest stay in Poland in
April-May 1976 ended in a stalemate in negotiations between
Warsaw and the Holy See on normalizing their diplomatic
relations. But his contacts with church leaders were even
closer than before. The shift in emphasis from the "worldley"
to the "spiritual" may be explained by the recent turn in the
Vatican's Ostpolitik which was becoming increasingly sober and
reserved. Another reason for the change was the deterioration
in church-state relations in Poland (see Chapter 7).

   Poggi's third visit to Poland in March 1977, in contrast to
the previous occasions, was not followed by any official communique, although he saw various Polish ministers. According
to Vatican sources, such problems as limitations imposed on
church construction and the independent Catholic press,
religious instruction and general discrimination against Catho-

lics were discussed in these talks. The reason for the
reticent reaction given to Poggi during his March 1977 trip by
all sides was to be found in the precarious situation in the
country in general and in church-state relations in particular
(see Chapter 15). The climate had been strained by the
appearance of a forged book of sermons by Cardinal
Wyszynski. In this, a nasty piece of forgery, significant
parts of the sermons had been altered to make it seem as if
the cardinal were expressing views favorable to socialism.
Under church pressure the government took the unprecedented
step of publishing a denunciation of the forgery in at least
four of its papers in February 1977.

By then the bishops were confident that the Vatican
would make no final move in interstate relations until conditions for Catholics in Poland were improved. "After all," it
was put to me "the Holy Father knows that here in Poland we
have perhaps the strongest, most united church in the world."
"Is coexistence really possible between Christians and
Marxists?" I asked. "The last 30 years in Poland have
proved that it is," said one priest. "We Catholics are loyal to
the state - all of us. But we reject the official ideology."

The leadership's plan to "socialize" society has been
closely related to the position and influence of the church. In
1974 Cardinal Wyszynszki(41) made the church's position absolutely clear: "For us, next to God, our first love is Poland.
After God one must above all remain faithful to our homeland,
to the Polish national culture. Above all we demand the right
to live in accordance with the spirit, history, culture and
language of our own Polish land...."(41)

The primate had no fears by now, as a Catholic journalist
told me, that Poland's national identity might one day be
"swallowed" by the Soviet Union. Ideologically, communism
was a dead duck. Ideology served only as a means of legitimization for the system, for the leading role of the Party and
for the fact that a minority Party was in power. Otherwise,
what had really counted, for many years in Moscow, was just a
plain game of power politics. There were not many people in
Poland who believed in communist system and its ideology.
Toward the end of Gomulka's era a popular joke made the
rounds in Warsaw: There is only one man who actually believes
in Communism in Poland. Who? Gomulka...but only in his bad
dreams. This joke was even more typical since Gierek took
over mainly because of the many changes subtly bypassing
some iron rules of communist doctrine. Even the Kremlin has
realized that if there is to be stability in a Poland within the
communist orbit, then there are two immovable forces to ensure
success: the minority Party and the most powerful church in
any part of Europe.

Both have to try to push a glacier moving without
causing an avalanche. "Fruitful cooperation," emphasized by

Gierek, will depend on the assessment by both partners of what lies in the national interest. There might not always be a basic conflict between them, except in ideological terms, but there have always been significant tensions between Poland's Catholics and at least some Party members. They may not be enough to endanger the Party or the system, but they have certainly been serious enough to generate a continuing rivalry. With workers playing a crucial part, the church is trying to push the Party "glacier" toward more liberal policies, opposing measures aimed at reducing citizens' rights and undermining its own position in society. Gierek, in turn, however pragmatic he is, remained a communist. And, by his long-term program of socialization of society is hoping to push, or at least to reduce, the size of the church "glacier." The Episcopate has been opposing socialization according to strict communist doctrine. When some Party leaders overstressed the orthodox and therefore defunct ideology, they came up against strong opposition from the church. There was no such opposition when they thought in terms of some real social transformation.

The leadership was aware that the church not only represented over 90 percent of the population but was also historically so intertwined with the fate of the Polish nation itself that the two sometimes seemed to be natural complements of each other. History fused the church and the nation in a way unknown in the rest of Eastern Europe.

When Gierek proposed to modernize the Polish economy and raise the population's standard of living he was fully supported by the church. However, specific programs such as the socialization of agriculture and an "ideologization" of the educational system were designed, in the long run to undermine the church's influence within society while expanding the role of the state. The church accordingly reacted strongly. As Rousseau wrote in Contrat Social, "The more the State expands, the more liberty diminishes."

A special chapter in the Party's socialization program concerned official policy toward the various lay Catholic organizations. Shortly after Gierek's accession to power, at a seminar for Party propagandists, Skarzynski, the head of the Office for Religious Denominations, assessed the value of the four main Catholic political organizations. He described Pax as the most reliable, socialistically minded organization, which had always supported the Party both in times of crises and successes. Caritas, a charitable organization, and the Christian Social Association were "of no significance." The Catholic deputies' club, Znak, was "antisocialist," but unfortunately had wide influence in the country and abroad and therefore had to be "tolerated" for the time being. The government, therefore, aimed at splitting the lay movement by isolating the more critical Catholic centers from their own organizational basis, and by granting special favors to any and all Catholic groups and even individuals, lay and clerical, who were likely to dissent from the Episcopate guidelines. This was certainly part of a wider attempt to strengthen the leading role of the Party in the remaining nonsocialist areas of society.

As the socialization program unfolded and, under external pressure, a drive toward ideological cohesiveness of the Soviet bloc gained momentum, the church's role in Polish politics has become increasingly evident as a type of political opposition. For both political and doctrinal reasons, however, the Episcopate wanted to avoid giving the impression that it was a political force agitating against the government. Instead it sought to use its influence with the government to press for measures that would advance the interests of the nation, its own interests, and most of all the respect for the civic human rights guaranteed by the constitution. The church leaders, knowing there was a time to keep silent and a time to speak, used their influence in a highly diplomatic way, often pressing for changes when no real church-state tensions were evident, and refraining from comment when strains in the society were the greatest. As some Catholic politicians and people closely connected with the Episcopate told me in 1976, the church does not want to be regarded as a fighting church or as always in opposition. The state and the Episcopate argue, agree or disagree. Sometimes the church would accept a compromise and even support the Party leader.

As a result of such an approach to crucial problems, the church can represent both a challenge to and support for government policy, depending on how it assesses the stability of the situation. The government has sometimes responded to this give-and-take approach, especially in its appeals for unity among Poles regardless of religion when social tensions seemed specially high. The result has been quite a subtle interplay of church and state initiatives.

If the church represents, as it was described by some observers of the Polish scene, a loyal opposition then it is not loyal to the Party. The Episcopate is uncompromisingly opposed to Marxist-Leninist philosophy. But the church is loyal to what it sees as the interests of the Polish nation as a whole. It sees itself as the protector of the country's national interests, the defender of the faith and of the nation, of the citizens' rights. This dual self-image has led the Episcopate to agree with the government when the overriding interests of the Polish nation were concerned. The church, for example, always supported the Warsaw claim to the former German territories, seeing the Western territories as indispensable to the Polish state. The bishops also recognized the necessity of finding a modus vivendi with the Soviet Union. But when the boundaries of strategic necessity are overstepped - or Warsaw seems, for example, to come too close to Soviet ideology or practices - then the agreement between church and state ends.

The communist ideology is alien and unacceptable to the church and to the nation but as there is no escape from the present geopolitical situation in which the Party and the church must coexist, realistic, pragmatic solutions have to be found.   By following responsible policies, the church has sometimes become indispensable to Gierek's policies.   The loyalty of its opposition has been important for Gierek and he has indirectly acknowledged this in his speeches.   But the Episcopate has also shown that it expects concessions in return for its responsible attitude, and that it can switch to the offensive if it feels its demands are not being heeded.

Seen from the outside, the Polish church may appear to be one of the most "pre-second Vatican council" churches, in its conservative and traditionalist attitudes.   It is only natural that given the external conditions created by the precarious status of a religious institution placed in the framework of an atheistic state, the members of this institution should adopt a conservative approach.   Such an attitude stresses the feeling of monolithic solidarity and hampers change.   But at the same time, the necessity for change is being felt as more and more urgent, both by the growing number of conscientious laymen involved in Church activities, and by the young generation of clergy as well as by younger bishops.

This feeling of a necessity for change, as Jerzy Turowicz, editor of the Catholic weekly, Tygodnik Powszechny, wrote "...is not due to the impact of the Marxist Leninist materialistic and atheistic ideology - propagated in Poland but without much efficiency and success.   Nor is it due to the impact of the mass media and the cultural progress of the lower classes.   A new mentality is being created."(42)

It is not the church's purpose to shape or change political regimes, but it is its duty to be present in every political situation.   As the changes occur it is its duty to adapt its activities and its influences to them.   Once it became clear that Party policy - despite any modifications that might be made in the interests of achieving short-term gains - aims at a long-term isolation of the church from believers, the church concentrated on its essential mission of shaping people's consciousness and transforming human society into a community of authentic brotherhood based on love.   Its impact on public life even in a communist-ruled country could therefore be much stronger, particularly since it is spreading its activities in the most modern ways among the workers and the young people.

It might seem paradoxical but a communist state might even benefit from the growth of authentically Christian values. The authorities are often worried by the declining morals in family life, by corruption, the spread of alcoholism, and the poor ethics of labor.   Secular ethics have often proved to be ineffective; thus, as Turowicz says, the communists are also becoming conscious of the help that they can get from Christians in public and social morality.

The second Vatican council decrees are however being implemented slowly in Poland. But many lay people and a growing part of the clergy are complaining that the spirit of the council should permeate deeper into the life of the Polish church whose structure is still, to some extent, authoritarian. There is no open crisis in the church, nor is there any open "contest." Institutional structures of the church and church teaching have not been questioned. What people are asking for, according to Turowicz, is a renewal of the language in the church teaching and preaching; more participation by the "people of God," lay and clerical, in decision making; and more sharing of responsibility. This process is slowly but surely developing. The position of the church in a one-party communist system cannot of course be compared with that in any other political structure. But, by trying to find some new solutions under those difficult circumstances and without disturbing the ecclesiastical structures, the Catholics in Poland may contribute to the universal search for an authentic renewal of the church.

THE PARTY, THE SEJM, AND THE GOVERNMENT

> Nothing is so galling to a people
> as a meddling government which
> tells them what to read, and say,
> and eat, and drink, and wear.
>
> Th.   Macaulay   in   Southey's Colloquies

According to the Polish constitutions of 1952 and 1976, the Sejm (the Polish parliament) is the highest organ of state authority, responsible only to the electorate. Described by the Party leadership in October 1956 and in December 1970 as the supreme authority in the land, the Sejm is elected for a four-year term and is composed of 460 deputies.

"Our Sejm is not the type of parliament one finds in Western democracies," Professor Stomma, the chairman of the Catholic deputies club, Znak, once remarked. "Our parliament is not a battlefield on which social forces vie for power."

More than one party is represented in the Sejm, but the overall majority of the Communist party is secured in advance, before the elections, by the selection procedure of candidates. All candidates, whatever group or so-called allied parties they come from, must in one way or another be approved by the Communist "leading" party. Apart from the Communist party representatives there are deputies from the United Peasants' party; the Democratic party; and nonparty deputies, including the three Catholic groups - Znak, a genuinely independent Catholic group (at least until 1976), the pro-Party Pax group, and the always amenable, tiny Christian Social Association group.

"I do not know if we will meet again in the new Sejm. That depends on the voters, those below, and those above," said Kisielewski, a widely known publicist, looking across at the government benches at the end of one of the debates shortly before a new Sejm election. This incident showed both the possibilities and the limitations of the Polish parliament.

Many Poles hoped in 1956 that the Sejm would develop along the lines of a parliamentary democracy, but this of course would have undermined the "leading role" of the Party, one of the imperatives of the system, which no one could seriously believe possible. And yet, in 1971, the Sejm did become something more than just a facade.

The real legislative work is done in the Sejm committees, where problems can be thrashed out on a man-to-man basis, which is not possible in the public forum of a plenary session. Furthermore the communist deputies are much more approachable in committee and have even been known to ignore the Party whip.

There is not much scope given to the noncommunist and particularly the non-party deputies, however. The only group in the Sejm to present a front and a standpoint of its own (apart from a few non-party experts) have been the Catholic deputies, particularly those belonging to Znak. At one time they posed most of the 140 questions addressed to the responsible ministers. Many questions are discussed and resolved in the lobbies at the Sejm, where ministers and members of the politburo of the Central Committee engage in informal conversations.

The Sejm is the only communist parliament in which a negative vote can be cast; this has happened not infrequently. On a number of occasions bills have been passed either with abstentions or with dissenting votes, mostly from Znak deputies, but also occasionally with a few other non-Party deputies joining forces with the Catholics.

The constitution provides for universal, equal, direct and secret suffrage. The electorate is presented with a single list of National Unity Front, which is dominated and organized by the Communist party, but which also includes the other so-called allied parties, various associations, institutions and groups. In the revised electoral law of December 1960, the number of candidates "may exceed the number of seats, but not by more than half." By imposing this policy, the Party sought to reduce the risk inherent in the basic provision of the electoral procedure, which remained unaffected: the right to delete names and to hold a secret ballot in a curtained booth by inserting voting papers in envelopes.

The first elections to the Sejm under Gierek's rule were held one year earlier, on March 19, 1972. He had already announced that there had to be a separation of functions between the Party and the government. The principle adopted was that the Party "inspires" and outlines the political and socioeconomic program. The government drafts the bills based on Party guidelines and submits them to the Sejm. The Sejm then discusses these draft bills and "proposals" in committee and finally at one of its rare sessions passes the legislative act. It is then up to the central and local government to implement the legislative acts and to administer the country. But, as Gierek implied at the sixth Party congress it would be impossible for the government, or for that matter the Sejm, which is supposed to be the supreme organ in the land, to do anything unless the matter has been discussed and decided in a detailed program by the CC of the Party.

By advancing the elections to the Sejm, Gierek certainly tried to consolidate his position, to maintain the impetus of the program of reforms he had undertaken, and, at the same time, to put the Party program over more widely to the nation as a whole in the preelection campaign. Against many hopes for a change he retained the old electoral law and therefore there were 625 candidates for 460 seats. Although there were also candidates from the other so-called allied parties as well as non-Party candidates, none of these could have the remotest chance of putting themselves up for election, let alone getting elected, were they not in agreement with the policies of the Communist party. At a one-day session in January 1972 the national committee of the FNU straight away accepted the program outlined by the sixth Party congress as its electoral platform. Neither the account in the Party press, nor reports by Radio Warsaw made it clear whether and when the participants of this session had time to get acquainted with the declaration, still less to discuss it. However, this sort of efficiency in "democratic processes" seemed to be a characteristic of the new leadership.

PB member Babiuch disclosed that it was decided to select Party candidates through a broader consultation than in the past including consultations with non-Party people. These consultations, according to Babiuch, involved some 150,000 Party activists and hundreds of thousands of people with no Party affiliation.(43) This sounded somewhat exaggerated. If it was claimed, for instance, that 150,000 activists took part in these consultations, this would be only a fraction of one percent of the total electorate of over 20 million. Another official claim that about 80 percent of Party members took part in these consultations in a number of provinces did not sound at all realistic. Considering the fact that the total Party membership was over two million and that the average Party membership in a province was 100,000, a figure corresponding to 80 percent would be out of all proportion to the 150,000 activists consulted; the number would be nearer 1,600,000 which was, of course, impracticable.

According to some Western observers in Warsaw(44) and from conversations I have had in Poland, there seemed to be little doubt that the actual selection of candidates took place at a much earlier date when the lists were prepared, checked and rechecked at the appropriate CC department and presented to the PB for final approval. According to an influential Polish official, the leadership absorbed more of the selection power than had been expected in order to ensure the election of reform-minded candidates against the opposition of more conservative Party members. On the other hand not one of the workers' leaders involved in the strikes after December 1970 was placed on the list of candidates and the number of non-Party members was kept fairly small, amounting to only ten percent of the candidates.

As in the past, the numerical distribution of seats between the Communist party and other "allied" parties and groups in the new Sejm was decided - in advance, of course - by the coordinating committee of the Party parliamentary clubs, which the Polish United Workers (PUW) party has always dominated.

The six-weeks preelection campaign was conducted very seriously, with varied and often significant discussions, and it also brought about amendments to the official lists of candidates. The elections were presented as a vote of confidence in Gierek, in the new leadership and policies. An attempt had been made to select more workers and peasants and also better qualified technical people. Since the result of the election was a foregone conclusion its main interest lay in the campaign. And this time the authorities conspicuously avoided appeals for people to drop the ballot paper into the box unmarked. Names on the ballot paper were not listed alphabetically but in order of precedence, and if electors did not go to a booth to cross names off, the top five or six out of seven or eight candidates were automatically counted. At ordinary election meetings people responded to the appeals for frankness by being more forthright than usual. For example, at one meeting, Prime Minister Jaroszewicz and the first secretary of the Warsaw Party committee, Kepa, were questioned for several hours by young people in Warsaw on tricky problems like housing and recreational facilities. The pattern was repeated around the country. Among the demands and suggestions put forth elsewhere, quite a number pertained to the future function of the Sejm and, in particular, to what a Sejm deputy should be like. The main bone of contention was whether the deputy should be a guardian of, and spokesman for, local or national interests.

It was all critical stuff, but mostly in a spirit of good
humor like that shown in an issue of the Party weekly,
Polityka, which had a joke about the three degrees of luxury
in Poland. They were: 1) a car, 2) a villa (this does not
exclude item 1), and 3) having your own opinion. This excludes both the first and the second items, said Polityka.(45)
The new mood also found its expression in preelection press
criticism of the old Sejm for neglecting its role as guarantor of
civic rights and duties. An article in the weekly,
Polityka(46), summed up for the first time those important
issues which became law without Sejm approval. In the Krakow
sociopolitical weekly, Zycie Literackie, a well-known writer,
Holuj, wrote:

> In our Constitution we say that in our country
> the working people are sovereign, exercising the
> supreme authority through their representatives in
> the Sejm and National Councils. I am, therefore,
> astonished by public assurances made by the execu-
> tive authority to the effect that this very authority
> is ready to give the Sejm greater rights. This is
> a confusion of ideas. The minimum of Sejm sover-
> eignty should primarily lie in the fact that the Sejm
> institutes its rights itself, if it is to institute the
> rights for the entire nation....(47)

But Holuj also looked realistically at the role of parliament
within a communist state. "I see no ticklish questions," he
wrote, "in the incontestable fact that the center of the main
political command is not on Wiejska Street [where the Sejm is
located] but somewhere else." (In other words, in the Party
headquarters.)
At some election meetings amendments were made to the
official lists of candidates. In Krakow, for instance, the
names of 14 candidates on the first list were removed. In
Wroclaw, nine out of 35 candidates were changed after consultation. In general the candidates were better known in their
districts, and either had some specific experience to offer or
were direct representatives of workers and peasants - "more of
those people who use trams and buses than an official
Mercedes" as one man put it to me.
Closing the election campaign on March 16, Gierek, in his
televised appeal, spoke as the leader of the nation rather than
as Party first secretary, and he saw to it that his words were
addressed to every citizen in Poland. Some of the passages
could have been pronounced by any political or even spiritual
leader. Gierek asked for full support for the FNU list of
candidates. It was a calm and dignified appeal, although it
showed some concern about a possible failure, not to obtain
the required majority, but rather, to obtain unanimity, or at
least something approaching unanimity, in the voting results.

It also contained some apprehensions about the possible reactions of Poland's eastern neighbor to the results.

With his constant promise that he would try to build "a second Poland," the emphasis on the family as a basic unit of society was particularly important. There were no ideological references, nor was the leading role of the Party mentioned. The family as a basic unit and the nation as a whole were clearly singled out by Gierek who on this occasion at least tried to appear as being above the political Party or parties. Gierek's dilemma boiled down to that everlasting problem in politics, the art of the possible. At one of his preelection speeches he said: "Our program is the building of socialism by the people, for the people." He promised that the Party would continue its wide-ranging dialogue with the people in the process of decision making. But he also warned that the essence of socialist democracy in Poland could not be reconciled with either an anarchistic disregard for interests of the state or with a rivalry of sectional interests. Building socialism for the people and by the people had its limits, in the context of power relations within the Soviet orbit, and Gierek was a pragmatist who firmly believed that the present system could be made to work efficiently.

The function of controlling the government by parliament was basic. Professor Stomma, the leading Catholic politician and Sejm deputy wrote in the Catholic independent weekly, Tygodnik Powszechny, that such a controlling function is a crucial factor and therefore in this sense the independence of the legislative body must be respected and strengthened. While the new leadership never mentioned the real independence of the legislative organ, since this would undermine the "leading role" of the Party, nevertheless, Gierek, according to his many pronouncements, intended to do all that was possible to make parliament more effective both as a legislative body and as a forum of public opinion. The regime had seen the great dangers that arise when Party and government authorities become isolated from the people. The enhancement of parliament was, therefore, part of the general efforts made during the preceding year to open up as many channels of communication as possible between the state and the government.

What then was the choice for the Polish voter? As voting is secret, people could express their opposition to the FNU list either by crossing out all the names, by using an ordinary piece of paper instead of the official ballot paper (which would make the vote invalid) or they could cross off the names of one or more individuals from the list. As a result, Communist candidates heading constituency lists have occasionally failed to secure the maximum number of votes. But there was never a danger of the Communist party losing its formal majority in any elections since 50 percent of votes cast was sufficient for it to be elected.

On March 19, 1972, voting began in brilliant sunshine in streets decked with small red and white national flags. Since Gierek had taken over, in all the offices the hitherto obligatory framed photographs of top Polish party leaders disappeared from the walls, as they did at each polling station. Here and there a small photograph of Lenin remained. Everywhere the atmosphere, while not enthusiastic, was relaxed, with a rush of voters going to the polls after church. One country church was so crowded that people knelt outside the entrance in the warm spring sunshine, as the priests reminded them of their duty to vote.(48)

The election results demonstrated that people were not afraid to use such rights as they enjoyed. In the old days, few dared to go into the curtained polling booth for fear of attracting attention; this time many not only altered their ballot papers in the privacy of the booth, but some did so conspicuously in public.

According to official results, out of a total electorate of just over 22,300,000 eligible voters, 97.94 percent cast ballots in the election, while just under half a million abstained. Of the valid ballots, 99.53 percent votes were cast for the FNU with just over 100,000 voters against the FNU's list. Although the electoral system hardly lends itself to "spontaneity," there was no doubt that the leadership could claim almost total support for its post-December 1970 policies. The distribution of seats among parties and groups, decided in advance of the election, was as follows: Polish United Workers party - 255; United Peasants party - 117; Democratic party - 39; and non-party deputies - 49. The non-party deputies included Catholic representation: the Znak group, loyal to the church hierarchy, led by Professor Stomma - five seats; Pax, a movement of "progressive" Catholics cooperating with the regime - five seats; the Christian Social Association, a small splinter group of "progressives" who pretended to be loyal to the church hierarchy - two seats; and, in addition, one representative of Caritas, a Catholic charity organization which was controlled by the regime.

Given the peculiarities of the Polish electoral system the election figures call for some explanation. Considerable use was made of one form of dissent, namely that of crossing off one or more of the preferred candidates at the top of the list, in effect simultaneously endorsing some or all of the "surplus" candidates at the bottom. The consequences of such negative votes was only apparent in the reduction of the total votes cast for the candidates, thus altering the order in which they were "elected." In political terms, this amounted to an expression of lack of confidence in certain individuals in the Party-dictated order in which the candidates were listed. As a result several leading Party personalities, who were heading the electoral lists in their districts, scored the lowest number of votes among those elected - not an electoral defeat, but an indication of public opinion. In only seven of the 80 constituencies did the top candidates manage to retain their orginal places.

The results showed that the unusually lively and critical spirit displayed at meetings during the campaign did not desert voters on the polling day. The final outcome was rather short of the "spontaneous expression of confidence" which the ruling Party claimed. Nevertheless, it was not an unqualified setback for Gierek, the Party leader. He himself romped home in the coal-mining constituency of Sosnowiec in Silesia, winning almost unanimously 99.8 percent of the votes cast. In fact, the election boiled down to a sort of popularity contest. Reading the results in this light, one saw that the people out of public favor were either well-known hard-liners (like General Moczar) or the secretary of the Warsaw Party committee, Kepa, or people compromised by close association with the previous leadership, and even some new men who were in charge of internal security or who had recently made unpopular statements.

In assessing the Sejm elections, one should not exaggerate the significance of the number of negative votes received by some high-ranking Party and government officials. Under existing regulations, elections provide neither an accurate barometer of popular sentiment nor a meaningful choice between candidates. The official reason for an earlier election was to gain popular approval for Gierek's leadership and policies. The popular vote seemed to signify support for this middle-of-the-road, pragmatic communism, with its promise of better living conditions, improved efficiency and greater involvement of the people in the running of the country. In 1971 Gierek said that the leadership would not hesitate to withdraw from chosen policies if it proved to be incorrect. In 1972, therefore, one should accept that the people thought and reacted in the context of the existing system.

If Gierek could now claim that he had received a national mandate, it was also obvious that he had secured the election of a Sejm that would be amenable to his policies. Of the 460 deputies elected, almost two-thirds were serving for the first time, while almost all the officials associated with the former regime had been removed. It was no accident that the majority of new members of parliament were new men, generally better educated, better qualified and younger than their predecessors. They were expected to play an active part in the affairs of their country. The days when the Sejm was simply a rubber stamp and a forum for formal speeches should henceforth have belonged to the past. The new deputies were to be involved in a fascinating experiment of trying to turn a communist state into an efficient machine, responsive to the needs of the people, drawing out their creative energies, and

in return giving them a decent standard of living and a modi-
cum of freedom.   All this, while the Communist party remained
the leading - in fact the only - source of power.   It was an
important experiment, which faded out over the years and
particularly in June 1976.

But in the hopeful days of 1972, as one leading intellectual and politician told me, the election "marked the end of a
period of transition and consolidation for Gierek."   Having
made the significant changes in the Party and government
hierarchy over the previous 14 months, he now transformed
the composition of the Sejm.   This process was completed on
March 28, 1972 when the newly elected Sejm met for its first
session.   In the officially proclaimed process of "renewal," the
triangular relationship of Party, Sejm, and government remained very much as before and coincided with Gierek's own
concept of the leading role of the Party.   Three days before
the Sejm session the coordinating commission of the parties and
political groups accepted Gierek's suggestions as to what
appointments and changes should be made in the government
and in the Sejm.   The day before the Sejm session, the CC
passed a resolution concerning choices for major state positions.   All these proposals were unanimously passed by the
newly elected Sejm.   At the session Jaroszewicz was duly
elected prime minister and Tejchma, one of the most intelligent
Party figures, released from his post of CC secretary, became
deputy premier.   The only other deputy premier "elected" was
Kazimierz Olszewski, hitherto the foreign trade minister.   The
new government presidium, consisting of the prime minister
and six deputy premiers was equivalent to something like a
cabinet and the aim here was to streamline the state executive
body,   increasing   its   flexibility   and   effectiveness.
Cyrankiewicz was replaced by Henryk Jablonski, former education minister, as head of state.

The second Sejm of Gierek's era was elected on March 21,
1976.   Again the resolution of the Party congress of December
1975 automatically became the electoral platform of the FNU,
and the selection of the candidates proceeded as before under
strict Party supervision.

During the intervening four years the promise of an
"enhancement of the role" of the Sejm was gradually disappearing into thin air.   The number of oral questions addressed
to ministers was rapidly decreasing.   The Sejm committees were
working hard, as in the past, but only slightly editing and
mainly introducing more precise legal wording to the draft bills
presented by the government.

As the years passed by so the hopeful glory of the Sejm
as the supreme authority in the land, as promised by the
leadership, was fading away.   The decline in the status of the
Sejm coincided with the growing, overriding need to strength-
en the leading role of the Party.   In 1975, for instance, Sejm

members learned about another more drastic reorganization of
local government from the newspapers and then proceeded to
pass a very complicated piece of legislation within a few hours
after it was submitted to the Sejm and just four days before it
was due to become fully operative. The Party CC had, of
course, discussed and approved all the details beforehand.
(See the following section, "Administrative Reform," of this
chapter). The most controversial constitutional amendments
were in 1976, again passed by the Sejm within a few hours
after having been approved by the Party CC. There was
perhaps seldom a more significant example of the conveyor-belt
relationship between the CC of the Party and the Sejm than in
December 1976. At exactly 1600 hours on December 2, Radio
Warsaw reported that a plenary meeting of the CC had ended
and that a Sejm session was "beginning." The economic plans
for 1976-1980 and for 1977 unanimously approved by the CC,
were passed on to the Sejm, which in turn approved them in
general and sent them to committees for detailed analysis. At
the same time the parliament unanimously accepted the changes
in the government suggested on the same day by the CC.
      During the preelection campaign in 1975, a Radio Warsaw
listener asked what role the Sejm played in the country's
political system, since, he said, it was well known that the
Communist party takes all the important decisions. After all,
the listener went on, there was no argument between different
parties in the Sejm, no confrontation of views and no parliamentary opposition whatsoever. Radio Warsaw told the listener
that he was quite right, but added that these particular features of bourgeois parliaments often hindered their work,
causing a crisis of state authority and holding back the country's development. In its answer Radio Warsaw did not mention the fact that much more severe and tragic crises were
caused in Poland, not because there was a bourgeois parliament which "often hindered the work of the government" but
because there was no parliament of any real stature and the
crises were caused, as admitted by the Party itself, by the
leadership of the "leading Party."
      In the 1972 election, 98.27 percent of the electorate cast
their votes and of the valid ballots 99.43 percent were passed
in favor of the FNU list. But the number of invalid ballots
cast in March 1976 nearly trebled the 1972 figures, while the
votes cast against the FNU list outnumbered the respective
1972 figure by nearly 23.3 percent. By adding the number of
absentees to that of those who voted "against" and to the
invalidated ballots one arrived at the figure of over 566,000
persons, who, in one way or another, could be considered
"dissenters." The number might seem minute but, in a communist system, it should not be underestimated as a sort of
"no-confidence vote." As one foreign correspondent put
it(49), quoting a Warsaw joke, "In Poland democracy starts
with the decimal point."

The distribution of the seats according to party affiliation was slightly modified in favor of the ruling Polish United Workers' Party (PUWP). Instead of its former 255 seats, it now had 261, at the expense of other allied parties. The non-Party group of deputies remained unchanged, and within it 13 Catholic representatives of various political creeds retained their seats although many candidates were new. The composition of the Znak group was drastically changed in favor of less independent and more amenable Catholic politicians.

Professor Jablonski remained the head of state in the new Sejm and there were only two changes worth noting. Jaroszewicz was reappointed prime minister and his ministerial staff remained virtually unchanged. Only two of the nine deputy premiers had departed; one of them, Szlachcic, was dismissed from the PB in December 1975 and regarded as the chief opponent of the present team.

Despite many promises there has been as yet no indication that the Party intended to moderate its powers even slightly in favor of a more effective and representative parliament. At all times in the triangle of Party-Sejm-government, the Party, in its position at the apex, insisted on reasserting its "leading role" at all costs, even within the framework of an increased emphasis on "socialist democracy." While reluctantly accepting this crucial imperative of the system, the people clearly and significantly demanded a more representative, efficient and more powerful parliament. Some enlightened communists, particularly of a comparatively younger generation, were frequently suggesting that there should be an opposition, perhaps another Communist party, or even a slightly social-democratic party, in the parliament and in the country. It would not undermine the basic foundations of the system but could present alternative programs, discuss them, introduce some controversy, and correct the mistakes unavoidably made by the "leading" Party over many years and on many occasions. In August 1971, the influential weekly, Polityka, insisted that within the socialist system there was a vast difference of views and all views should be respected and given expression because it is this variety which provides the propulsive power of society. The weekly then advocated the right to choose freely from a variety of socialist systems and to apply only economic principles for their establishment. Small wonder that these propositions came under very strong attack from some Party quarters as bourgeois, anachronistic and antisocialist. What they seemed to prove was that when the country found itself with a choice of directions, conflicting political undercurrents revealed themselves within the Party. And one of these currents was certainly a suggestion, voiced privately more than once during my many conversations in Poland, that within the existing system there should be scope for an official "loyal opposition," active and having a voice in adjusting and readjusting policies imposed by the "leading" Party.

In 1973 one of the leading Catholic politicians and member of the Znak group, Zablocki called in parliament(50) for the setting up of a broadly based Catholic lay movement with the approval of the Episcopate, which would enable believers to be really active in public life, under the auspices of the communist-dominated FNU. The Party, he was told by a high official, could not accept such a proposal because it might be tantamount to approving a new and powerful political party. This was obviously out of the question, because there was no place for an opposition party.

Since the end of 1975, demands for a recognized opposition in parliament and outside it were more and more loudly voiced by small loosely organized groups of people and by growing numbers of dissenters. Very often these demands went unrealistically far. The so-called Polish League for Independence (PPN), for instance, in a declaration circulated clandestinely within the country, believed that the supreme authority in the country should rest with parliament elected on the basis of universal, equal, secret, direct and proportional votes.(51) In an open letter to Gierek, published in the French press, Professor Edward Lipinski(52), still a member of the PUW party, warned that in Poland a government imposed by a minority had an in-built tendency toward totalitarianism. That is why, he argued in his letter, "we need a legal opposition with the rights of freedom of association and assembly guaranteed by the constitution. The contradictions should be allowed to express themselves and manifest themselves freely. The system of parliamentary democracy is the only one which allows that to happen."

This, of course, meant transplanting pluralism which already existed to a substantial extent in the world communist movement into a particular country ruled by the Communist party. As such, the proposition was, in the present circumstances, unacceptable to the Soviet leaders unless they displayed greater political maturity than hitherto. Although politically unrealistic, the suggestion of pluralism in the country does not necessarily mean the abolition of existing political structures but it certainly means that there are undercurrents aiming at a substantial upgrading of the role of a truly representative parliament and other bodies. This could lead to what might be termed consensus socialism, in other words, to a much more effective consultation in policy matters with the people and their real participation in decision making. The aim would be to improve the system from within and to change it in time perhaps beyond recognition.

Such, at least, were the feelings I came across in Poland. All this is anathema to the Soviet leadership, even if they now think exclusively in terms of power politics which, nevertheless, they try very hard to justify by ideological dogma for the sake of appearances. And one of these is the imperative

"leading" role of the Communist party. Lenin said so; but the
trouble with Lenin and what he said and wrote has been that
there are so many contradictions in his various assessments
and suggestions. He can be easily quoted to justify Soviet
policies which the Chinese condemn as social imperialism, and
at the same time to justify whatever Peking is doing which,
again, the Kremlin regards as treason of socialism. The fact
remains, however, that in Poland even some farsighted communists would argue that in a country so closely linked with
Western civilization and culture, a variety of views is unavoidable and only the freedom to express them could contribute to
a very much needed political restructuring and modernization
of the system. No political party anywhere in the world has a
monopoly of wisdom and infallibility. It could even be argued
that the ruling Communist parties in Eastern Europe and in the
Soviet Union have a lesser claim to this sort of "wisdom" since
their "leading" role has led in the postwar years to many
tragedies and had produced many disastrous effects.

ADMINISTRATIVE REFORM

The hallmark of Gierek's general policy has been the search
for administrators, industrial and economic managers, Party
and government officials who, apart from being committed to
the program of the leadership, had the necessary professional
qualifications as well as the capacity to tackle problems in a
fresh and imaginative way. This basic principle was very much
in evidence in the reform of the local government.
    The system, which had been in existence for over 20
years, was inefficient and cumbersome, and consisted of three
tiers: provinces (voivodships); districts and primary units in
the form of small villages; and settlements and communes.
There was in each of them an elected national council with its
committees and an executive presidium. The entire system was
linked by vertical lines of subordination. The leadership
decided to reconstruct the edifice of local government starting
at the lowest level. The decision to introduce major reforms
stemmed from a conviction that many problems resulted not
only from inadequate resources, but also from poor administration and mismanagement of existing resources, and misuse of
personnel. The communes have generally been acknowledged
to be the worst functioning units in the entire system and this
was so much more damaging in that by definition they were in
rural areas and were, therefore, mostly responsible for agriculture and its performance.
    Breaking with the largely fictitious Soviet model of
"people's councils" the plenum of the CC meeting in September
1972 introduced the country's most ambitious reform of local

government.(53)   As of January 1, 1973, the 4,313 existing
rural communities were replaced by 2,381 parishes - a much
larger administrative unit with a clear division of responsibilities between elected legislative and nonelected executive
authorities. This was a clear deviation from the Leninist
dictum: all power to the Soviets. This move was designed to
facilitate the integration of neighboring villages and small
towns into naturally bounded economic microregions equipped
with all locally needed economic, social and cultural services.
The elected parish councils retained their former legislative,
supervisory, coordinating, organizing and controlling powers,
but relinquished their day-to-day executive powers. These
were invested in a parish office headed by a chief or executive
manager appointed by the chairman of the Provincial National
Council. He became the central figure in solving the problems
of the development and in satisfying the needs of the population of his parish. And he had to have higher educational
qualifications in agronomy or economics.

The vesting of authority in a single person rather than a
collective body was intended to clarify the question of responsibility and introduced strong leadership into rural administration. One of the intentions of the reform was also to shorten
the distance which the farmer must travel to government
authority, both physically and psychologically, and to decrease
the amount of red tape and time involved in settling his business. According to one estimate there were over 15,000 laws
and executive orders which had to be revised to carry out the
reform. The reform of rural administration and the restructuring of the Party organization in the countryside accordingly
offered an opportunity for large-scale personnel shake-ups. It
thus contributed to consolidating the hold of the Gierek forces
over the Party.

The national Party conference in October 1973 decided to
go ahead with the next stage of the reform involving the
country's districts and provinces (voivodships). Legislative
and executive functions were again separated.

At every level, executive function was carried out by an
appointed administrator, under the general supervision of the
elected National Councils. In order to secure the Party's
day-to-day influence over local government affairs, Gierek
decided that the first secretaries of local Party branches would
serve as chairmen of the National Councils at every appropriate level of local government hierarchy. The Party leaders
installed regionally as chairmen of National Councils provided a
single point of contact for administration. It certainly made
local government more responsive to central direction but it
also contradicted Gierek's early promises of separation of Party
and government functions by spreading overall Party control
much further and deeper.

And then, quite unexpectedly in 1975, came something which one Polish journalist described to me as "the fourth historical partition of Poland." It all began on April 25(54) at a press conference when Gierek disclosed a bold, imaginative move designed to reform fundamentally Poland's cumbersome administrative structure in an effort to create a bureaucracy flexible and streamlined enough to match the country's dynamically expanding economy.

This was really the third and final stage of the operation, the most radical of them all. The intermediate tier of the local government, the 314 districts, were all abolished. The number of the provinces (voivodships) was increased from 22 to 49 including the three autonomous cities of Warsaw, Lodz and Krakow. The newly created Ministry of Local Administration, Area Planning and Environmental Protection, became responsible for the whole structure of local government.

Gierek acted with characteristic efficiency but also with unusual speed after careful preparations carried out almost secretly without any real consultations within the Party. Well before the CC approved the reform on May 12, special organizational teams were set up, in all existing 17 voivodships, to sort out the problems which would arise.(55) After the approval of the reform by the CC plenum, special "task forces" went to 49 proposed voivodships to prepare the ground for the changes. On May 13 the Council of Ministers approved all the necessary draft bills and sent them to the Sejm which passed the appropriate legislation on May 28. Two days later the Council of Ministers adopted several executive orders and regulations as acts corollary to the reform law. On the same day the new chief administrators or "voivods" were presented in Warsaw by the prime minister with their nomination acts, while the new provincial Party leaders gathered around Gierek for a final briefing before being sent out to their respective provinces to get their committees ready for the plunge. On June 1, 1975, the reform became operative and the new bodies in all 49 voivodships reported in unison: open for business as usual.

As at the rural level, the separation of legislative coordinating functions of the new National Councils from the executive functions of the chief administrator became very clear. The first secretaries of the new VPCs became the chairmen of the new voivodship National Councils. Most of the executive functions of the abolished districts were taken over by the lower of the two remaining tiers, i.e., the parishes, and their control prerogatives passed to the higher level, i.e., the voivodships.

The question everybody naturally asked was: Why such a rush, such secrecy?

The reform meant a tremendous upheaval not only in the local government, but also in the structure of the Party appa-

ratus.   There were substantial controversies within the Party
with regard to the reform and the reasons for secrecy could
be found in the Party apparatus' resistance to the change.
The reorganization was undoubtedly a big step forward in
streamlining and modernizing the structure of local government.
But it had two very important political implications.   The chief
characteristic of the reform was in fact centralization.   Here,
Gierek made a rather revealing remark: "The reduction of the
distance between centers of control at a national level and
basic units should strengthen and intensify the links between
them."   In other words, much stronger central government and
central Party control over the regions would be possible.   The
new voivodships, which were, on the whole, weaker, found it
more difficult to resist pressure coming from centralized government.   At the same time, now that the compartmentalization
caused by the existence of districts had disappeared, they in
turn were better able to check the activity of the basic rural
parishes.   Hot lines between the 49 voivodes and the first
secretaries of the new VPCs and the Party headquarters in
Warsaw were established.
     Another political implication was undoubtedly Gierek's
intention to curb the local government and Party apparatus,
particularly at the district level.   He had decided to start
fighting bureaucracy, including the Party one.   The increase
in the number of voivodships was a hard blow to the local
"chieftains," i.e., first secretaries of big and strong VPCs,
because at this level it was possible for central policy to be
challenged.   While the reform contributed to more effective
administration, it was certainly a move toward stronger centralized Party control.   One of its main purposes seemed to have
been the elimination of any regional power centers which could
challenge Gierek as he had challenged Gomulka in the past.
By eliminating the middle tier of administration and creating
more, smaller voivodships, Gierek cut down the size and
influence of the larger provinces and installed his supporters
in important new positions in the restructured local Party
organizations.   The editor of an important Party publication
told me: "It would be very difficult for someone now to organize any opposition against Gierek's policies. The main idea is
to make this leadership stronger."
     The thorniest problem of all involved the regrading of the
121,000 or so civil servants who used to work for the districts.
The Party leaders were at great pains to avoid criticizing the
middle-level officials whose aversion to change was notorious,
but they had been told in no uncertain fashion by Party
leaders that many of them would have to be moved into other
sectors of the economy and change their working methods.   On
the whole, about 15,000 administrative jobs disappeared and
over 13 percent of civil servants both in local government and
Party officials resentfully lost their status.

Some question marks remained. The changes carried with them the price of discontent within the Party which was not consulted about the reform. The personnel switches not only installed many of Gierek's supporters into positions of influence, but also demoted those with differing views. This could also be the basis for some discontent, and since those who were most problematic to the leader before were now stripped of their positions of Party power, the possibility of opposition taking forms other than party infighting increased.

EDUCATIONAL REFORM

The drastic school reform at primary and secondary levels formed a part of Gierek's modernization program for the country. The system of education hitherto was obsolete, costly and inefficient. The university authorities constantly complained about the low standards of education of the candidates who applied for places in higher schools.

A commission of 24 experts on education, chaired by a distinguished sociologist, Professor Szczepanski, helped by over 200 scholars representing all branches of the social sciences, was formed to analyze the situation and to propose improvements.

In its voluminous report, the commission, while sensibly and rationally assessing the deficiencies of the existing system, did not produce a uniform blueprint for reform, but instead presented four various and different options. Whatever the options presented by the commission the proposed reform was two-pronged: 1) the introduction of afternoon classes and the organization of a network of big comprehensive parish schools in the bigger villages, and 2) the new uniform ten-year curriculum in both urban and rural schools in which educational objectives would be defined by the socialist state alone. In the Sejm debate in April 1973, Prime Minister Jaroszewicz outlined three main factors in what he described as the "great complex of the content of ideological education," namely: the importance of acquired knowledge and professional qualifications; well and properly performed work; and high professional, social and state discipline. Broadcasting over Radio Warsaw he stated(56) that "antisocialist forces do their best to reach youth, counting on its immaturity and political inexperience. This is of particular importance now as the ideological confrontation of the two systems becomes more intensive with the development of international cooperation." The Sejm passed the resolution with the Catholic deputies' club, Znak, abstaining from voting.

Between the publication of the commission's report and the final adoption of the resolution on educational reform by the Sejm in October 1973, a "nationwide discussion" was launched in the official media. This proved to be more a propaganda campaign in favor of the proposed measures than a factual assessment of the relative merits of alternative suggestions. The total absence of the voice of the church authorities from the public discussion was particularly telling. As an institution deeply concerned with problems of education and upbringing and one which represented the views and wishes of millions of Catholic parents and pupils, the church obviously had a highly relevant voice on matters of school reform. It was not, however, regarded as a partner in the "discussion" and its objections to some of the measures proposed by the reformers were not allowed public expression.(57) But the church spoke firmly and frequently (see section, "The Church: A Key Force in the Country," in this chapter). The Catholic Znak group's leader, Professor Stomma, whose Sejm speech was not allowed to appear in the press, put the case simply: the leadership should never forget that its admitted mission is to "build a Poland, both politically and economically strong, and to do so while taking into account all the realities" of the situation. The fact that 90 percent of the population is Catholic deserves to be regarded as "one of these realities."(58) Even the chairman of the committee, Professor Szczepanski, admitted that various professional groups, directly or indirectly involved in school policy problems, viewed the reform with distrust, and that in the Party apparatus itself there were those who saw in the school system only an instrument of political indoctrination.(59)

The Sejm resolution on the reform (60) of the new school system provided for the gradual introduction of free, compulsory ten-year general education (instead of the present eight years), based on a uniform program in urban and rural areas. University courses were to be considerably shortened and streamlined. In the rural areas many of the small village schools, badly equipped, staffed with poor quality teachers, and attended by only a few pupils, would be closed in favor of comprehensive community schools in the larger villages. These schools would only employ teachers with university training and would expand their curriculum by offering afternoon classes as well.

Theoretically the quality of the proposed changes remained unquestioned, but their practical implementation and their ideological contents met with serious difficulties and complications. The leadership consequently had to slow down its reform drive at least for the time being. First, under the strong pressure from the Church (see section, "The Church: A Key Force in the Country," in this chapter; and Chapter 7). Opposition came also from the teachers who would be forced to give up their homes in the villages and establish temporary ones near the new comprehensive schools, where adequate housing was lacking. The Teachers' Charter, adopt-

ed in 1972, gave teachers an assurance of the Party's support
in their important and difficult task of educating the nation's
youth; at the same time a 20 percent increase in their salaries
was granted, and their old-age and disability pensions were
increased. But by the end of 1975 about 15,000 of them were
still leaving their classrooms every year. This was a significant contributory factor to the acute shortage of dedicated and
qualified personnel which remained a nationwide problem.
    The new system also met with considerable criticism and
opposition from parents, mainly on the grounds of the excessive distances the children had to travel, together with the
lack of an efficient and safe transportation system.   Since
spring 1974, even according to Party newspapers, "parents'
protest committees" started mushrooming in an effort to persuade the authorities not to close local schools too hastily.
Comprehensive schools could not, in their view, be nationally
imposed before the necessary infrastructure was completed.
    Still another problem was that of school textbooks. By
176, the state educational publishing house provided only 45
percent of the school books needed. The reformed schools
would require a set of completely new books by mid-1978 which
would fully exhaust both the production capacity of the printing industry and the stock of paper available.
    And finally, by the end of 1976 more than 160,000 teach-
ers, almost half of the total teacher force, still failed to produce academic diplomas which were required within the school
reform.(61) The government's effort to influence the teaching
profession ideologically was visible in increasing Party membership figures. But, what was worse from the Party's viewpoint, was the result of two public opinion polls which showed
after 1973 that among those teachers interviewed for the purpose of the polls, 85 percent declared themselves to be believers and only five percent to be atheists.
    The crucial importance of the educational reform for the
success of the social and economic transformations planned by
Gierek was obvious. The country would need, for the decades
to come, a growing body of highly educated and trained young
workers, technicians, and managers to cope with the ambitious
plans to expand and modernize the economy.
    But the Party's drive to inculcate materialistic, socialist
attitudes in all the children of a predominantly Catholic country was bound to face difficulties and depending on its course
could have sociologically and politically destabilizing repercussions. While the basic and drastic reform of the educational
system remains a must if the country is to make further progress, the overriding ideological ingredient in the schools'
curricula, (one of the imperatives of the system) is bound to
produce damaging effects.

THE WORKERS: THEIR STRENGTH AND THEIR PRESSURE

In the absence of any forces acting on it,
a body will continue in its state of rest.

Newton's   first   law

"We convinced ourselves in those December days that power
lies with the people," said one Gdansk worker to me. This
was the problem in a nutshell. There was a rich tradition of
both economic and political militancy in the history of the
Polish industrial working class over the last century. Factory
occupation and control was a common feature of workers'
actions in Poland after both world wars. But if such militancy
was explained by Party ideologists as a result of the capitalist
exploitation, it was much more difficult, if not impossible, for
them to explain why this militancy in a much harsher form
persisted in a socialist system when the only ruling and "leading" Party was supposed to represent the interests of the
workers. And, since the workers in a socialist system are
acknowledged as co-owners of the economy no conflict could
arise between the Party and state on one hand and the working class on another. Such, at least, is both the ideological
dogma and dilemma.

In contemporary Poland there appears to be a consensus
that the country's goal can only be socialism, but the unanswered question which led to confrontations and tragic conflicts was: What kind of socialism and how do we go about
achieving it? It was certainly clear that the workers rejected
Soviet-type "socialism." The December 1970 explosion proved
the determination of the working class to be really, not just in
theory, primary guardians of the Polish road to socialism.

In 1970 and in 1971 the workers rebelled, not only against
deteriorating economic conditions and appallingly low standards
of living, but against a system that provided no effective
channels for the transmission of legitimate grievances and
which prevented their having any influence on policy. The
main issue for the Polish workers was their dependence on an
autocratic, centralized and highly impersonalized bureaucracy,
with very little scope, not only for individuals, but even for
group initiative. They now demanded to be allowed to negotiate as equals with a Party that proclaimed itself to be the
leading representative of the working class - phenomenon
without precedent in Eastern Europe. If a younger worker
could boast to me that "now we know how to push them back,"
then it was clear that the Communist party had to come to
terms with that self-confidence of the working class and to
apply more literally the words "dialogue" and "democracy" that
were so widely quoted in Party propaganda.

Immediately after December 1970, Gierek's response to workers' demands was confined to the alleviation of certain of their hardships, to firm promises fulfilled over the period of the next five years of raising the standards of living, but at the same time ignoring the workers' demands for institutional representation and self-expression. Up to the beginning of 1976, Gierek had done more than any other communist leader to improve the material and social conditions of the workers – in this, his policies were dictated by a genuine concern for the workers' well-being. At the same time he fully realized that Soviet support for him remained conditional on his ability to maintain political stability and Party control. These, in turn, were ultimately dependent on working-class support, or at the very least on the absence of working-class hostility. In order to achieve this support he went so far as practically to mortgage Poland's future for the benefit of the workers.

This contrast between clear improvement in living and material conditions on one hand and the lack of political changes on the other was summarized to me rather aptly on two occasions. Three workers in Szczecin simply said: "There is a big difference between Gomulka and Gierek. Under Gomulka you were promised jam tomorrow – jam which you could neither see in terms of time nor quality." On the other hand a trade unionist in Lodz told me: "We are watching Gierek everyday; we are waiting to see whether he keeps all his promises." In fact, throughout 1971, the mass media frequently reported the dismissals of managers under workers' pressure as well as court actions against administrators of state-owned enterprises in defense of workers' interests.

In December 1970, and after, Gierek felt unable to challenge the "dictatorship of the proletariat," that is to say the powerful workers, who evidently did not accept either the Party policies or the leadership or both. What he did in those days was unprecedented in any communist-ruled country and was even criticized by some "friendly" parties in power. The new leadership publicized its "new methods of political work" designed to demonstrate its accessibility to the public and its genuine concern for popular wishes and opinions. The practice of conducting direct discussions with workers to review their grievances continued. But in time, more and more of these visits and this "dialogue" transformed themselves into meetings with local Party activists. This obviously was no substitute for workers' demands of autonomous and fully representative participation in decision making.

The alarm bells began ringing almost without interruption. There were hundreds of small stoppages all over the country until at least the middle of 1972.(62) In the coastal cities work stoppages and slowdowns occurred at the end of 1973, then both in the spring and in July 1974, with over 8,000 men, mostly stevedores, involved.

The official media at first firmly denied reports of dock
strikes but stated that "some difficulties, had been caused by
rain in July."(63)   But then the Gdansk Party newspaper,
Glos Wybrzeza, in a series of interviews, learned from the
workers that in fact there were "other reasons for stoppages
and other problems than the inclement weather which disturbed
the normal pace of work."   The unrest continued in Gdansk,
Sopot and Gdynia in September 1974, when the dockers stopped
unloading   several   ships   inside   the   harbor   and   again,
according to official media, this was due to "heavy rainfall."(64)   Whatever the media have said, the fact remained
that at this very time because of "heavy rainfall" or perhaps
for "other reasons" both Gierek and PB member Babiuch
visited coastal towns to discuss, as officially reported, the
"prospects of...the harvest."(65)   There were several protests
and strikes after the price of gas had been increased at the
beginning of 1974, among them a three-day demonstration by
taxi drivers in the large textile town of Lodz, where a gas
station was attacked and set on fire.(66)
     The strikes and stoppages not only continued but were
almost tolerated.   In retrospect, given the exigencies of the
first months, many of the concessions made seemed tactical and
many of the promises rhetorical.   This produced among the
workers an attitude of deja vu although this was slightly
unfair, for Gierek's achievements, especially the performance
of the economy and the material benefits which accrued to the
workers and the population as a whole, had been significant.(67)
     Gierek had to face an entirely new working class.   First
of all the mass migration of rural population into towns
changed the face of the country.   The process of integration
is, of course, a long and extremely difficult one.   But what
the new generation - in many cases, the first generation - of
industrial workers proved, was their political maturity.   Not
only was the working class numerically very strong, but a
high level of social mobility had considerably expanded the
scope of social contacts and influences available to the workers.   They now had friends and relatives almost everywhere.
At the same time the mechanism of political indoctrination
among the working class had functioned inefficiently and in
their attitude toward the communist ideology they have remained, to say the least, lukewarm.   In addition, the working
class became increasingly better educated and the workforce
was accustomed to handling increasingly sophisticated machinery
in the factories.   Consequently it has become more self-
confident and impatient with any shortcomings in the sur-
rounding way of life.   A survey taken in Warsaw and Kielce in
central Poland in 1973 revealed that as people became better off
they become more interested in taking a share in running the
country; and the less they earn the more importance they at-

tach to economic equality.(68)   Better educated workers read
many good books, watch television programs, and com-
municate with their numerous relatives who live abroad; and
consequently they are not easily satisfied. They compare their
situation with that of people in other countries, seek a better
life and are increasingly critical of many of the ineptitudes of
the Party measures. As a distinguished journalist told me in
1976, new generations of workers are growing and they want
something new and better, but the Party has not changed and
has no intention of undergoing a basic change.

The workers' approach seems to be very simple: nothing
about us without us; in other words, no decisions about our
situation and no changes without consultation with us and
without our participation in decision making. Gierek had to
choose between the leading role of the Party and the vaguely
semi-independent, semi-autonomous workers' organizations,
properly institutionalized. He chose the Party, for obvious
reasons. A good deal has been done to try to bring the Party
closer to the workers. More workers have been recruited into
its ranks, and the Party can boast the largest shop-floor
representation in their CC of any ruling Communist party.
But the Polish leaders have consistently refused to acknowledge that there might be a conflict between the workers and
the Party within a socialist system and therefore refused to
grant this fact of life institutional recognition.(69)

This, in turn, stems from the leaders' refusal to recognize the existence of workers' alienation from the production
process and thus from the system as it exists. This is at the
root of the Polish workers' lack of faith in the Party and
government and his unwillingness to subordinate his immediate
material interests to overall Party policies. The leadership's
decision to neglect the fundamental problems of alienation and
rely on a combination of controls and material incentives has
only encouraged the workers in their extractive attitude
toward the regime. Moreover, because of the lack of proper
representative and realistic participation channels, the leadership's attitude has taught workers that they have the political
and economic muscle to safeguard what they have come to
regard as inalienable rights: unconditional security of employment, relatively light labor discipline and, most important, a
steadily rising standard of living. As a result, they have
found themselves in a bargaining position unprecedented anywhere in Eastern Europe except perhaps in Yugoslavia, yet
without any effective organization to press their demands,
simple because where real participation increases, the leading
role of the Party must necessarily retreat, and vice versa.
Yet if stability in the country is to be maintained, a compromise solution must be found.

As Gierek's position grew more secure, Party hegemony
over any intermediary organizations such as the workers'

self-government and the trade unions became more monopolistic. Gierek felt that his ambitious program of dynamic economic development coupled harmoniously with a steeply rising standard of living could be implemented without far-reaching reforms that would reduce the Party's preeminence in all aspects of public life, particularly in relations with the workers.

The leadership committed itself(70) to making the system and the existing workers' organizations work better, an effort that, while offering some relief in the short term, was no substitute for the fundamental changes that were required. In the post-December days the workers themselves blamed the trade unions for everything, describing them as "indolent conveyor belts of the Party" and demanded new, freely elected, truly representative workers' self-government bodies, particularly workers' councils. These had spontaneously mushroomed all over the country in October 1956 and had played an important part in worker-management relations. But by 1958 Gomulka had decided that enough was enough and, to strengthen Party influence, promptly created the so-called workers' self-government conferences which consisted of three main pillars: the local Party organization, the local trade union work council, and local workers' council. The workers' councils had been, therefore, downgraded to such a degree that as a rule the local Party secretaries became chairmen of the workers' self-government conferences. Their main duty as such amounted to supervising the fulfillment of the plan.

In December 1970 Gierek was also faced with some changes which had already taken place on the coast and in many other enterprises, where new workers' councils, local trade union organizations and even Party organizations had been purged of discredited officials by the workers themselves and new leaders had been elected in many instances. A new form of workers' organizations had also appeared: the efficient and extremely active strike committees. Gierek sensed the urgency of the requests and incorporated them into a solemn declaration of intent when he confronted the shipyard workers in Szczecin in January 1971 with these words: "I promise you that we will do more to bring the workers to rule the country; you can be sure of this." Countering the workers' demands for thorough organizational reform, it was asserted that "the Party ensures for the trade unions conditions for the implementation of their statutory rights and observance of their power which constitutes a guarantee for the independence of the trade unions."(71) This was one of the most paradoxical and contradictory statements ever made in this respect.

The demands to revitalize workers' councils were the strongest. Because of their past history and because the workers preferred freely elected workers' councils as the main organization representing them and defending their interests, at the expense of trade unions, there was a sharp conflict between the two. In a public opinion poll in Silesia, organized by the fortnightly Rada Robotnicza, only one voice in over 2,000 was cast against workers' councils. All the other interviewees pointed out that if workers' councils did not work properly, it was only because no proper conditions were created for them, and no proper people were elected to them. In fact, I was told, in the whole of Silesia there were only two really active and efficient workers' councils. Why? Because, after so many years of Gierek's rule as first secretary of the VPC in the region, the decisive and overriding role of the Party had been imposed so strongly in Silesia that there was no room for any active independent workers' councils.

In July 1971, a Party official told me that the Party did not really know what to do about workers' councils. They were afraid of them as potentially important factors in economic administration, but they also had to take into account the workers' demands in December, the more so since many spontaneous workers' organizations set up then were still influential in both the various enterprises and in local government. Only in 1972, slowly and gradually, the former leaders of strike committees, the freely elected chairmen of workers' councils and other representative activists were quietly moved to work in other parts of the country.

The basic principle of the "new course" was supposed to be that the trade unions not only had to make sure that the production plan was fulfilled, but they also had to defend workers' interests; the emphasis was to be on the "human element." They seemed to be discovering America in the twentieth century. Some officials in the CCTU in Warsaw stressed that the "evil" of the past had been the identification of the trade unions with the Party and the government. Workers' self-government should exist, according to CCTU officials, only in those establishments where the workers were mature enough and the system could not be decreed from above. The real solution would be in what was called "workers' democracy" on the shop floor, with trade union organizations looking after the workers' interests and representing them. Thus, there would not be any real need for workers' councils.

When the trade unions congress finally assembled in November 1972 it became clear that there would not be any new institutional forms of workers' participation. Only the methods were to be changed, as well as those people who had not proved to be up to the required standard. The leading role of the Party in the unions was emphasized more strongly than in the past but its leadership was to be exercised in a way less hampering to the initiative of the lower level organizations. In an atmosphere of caution as to how far to allow workers real power, Gierek warned that the unions must

not allow "differences to degenerate into conflicts," and offered a partnership with the administration in improving living
conditions and solving selected problems of social policy. The
main test of the efficiency of the unions was to be the "elimination, in time, of causes of tension and the prevention of
conflict in places of work."(72)

On balance, the congress, after many promises and still
greater hopes for something like a really independent trade
union movement, was a complete anticlimax. Reforms which
might have resulted in greater autonomy, such as, for
example, the veto right that the trade unions were promised
soon after Gierek came to power, failed to materialize. Early
demands for the revitalization of workers' self-government
organs were also conveniently forgotten. Despite, or rather
because of, the workers ultimately decisive power, the Party
leadership persistently refused to allow any institutionalization
of the de facto situation. For it was a fact that all that the
workers had gained since December 1970 was due solely to
themselves. But it was also an undeniable fact that the decisions in these matters were made, under workers' pressure,
by the Party and would have been made regardless of whether
or not the trade unions existed. What happened was that in a
time of severe social tension, the Party abandoned an inert
and badly compromised union apparatus and become the first
and final court of appeal.(73) It was clear that it did not
want to surrender this role, and the status quo was likely to
remain unchanged.

Nevertheless, in some enterprises by 1973, local trade
unions had increased their influence. This was not the result
of the resolutions of the 1972 trade union congress, but
depended on the people who were locally in charge of trade
unions. If they were strong and courageous enough they did
influence managerial decisions. But in the overwhelming
majority of industrial enterprises criticism by the workers of
the unions, the government or of Party measures was as a rule
condemned as "subversive" and workers' complaints were
quietly shelved.

In January 1975, after over four years of drafting and
redrafting the new labor code was passed by the Sejm.(74) It
observed strictly the principle of centralized management and
did nothing to increase the powers of workers' self-government
and the trade unions. In a few instances it increased the
prerogatives of plant managers who in effect represented state
interests. The labor code thus not only failed to extend the
prerogatives of the trade unions in the area protecting
workers' interests, but did in fact approve existing practices.

At the trade union congress in 1972 Gierek rightly said:
"We must fight for time and lengthen the pace of our march
toward progress, because the whole world is quickening its
development. The slogan of modern times is: better and

quicker."(75) The problem was that this fully justified and
absolutely necessary aim could not be attained without structural political reforms within the existing system. Nothing
that was done in the area of the relations between workers,
Party and government during the five years was likely to
accelerate the necessary political reforms.

THE INTELLECTUALS: THE CONSCIENCE OF THE NATION?

> The Power least prized is that
> which thinks and feels.
>
> William Wordsworth in "Humanity"
>
> Fear makes an enemy
> of truth itself.
>
> J. Davidson

The intellectuals had been among Gomulka's most bitter
antagonists; yet, in December 1970, having suffered from the
cumulative effects of severe censorship, administrative
measures and professional intimidation, they watched in silence
as the workers on the Baltic coast brought the Gomulka era to
an end.
In July 1971, I had a long talk with Antoni Slonimski, a
most distinguished Polish poet, essayist and publicist who died
in a car accident in 1976. He was a leading figure, respected
and even revered in Polish intellectual circles. Condemned by
Gomulka, he was always active as the most liberal and the most
outspoken critic of Party dogma, repressive measures, and
disregard for human and civil rights. The situation in
December, he told me, was so tense and dangerous that
writers decided to "abstain" from involvement. Also there was
a real danger that any support from the writers could give
General Moczar a chance to play again, as he did in March
1968, his antisemitic card - disguised as an imaginary "Zionist
plot." December was exclusively a workers' protest, Slonimski
maintained, strong enough to shake the Party by itself, without the intellectuals' participation. Besides, for "external,
political reasons" it was better to leave workers alone.
In 1971, the Polish intellectuals, taking two steps forward
and one step back, began meekly emerging from the shell that
was thrust down on them in 1968. Even before the new official Party cultural policy had been outlined, Gierek moved
slowly to mend the Party's fences with them. He has never
repudiated the repressive measures taken by Gomulka against
writers and students in 1968, but Deputy Premier Krasko,(76)

responsible for cultural affairs, appealed to the intellectuals for "prudent activity, not marked by thunderous declarations or making unrealistic demands, but documented by creative work and constructive contribution to the socialist development of the fatherland." He made it clear that the general lines of the state's cultural policy would not be changed, although there had been "errors" in some areas in the past. One thing had changed, said Krasko: "The Party has understood that the arts cannot be commanded to do this or that, and this opens possibilities for more intellectual freedoms."

Slowly and gradually the climate was changing. Distinguished Polish writers and artists, living abroad, like film director Polanski, famous playwright Mrozek, and Dejmek, producer of "Forefathers' Eve," banned in 1968 were invited to return to Poland, since their works "were an integral part of Polish culture." A number of prominent writers and critics, silenced and condemned by Gomulka after March 1968, like Slonimski, Kisielewski, Andrzejewski, were allowed to publish once again. A new historical book by the late Pavel Jasienica, strongly accusing Gomulka of various sins, was published. A high official of the Polish Writers Association board, told me they were allowed to print almost anything with the proviso that it was not antisocialist nor anti-Soviet.

The self-confidence of the intellectual community was able to develop within the generally more relaxed atmosphere created by the "renewal" process. This resurgence of spirit has been manifest in some dramatic ways. Slonimski, for instance, wrote a courageous response to the accusations launched against him in 1968 and this was published.(77) Shortly afterward, 17 distinguished writers protested to the Ministry of Justice about the trial of a small student group known as RUCH, who were sent to prison for opposing Gomulka's regime and having, among other equally ineffectual activities, desecrated a statue of Lenin. The ministry reacted to the protest by inviting five writers for a talk and giving them access to all the files.(78) Andrzejewski wrote a personal letter to Gierek on the same subject and immediately the Party leader telephoned him to discuss the case. As a result of an appeal court judgment, the young people of the RUCH group were released.

The gradual emergence of intellectuals from the Gomulka dark age could also be seen in the increasing assertiveness and intensity of discussions within the literary community. In the Polish Writers Union's periodical Wspolczesnosc, Marek Jaworski bluntly referred to the "paralysis" in the literary movement and to the fact that, "whereas our reality has been extremely political for years, our literature has become increasingly apolitical." Slonimski caustically remarked to me that the only good thing about the present Writers Association board were the apple pies served in their refectory. A well-known writer, Konwicki, asked what he hoped for in this atmosphere of attempted "renewal" answered: "I expect our literature to become more "sided," to have fewer blanks, to be a richer by the presentation of various writers' attitudes and world out-looks."

Gradually the mood in 1971 became bolder. The fort-nightly journal of the Polish Students Association, Student, published a serious and outspoken series of articles by well-known writers. In one of these the author tried, under the title "Depraved Literature"(79) to analyze the "persistent silence of Polish literature and political journalism" in the wake of the "startling and violent evolutions in Polish political and ideological life." In another bitter analysis called "Against Tamed Literature," Witold Nawrocki, attacked the "loud and pompous talk" about the role of literature, which only con-cealed a vacuum. "The painful experiences of December 1970 exposed a range of dramas ensuing from a disregard of reality and a misrepresentation of it."

In the freer atmosphere in the country the old question of the function of the intellectuals has once again been revived. The preference given by the authorities to political loyalty over intellectual and moral qualifications has come under heavy fire. A well-known sociologist, Piekara,(80) minced no words in suggesting that a proletarian background and membership in the Party should not be the only criteria for placing people in positions of influence. Professor Jerzy Bukowski of the Warsaw Polytechnic(81) argued that bourgeois attitudes show up as frequently among Party members as among the non-Party members, and he condemned the tendency to set intelligentsia apart from the rest of society. The students' paper, Student, advocated more prominence for intellectuals.

The priority accorded to socioeconomic problems may in part explain the leadership's failure to articulate for almost a year any definite policy toward the intellectual community. Its attitude seemed to reflect both the technocratic mentality on the ascendant in Warsaw, and the limitations imposed by doctrinal considerations. This came out in Gierek's speech at the sixth congress of the Party in December 1971 when he stated that: "The sole criterion in judging the arts is the ideological, social and artistic value of the work, its con-tribution to the consolidation of the nation, its internal strength and international position." Even more significantly, he singled out the period 1956-1959 as one in which, "the necessary elimination of specific dogmatic and sectarian errors" had been accompanied by "compromises with revisionism."(82) Although not spelled out, the implication of the statement for the intellectual community, whose euphoric performances in those earlier years had been an essential ingredient of the post-Stalinist thaw, seemed both direct and ominous.

The new leadership's cultural policy seemed at first sight
to be something of a paradox. It was the tone but not the
substance that differed completely from what was the norm
under Gomulka. Then the writers had been harried and
prevented from offering criticism by wholly arbitrary censorship. Consequently, those intellectuals who were regarded as
the "conscience of the nation," were alienated, demoralized and
even to some extent intimidated. Gierek had recognized that a
wholly alienated intelligentsia is of no service to the nation.
Consequently, whereas Gierek had changed the official line
toward the intellectuals, it was in the way in which the writers
were treated, rather than in any liberalization of the substance
of policy. The tact with which Gierek handled cultural policy
did emerge fairly clearly at the Polish Writers Association
congress in Lodz in February 1972. In the selection of
delegates for the Polish Writers Association congress many
hard-liners had been thrown out and those who had been
persecuted or condemned by Gomulka were elected. The
congress has produced the same tentative opening toward
reform that had characterized Gierek's period so far. Minister
of Culture Wronski restated(83) the basic principles. There
would be preference for "works advocating progress and
socialism" and the prevention of the "penetration of works
which were hostile to socialism and which would undermine our
fraternal alliance with the socialist countries." However, he
stressed that "apart from conditions of this fundamental
political nature, we do not, and will not, restrict the freedom
of creative work in culture." He noted that the regime's
cultural policy would not ignore the intellectuals' right to
various creative experiments, to an individual viewpoint, and
to a polemical approach to various programs. At the same time
he condemned previous bureaucratic interference and rigidity
although he added that "there have also been examples of the
abuse of writers' freedom for political purposes contrary to
socialism."

The reaction of the writers was twofold. They elected
two-thirds of their liberal colleagues to the new board of the
union. But to accentuate the tendency toward compromise,
Iwaszkiewicz was reelected for the eighth time as chairman of
the union. He was seen as a symbol of immobility, of conformity, of active and passive compromise. Iwaszkiewicz was a
respected and gifted writer of great talent which he knew how
to apply with grace and ease to situations calling for supreme
diplomatic skill in maneuvering between the wrath of the powerful authorities and loyalty to his colleagues. The secretary of
the union's Party organization, a well-known hard-liner,
Putrament, was reelected as one of the deputy chairmen. But
while the key posts remained in the hands of people loyal to
the Party, several figures who had taken a hard-line stance in
1968 lost their seats on the board and were replaced with
well-known liberals.

The discussion at the congress focused on the issue of the latitude to be allowed to writers in dealing with topical subjects and several of them criticized the negative impact of censorship of Polish literature.(84) As one writer said: "What immense areas of our history and our contemporary life have become taboo - a burden on our souls which prevents us from writing what we think." The main taboos have always been anything antisocialist; anything against the leading role of the Party; anything anti-Soviet, even if only slightly critical; and anything anti-Warsaw Pact - in short, anything anti-establishment. The literary critic, Artur Sandauer, asserted(85) that: "We are able to speak only half truths and we can never read the whole truth."

On the other hand, the grand old man of arts, Slonimski,(86) spoke about a new "climate of hope." He emphasized "the possibility of finding an area of agreement between the authorities and the creative circles," and characterized a compromise solution as "not only possible, but necessary, if we are concerned about the development of our culture." However, he stressed that any compromise would have to be a reasonable one, and that an open and honest opponent is always better than an ever-willing boot licker. Slonimski, the author of "Ashes and Diamonds," Andrzejewski, told a Western correspondent: "We must be realistic and avoid provocation. We should not make it more difficult for our politicians." In seeking a modus vivendi with the intellectuals, the Gierek leadership made certain concessions, expecting in return the benevolent neutrality, if not the active support, of the literary community in dealing with issues of a fundamental political nature. Now, the writers acted in such a way as to avoid a conflict with the authorities and the basis for a compromise agreement was outlined. What was clear, however, was that the intellectuals would seek to probe the regime's level and limits of toleration.

In March 1972 a memorandum(87) signed by some leading Polish scholars, including the noted philosopher, Professor Kotarbinski, and addressed to Gierek called his attention to the critical situation of the teaching of science and Polish universities. The authors pleaded that the social origin of the scholars and their political commitment should not be the criteria for their evaluation by the political authorities. In an interview for the Warsaw weekly, Professor Kotarbinski(88) emphasized even more strongly the need for teaching and research free from interference by the political authorities. "A light that is limited in scope becomes a laser, it can cut but it can no longer help us to see."

The Polish intellectuals have thus tried to act as a pressure group. They tried, in one way or another, to influence those in power and to participate in decision making in social, cultural and even political matters. Those aspirations came clearly to the surface in an article published by a well-known sociologist, Jan Strzelecki, in which he argued that in order to mobilize all the social energies necessary for a scientific and technological revolution in Poland, needed for its progress and prosperity, it was necessary for the country to evolve in the direction of democracy.

Obviously, some Polish intellectuals, particularly writers and academics, hoped that a spectacular advance in the economy might be matched by a real liberalization in culture. They felt that Gierek had the strength, the popular support, and most important the confidence of the Kremlin, needed to throw back the shutters and let in the light. It might be argued that Gierek and his colleagues judged soundly in deciding that a rapid rise in living standards was the first essential and since this was going to entail far closer trade relations with the West and an internal reform of the economy, Poland might be better advised to avoid all suspicion of receptivity to disruptive ideas from abroad.(89) Thus some of the more optimistic intellectuals have been disappointed, particularly when in 1973, and more so in 1974, Poland, in common with the rest of the bloc, found herself engaged in a kind of ideological rearmament designed to withstand the presumed onslaught of "subversive" petit bourgeois ideas from the West as detente got under way.

In May 1972, shortly after Gierek's meeting with representatives of creative and cultural organizations, the Party paper, Trybuna Ludu warned the writers against acceptance of ideologically alien ideas, and against the inclination to overemphasize the "European character of Polish culture."(90) In contrast to the previous year's pronouncement this tended to narrow the options.

By 1973 culture was definitely viewed by the leadership as an important means of shaping popular attitudes. And the Party, therefore, sought to encourage a cultural product which corresponded to, and therefore assisted, its political, social and economic objectives. In the most elaborate statement of the leadership's view by a high Party functionary, PB member Szydlak, writing in Trybuna Ludu, censured Polish intellectuals for having failed to pay enough attention to work and the workers as a motive in their creative activities. He accused some writers and film directors of "Europeanization," of blindly imitating themes and trends that were alien to Polish traditions and ideas, and of merrily wandering through the marginal fringes of life. This was not the way to fulfill the social mission. Then he spelled out what the Party expected: "There is absolutely no justification for the absence of any

artistic reflection of that optimistic vision of the future which
we have emphasized and are implementing." In this process
the Party, he stressed, must be the director and judge.
There certainly was a further intensification of ideological
control and official pressures, but, as often happens in
Poland, with mitigating loopholes.

When I discussed this problem in Warsaw with some intellectuals and journalists, doubts were expressed whether the
ideological and political clampdown could be fully applied in
everyday life. Limits are imposed, a writer said to me, but
this is rather a "leveling down" process and, besides, the
"high waters" of detente bypassed these limits every now and
then and new limits had to be built up.

In 1974 a well-established writer complained to me in
Warsaw about the heavy hand of censorship strongly felt in
literature, theater and especially in films. His theme was that
while older, established writers like himself had ways of
getting round the censorship, and could publish an unorthodox
book, providing that it did not offend "the great neighbor,"
and particularly when they had a friend in the PB, the
younger writers could not.

Opposition to the ideological offensive was quite often
voiced - sometimes in strong words, more often very subtly.
In an interview published in the weekly, Polityka, the well-
known poet, Herbert, defended the role of art as a valid
aspect of history, and demanded respect for the "irrational
factor in human beings." He rejected as "naive" the Marxist
philosophy of progress and said that conflicts would not disappear in human society. In an article in the Warsaw daily,
Zycie Warszawy, Andrzej Micewski insisted on intellectual
freedom and diversity. Some of his comments were directed
implicitly but unmistakably at the dangerously narrowing
effects of an intellectual life where the main lines of discussion
and discovery were prescribed and conflict proscribed. A
popular essayist, and a Catholic writer, Kisielewski, wrote:

> What is clear is that the Party is far less in-
> terested in providing a fertile milieu for the devel-
> opment of genuinely high-quality literature than in
> eliciting a cultural product from the country's
> artists which convincingly mirrors and generates
> support for its own political objectives.(91)

Political criticism in the country at large centered, therefore, on two issues: a narrowing of the permitted range of
expression and a tightening of Party ideological control in all
areas. A sort of cat-and-mouse play began between the
authorities and the intellectuals. Behind the facade of
ideological offensive and conformism, many things have happened which could mildly be described as unorthodox and

perhaps unique in Eastern Europe. The official reaction to these "happenings" was either muted or contradictory, which again pointed to some diversifying trends within the Party hierarchy.

There was, for instance, the case of Professor Maria Turlejska, a historian known for her long and close association with the communist political establishment. In her book, A Record of the First Decade published toward the end of 1972, she put the blame for the start of the cold war on the Soviet Union and ascribed its ending to the changes which took place after Stalin's death. She also quoted without comment Mikolajczyk's opinion, that the results of the first postwar elections in Poland were faked. The main Party paper, Trybuna Ludu, highly praised Turlejska's narrative of the postwar decade for demonstrating the magnitude "of our lack of knowledge." But very soon the book was withdrawn from sale and became the target of a stinging attack in the Party theoretical monthly, Nowe Drogi. This official review made it clear that the historian had overstepped the bounds of scholarly license and that the book and its publication were regarded as serious infringements of the political-ideological norms.

The whole story of publication, praise, withdrawal, and condemnation suggested that there was disagreement and confusion or perhaps both at whatever level the Party censorship and approval mechanism had handled the manuscript. This was at a time when some previously classified documents had been made accessible. Some of these revelations were posing a serious threat to the existence of many historical theories which up to now had been regarded as sacrosanct.

In January 1973, PB member Szydlak(92) emphasized that there had been some attempts to interpret falsely and tendentiously past experiences "in the spirit of theories and patterns ideologically alien to us." Shortly afterward, Gierek stated bluntly: "A correct assessment of the historical past must be based on a Marxist-Leninist analysis."

But the historians have not stood by in silence. For example, Professor Henryk Wereszycki(93) wrote that historians must search objectively, impartially and dispassionately for historical truth "as opposed to an adjustment of the image of the past to some nonscholarly requirements." Another writer, in an article in Zycie Warszawy rejected the tendentious and often obscurantist historical writing of the fifties and stressed that the historians should not bend facts to suit a selected interpretation of historical reality.

The case of historians was only one of many. In December 1974 at the top-level ideological meeting in Moscow, Suslov laid down the cultural line for his East European colleagues and he was critical of Polish cultural life, mainly because of its nationalism. In two major speeches, Lukas-

zewicz(94), the CC secretary in charge of press and propaganda, made it clear that in the Party's view detente
demanded still greater vigilance against what he termed
"imperialist subversion." Nor, according to him, could writers
and artists who were unprepared to further the Party's aims
expect to avail themselves of the facilities it alone controls.
But, even in this official atmosphere the Poles were very
subtly able and willing to find ways and means of expressing
themselves more freely than their neighbors in other East
European countries.

For instance, while the authorities had repeated their
hopes for a topical, "political" socialist theater, even CC
member Lomnicki, rector of the state drama school in
Warsaw(95), expressed serious concern about the existing
conditions and climate which obstructed the development of
contemporary Polish drama. Being unable to create a political
theater worthy of its name, Poles have found a peculiar outlet
for their feelings of frustration and rebellion against the
existing political establishment.(96) The traditional historical
plays by nineteenth-century Polish poets and playwrights,
such as Adam Mickiewicz's Forefathers' Eve, or Wyspianski's
Wedding Liberation and November Night were being performed
in some of the leading theaters, directed by Poland's most
distinguished directors, such as Wajda, Hanuszkiewicz and
others. They provoked heated discussions in the press as
they dealt with sensitive "political" subjects: personal,
religious, national freedom in Poland; submission to Russian
and other foreign oppression, etc. They formed a specifically
Polish substitute for an overt on-stage discussion of current
political and social conflicts.

This return to the great Polish classics of the last century was one striking aspect of the intellectual climate of
Giereks' Poland.(97) They were written in bitterness and
protest against Czarist domination, and the audiences vividly
and loudly applauded all the anti-Russian passages. This flight
into the past is partly explained by the lack of good stage or
screen material dealing with the contemporary problems of
Polish life. Gierek recently repeated that the Party was still
waiting for the great works of literature which would do
justice to Poland's construction of a socialist society. Meanwhile, in the classics, young Poles were in a sense redis-
covering themselves and their past. It was an atmosphere in
which the mature generation of young Poles, who knew no
other system, felt sure enough of themselves to speak out
openly, and sometimes critically, of improvement and progress,
not with any reversal of the system.

It was against this background that the dramatic call for
a truly political, contemporary theater published by the noted
critic, Grodzicki, amounted to a sort of manifesto:

> No great literature, including drama, originates from
> conformism, accommodation with the establishment, or
> a polishing-up around the edges....Half-truths are,
> in fact, not only halves of the truth, but falsifica-
> tions. Nothing good can result from a situation in
> which a play-goer or reader knows more about a
> given subject than the author wants to tell him.(98)

Even in the most modern and fascinating production of
Goethe's Faust, directed by a young and distinguished Polish
director, Szajna, the accents on contemporary issues, very
critical in tone, were clearly detected.

While the leadership repeatedly affirmed that the friendship between the Soviet Union and Poland was vital for the
country's well-being, the Poles were not discouraged from
taking pride in their national heritage nor in the long history
of resistance to Russian and other occupations, which inspired
some of the great dramas of Poland's past. Some celebrated
historical novels were being made into films - for instance,
Sienkiewicz's Deluge, and Colonel Wolodyjowski or the famous
novel The Promised Land which dealt with labor conditions and
intrigues in Poland's pre-World War I textile center, Lodz. In
all these productions, contemporary problems were subtly and
cleverly in focus, in a critical way and by implication some
current policies were strongly condemned.

Perhaps nowhere else was criticism presented in such a
subtle form, than in some student theaters and cabarets such
as the "Pod Egida." This political cabaret, known for its
courageous and sharp wit, was housed in very small and uncomfortable premises, and filled every night to capacity. Texts
and songs were written, spoken and sung by young people,
their jokes currently directed against the Polish mass media
and the archtypal Party "apparatchick." They did not
hestitate to criticize higher placed Party men and, indirectly,
even the Russians. The real motivational force of the cabaret
was a brilliant young intellectual, Jan Pietrzak. The cabaret
had been tolerated since 1972, but finally the last program was
withdrawn by censors' orders at the beginning of 1976 and the
cabaret ceased for the time being to exist.

Despite a good deal of huffing and puffing from the Party
ideologists, film directors and critics I talked to made the
point that, although scripts had to be approved in advance,
the production was state subsidized, the most striking recent
films made in Poland could hardly be said to fulfill the
strictest requirements of Party dogma or the function of the
so-called socialist art. For example, a film depicting the
tragic heroism of a lone Polish unit which refused to surrender
after Poland was overrun by Hitler's armies in September 1939,
has had a remarkably good reception from young people to the
surprise of its maker. The film Hubal shook off some of the

trappings of orthodoxy, by ascribing a genuine role to the aristocracy and the church in the early days of the fighting. It played to packed houses. But by 1974 all except statistical mention of the film had been banned from the Polish press. Some other films, for instance, those directed by Zanussi, whose subjects were some contemporary problems treated in an honest and potent way, appeared on the screens; but the censors banned many films with a sharper edge of criticism, although these films were fully completed and ready for showing. The prominent film director, Wajda, used to say: "The art of making a film in Poland is the art of constant resignation." Nevertheless, these films were being shown in so-called studios, in other words in film clubs of which there are many, particularly in Warsaw.

All these examples are proverbial in the huge unwritten textbook on censorship evasion. Writers compromise in various ways. Most of the contemporary Polish literature resembles an enormous cypher. Everything is an illusion. To discuss your book, to play with meanings and obscure them, to pretend that you are saying something different or contrary to what you are actually saying, to avoid being straightforward - these are the tools of self-censorship, of fooling the censors, but also fooling sometimes the readers, or the audience in the theater.(99) One has to be well acquainted with current and political social gossip and has to know various personal connections and constellations to be able to comprehend some of the books by talented young writers like Glowacki, Iredynski, Nowakowski, or Bonarski.

It became part of a new cultural policy after 1970, not to erase names as such from the cultural map, in order to neutralize possible criticism from the West and to avoid creating martyrs, but to erase those works which were unacceptable to the Party. Some books, banned by the censors in Poland, can be published, and were published, abroad. The difference between the Gomulka and Gierek eras was that their authors were still in Poland, could still publish in Poland, and although they were condemned for sending the manuscripts to "subversive" centers abroad for publication, nevertheless, this was all that happened to them.

Mysia Street in Warsaw is famous only because of one building there, namely the headquarters of the official censor. Its full name is the Main Office for Control of Press, Publications and Performances. It has agencies in all the bigger cities and itself is controlled by various departments of the CC of the Party. The official censorship, by the way, contradicts the principles of the Polish constitution. The trouble and the difficulty of the censors, of course, has always been that political permissiveness can change overnight, depending on the policies of the Party. A good example of how the censorship works is the case of weekly, political, literary,

social magazines, e.g., <u>Kultura</u> or <u>Literatura</u>. Every issue of
the magazine is sent to the printer on Friday afternoon. Over
the weekend the galley proofs are prepared and on Monday
they are handed to the censor. There is a new censor every
week to prevent the relationship between him and the editors
becoming too friendly. The censor reads the proofs and makes
his corrections; then, marking them with a special seal and his
signature he hands the proofs back to the editors. Without
that seal nothing can be printed, the censor's copy of the
proofs being obligatory for the printer.

A similar procedure operates in the case of books, stage
plays, television, films, etc. A book has its own screening to
undergo before it gets to the reader, if it reaches him at all.
The writer delivers his manuscript to a publishing house and
then waits. He may wait a short time, or much longer -
perhaps a year - depending on his current standing on the
ladder of grace. The writer then meets the publisher and is
told what will happen to his book. That is the first level of
censorship. If the writer accepts the suggested changes, then
his book goes to the printing house, one set of the galley
proofs being sent by the publisher to the censor's office. The
censor reads it and makes alterations, as do some officials from
the Ministry of Culture and from the Party CC and finally the
book is printed. It may happen though, that by the time the
book is ready to be distributed to the bookshops the political
climate may have changed and the book suddenly becomes
undesirable. Or the writer might blot his copybook, as for
instance, by protesting against the invasion of Czechoslovakia
in 1968. A book which has been rejected by the censors may
be lost forever, or it may be printed some years later like the
books written during Gomulka's period that appeared after
1970. Even a slightly controversial book might be printed
quickly if the author is on good terms with, for instance, a
member of the PB and has persuaded him that the book is
worth publishing. On the other hand, very much depends on
the ever-changing climate within the Party and on who, at a
given time, has the upper hand in cultural matters within the
Party hierarchy.

Official censorship sometimes amounts to a farce. The
censors, for instance, went so far as to cut out certain passages from the 22-volume complete edition of Joseph Conrad's
works published recently in Poland. They cut out a number
of passages which might cause offense to the Soviet Union.
One such example was in the <u>Last Essays</u> and <u>Uncollected
Pieces</u> from Conrad's letter to the <u>Times</u>, when the sentence,
"a charge of lying occurs naturally to the Russian mind," was
cut out.

But there is also another channel of censorship which was
confirmed to me in my many conversations in Poland. The
Soviet ambassador, Pilotovich, has acquired fame as a censor

in his own right, ready to come down on editorial offices or
film production units personally or through his officials. He
has intervened on many occasions even in cases when the book
or a film has been passed by the Polish censorship office. For
example, in May 1972 the monthly magazine, Photography had
been devoted to the memory of a famous artist, Jan Bulhak,
who was a pioneer Polish photographer at the beginning of the
century. The editors printed a retrospective anthology of his
famous photographs, and included one which caused quite a
stir. Bulhak happened to be in Wilno (now Vilnius, a Polish
city incorporated into the Soviet Union, in 1939) during the
Polish-Soviet war of 1920 and photographed Polish soldiers
capturing the city. He gave his photograph the title "Wilno -
ours again" and the photo, with the same caption, appeared in
1972 in this anthology in a "socialist" magazine. The Soviet
cultural attache called it a provocation and late in the night
rang some Party officials. The censor responsible was the
first to be punished and was dismissed the same night. The
entire circulation of that issue of Photography was confiscated
and the next day the whole editorial committee was dismissed.

At the height of the ideological offensive, the leadership
attempted a new form of compromise in the cultural field.
Minister of Culture Wronski was released from his post in 1974.
An educated, but nevertheless crude bureaucrat who was
closely linked with General Moczar and his ideas, he left
unlamented by the intellectuals. His replacement was Jozef
Tejchma, one of the best brains in the Party, an able
pragmatist and within the communist context a liberal.
Wincenty Krasko, newly appointed secretary of the CC
responsible for the "cultural front," was also a man of
educated taste and manners with a certain standing among the
intelligentsia. It was only the simultaneous appointment to full
CC secretaryship of Werblan, a hard-line ideologist, who had
been in the limelight since Stalin's time, that indicated that the
leadership meant to balance a new degree of urbanity with a
stress on the old Party virtues.

At the Polish Writers Association congress in February
1975 in Poznan, Tejchma, eloquently outlined the cultural
policies of the leadership:

> We would like to understand ever more deeply,
> in the whole solemnity of cultural life, the functions
> of literature, which not only reflects reality as per-
> ceived today, but which also signals new phenomena
> of tomorrow, not excluding the dangers which may
> grow up if they are not laid bare and overcome in
> time. Hence there is room for both firm acceptance
> and critical restlessness in literature, as in all our
> activities.(100)

Iwaszkiewicz, was elected chairman of the association for the ninth time. The new board of the association underwent a "face-change," as one of the participants said. The left had consolidated its position. Some of the writers, particularly the liberals and those who took part in various protests, were dropped and replaced by people much more amenable to the Party directives and much closer to the official approach to cultural policy.

A new problem which was not discussed but only mentioned in a few sentences by Iwaszkiewicz was the problem of young writers and poets. Just before the congress two young Krakow poets, Julian Kornhauser and Adam Zagajewski, had provoked a discussion with their recent book, The Word Not Represented, in which they dealt with the failure of present-day Polish literature to represent or reflect existing realities. These two and many other young writers, mostly poets, were known from their poetry readings in various towns and from several low-circulation collections of poems and essays sometimes delayed by the censors for many months. This could be described as a "new wave" represented by young intellectuals born after World War II, whose vivid memories included the student and intellectual rebellion in March 1968, and the workers' revolt in December 1970. They do have searching and suspicious minds, not taking anything for granted, querying and critically analyzing existing reality. They call themselves, the "intervention group," "the seekers of the truth," "the unmaskers," and "the contesters." They oppose opportunism and what is called the attitude of "life on bended knees."(101)

The two youngsters, Kornhauser and Zagajewski called for literature, and in particular poetry, to put its imprint on current events, and to shape cultural awareness. The crisis in Polish literature is not in their opinion, caused by a lack of talent or of well-written books, but by a lack of courage "to tell the truth," to face the world.

The creed of the new wave was defined by the poet and critic Baranczak as follows: "Our challenge should be expressed by the mistrust, criticism and unmasking of evil. It should be expressed thus until the very last lie and demagogy, the last act of violence, shall have disappeared from this earth." Challenging "little cultural stabilization," one of the young poets wrote: "Less prevarication and more perturbation." At the time when the Party leadership had been advocating the need for involvement, the poet Jacek Bierezin criticized the familiar landscape of present-day reality: "Drunkards fighting in the streets, mobile radio units, patrols, buildings with the plaster flaking off their facades, and a neon sign proclaiming: 'the Party - the leading force of the nation' in which several letters fail to light up properly." The voice of these young writers was not heard at the writers' congress in February 1975.

The problem with intellectuals had always been twofold in postwar years. Too often too many of them adjusted immediately to changing political circumstances. Many were most loyal, perhaps occasionally even more loyal than most communists themselves, in Stalinist times, and some of them remain, within the communist context, "conservative and loyal" to this very day. Very many of them changed overnight, in October 1956. Then, there was the abortive rebellion in 1968 after which the intellectuals somehow withdrew into their own shells, becoming partly more compliant, with reservations, partly detached, and only partly opposed to the cultural trends and policies of the Party.

The other problem was, and perhaps still is, the social profile of the intellectuals which is probably largely responsible for their continued insistence on being "the conscience of the nation." This social group represents a unique intellectual, spiritual and political cultural blending of outstanding personalities from different social groups, and from different ideological and spiritual backgrounds. There are among them descendants of the Polish nobility and descendants of the traditional old intelligentsia, themselves often originally minor nobility. There are also the people of upper or lower middle class, often of foreign extraction, but assimilated two or three generations ago. There is a growing number of intellectuals of the first, or at the most second, generation of peasant or worker origin. Their outlook is rather conservative, and conformist, but even they became perturbed, "opposed" and very many of them, even including Party members, disappointed and frustrated. The process of integration is slow and difficult, but it is unavoidable. There must be harmony within the intellectual group of the nation if they want to represent the conscience of the nation.

In the autumn of 1975, the Poles were concerned about two things - officially with the Party congress and privately with prices and wages. Quite unpredictably, however, in the middle of all this, crowds were flocking to an exhibition of nineteenth- and twentieth-century romanticism in Poland. Those were the times, particularly during the nineteenth century, when on one side intellectuals and on the other, the church were the only people who, in the absence of a Polish state or political parties, could reflect national aspirations. Why this interest in outdated romanticism? One critic has called the exhibition a national "psychoanalytical session." Another said it provided a stock list of national identity. If this need to freely express the national identity is widely felt as it seems to be, the intellectuals have an important role to play.

Among the signatories of various protests and memoranda which began to appear again in 1974, were not only the names of old-style intellectuals, but also the names of the very young

writers of the "new wave," together with the names of those
who came from a proletarian and peasant background and were
educated in postwar Poland. In December 1974, acting on the
initiative of Slonimski, 15 intellectuals signed an appeal sent to
Minister of Culture Tejchma,(102) calling on the Polish government to intervene with the Soviet authorities "to enable Poles
in the Soviet Union to obtain the same rights as those enjoyed
by our countrymen living in other countries."   According to
official Polish sources, 1,430,000 Poles are living in the Soviet
Union but they have never taken part in various congresses
and conferences organized in Poland for Poles from abroad.
This appeal broke the tradition of near silence in Poland on all
matters relating to conditions in the eastern half of prewar
Poland which was annexed by the Soviet Union in 1939.   It
was, therefore, an unprecedented public expression of Polish
concern,
     A year earlier Slonimski had protested against the im-
prisonment in a labor camp of Andrei Amalrik, a Soviet historian and poet.(103)   At the beginning of 1975 five Polish intellectuals sent a defiant letter of congratulations to the Soviet
dissenter Andrei Sakharov, whose Nobel Peace Prize was
described by Frelek, secretary of the CC, as "an example of
the sharpening of the ideological struggle by anticommunist
forces." After almost six years of silence or "abstention,"
some intellectuals had reappeared on the scene as champions of
human and civil rights.

MASS MEDIA: THE INSTRUMENT OF THE PARTY

> A censored press remains bad, even
> when it produces good things.
>
> Karl Marx in Das Kapital

     One afternoon, sitting comfortably in the editorial office
of a Warsaw daily newspaper, I discussed with the editor the
treatment of news and comments in the Polish press. Sipping
Georgian brandy and chasing it with innumerable cups of black
coffee, I queried in particular why the Polish press either kills
or publishes, with a two- or three-day delay, an important
news item which has already been reported by all the world
media.   There is sometimes, he replied, a politically touchy
item and we first have to assess how to comment on it from a
"socialist" point of view. Only when such a "socialist" comment is forthcoming from our Party do we publish the news
item with the comment.
     There could hardly be a more telling comment on the
limitations of the Polish mass media. All the journalists I have

met over several years admitted freely: "We suffer terribly
from censorship, and we hate it." Obviously if some of the
editors are clever enough they can occasionally slip in some
unorthodox passages because the censors are, in one man's
words, "plain stupid." The problem was that in addition to
internal censorship there was also strong "censorship pressure
from our Soviet friends." For instance, the Tass report on
the Soviet-Chinese clash on the Ussuri River came one day
after the event and was embargoed for another 24 hours,
despite the fact that all radio stations in the world had reported this event immediately. Details of the crash of a Polish
plane near Krakow were not reported because the official
communique spoke about the pilot's dying of a heart attack -
although, as the autopsies revealed, and this was common
knowledge, all three crew members had been shot in the head.
In an article on the reformist movement within the church half
a sentence saying that the Polish nation is overwhelmingly
Catholic was cut out by the censors. When the Polish commentator spoke on a direct transmission of the Apollo 11 lift-off
for the first manned moon landing, he dwelt almost all the time
on the Soviet cosmic efforts, Luna 15, and the fact that the
Soviet cosmonauts paved the way for the American moon landing, although they had never landed there. When I asked a
high official, with whom I watched this direct television transmission, about this Soviet slant on an American achievement he
just replied: "We were instructed to do just that." A few
days later I had a dinner at a well-known Krakow restaurant
and we were told that all the kitchen staff were watching the
television transmission of the moon landing. Suddenly a waiter,
excited and smiling, rushed into the restaurant room and
shouted, "They have landed! They have landed!" Champagne
corks popped in celebration and there were lengthy conversations at all the tables about what had happened.

These were pre-Gierek times. But in 1973 I listened to a
Warsaw radio news bulletin during the Israeli-Arab war and to
a news item which described the action on the battlefront in
the following words: "The imperialist Israeli aggressor forces
viciously attacked defensive Egyptian positions." Here was a
completely blurred line between the reporting of facts in a
news bulletin and a comment. The news bulletin had to be
adjusted to the official assessment of the situation. Again
when the announcement of the Nixon's first visit to China made
the headlines all over the world, an editor of a press agency
in Warsaw objected to it very strongly and asked me, "What's
all the fuss about?" When I replied that, after all, on this
very day, this was the top news story, he said, "Yes, perhaps, but it does not contribute to detente between East and
West!" In the autumn of 1976, one of the journalists told me:
"I can talk freely with you, perhaps with some of my colleagues, perhaps with other foreign journalists, but I cannot
write what I really think and what I really feel."

These may be extreme examples but they illustrate the
problem which the mass media face even if many Polish journalists are more clever and subtle than their colleagues in
other East European countries in devising ways and means to
comment more realistically. To understand it fully one has to
learn to read between the lines.

Whenever any upheaval occurs the long-suppressed feelings of true, professional journalism come to the surface. In
December 1970 many sensitive issues were openly discussed
and sometimes highly unorthodox articles questioning the
nature of the political system itself appeared in some papers,
although it was, at this time, a pale shadow of the
free-wheeling journalistic debates of 1955-1956. One felt the
existence of substantial limitations - self-imposed and also
external. Even so, during the tragic and chaotic December
days, the broadcasting staff in Szczecin and Gdansk were left
completely on their own and for the first time in many years
they felt free to do their job properly. In those brief, heady
days no censorship existed. Many journalists lived then
through an internal conflict of conscience between their loyalty
to the Party and journalistic honesty in reporting and
commenting. As a reporter on the coast told me: "We could
not condemn the workers' protest, because we were convinced
that it was fully justified. Yet we were hesitant to say so
openly because that would have implied that we would have
rejected the assessment by the Party and this would be a
violation of Party discipline." Finally, however, they decided
to "say it openly," both in radio and in the press.

In June 1971 Gierek attended the congress of the Polish
Journalists Association for the first time. He praised the
press for its role and attitude during the December events. A
well-known commentator and television personality,
Malcuzynski, (as reported in Prasa Poliska in June) offered a
vote of thanks for this praise, but emphasized that during
the students' demonstrations in March 1968, and again during
the riots in December 1970, the slogan "the press is lying"
appeared everywhere. So while it was gratifying, he said, to
hear the first secretary praising the press, something must
be wrong somewhere. He suggested that censorship might
soon be eased, underlining the importance of such a move if
the public's confidence in the press was to be restored. A
newspaper cannot be edited with an eye open to only a
narrow section of the Communist party, he said, and continued:

> We are facing the task of restoring the damaged
> link and the damaged credit of social confidence in
> our press, in our information system, in the credibil-
> ity and honesty of our arguments....The critical
> December week demonstrated in a most drastic way

> the inefficiency and weakness of the propaganda
> methods as well as the stifling and paralysis of the
> information channels between the leadership of the
> Party and its own sources....We found ourselves
> torn between the sense of loyalty and discipline...
> and the internal conviction that the decisions taken
> by the leadership were wrong and even leading to a
> catastrophe.

What Malcuzynski suggested was not that the Party Press
Office but journalists themselves should map out and outline
the targets and then analyze and assess their execution by the
mass media. The press should be a channel of transmission,
he argued, in both directions - from below to the top and
from the top of the masses.

In July 1971, after the initial and short-lived freedom in
expressing various views, the mass media quickly came under
close scrutiny. Refreshing polemics and lively discussions
became rare. No polemical accents were allowed by the censor
in foreign, inter-Party policies or in comments on anything
connected with the Soviet Union and for that matter, any other
country of the Warsaw Pact. Some news items, particularly on
internal Party conflicts, were simply suppressed, I was told by
several journalists.

One journalist explained to me that in the 1971 atmosphere
of fluidity, while everyone was "waiting for Godot" - in other
words, for a comprehensive program of reforms and further
economic progress - the mass media were rather in a state of
uncertainty. Censors were perhaps more amenable, but,
according to some journalists, the future did not seem to be
very hopeful in this respect. In the subcommittee of Szydlak's
commission (see section, "Defusing the Situation: Phase Two,"
in Chapter 3) on mass media a suggestion that some subjects
such as theater and film reviews, sport, science and technology, should be exempted from censorship, was strongly rejected. The then chairman of the Polish Journalists Association,
Mojkowski (as reported in Prasa Polska, June 1971) noted at
the journalists' congress that the political crisis in the Party
had gravely affected the work of the media, but apologetically
claimed: "Come hell or high water, we were always with the
Party, we tried to embody its teaching reasonably in life."
Such an attitude could hardly serve to restore the credibility
of the press.

Information made available to the public began to be
carefully screened. The leadership's promise to reveal all the
facts about the brutal repression of the workers' demonstrations in December 1970 was not kept. A special issue of the
Party theoretical monthly, Nowe Drogi, containing a record of
the debate that took place on this subject at the eighth plenum
of the CC in February 1971, was never put on sale and circu-

lated only to a very restricted number of Party activists. PB
member Szydlak was greatly embarrassed when he appeared on
national television in June and was repeatedly asked to explain
this. Two highly placed journalists admitted to me in July
1971 that the press once again had a very limited impact on
society. Mass media did not cover news properly nor did their
comments on topical events; so the people looked for information elsewhere, primarily to foreign radio stations, the BBC,
and Radio Free Europe, as, incidentally, they always have
done in the past. Too many views were still suppressed about
the real political situation in Poland and certainly in other
"socialist" countries. And besides, there were generally too
many taboos, I was told by several journalists.

In his initial statements to the nation, Gierek committed
the leadership to a dialogue with the people by all means
available, including mass media, and to policies that would be
"clear, understandable and explained to all."(104)   Even if
these initial hopes were not fulfilled some changes in information policy have been forthcoming. In 1971 "Citizens' Tribune," a television series of question-and-answer sessions with
prominent leaders was inaugurated. The problems to be discussed were advertised in advance in the press. Questions
from listeners were sent in by mail but there were also 16
telephone lines in the studio, allowing people to phone in from
various parts of the country during the transmission. When I
watched one edition there were also three mobile television
units out in villages, and during the transmission the anchor-
man went over to them for questions on the spot. On this
occasion questions on agriculture were answered by the CC
secretary, Barcikowski, and three ministers. Some more
general questions proved to be rather grilling and unpleasant,
as for instance, one from a peasant who asked: "This so-called
renewal has been widely proclaimed in the last six months, but
our local authorities have merely changed the phrases they use
and have even strengthened their old bureaucratic attitudes.
Is, therefore, this "renewal" just another common fraud?"
Other questioners referred to more detailed and personal
problems which had not been solved and they wanted to know
why. Barcikowski and the ministers tried to answer all the
questions, sometimes evasively, but showing at all times ner-
vousness and every now and then apprehension. There was
no doubt in my mind that this was a live and spontaneous
program. But this unique experiment was discontinued after a
few editions when the questions became more and more embarrassing and politically unacceptable - perhaps even unanswer-
able.

Another innovation was the appointment in March 1971 of
a government spokesman with the rank of minister, Wlodzimierz
Janiurek. The activities of his office consisted of: one monthly conference given by Janiurek himself for the benefit of

Polish media; informal meetings with some editors in order to explain and interpret government decisions; reacting to journalists' queries over the phone; and preparing irregular bulletins for the prime minister and some ministers, dealing with special problems arising from complaints and questions put forward by the ordinary people. The government spokesman was also expected to exert pressure on the ministers to give their own press conference when justified by events. Only two such departmental press conferences were given.

The spokesman dealt exclusively with socioeconomic problems, because "the government was concentrating on them." He ventured into more politically delicate issues after the events of June 1976.

In addition, for the first time in the Communist party history, brief communiques have been issued regularly on the activities of the PB and the CC secretariat. But at a meeting with journalists, Gierek agreed that the communiques were laconic and described this as "an oversight on our part"(105), promising that more detailed information would be added to the communiques so that the journalists would be much better informed. This has not happened.

Finally Gierek himself inaugurated press conferences. At first these were very occasional, but since November 1974, they have become more regular. These were rather confidential briefings, and some information was supplied by Gierek for background only. Certain statements by Gierek were addressed exclusively to this selected circle of invited journalists, "for reasons of state." This was actually, as the weekly, Polityka, wrote, one of the conditions governing the openness of exchanges during the meeting. Nevertheless quite a lot of this "background only" confidential information leaked out from these meetings, deliberately or because of the specific Polish atmosphere in which journalists were inclined to divulge to their colleagues and friends what was said. In other words, this proved to be in the long term an unofficial extension of a channel of information, sometimes tacitly approved by the authorities, often against their will.

In 1971 Gierek outlined the tasks of the mass media as he saw them: "Avoid going to extremes but at the same time beware of exaggerated optimism." A black outlook and pessimism and the negation of the achievements, he said, is as bad as too much optimism and the feeling of self-satisfaction. These were sensible and rational words. But, in the following years the hopeful propaganda of success overshadowed anything else, even cautious warnings and sober, realistic assessments of the economic situation.

The importance of many original initiatives outlined above was diluted, however, by the leadership's essentially conservative approach to the role of the mass media. Although there has been a visible increase in discussion and criticism in the press both have been confined within limits acceptable to the Party. As was reflected in the resolutions of the sixth Party congress in 1971, the mass media were "instruments of the implementation of the Party's program(106). Exposure of "shortcomings in socioeconomic life" was to take place only within "the field of criticism extended by the Party." This was not a very wide field. A freer press was welcome when it criticized the previous regime. It was less welcome now that Gierek's men had to account for the shortcomings. PB member Szydlak, responsible for the so-called ideological front(107), stated clearly: "It is our intention that the concerted efforts of all Polish journalists should promote still more effectively the ideological unity of the people, rallying it around the program of the Party and the interests of our socialist state." This has meant greater standardization and centralization, with the main Party organ, Trybuna Ludu, serving as the model. In the words of its editor, Barecki, the paper's objective is to "fulfill more comprehensively its tasks as a propaganda organ, agitator and organizer, the classic functions of the socialist press."(108)

What were these classic functions? In December 1972, Szydlak listed(109) four taboos for writers and journalists: 1) criticism of the leading role of the Party, 2) socialism, 3) Poland's alliances, and 4) spreading antipatriotic ideas. The time soon came, at the end of 1972 and the beginning of 1973, when Moscow was also exerting pressure throughout Eastern Europe for greater uniformity and tighter ideological control. Immediately on at least two occasions Szydlak instructed journalists to use criticism only in accordance with Party policy, bearing in mind its program and strategy.

There were several reasons for this tightening of ideological screws in the mass media. With the Helsinki conference in mind some of the more orthodox communist officials and journalists argued with me that they must have time to educate the nation themselves and to influence people's attitudes before a full frontal confrontation with the West. Otherwise the people might, in full contact with the West, become influenced by false ideas about socialism and might think about too many different solutions of Poland's own problems, especially since the Western foreign broadcasts were full of subtle and suggestive hints. The other argument advanced to me by more liberal and forward-looking journalists ran something like this: The trouble is that the people at large have too high hopes. While they are not too optimistic about the freedom in human contacts, exchange of ideas and information, they expect, nevertheless, a marked improvement. They also expect the scope of the exchange of information to grow. This, of course, conflicted sharply with the attitude of some people in the Party who maintained that to relax controls too far would be to court the danger of conflicting views and opinions. In this assessment this would threaten the existing system.

Some limits on free exchange of information and on freedom of mass media must, according to them, be imposed although these were resented by at least some journalists I met.
The officials argued that some foreign broadcasts are influencing public opinion in Poland and they resented it, since, as
they said, "This is our job."

Everyone can listen to foreign Polish-speaking radio stations, but in the last two years before 1976 more and more
people who listened to foreign broadcasts, and particularly
those who wrote to foreign broadcasting organizations, were
interviewed by the security police and even cautioned. Foreign communist newspapers are available in Poland to anybody
who wants to read them, but they are most unrepresentative of
the public opinion in foreign countries, except perhaps Italy
and France where the Communist parties represent a strong
force. Other newspapers, like Le Monde, the London Times,
the Guardian, the Herald Tribune, and German and Italian
newspapers, could be bought in kiosks in the hotels where the
foreign guests were staying or read in the university libraries
and in international press reading rooms. Access to them is
therefore very limited. For instance, in one of the most
fashionable hotels in Warsaw, I could not obtain a copy of the
London Times since the whole supply of English newspapers
amounted to only five copies. Besides, the censors block
wider - or even any - circulation of any product of the Western press if it contains criticism of the Soviet Union or is
otherwise ideologically unacceptable. The official bulletin "S"
of the Central Customs Office in Warsaw (which has reached
the West, having been released on February 28, 1976, after
the Helsinki agreement)(110), marked confidential, gave a list
of 488 periodicals denied entry into Poland. It also deals with
magnetic tapes and issues instructions concerning the prevention of the export of "materials that can serve purposes contrary to the interests" of the state. It mainly concerns the
outgoing flow of Polish writers' works which have been denied
by the censors publication in Poland and can be published
abroad.

Then, quite suddenly, the central censorship of the main
Party organ, Trybuna Ludu, and of the most interesting and
best-edited sociopolitical weekly, Polityka, were abolished in
April 1973. Polityka was known for many years for its more
provocative style, its courageous stand on several crucial
issues and sometimes its unorthodox assessments of events,
often going much further than Gierek in his statements.
Official sources described this measure as an experiment and
said that the responsibility for the content of the newspapers
lay with individual writers and editors.(111) Government or
military secrets were still subject to censorship. In the case
of Polityka, this created more problems than it solved. While
in the past some unorthodox articles could be subtly slipped

through the censors because of the latter's witlessness and low
level of intelligence, now of course when the editor himself had
the ultimate responsibility, journalists had to avoid some sensitive subjects knowing that the responsibility ultimately lay with
them and not with the censor. The weekly, Polityka, took
advantage of this new elbow room on at least two occasions.
Once it published two lengthy articles on the life of the dis-
enfranchised aristocracy in today's Poland which presented a
generally sympathetic view.   On a second occasion, the paper
printed extensive interviews and articles on the situation in
some mining areas, and on frustration as well as dissatisfaction
among some miners.   The weekly was strongly attacked and
even condemned by most Party papers.   On one occasion even
Gierek intervened with the editor and on another, Polityka
responded somewhat contritely that the intended irony of the
article on aristocracy had not been clear enough.   Thus, the
journalists' no-man's-land created by the removal of censorship
of some publications was occupied by the Party.
     There was another channel of censorship: the constant
interference with particular articles and with some papers by
the Soviet ambassador and his staff.   Among the many specified taboos there was one which, to any outside observer,
seemed particularly childish.   Nothing even slightly critical
about anything Soviet must appear in the Polish media.   Thus,
as far as Polish journalism is concerned, there has never been
anything wrong at any time with what the Soviet Union has
been doing or will be doing: the Soviet Union is the best and
the greatest, the most infallible; it knows all the answers and
sets the example!   All this became nauseating at times.   Nowhere in the world, except in some fascist distatorships could
an ally, however strong and however politically unavoidable,
be so ideally and absolutely right in everything as the Soviet
Union has been in the Polish media.   This, of course, was not
the fault of Polish journalists, perhaps not even of the Party
leadership.   It stemmed from a Byzantine attitude on the part
of the Soviet leaders who would not tolerate any criticism, any
realistic and objective assessment of what they were doing if
this assessment did not agree with their official line.   Every
now and then, as for instance at the time of Brezhnev's visits
to Poland, the Polish press has engaged in an impressive
spreading of "Sovietomania."   This, as some sources explained
to me, was thought to be a sort of facade satisfying the demands of the "Soviet friends," a smoke screen behind which
Poles might hope to gain more elbow room for their own domestic or even foreign policies.
     Whatever the reasons, since about 1973, the principal
victim of Party policies has been the press, which has grown
increasingly gray, and with only a very few exceptions, was
no longer more interesting than that of other East European
countries. Polityka has nearly closed several times since the

lifting of official censorship. The paper has become an easy target for all its professional opponents who used any pretext to argue that the lack of censorship shows the true face of the editor and his "revisionist clique." The team of editors at Polityka have always tried to remember that the fundamental right of the press is to criticize and oppose, but then they were called "squalid." Criticize? From what standpoint? Criticism must be constructive.

This "constructive criticism" was a theory launched by Party propaganda experts which made it possible to criticize the minor symptoms but never the malady. Even in these circumstances, the team of Polityka managed to establish their position as "an independent" weekly within the existing context of ideological tightening up. But another popular daily paper in Warsaw, Zycie Warszawy, has, since the new editor, Rolinski, took over, become more dull with each passing day except for the foreign news coverage. Many of the best writers and journalists have left the paper. The editors of two of the liveliest weeklies were dismissed in 1975 for insufficient conformity. They were Gustaw Gottesman, managing editor of Literatura, and Krzysztof Toeplitz of the satirical magazine, Szpilki. On one occasion eight articles in one single issue of Literatura were censored in full. The charge against Gottesman was that he published too wide a variety of subjects currently fashionable in Western countries. It was noted that Literatura resisted pressures to print articles attacking the exiled Soviet writer, Solzhenitsyn. The magazine had also clashed with censors over its desire to reply to articles in a publication of the Academy of Sciences, purporting to give economic justification for antisemitism in prewar Poland. The Party apparatus contributed still further in 1975 to reducing the liveliness of the press when an article in the theoretical monthly of the Party, Nowe Drogi, by PB member Szydlak, in effect told the press that the Party did not need its advice.

The situation certainly deteriorated when Lukaszewicz was appointed secretary of the CC responsible for mass media and Rokoszewksi as head of this particular department in the CC. I have met some of their more prominent officials and I have seldom seen more conceited and arrogant people. As self-styled arbiters of news and views, they knew best what the people should know and should learn and how. It was not a journalist, still less an editor, but no less a person than the Party activist who was to be responsible for mass media, who was really the man to decide how and in what way public opinion should be shaped. For him the facts and the realities of life did not count. What was important for him were the Party directives. The press must march with its leader, the Party, and there is no alternative, one of them told me. A naive and ignorant reader of the present Polish press might

easily think that he lived in the healthiest, richest, most
important country in the world. But, of course, the Polish
readers were neither ignorant nor naive.(112) They were
more politically mature than many people in other countries.
They have their suspicions, they know how to read between
the lines, and what is most important, they see the discrepancy between their everyday life and the newspapers'
fairy tales.

The importance of the press as the main tool in brain-
washing the public, however inefficiently, has never been
underestimated by the Party. Slowly but steadily, everything
seemed to revert to normal after the heady post-December
days. Chairman of the Committee for Polish Radio and Television, Szczepanski, stated bluntly at a closed meeting of
Party activists: "Every press system depends on its mandatory
power. There is no independent press anywhere in the world.
In every political system, the press is an instrument of some
power and of some class command." What he conveniently
failed to say was that nowhere in the world, except in
totalitarian systems, is the press forced to express the views
of one single small minority political party. He conveniently
forgot to tell the activists that in a Western-style democracy
all views, ranging from Trotskyite to fascist, appear in print
and that sometimes antiestablishment ideas receive more
coverage in the media than those that conform - no matter
which political party or parties are in power at a given
moment.

The journalist in Poland and especially the editor may
"sin" either by commission or omission. It is, for instance, an
even worse mistake to forget to celebrate the anniversary of
the 1917 Great Revolution with the customary huge front-page
article than to write something sympathetic about Israel. On
the other hand, there are still very many "sinners" among
thousands of Polish journalists. They are certainly among the
most intelligent, knowledgeable, distinguished and honest
journalists I have met anywhere in the world. As journalists
and experts they could easily compare with the best brains in
the West. Some of them have an even wider vision and more
realistic assessment of the situation because they have lived
through so many pitfalls and because they worked for so many
years under a Communist party rule. They know what that
means and they know how the system and the conditions of life
could be improved.

Meanwhile the censorship, except in the two cases already
mentioned, has remained in full action, Helsinki or no Helsinki.
The internal documents of the Polish censorship, which have
reached the West,(113) reveal for everybody to see, that in
order to keep all distasteful or politically unacceptable subjects
out of the mass media, the Party has to issue list upon list of
absurdly detailed instructions and to employ a whole army of

bureaucrats (see section, "The Intellectuals: The Conscience of the Nation?" in this chapter). In Poland it is not easy for them to impose obligatory perception and uniformity of expression. They can expunge independent views from the media, but they cannot suppress them altogether. Even the self-censorship is being subtly eroded by an increasing number of people who cease to exercise it and are no longer subject to "double-think."(114) Both censors and censored alike must be perfectly clear in their own minds that this is a game. There is no indication in these documents of any belief that what is officially printed or broadcast has anything to do with the objective truth, or that what is cut out is cut out because it is false. The authors of the instructions know and assume that those they are addressing also know what the truth is. Poles do not believe what they are told by their official media. They do not have to, for they have other sources of information. They travel abroad massively and listen to foreign broadcasting stations. What is then the object of this exercise? The Party simply does not want certain facts to be officially disclosed. Both censors and censored "are peddling," as the London Times put it, "an ideology which has no hold over their own minds. They are salesmen who do not believe in their product."

Now what about journalists? Usually the editors themselves are the first censors, and they tend to be severe because they know they cannot risk their own safety before hostile censors, rivals, and Party bureaucrats. It is an instinct for survival. Moreover, they usually have their own political ambitions, they play their own cliques' little games; therefore a vast majority of them can be described as gamblers. I have come across this description very often. The censoring process initially starts with the author, or the journalist writing his story. If he has any honesty left, he will apply the rule which in his case says: sell three truths, squeezed among seven lies. The editor, reading the piece later, will spot this device immediately, but he will approve it, for such are the rules of the game. More often the author is not likely to bother with any subtle devices, preferring to meet the expectations of his bosses half-way.

Journalists in Poland have no illusions about the work they are doing. A journalist told me he has to lie and is constantly encouraged to do so. He does not read newspapers himself because he knows they are rubbish. He reads the bulletins instead. There are many different bulletins published by the official Polish Press Agency (PAP). The ones the journalist reads are secret, only for so-called "internal" use. But not even this bulletin gives all the information, the naked truth, although it is certainly much richer in information than the ordinary newspaper. The real source of true information for a journalist trying to work honestly for

his paper is bulletins issued by the monitoring service, which
cover the Polish transmissions of the many Western stations.
Here again, there is a sort of security clearance of the bulletins. The full bulletins carrying every word that was said
are circulated only to a very selective group of top editors as
well as to top Party members. Another much more diluted
bulletin, already censored by omitting delicate subjects and
more sharp comments is circulated much more widely. Very
many journalists, before they start their daily work, listen to
the BBC's early morning transmissions to learn exactly what is
going on in the world and what the foreign press is writing
about topical events.

The appalling thing about a Polish newspaper is its
language. The journalist's verbal gimmicks, the censor's
activities, the phoniness of Party jargon, have combined to
create a news sheet often divorced from reality, meaningless,
obscure and sometimes ridiculous. It proves George Orwell's
remark that "Clear thought is dangerous to orthodoxy." The
ever-present patriotic and ideological struggle, together with
the optimistic attitudes, made it impossible, even for the
weather forecasters, to write simply about the weather. The
weather reports sounded more like dispatches from the battlefield. There was always "winter's heavy invasion," which had
been "bravely counterattacked" by our "heavily armored snow-
men." But even here the typical Polish humor appeared occasionally. In once listened to the following weather forecast
warning listeners to: "Be careful, beware, strong eastern
winds are approaching tonight!"

Television and radio provide a chapter apart, particularly
since they have been taken over by the new chairman of the
Committee for Radio and Television, Maciej Szczepanski, the
former editor of the Party's main paper in Silesia, who was
for many years, in this capacity, a close associate of Gierek.
He certainly proved to be a tough and good administrator,
but, unfortunately, he had his own ideas about programs and
who should prepare them. His subordinates called him:
"Bloody Maciej." Having several times exhorted them to serve
the interests of the state, and having reinforced his words
with the threat of dismissals, he turned the television staff
cuts, ordered largely for economic reasons earlier in 1974, into
political purges that got rid of some 300 people. The purges
brought duller men to power. Among his "brighter" program
ideas was a directive that all the news and comments must be
based on Soviet Tass agency and PAP dispatches and assessments, and that the mass media must provide a reliable and
strong instrument to put over the policies of the Party. This
rule limiting the coverage to Tass and PAP was slightly
relaxed as the months went by because it proved not only
ridiculous but also impracticable.

One of the vice-chairmen of the Committee for Radio and Television, Szczepanski's assistant in charge of television, was known to brake hard on the more lively and sometimes controversial current-affairs programs. There were two particularly popular programs: "Monitor," edited and presented by the well-known commentator and television personality Karol Malcuzynski; and "Poland and the World," presented by the editor of Polityka, Mieczyslaw Rakowski. Unfortunately, as it was explained to me, there was no room in these programs for Western correspondents to take part and freely discuss topical problems. Only occasionally were journalists from socialist countries "admitted." When I raised the same problem of coverage of foreign news in domestic radio service, I was assured that they would very much like to use Western correspondents in their current-affairs programs, but "there were technical and editorial difficulties" preventing them from doing so. There certainly must have been editorial difficulties because in this day and age there were no technical difficulties to prevent anyone talking on the line to a Western correspondent in a foreign capital.

The mechanism of censorship in a broadcasting department was described to me in detail. The editor responsible, for instance, for the youth column, commissions a talk from one of the subeditors. He has to read the text, correct it according to the Party line, and sign it. Then it would be reread and signed by the following people in this order: the inspector of programs, the director of the radio station, and finally the censor. From the censor it comes back to the director, who has to initial it again and then it might go on the air. As a rule there were no live programs broadcast except sporting events and some official gatherings, if they are covered by "reliable" commentators. Everything is recorded and edited, sometimes even the news bulletins. So much for the topical and up-to-date coverage of events, not only in Poland, but also in the world.

Watching news bulletins on Polish television or listening to them on the radio must stretch the patience of the audience to the extreme. When Gierek went to Washington at the invitation of President Ford, a visit which was described and regarded as most important and prestigious, the television news headlined its bulletins with reports from a selected number of factories in Poland describing working conditions, the production pledges, etc. But, when in the autumn of 1976, Soviet Defense Minister Ustinov paid a visit to Warsaw (one of the several Soviet ministerial visits in Poland), half of the television news bulletin at the very beginning was taken up by Gierek's and Ustinov's speeches, by the decoration of the Soviet minister with a Polish order, and by the ceremonial departure of the Soviet delegation. Seldom have I seen a more boring coverage of current affairs in a news bulletin, nor one more out of touch with events in the world.

In 1971, Gierek had said two things to the representatives of the mass media - that it was impossible to expect
all people in Poland to have identical opinions and to "beware
of exaggerated optimism." If only the Party would have followed these two clear-cut and certainly correct statements, the
mass media could have been much livelier, much more representative of various opinions in the country and much more
efficient in transmitting the objectives of the leadership and in
persuading the people that even if some of the things are bad
or incorrect, there are some others worth praising and certainly useful and beneficial. This could even have been squeezed
into the framework of the imperatives of the system, and it
would certainly have shown that the Party, while officially the
"leading force," is not infallible and makes more mistakes than
many other political parties. But it would have also shown
that the Party lags behind the times, and is unable to readjust
itself to the changes not only in the world but in the country
itself.

THE YOUNG GENERATION: THE FUTURE OF THE NATION?

The Youth of a Nation are the Trustees of Posterity.

Disraeli in Sybil.

A man that is young in years may be old in hours,
if he have lost no time.

Sir Francis Bacon in Of Youth

When Gierek took over in December 1970, five youth organizations existed semi-independently, at least organizational-
ly - a unique phenomenon in Eastern Europe. The Socialist
Youth Union and Military Youth Circles were strictly under
Party supervision as training ground for future Party activists
and leaders. The Polish Rural Youth Union, associated with
the Peasants Party was active mostly in the countryside. The
Polish Scouts Association, with a long prewar tradition was
by and large a typical scouts' movement. Finally the Polish
Students Association, the only more or less nonpolitical organization, embraced almost all the students at higher
education schools, cared for their well-being, social conditions,
for their grants, accommodation, etc. In all the academic
centers in the country, students' clubs, theaters, cabarets
and discussion circles abounded, all organized by the Association. Students gathered together in their clubs to
discuss the problems, to make arrangements for future activities, drinking Coca Cola or lemonade, tea or coffee. In the
Baltic resort of Sopot, particularly during the summer months,
pop groups performed nonstop in a cafe filled to capacity. In

Wroclaw in southwestern Poland, I came across an open-air pop
concert given in the city square with thousands of young
people milling around listening and dancing. There was in the
middle of 1971 an atmosphere of cautious optimism among many
of the leaders of youth organizations and ordinary students
whom I met in their clubs in Gdansk, Szczecin, Krakow,
Warsaw and Lublin.

In the coastal university cities, for instance, the students
seemed to be looking forward to a much wider range of reforms
in political terms.   The electoral law in Sejm elections had to
be "radically changed" said one of them.   The people were
represented by "appointed delegates" whom nobody has elected.
Enough of that, they argued: we want to be truly elected,
because we have better solutions to offer than the ones we
have seen so far.   Without revolution, but in a process of
quiet and calm evolution, they wanted to be admitted to really
responsible positions on a wider front.

Very cautiously, but nevertheless steadily, they pressed
throughout the country for the removal from the universities
and other high schools of special Socialist Youth Union and
Rural Youth Union student circles.   So far, these "political"
bodies had no alternative but to cooperate with the Polish
Students Association.   The association should, however, it was
suggested to me, be the only mass student representation
since they genuinely defended students' interests without
political undertones.   "One cannot and should not live by
politics and ideology all the time," a student leader on the
coast told me.

This was, in 1971, a growing consumer-oriented young
generation.   They wanted to learn, then to get a good job,
and earn money to improve their living standards.   But, at
the same time, they were undertaking a lot of voluntary
charity work during their studies.   Thus a materialistic and
sometimes cynical approach was interspersed with idealism and
an urge to help people who could not help themselves.   In
Krakow, for instance, the students organized a cooperative
successfully filling the gap for various urgently needed services such as, television and radio repairs, agricultural
machinery repairs, garage services, etc.

Students complained of difficulties in finding work for
which they were qualified.   There was less difficulty for
science graduates, but arts graduates were being left out in
the cold.   Very often a graduate historian or philosopher
would be sent to work behind the counter in a public library.
There was still no chance of an equal start for them in state
and economic administration since, as many students told me,
there were too many of the "old guard" who should have
retired long ago.

Within the universities, students insisted on full participation in preparing programs of study and within the Polish

Students Association insisted on having a say on all economic and social problems affecting students. While they were prepared to be very active and waited to be accepted as such the authorities were reluctant. When I spoke to rectors and prorectors at some universities, they maintained that students representatives in various departmental councils were passive, did not show initiative, and did not make constructive suggestions. The explanation of these two contradictory attitudes might lie in the fact that the rectors were representing the establishment and were talking in terms of the accepted Party line.

In the ancient, royal city of Krakow, which miraculously escaped the damage in the last war and is still spared the devastation of uncontrolled car traffic, one finds among the Gothic basements in the Old Market Square, youth and student clubs as well as many renowned and popular cafes such as "Under the Lizard's" or the "Michalikowa Cave." Just above the Lizard's club were the editorial offices of a student newspaper, Student. Here a new type of collective voice of the young generation was emerging in 1971-1972, saying things which were both new to postwar Poland and of considerable potential significance for Eastern Europe.(115) These were students who new something of the West and expressed themselves, students who were unconvinced at what they saw, yet who believed that political change was possible within their own society. They neither despaired nor did they want to act in what they saw as the futilely romantic way of Czechoslovakia, Paris or even Warsaw 1968, which had all proved counterproductive. Poland, according to them, needed reform, not revolution; but, unlike the politically switched-off students in some other Eastern European countries, those in Krakow believed reform is possible.

The movement's voice was Student, the fortnightly journal of the Polish Students Association which shortly became a weekly by popular demand and with official blessing. Because of its bold articles it won a wide following in spite of its small circulation - which was the main reason why Student has been allowed to print articles attacking the regime's excesses in 1968, for example, or deploring the effects of overly rigid censorship of Polish literature, articles which could not have appeared elsewhere. "We want to speak openly," they said to me, "we reject the cat-and-mouse games of the past and the patronizing attitude the authorities had toward youth." What they were trying to create was an intriguing synthesis: the Christian ethics in a socialist context. Their attitude certainly represented, in 1971-1972, a commitment to change, to radical improvements, and, consequently, to a long-range optimism that was barely conceivable at the end of the dark year of 1968.

By 1972, even some articles in the Party newspapers were
making it clear that not everything was as rosy as the Party
would have wished in the student and academic circles.   As
one author of an article in the Zycie Warszawy observed,
university students were more and more inclined to "average
performance," outstanding work being recompensed neither
during their studies or later in their professional careers.
Student grants, choice of employment, and starting salaries
were the same for all, irrespective of academic achievements.
The paper called for more flexible diversified criteria capable
of spurring students to more efficient and more independent
work and the necessary steps ought to be discussed, not only
with representatives of youth organizations, but with what the
paper called "informal leaders of student groups" as well.
    A study published in winter 1972 provided an illuminating
picture of young Poles' hopes and ambitions.   The generally
expressed ambition was to found a family as a haven of love –
a harmonious joint life of a married couple and a source of joy
from their children.   On the average one out of every four
respondents selected this family-orientated goal as superior to
the others available.   Other respondents selected, in statistical
order, the following social values as their main goal and inspiration: 1)   a desire to obtain a college degree;   2)   a
response to various aspects of social prestige mainly apparent
in social or political activity;   3)   a desire to become highly
qualified and to obtain an outstanding position in one's profession; and   4) fascination with material wealth combined with a
strong desire for security, guaranteed by a well-furnished
house and an easy life.   Each of the above groups included
"family happiness" as an accompanying value.
    Some of the officials, Party activists, and journalists I
spoke to in post-December months were both apprehensive and
skeptical about what the future held for Polish youth.   After
the "blow" in 1968, there was no more political discussion,
exchange of ideas, nor any arguing of new revolutionary
solutions, among the students.   They were, on the whole,
passive and dormant, and this was deeply regretted.   Others
maintained that qualified and enterprising young people should
certainly be admitted to responsible posts in the Party, in the
state, and in the economic administration.   But, as one
sensible and logical member of the CC told me, there unfortunately remained a great danger that once they were in the
Party, and came face-to-face with a "blank wall" of bureaucracy and routine, they might readjust to the existing passive
attitude of the Party apparatus.   Others complained that young
people were now taking everything for granted because they
had not lived through the most difficult years, and therefore
they expected much more from the state than the state could
offer.   But the main worry of those who were thinking strictly
in Party terms was summarized by one Party journalist who

said: "I am afraid that the Party will not be able to find a common language with the present young generation." Most students I met agreed that the new leaders were more human and had sometimes an informal, direct approach, but that infinitely more had still to be done.

From the very beginning of his leadership, Gierek had emphasized the role of the young people and the hopes which he attached to their commitment and involvement. In his speech to the eighth-Party plenum in February 1971, Frelek, head of a CC department, said, "The problem of the younger generation is the key issue." Referring to the March 1968 student revolt and to the December 1970 workers' rebellion he stressed that "These two events have only one point in common: in both cases, young people appeared in the streets. In March exclusively, in December mainly. This is a matter for deep thought."(116) In December 1970 students as a body virtually "abstained" from the riots after what hit them in 1968. The new five-year plan included specific indications of concern for the younger generation, e.g., assurances of full employment, increased housing possibilities, better living standards. Gierek also met student representatives and assured them that "there were no problems on which it would not be possible to find a common language with the Party and government leadership."(117)

In over 25 years of communism, the Party had never managed to gain the support of succeeding young generations. This was deeply worrying, for the Party knew that when inspired by hope for a more democratic way of life, the young people, and particularly the students, represented a real political force. This was the case in 1956 and in 1968. Gierek was aware that if the Party had ambitious plans for transforming Poland it needed the cooperation of the young.(118) At the national Youth Rally held in Lodz in July 1972, Gierek called on the young people to speed up the rate of the country's economic development, a program which, "we share with you in mind." Its implementation, he said, depended greatly on the young people's work and their ideological attitude.

But at the same time he emphasized that a reorganization of the youth movement would be required to work out the best possible scheme for the future ideological development of young people. The significant word in Gierek's speech was the "integration" of the youth organizations. The question remained: What kind of integration? In a television program, "Citizens' Tribune," CC secretary Olszowski, while answering a question put to him, suggested that "the existence of a single united youth organization would guarantee a more efficient representation of the young people's interests. It would also make it easier to define the main lines of ideological indoctrination."

The long-promised and oft-postponed plenum of the CC on youth problems assembled finally late in September 1972.

There was certainly a conflict of attitudes within the Party
between those who advocated, as Olszowski did, a comprehensive integration of all existing youth organizations into a
single mass organization, modeled on the Soviet Konsomol and
on the former discredited pre-1956 Polish Youth Union, and
those who opposed such a return to dogmatic schemes. Moreover the planned merger aroused unexpectedly strong opposition among existing youth organizations, which enjoyed a
long tradition of strong support in certain groups of society
such as the Boy Scouts, the Students Association and the
Rural Youth Union.(119)   While the top leaders of these organizations were more or less Party nominees, some of the
activists in the lower ranks and certainly in the rank and file
strongly opposed the loss of what was still left of their organizational independence.   The Party had, indeed, every
reason to feel uneasy about the youth activists' unwillingness
to give up their semi-independence on the one hand, and
about the younger generation's noncommittal attitudes, common
to students and workers alike.   Opinion polls published in
October 1972 by two papers (120) clearly showed that noncommittal and noninvolvement attitudes prevailed among
students and young workers and that there was a lack of any
great ideals, including the Party program, capable of inspiring
them.   The problem, therefore, which faced the Party was one
of inducing the younger generation to feel committed to the
tasks assigned them by the Party.

The CC plenum on youth in November 1972 produced a
bulky document with a modest content, further diluted by the
dogmatic verbosity typical of a Party pronouncement, and very
often with some childishly naive statements.   In short, it
called for a radical modernization of teaching methods, for
solidarity and harmonious cooperation among the family, the
schools, the youth organizations, the army, the factories, and
the mass media.   A special task in this process was assigned
to youth organizations, which "were important links in the
ideological-educational front," and "the Party's allies and
helpers."(121)   The theses produced by the plenum showed a
serious attempt on the part of the leadership to curb the
unruly, refractory element which became the postwar generation, and to set it to work for its socialist fatherland.   This
would be achieved by persuasion, including a considerable
increase in ideological work aimed at the "immunization of the
young people against ideological pollution from the West."   The
only concrete suggestion made at the plenum was that there
should be a federation of youth organizations as a basic
concept and a uniform organization of all university youth.

There was significant student unrest in Warsaw during
the week preceding the plenum on youth, when demonstrations
were held(122) in protest against this proposed swallowing up
of the Polish Students Association by its tougher counterpart,

the Socialist Youth Union. After the plenum, according to the Warsaw students' paper, ITD, stormy discussions took place throughout the academic world, while petitions in favor of maintaining the present form of the association were being studied and demonstrations organized. The discussions revealed substantial divergences of opinion among the students and added to the general disorientation. A girl student from Warsaw's Higher School of Planning and Statistics admitted openly that what they feared most was that the "fine words" used by the apostles of integration would prove empty. In addition most Catholic students had serious misgivings lest the idea interfered with their religious beliefs. Finally, the students appeared to be emphasizing their movement's achievements in intra-organizational democracy which, they said, should "on no account be curtailed."

The meeting of Warsaw University students passed a resolution(123) in which the students vigoruously protested against the regime's methods of suppressing student criticism of the merger, and against "depicting the views of youth organization officials as the authentic voice of student opinion." The resolution called for a student organization "based on trade union principles," dedicated primarily to the protection of students' social and cultural interests, and for a public student referendum on the question, following open discussion in all academic institutions throughout the country.

The Party leadership was well aware of the ferment in the student community, and was prepared to do anything in its power to avoid a direct confrontation. The congress of the Polish Students Association, which was to lead to the merger, was convoked during the vacations, when many students were with their families and away from Warsaw; it coincided with the coming into force of the new regulations on improved government grants for students. This timing, obviously designed to placate the students, was reinforced by repeated insistance on the new organizations' ambition to grant students more say in matters concerning their schools, and to make them partners and subjects rather than objects of education. But the fact remained that the diverse, pluralistic character of the student movement in post-1956 Poland, which was unknown elsewhere in Eastern Europe, had now come to an end. What started on March 26 in Warsaw as the eighth congress of the Polish Students Association, became just a few hours later a congress of Polish students, and closed on March 28, 1973 as the first congress of the Socialist Union of Polish Students. This new organization consisted of the former Polish Students Association, as well as of the Socialist Youth Union and Rural Youth Union University circles. Just before this transformation of the generally independent Polish Students Association, two other youth organizations, namely the Rural Youth Union and the Military Youth Circles, also convened extraordinary con-

gresses and added the "socialist" adjective to their respective
names.

In April 1973, the presidium members of the five youth
organizations(124), meeting in Warsaw, finally created what
was called the Federation of Socialist Unions of Polish Youth
and signed a constitutional document.   This umbrella organization represented a decisive step on the road toward the
long-heralded integration of the Polish youth movement - in
other words the destruction of whatever remained of the particular organizational and traditional character of these organizations.

An interesting insight into the attitudes of the young
people at the end of 1975 after all the mergers, integration
and addition of "socialist" adjectives was given by Gierek
himself, at a youth rally in Koszalin on the Baltic coast.   He
appealed to Poland's youth to abandon what he called their
"barren discontent" in favor of a "passion to transform
reality," and then dwelt extensively on the achievements of his
policies.   Realising, however, that he was speaking to an
impatient and suspicious audience, the Party leader added:

> Human expectations and hopes always grow
> faster than the possibility of realizing them.   This
> human characteristic has its good and bad points.
> When it produces creative anxiety and encourages
> greater efforts to carry through new and ambitious
> tasks, it is the driving force of progress.   But
> when it leads to barren discontent and to demands
> that cannot be justified by its own work it becomes
> a hindrance to any society.

This was a realistic statement which could be accepted by
anybody and certainly by the young people who were indeed
showing this creative anxiety and wanted "greater efforts" -
but without the ideological and political supervision of the
Party.   Symptoms of this barren discontent Gierek said,
should be energetically opposed and he told his audience that
their "critical attitude" should be exchanged for a passion to
transform reality by perseverance and honest work.   Here
again he touched upon a very delicate point; there has always
been a critical attitude among the young as well as a passion
to transform reality in the sense of improving and making the
system more efficient and more humane.

Judging from past experience in post-war Poland re-
structurings involving names and organizational methods would
not change the substance.   The results of an opinion poll
published in Warsaw in 1976 clearly demonstrated that these
young people born and educated in a socialist state still
thought and behaved much like their parents, and remained
practically untouched by the regime's repeated appeals that

they "rally round the Party's program." In the weekly, Polityka, Professor Stefan Nowak of Warsaw University's Institute of Sociology concluded that the "committed attitudes" and enthusiastic appraisal of the Party's bold socioeconomic program remained but wishful thinking. Asked about what they valued most in life, they listed "love and a happy family" in first place (90 percent); then "good relations with friends" (60 percent-80 percent) within small informal groups; and an interesting job which provided personal satisfaction and a good standing in life. Asked what a good political system could be like they listed, in this order, the following points: 1) equal opportunities for all, irrespective of social origins; 2) freedom of speech and a right to express differing opinions; 3) all citizens together determining government policies; and 4) economic efficiency. The problem was made even more acute by the fact that it affected more than half of the country's total population - 52.9 percent of all Poles are under 30 years of age.

In 1976 some journalists and a Party official put the problem to me in a nutshell: the Party has lost the young generation; despite continuing efforts at indoctrination in the schools and at the universities the young generation seek other ideals. They were still prepared to listen to Gierek - a student told me - but only if he talked sense. If he succeeds in rationalizing and modernizing the country's economy and getting rid of dead wood and bureaucracy he still might have an honored place in Poland's history. For the time being, said another student in Warsaw, we are not rebelling against Gierek, we are rebelling against the order established by the Party and to a very great extent Gierek seems to many of us to be the prisoner of the Party. It may be argued whether this assessment of the Polish leader was justified or not, but there was no doubt that they were highly cynical about politicians:

> This self-perpetuating establishment trying to enforce on all of us the mythical, so-called leading role of the Party. We have to push them as far as possible. We know there are certain limits imposed by the Soviet Union but we are sure that there is quite a wide scope of freedom which is unused because of the stubborness and stupidity of some Party leaders.

Of course, as in so many countries, there are the problems of alcoholism (particularly in some small towns), drugs, vandalism and crime. But by and large in Poland these are on a small scale, except alcoholism. Of course, these young Poles born after the war take much for granted. They do not have the memories of the tragic days in the

forties or even the fifties, but they have already lived
through 1968 (see Introduction) and 1970. They are hoping
that the system can be restructured, renovated, and improved. Some of them are convinced that Gierek could do it if
he were not hampered by the Party and some hard-liners in
Moscow. But most of them think they, themselves, can change
the system once they are in key positions in the country.

What impressed me most when talking to students in 1976
was the freshness of their approach, their harsh assessment of
the Party apparatus, their hatred of bureaucracy, and the
rejection of the overbearing control by the Party. "Gierek's
vision of a second Poland," a student in Warsaw told me, "is
most attractive, and certainly realizable if it were not for the
fact that all this was strictly related to some ideological com-
mitments which we are unable and unwilling to accept." "Don't
you think," I asked, "that in view of the geopolitical situation
of Poland, some sort of ideological facade, if it is a facade, is
absolutely essential?" "Yes," came the answer, "but how long
can you live behind a facade? How long can you apply
double-think and double-talk?"

In the past the imperatives of revolutionary transitions
provided the regime with useful excuses for almost everything
from show trials to economic shortages and censorship. But
now new generations of Poles are growing, who are neither
impressed nor frightened by all this. They now demand what
the system used to promise in the "golden future"(125) and
they want more of it every day. There is this ever greater
yearning for a qualitatively different way of life.(126) The
question, of course, is: Who is best equipped to understand
such new aspirations? It is surely time for the generation of
old "apparatchiks" and civil servants as well as for the middle-
aged former Polish Youth Association generation to make way
for young graduates bursting with bright modern ideas. The
take-over is inevitable, and in terms of the vitality of the
country it is fully justified. Judging by the quality of the
young people, it is also most hopeful.

But the problem which present-day Poland is facing is
that of the successors to the present young generation.
These children now, and young men and women within the
next few years, could be still more rebellious. The danger is
that while they are going to have a considerable impact on the
situation in the next decade, they may not be fully aware of
the limits which cannot be overstepped. On the other hand,
the world is changing constantly and fast, and in the next
decade or so the political realities in Eastern Europe and
particularly in Poland might create opportunities for coming
generations to fulfill their hopes and to change the face of the
country. So far, after over 30 years of socialist Poland, ruled
by the Communist party, there is no evidence that the en-
forced communist ideology has left any indelible mark on the
young people.

THE ECONOMIC MIRACLE

> In economics all roads lead to Socialism, though
> in nine cases out of ten, so far, the economist
> does not recognise his destination.
>
> George Bernard Shaw in "Unsocial Socialist"

When Gierek took over in 1970, Poland had the lowest
rate of development of any country in the Soviet orbit. The
main thrust of his economic policy was to link industrial development, economic modernization, and up-to-date technological
know-how with a steady improvement in the population's
standard of living. This reversed an earlier policy of
economic growth and priorities in which a policy of compulsory
austerity had lain the heavy burden of the nation's economic
growth on the Polish consumer. The trauma of 1970 was
continually seen as the touchstone of economic policies and
decisions. The only difference was that Gierek's leadership
endeavored to make a virtue of necessity by wholeheartedly
embracing an approach to economic development which delivered
the goods and promised further consumer and social benefits.
It was a high risk since Gierek's leadership had mort-
gaged its own political legitimacy and the country's economic
future as well, including her national resources and future
industrial potential(127), not only because of the growth based
on credit but also because of several cooperation agreements
and joint ventures mostly with Western firms (see Chapter 3).
The boom, Gierek's "economic miracle," started almost from the
very beginning of his leadership.

Industrial Development

Touring Poland during those five years I was struck by the
look of the country as a giant construction site, with new
apartment blocks, modern coal mines, new factories (mainly
imported from the West), and roads being built everywhere.
The cities buzzed with Polish-made cars, new residential blocks
edged gradually out into the countryside. There were some
other remarkable successes. In 1972, 96 percent of new
investment projects were completed on time, after the government had introduced a special bonus system for completion
of investments within their planned time limit. But this unprecedented success was followed by a severe setback in the
commissioning of new plants and their achieving full production
capacity. Projects that used to take five or ten years were
now completed in two or three, like the Katowice steel works,
or the Trasa Lazienkowska (an urban highway cutting through

the center of Warsaw). The newly build and most modern northern port of Gdansk has one of the most up-to-date unloading facilities in the world.(128) Everywhere I went during those five years in Poland, I found great pride in what was being achieved, a high degree of expectation that the economic future of the country would be brighter still.

While the average Poles "have never had it so good" their starting point in 1970 was extremely low. They were among the lowest paid in the whole communist orbit. In its economic policies the leadership had, therefore, to face what was described to me by an economist as a "consumers' imagination" on the part of the people. If socialism is really such a good and human system, one journalist and active communist told me, the people simply want to feel immediately and repeatedly in their everyday life the tangible gains and improvements brought by work and sacrifice. Twenty-five years of waiting and denial had been more than enough.

The sharply raised targets of the 1971-1975 plan were in most cases reached by the end of 1973 and 1974. The concessions made to the consumer were unprecedented in the Soviet bloc. Whereas in 1973 heavy industry had barely quickened its pace, registering a 10.4 percent annual growth rate over the previous three years (compared with 9.3 percent per annum over the previous five years) light and consumer industries were speeded up to a 10.7 percent growth rate compared with 6 percent before. This was all the more remarkable since for the first time in the Soviet sphere a Group B (consumer goods) rate of growth had exceeded that of a Group A (capital goods).(129) The net result was that by 1975 real earnings had increased by over 40 percent, more than double the planned figure, and investments also rose more than twice as rapidly as planned. Although Poles like to grumble, they had to admit that in five years they had become richer, better fed, clothed and housed, and more abundantly supplied with everything from Coca Cola to cars than they would have dreamed possible in 1970.(130)

Part of the answer lay in the shock which the Party suffered in that winter of discontent in 1970. Every local Party boss now knew that his headquarters could be set on fire by an angry crowd. The factory manager and the local planner both learned that a superior's blessing is not the only yardstick of success. Therefore, the leaders in Warsaw were aware that if tensions were allowed to reach the same pitch once more, the whole regime could disintegrate.(131) The overriding priority given to economic development was seen not only as a means of making people happier, but also as a way of asserting Poland's influence in the world, particularly in the Soviet-dominated world. A strike-ridden, economically backward Poland would carry little weight in international communist councils. But it was especially important that Polish national interests should be taken into account at a time when Moscow was engaged in a policy of detente and in a direct dialogue with Washington and Bonn.

With total investments nearly doubling during the five-year plan and far exceeding their targets, the industrial sector was now in high gear, widely modernized and backed by strong material resources. By 1976 half the machinery and equipment in industry had been built or imported less than five years before. In those five years nearly half the funds earmarked for investment were channeled into industry. As a result, industrial fixed assets increased by more than 60 percent and more than one-third of these fixed assets were modern machines and equipment. Half of these had been imported, mostly from the West. The average annual growth rate in industrial production (11 percent against the world average of 6 percent) put Poland's overall output in tenth place in the world.(132) Mechanization and automation, which in 1970 equalled 168,000 zlotys worth of fixed assets per worker, exceeded 270,000 in 1975. More than 50 percent of all licensed foreign purchases over the previous 30 years were effected during 1971-1975.(133)

Polish shipbuilding ran twelfth in the world, but second in the construction of fishing vessels and the country accounted for some 24 percent of the global output of sophisticated vessels like mother ships and factory trawlers. The car industry developed dynamically. In 1975 Poland produced 290,000 vehicles including 172,000 cars, made mostly under an Italian Fiat license. The country became Europe's sixth producer of building machines and massive production of tractors was launched.

Expansion and modernization of consumer industries was speeded up. Industrial production during the five-year plan went up by 73 percent but deliveries of consumer goods to the market went up by 79 percent. The share of light industry in overall production was 12.4 percent, including the textile industry's 7 percent, making it an important part of the Polish economy. In those five years, 74 new light industrial plants were built, and a further 130 modernized. The engineering and chemical industries, both important for technical progress, accounted for 40 percent of total industrial output, and continued to grow.

But success brought its cost as well. In trying to cure industrial problems the leadership had aimed at bigger material incentives. In 1972 almost ten and one-half million employees received generous wage increases, while sickness benefits and family allowances, retirement and disability pension for one million people were raised. Further increases for lowest paid workers and in social security benefits came in 1974. A huge growth in peasant incomes resulted from the concessions granted to the peasantry (see the next section of this chapter,

"Agriculture: Private or Socialized?"). All this, on top of the
five-year basic foodstuff price freeze and the initial package of
economic concessions granted by Gierek immediately after
December 1970, produced an excessive money supply.(134)
Most of the welcome measures were politically necessary,
socially justified and long overdue. Yet every year the actual
supply of money, in the form of purchasing power available to
the population, far exceeded the planned targets. Despite an
annual growth rate of about 11 percent in industrial output
and a very rapid increase in supplies of agricultural products
in the first three years, this huge increase in purchasing
power could not be absorbed by the goods and services earmarked for consumption.

The situation was aggravated by the inherent inability of
an economic system, which still remained in essence a command
economy, to adapt its industrial output to the evolving structure of effective demand. Moreover, producers were already
working at near capacity level and could not satisfy quickly
the unprecedented upsurge of mass demand for many consumer
durables which for years had been considered luxuries beyond
the reach of the masses. It was clear that the inability of
domestic industry to supply the type of goods for which the
suddenly more prosperous Poles were looking was seriously
aggravating the market disequilibrium and the problem of
oversupply of money, and was thus also contributing to the
growth of inflationary pressures. Imports were used in the
initial period as a stopgap measure to prop up the standard of
living. Once this policy had been introduced, however, imported goods soon became an integral part of consumption and
growth. But most of the hugely increased imports were mainly
used for productive investment purposes. This in turn
produced a growing foreign-trade deficit and increasing indebtedness, particularly to the West.

Nevertheless, the pace at which investment in industry
was put to work was relatively slow, partly because of shortages of construction materials and partly because of sheer
inefficiency. The average investment cycle in Poland was, as
a rule, much longer than in the West. Since 1971 there had
been an initial improvement but certainly not enough. While
selected priority investment projects were keeping more or less
to schedule, others, and particularly nonproductive investments, were tending to lag behind. Moreover, the leadership
was unable to put an end to the very widespread practice of
starting more investment projects than the available investment
resources warranted. Surprised at the ease with which they
could obtain loans, many managers went on an investment
spree, whatever the central planners might have resolved.
The net effect was that the country's available investment
resources were being used up at a much quicker rate than had
been foreseen in the national plan.

In the middle of the five-year plan it became imperative to reallocate the remaining investment resources to a small number of priority investment projects, and others were either abandoned for the time being, or work on them was substantially slowed down. On the other hand any trimming of the sails necessitated by the rapid development was bound to hit consumption, and, on the evidence of December 1970, Poles could react sharply to any downward adjustment of their economic situation. Because of the shorter investment cycle which should have been made possible through the introduction of foreign up-to-date technology, the planners calculated that many of the investment projects started at the beginning of the five-year plan would be paying themselves off by its end. However, this was not the case. In 1974 over 60 percent of these investments were unable to pay off their initial debts through exports, since domestic demand had, in the meantime, grown so strongly that production had to be diverted to the home market.

Another major problem was that of the diminishing labor force. The 1971-1975 period saw an increase of 1.8 million people. However, in the next five-year period, 1976-1980, the increase will be only 1.3 million and beyond 1980 even smaller than that. In order, therefore, to keep the same rate of growth, the process of production had to be not only modernized but investment cycles sharply speeded up. The worldwide inflation also began taking its toll on the Polish economy. In a sense the trade shift toward the West could not have taken place at a worse time (see Chapter 10). Poland was exposed to world inflation on two fronts: higher Western prices and at the same time increased cost of raw materials from the Soviet Union.

In this situation exports became of vital importance, but exports to the West grew very slowly. There were several underlying reasons. Labor productivity was still low and industry was plagued by absenteeism and alcoholism. The leadership initially worked on the principle that greater material rewards would automatically yield greater labor efficiency. Yet by 1975 it had become evident that larger material rewards could be counterproductive. In the longer term, a foreseeable drop in the supply of new labor meant that the economy would have to produce more per worker merely just to stand still. Perhaps Gierek's greatest mistake was to give away too much too soon, especially if he has to continue buying people's gratitude in the future.(135)

The symptoms of the workers' underlying alienation were treated as products of idleness. Gierek insisted on what he called a "social contract" between the people and the state. Its value was not just to reduce tendencies toward anarchy and instability but also to get the people to work harder, more efficiently and better. No leniency toward "laggards" was to be tolerated. Instead of measures designed to involve the workers more closely in decision making, penalties, controls, and a tightening of discipline were imposed or increased. Gierek's decision to neglect the fundamental problems of alienation and rely on a carrot-and-stick combination of controls and material incentives only encouraged the Polish workers in their extractive attitude toward the regime.

The leadership tried hard to change the spending pattern. A long-range housing program in 1972(136) envisaged a self-contained flat for every family by 1990, at least 7.3 million new dwellings. Private building over the next few years was expected to produce 30 percent of the planned total for the period and banks granted long-term loans covering up to 80 percent of the building costs. According to Gierek all dwellings "should increasingly become the personal property of citizens, fully supported by our socialist system and legally protected."(137) Here, then, was the incentive to save money not only to build private villas or flats, but also to purchase flats in housing cooperative systems. A Warsaw housing official, asked whether it was true that there were Poles with a million zlotys to spare to buy homes in cooperatives replied: "I can assure you that if I have five thousand apartments to offer for a million zlotys each, I would not need to look around for customers."(138) Another direction in which the leadership tried to divert purchasing power was to the popular small car, Fiat 126P, once it started rolling off the assembly lines in Silesia.

Despite all this, the Poles still spent almost half their income on foodstuffs, particularly on meat. Yet, in order to carry the growing costs for imports needed to sustain growth, supplies of meat were shifted from reserves on the home market to increased exports of Polish meat-based products. Food exports had risen sharply since 1972 and 55 percent of all production, mostly meat, was sold abroad by 1975. Popular anger in January and February 1975, incited by the gradual worsening of food supplies in general, finally broke out in March. Windows in several Warsaw stores were smashed.(139) People were lining up from midnight, or at the latest from 3 a.m., to get meat. In Warsaw, wall cartoons appeared showing Gierek wheeling a cart labeled "meat" to waiting aircraft, one of them bearing Soviet Aeroflot markings.(140) Interestingly enough, the cities in the sensitive areas along the Baltic coast and Silesia were, on the whole, quiet because meat supplies from army reserves were placed on the market at the right time. When shortages in Warsaw and Lodz did not receive such prompt attention, wildcat strikes occurred. Poles revelled in telling stories such as:

Question: Why is it impossible to find meat in our shops?"

Answer: "We are striving so fast toward communism that the poor animals can't manage to keep up with us!"

What the people now demanded was not a new policy but
simply the realization of the promises of the present one.
Admittedly the small-scale disturbances which occurred in 1975
were precisely what Gierek's entire strategy was designed to
avoid. Their recurrence after years of economic boom underlined the continually conditional nature of the leadership's
popular support.

To understand the situation in 1975 one has to take into
account the prolonged existence of three different markets: 1)
the official state market; 2) the free private market; and 3)
the foreign-currency market in special shops where, if you
had foreign currency you could immediately buy anything from
basic foods to cars and even apartments. The prices on the
free market were, of course, much higher than in the state
shops. While talking about the necessity of a flexible price
policy, the leadership, for political reasons, had maintained a
freeze on basic food prices for a full five years. Low prices
made certain items ridiculously cheap compared with the
people's stronger purchasing power and this in turn put
intolerable pressure on the suppliers. Worse still, the freeze
killed off some of the market forces that shape the economy
naturally.

Many economists suggested that prices be allowed to rise
all around and more rapidly if the momentum of the economic
upsurge was not to be stifled for lack of funds. In 1974 the
price of various services went up between 10 percent and 25
percent. Some new or even just slightly altered goods, re-
packaged and renamed, were introduced at substantially higher
prices - an interesting example of essentially Western marketing
techniques. All prices in restaurants went up by varying
margins. Internal air fares rose by 75 percent, alcohol by 40
percent, and gasoline rose by a massive 80 percent.

Against this wages were rising very fast, bringing the
average Pole a substantial increase in living standards, but
now and then wage increases were inevitably forgotten as
prices constantly went up and the Poles were quite prepared
to argue that they were worse off than before. While domestic
prices were rising, the international inflation was being spread
like some medieval plague together with its symptoms of
soaring import prices. Of course, prices for Polish exports
also rose with the inflationary tide, but not as strongly as did
those paid for the products Poland was importing. Although
this was helpful, it was neutralized by the far more rapid rise
in imports than exports.

Most of these problems and distortions were already
apparent when the balance sheet was drawn up at the national
Party conference in October 1973. The leadership was
surprised by the dynamic development it had itself initiated,
and which had gone much further than planned. It became
clear that only continued foreign credits seemed able to sustain

the broad investment policy already in gear and the rising consumers' expectations. The leadership was willing to take economic risks that would have been unimaginable a few years previously.(141) It would, however, be wrong to begrudge this search for prosperity to a people who have been through so much suffering and austerity. Gierek was gambling on his massive investment program bearing fruit before disenchantment became too deep.

The initial euphoria was certainly over by 1974 because, politically, the country had changed little since Gierek was swept to power and few of his promised reforms had materialized. The country had been through a social as well as a political revolution. But in spite of this, or perhaps because it could just as well have been achieved by a noncommunist government, the present leadership had undergone a perhaps inevitable alienation from the people, although Gierek was still more popular than anybody else and certainly well ahead of the Party itself which was regarded as an instrument hampering real progress. That meant that the leadership would have to pay an even higher price for the people's support.(142)

But the picture was not wholly black. A large proportion of imports consisted of modern equipment. In this sense and to a great extent the Polish leadership has been using its credits responsibly, applying them to productive investment which will eventually guarantee a return. The question, therefore, at the end of 1975 was not how far Poland would go into debt, but how soon the new capacity it was busy building would come into operation and even affect the trade picture and the standard of living.

Polish leaders were undoubtedly saying quiet prayers for Western capitalism's quick recovery. Poland was anxiously looking for an upturn in the Western economy to stimulate demand for its products and bring stronger trends in raw material prices. With more attention being paid to exports, the country was better equipped to take advantage of the world's trade boom than just five years ago, and the strong links it has forged with many Western countries since 1970 provided a good foundation to build on.(143)

Agriculture: Socialized or private?

> In agriculture, if you do one thing
> late, you are late in all things.
>
> Cato

In farming Poland remains the odd man out in Eastern Europe. The countryside is a patchwork of small fields grouped around villages and farmsteads, and not, as in other communist-ruled countries, an open expanse of collective and state farms. When Gierek took over in 1970, just over 84 percent of the land was privately owned by individual farmers and just under 16 percent remained in the socialized sector, which meant collective and state farms. At the end of 1975, the area owned privately by the farmers decreased to 81 percent and the area of the socialized sector increased to 19 percent.

By the end of 1975 private farms produced the bulk of agricultural output. They accounted for 85.6 percent of the output of the four basic grains, 91.7 percent of potatoes, 77.5 percent of the sugar beet crop, as well as 78.3 percent of cattle and 79.7 percent of the pig population.(144) In grain production the private farmers achieved better yields per hectare output than either collective or state farms.

Without fear of exaggeration, one can say that a real revolution has taken place in the Polish countryside, after forced collectivization was abandoned in October 1956 and most of the collective farms disappeared overnight. Traveling, many times, through Polish villages, I was impressed by their look of prosperity - new brick buildings, the prosperous appearance of the peasants and their womenfolk, near total electrification, television aerials in many villages, and quite a lot of motorized transport.

For a number of years, the Polish private farmers produced comparatively more than the fully collectivized agriculture in other East European countries, including the Soviet Union, although productivity was much lower when compared with Western standards. There were three main reasons for this: 1) fragmentation of the land, and no effort on the part of the authorities to consolidate the landholdings, 2) lack of mechanization, and a disastrous underinvestment in agriculture. In 1971 almost 65 percent of farms were only up to five hectares, over 24 percent were between 5 and 10 hectares, and only 11 percent of farms were over 20 hectares. For many years the agricultural machine industry was geared to produce huge combines which could be used only on large, state or collectivized farms and were, therefore, of no use to small farmsteads.

Agriculture has become a key political and economic factor. The peasants who had to deliver their products to the state could easily blackmail the authorities as they very subtly did on more than one occasion. They could reduce the deliveries and there was no possibility of forcing them to do otherwise since there were too many private farmers. Once they reduced the deliveries, industry would suffer and theoretically the whole industrial machine would grind to a halt.

From the very beginning Gierek showed a realistic awareness of agriculture's importance for raising living standards.
The point was, however, that a modern and efficient agriculture could only develop on large, fully mechanized farms.
A major feature of Gierek's policy has therefore been a drive
to modernize private farming, to raise farmers' morale and at
the same time in the long term to transform agriculture into a
state-run industry.   These seemed to be two contradicting
aims: the leadership therefore had to tread carefully, not only
because of the justified suspicions of farmers who had lived
through experiences of forced collectivization before 1956, but
also because private farms accounted for more of Poland's total
grain output than the proportion of total farmland that they
represented.   Besides, since Gierek wanted to raise the
people's living standards quickly, he had to make the sharp
increase of agricultural production the number-one priority
which would take precedence over the long-term plans of
socialization of agriculture.   At a time when food shortages
were prevalent and Polish agricultural exports earned much-
needed hard currency, the state could not afford the losses
that would result from a rapid transformation of agriculture.

In April 1971, Gierek launched what was described to me
as a historical agricultural policy, to become operative as of
January 1, 1972.   Compulsory deliveries of the main agricultural products to the state were abolished.   In these the
farmers hitherto had to sell to the state a considerable part of
their produce at prices below their own production costs.
This was a bitterly resented and unpopular form of "legalized
robbery" by the authorities of part of the farmers' output.
The supplies to the state were now to be based exclusively on
contractual agreements between the state and the individual
farmer with emphasis on long-term two- to three-year contracts, at prices which assured profitability and which were
several times raised by Gierek.   The rate of taxation became
lower, with special tax relief for those who wanted to expand
their farms or to put new areas under cultivation.   The
leadership was to encourage the individual farmers to buy more
land, and to increase their holdings up to 30 hectares by
granting credits to those who wanted to do so.   The scope of
the free-market policy, in the rural districts, has been
radically broadened and the average farmer has been given the
possibility of influencing the profitability of his farm.   For the
first time the farmers had been included in the national health
service and were also to receive social security benefits.   The
scheme(145) covered six and one-half million farmers and
members of their families who, hitherto, had not been covered
at all.   Finally, by an act of parliament, about one million
farmers who held and cultivated their farms without any valid
property rights now became legal and rightful owners.

On balance, during the first 18 months more was done to encourage greater profitability in agriculture than at any other period in the past. The measures gave the private peasants a greater sense of security and social standing and this plus the favorable weather conditions made a significant contribution toward a successful harvest in the next two years. It was a paradox that Gierek, an ex-miner, had introduced more sense into the agricultural economy in the space of a few months than Gomulka who was hailed by his contemporaries as the "healer of Polish agriculture," had introduced over 14 years.

The theory about self-sufficiency in grain production was abandoned. The new policy was based on simple commercial calculation, which pointed out the obvious advantages of importing grain for the purposes of animal breeding no matter whether such a move would result in an increase in the export of meat or whether it would merely make it possible to diminish imports of this commodity. The leadership succeeded first in stopping the decrease and then in stimulating animal production, and increasing its profitability. This provided incentives for specialized farming. Since the abolition of compulsory deliveries in 1972, about 100,000 individual farms have switched to specialized animal or plant production. There has also been evident a considerable awakening of farmers' interest in acquiring land. At the end of March 1972 about 35,000 applications for the acquisition of a total area of 120,000 hectares of land awaited legal approval.

As a result of all these changes, agricultural output has risen steadily by over five percent a year against three percent in the sixties. And in five years farmers' earnings have risen by 34 percent and costs only by 10 percent, making the agricultural sector one of the better paid, if also the hardest working sector, in Poland.(146) For the average Pole this has meant a rise of personal meat consumption from 53 kilos in 1970 to 70 kilos in 1975. But even this spectacular increase did not noticeably ease the meat supply situation. Meat shortages occurred many times and demand was rising enormously with the rise in personal incomes, spurred on by the very low price at which the meat was sold.

While helping private individual farming, Gierek has not given up strengthening the existing forms of socialized agriculture. In February 1972, the government began subsidizing between 40 and 80 percent of the cost of major investments in collective farms. The private farmer, although much more secure and profiting in many ways from the new policy, remained - as East European farmers always do - rather suspicious. When one of the weeklies interviewed a group of farmers, they expressed the fear that the officials: "will think up something again and slow down the good changes."(147)

In November 1974, Poland had just become the first East European country to adopt a long-term plan on food production which, it was said, would put a fatter chop and a brighter salad on everyone's plate. Agriculture was classed as a priority industry of national importance and the new program envisaged the doubling of agriculture output by 1990. Farmers received 20 percent more for their products in contractual arrangements with the state. Gierek assured them that they should not worry about possible collectivization.(148) But, at the same time, the CC plenum emphasized that the primary task of the Party's agricultural policy was the guaranteeing of a consistent increase in agricultural production and of social changes in agriculture along socialist directions.

How, then, were the authorities proceeding in trying to achieve these two contradicting aims? Despite their predominance in terms of area owned, the private farmers were enmeshed in the whole network of socialist economic planning. The shaping of the dynamics and the structure of agricultural production, investments and income of the peasant sector of farming were determined by state-made plans. Though theoretically independent, the peasants were subject to the indirect effects of planning, since the state regulated the supply of means of production, credits and machinery, purchased much of the farm products, influenced levels of incomes, and controlled the rate of introduction of technical progress.

One of Gierek's most important innovations included a speedup in the mechanization of agriculture. With Western help, production of tractors was to be increased from 55,000 a year to over 100,000 - a high target given that there were only 370,000 in the whole of Poland at the end of 1975. The hopeful sign here was the Ursus contract with the British firm of Massey-Ferguson-Perkins which was intended to help standardize production, and improve not only the export position, but also make for easier repairs and service to Polish users. As the current planning had anticipated that one and one-half million people would leave the agricultural sector within the next 15 years, while production of food was to double, the key to achieving both these targets lay in increased mechanization. Though the number of tractors in the individual sector was more or less equal to the number in the collective and state sectors put together, very few of them were new and reliable. Besides, the fact that state and collective sectors together represented only one-sixth of all agricultural land in Poland deflated the seemingly impressive number of tractors in the individual sector.

To coax private farmers into voluntarily relinquishing their holdings several schemes were set up. Given the advanced age of most farmers, the popular scheme was the exchange of a farm for a state pension and a right to continue living in the farmhouse if desired. The land then went to the state land fund. At the beginning of Gierek's era, farmers were encouraged to purchase land from the state land fund, but as the years went by, more and more obstacles were created by local Party officials to this scheme. Moreover, in 1974(149) at the CC plenum the state land fund was directed to pass the land taken over from poor and uneconomical farmers, to state and collective farms, agricultural circles and their agricultural cooperatives. As a result of these measures in the last few years one million hectares of agricultural land have been taken over by the state from the private owners. In the same period, over 170,000 owners either abandoned their farms or opted for a pension. But most of the land taken over by the state remained uncultivated because the socialized sector was unable to use the land properly.(150)

With the state's clear encouragement there was a distinct increase in the number of private farmers who engaged in some sort of cooperation. For instance, there were 32,000 teams of individual farmers who combined together for a specific purpose, such as crop production, livestock breeding, general farming, or for the joint use of agricultural machinery.(151)

Another curious phenomenon emerged. Rich farmers who acquired new land, sometimes up to 50 hectares, were now organizing themselves into agriculture voluntary cooperatives, which were in accordance with pronounced Party policies, but had in fact a completely different character. They were truly voluntary. These rich farmers formed cooperatives to ease the burden of work and to make more profit. The Party had nothing against this because they delivered the goods. However, some Party functionaries at local levels tried to persuade them not to buy but to rent land so that in the future it could be truly collectivized.

The last collective sector group are the agricultural circles, orginally formed to provide services and agricultural machines to the individual farmers. Instead the circles have been used to force individual farmers to conform to the authorities' rules and regulations, since nonobservance of these would totally deprive the peasant of the Circle's services, such as they were. During a difficult harvest in 1972, the Agricultural Circles managed to help the individual farmers to harvest only five percent of the total.

The private sector in Polish agriculture also included the so-called peasant-worker. About 32 percent (or 3 million) of all individual farm owners have a permanent secondary occupation outside agriculture.(152) In fact the peasant-worker has become a kind of "Gastarbeiter" of the great industrial and urban civilization, people who work hard for little pay but without whom railways and buses would not function, municipal sanitary facilities would flounder, and transportation and building would be seriously affected.

Another unique feature is the vegetable and flower growers, mainly around Warsaw but also in some other parts of the

country. They have large greenhouses and large plots of land
on which they grow vegetables and without them Warsaw, for
instance, would not be supplied with vegetables at all. They
have their own villas and cars and are regarded, quite
rightly, as millionaires.

In the socialized sector of the agriculture, the state
farms, which in 1975 accounted for just over 16 percent of
land, supply agriculture with production means, produce
selected seed grain, pedigree cattle and pedigree sheep, and
are fully supported by the state.

Although the state farms serve an economic and ideological end they have yet to prove their economic value.
Apart from the fact that individual incentives on a state farm
are weaker than on a private farm, economists have found(153)
that economies of scale do not always work. This is mainly
because much agriculture is still labor intensive and state
farmers lack hands, especially at harvest time. In 1972 and
1973 the army and young people were mobilized to help state
and collective farms with the harvest. By contrast, a private
farm can call on the loyalty of a whole family which will work
all night without extra pay.(154) The high cost of capital
related to labor means that simple private farms still compete
quite strongly with their giant mechanized counterparts in
terms of production cost. In addition, private farms are
almost totally self-supporting and cost the state very little,
whereas state farms make heavy demands on the budget for
credit finance, technology, and equipment.

The collective production farms (the most significant unit
of a collectivized agriculture) accounts in Poland for only 1.7
percent of land.(155) The importance that the state placed on
the collective sector as a spearhead of the "gradual socialization of agriculture" may be gauged from the rate of increase in
collective members' income in 1971-1975, which far exceeded
that of the industrial sector. In 1975, special measures were
introduced to extend the stake of the collective farms and the
supply of building materials and capital goods was increased.

The main problem is the lack of manpower in the countryside, in both the socialized and the private sectors. Hardly
anyone of the young generation wants to stay in the villages,
and the huge industrial investments provide ample opportunities for employment. By 1976 the number of those actually
working in agriculture had decreased dramatically to just
under 28 percent of all persons employed in the country. The
average age in the villages has risen to the point where now
nearly one-half of the population is about 50 years old, and
about 500,000 farms no longer have young people to whom the
private land can be passed on.(156) These demographic
changes and time will, the authorities hope, help them in the
socialist transformation of agriculture.

Yet, if agriculture is to assume a modern image and structure, it must go through a still further slimming process. And here mechanization is the answer. It is an essential factor in feeding an expanding population from ever-shrinking land and human resources devoted to agriculture. According to an agricultural economist I saw in Warsaw in 1976, there is a limited scope to the further development of the state sector, and he saw the future of Polish agriculture within the private sector, which, though socialized to a degree, was built more on an individual cooperative basis than on the doctrine of compulsory collectivization. According to Professor Manteuffel, the trisectoral structure of agriculture - individual-private, state-collective, and voluntary-cooperative - has to be accepted by the authorities.(157) If that is so the individual peasant should be treated more equitably - in the purchase of land and in their share of mechanized equipment. They are and will remain for many years to come the main suppliers of food.

The Raw Materials Base

The country's economic might still lies in raw materials and will do so for years to come. The dramatic changes in world energy scene since 1973 have to some extent favored Poland. The decision taken a long time ago to base as much energy production as possible on the country's vast coal reserves in Silesia has been completely vindicated. The output of 172 million tons of hard coal in 1974 put Poland in fourth place(158) in the world as coal producer after the United States, the Soviet Union and China, and as the second largest supplier of coal to the world market after the United States. Coal accounted for three-quarters of Poland's energy sources and 95 percent of all power and has even enabled the country to export electricity to other Comecon states, to Switzerland, Austria and West Germany. It was also the largest single foreign-trade commodity, accounting for some ten percent of foreign revenues, twice as much as shipbuilding. Poland was exporting an average 44 million tons of coal per annum. This commanding position followed years of intensive investment in the coal industry, and Polish mines are now among the most modern in the world.

Moreover the leadership launched a major program to open up new coal fields near Lublin in eastern Poland, with an expected capacity by 1990 of 250 million tons a year and with deposits estimated at 4,000 million tons. When the Soviet Union was unwilling to promise credits to help the exploitation of these deposits French and Italian initial credits were secured, linked with long-term deliveries of Polish coal. While the lack of domestic oil resources was a major weakness, the hunt for offshore fields in the Baltic was being intensified with the help of East Germany and the Soviet Union. Meanwhile, exploitation of lignite was also advancing with the aim of doubling the present output of 40 million tons by 1980.

Poland's second postwar bonanza was copper. The resources rate among the world's ten largest, but their geographical proximity to the world's major consumers makes Poland potentially more important than remote producers like Zambia, Chile and even the Soviet Union. In order to secure a major loan to develop its copper resources, in April 1975, Poland decided to shed light on its balance of payments by producing a prospectus giving full details of copper production and export plans. This striking departure from Comecon secretiveness secured Poland one of its biggest Eurocurrency loans for 240 million dollars.

Poland's other principal metal products are zinc and lead. Progress was also being made in the production of sulphur of which Poland is the second largest producer in the world after Canada.

Foreign Trade: The Instrument of Growth

A drastic change in foreign-trade patterns and reliance on mainly Western credits became absolutely necessary for a dynamic growth of the economy based on modern technology and at the same time for a rapid wage growth. The Comecon countries have all opened their trade doors to the West. What singled Poland out from the others was the extent to which Warsaw has pursued trade with the West in 1971-1975 and the dimensions of its present entanglement in the web of international trade, finance and politics. In this respect, Poland's activity was unprecedented by East European standards.

"Before 1970, foreign trade was just a little something we did on the side. Today our whole economy is geared to foreign trade, and will stay that way," an official told a Western correspondent in 1975.(159) This shift was a natural consequence of Gierek's drive to modernize the Polish economy as rapidly and along as broad a front as possible to make up for the gap of previous years. Up to 1975 Poland had imported several billion dollars worth of machinery, everything from complete chemical plants to fizzy drink machines. It has, for example, set up car and bus factories, greatly expanded tractor production and the plastic industry, and invested heavily in coal and copper. On the consumer goods side, large sums went into food processing, textiles and household items, as well as into the importing of some luxuries that would have been virtually unheard of before. Some of these purchases were made on the basis of industrial cooperation with Western companies accepting partial payment in production from the equipment they supplied. Part of it was covered by joint ventures, but Poland also had to draw heavily on Western credits, both government subsidized and commercial.

Industrial cooperation included several joint ventures. Foreign ownership of property, land and fixed assets was not allowed. But the key elements of joint ventures were: joint management of the plant, with foreign staff living in Poland; joint sales and marketing management; and manufacturing programs tied in with foreign plants. And, most important, a joint venture contract guaranteed(160) the transfer to the foreign partner of its share of profits and interest, and also the ultimate return of the overseas capital investment to that partner. In 1973 a deputy director of planning, Ostrowski, said: "We stick to the rule that we must take at least a 51 percent stake in a venture. But this does not mean that we cannot grant contracts which give full equality of management. In due course joint ventures comprised not only the manufacturing side, but also some experiments in the field of raw materials.

In 1971-1975 Poland signed long-term, ten-year, economic cooperation agreements with all the major Western industrial countries. Within these framework agreements between governments specific industrial cooperation transactions were signed between Polish state enterprises and Western firms. Poland, trying to boost its export earnings and to continue to finance a high volume of imports, supplied either raw materials or components for sale in world markets, large finished products like ocean-going ships or sulphur and sugar plants in which the country specialized.

For instance, Poland was now manufacturing the small economy Fiat 126P under Italian license in new factories in Silesia. The Italian company will eventually share with the Poles a turnover of 350 million dollars. This car, Poland's first move into bulk production, was also to be sold in third markets. In other motor vehicle ventures Poland started producing large buses made under license from the French Berliet group; was supplying components for the Swedish firm of Volvo; and began assembling parts of heavy dump trucks for the Swedish firm Kockum. The Ursus tractor plant awarded Massey-Ferguson-Perkins the main contract for the building of up to 100,000 tractors a year, partly for the foreign market. General Motors were considering manufacturing half-ton trucks in Lublin. A modern Polish oil refinery near the coast, which was linked with the new northern port in Gdansk, was built according to an Italian plan and used a large share of imported equipment. In 1973, for instance, altogether about 12 percent of engineering exports from Poland to the West came from joint manufacturing ventures.

Foreign trade reached the point where overall imports were increasing in 1973 at 28 percent a year and imports from Western countries at a staggering 60 percent while exports

were only rising at 15 percent. A fair proportion of the
increase represented inflation rather than volume. In 1970,
only one-third of Poland's imports came from outside Comecon.
In 1974 this figure had leapt to 57 percent including over 50
percent from Western industrialized countries. Foreign trade
with the developed Western countries in 1970-1974 rose 2.2
times faster than trade with Comecon.

But at the same time the foreign-trade deficit began to
increase at a very rapid rate. It amounted to about 283
million dollars in 1971 and at the end of 1974 Poland's trade
deficit with the West stood at 2,250 million dollars. By 1975
the Western share in Polish foreign trade exceeded well over
50 percent while in 1971 it was merely 25 percent. The export
side of trade became most vital. Although the growth in
exports to the Comecon countries kept pace with socialist
imports, exports to the West grew at only one-fifth of the rate
of imports from the developed capitalist world. Poland was
pinning its export hopes on raw materials: coal, lignite,
sulphur, copper, and on agricultural products like sugar, meat
and other foodstuffs. But industry was also to play a still
bigger role, in particular shipbuilding and ship repair services, building equipment and the expanding electronics industry. Besides this, factories bought on compensation deals
will also come on stream and supply Western companies with
products to work off loans and credits. The officials I talked
to stressed that by 1975 they want to maintain a high rate of
imports, but with the important condition that exports will go
up too. This policy was dictated partly by the obvious benefit
a country of Poland's size and structure can derive from
greater participation in the international division of labor, but
a more urgent consideration was the large debt accumulated
over the previous five years. Although Gierek's initial economic strategy was one of moderate growth to satisfy what was
then expected to be a moderate increase in demand, by 1973
this growth strategy had been transformed into one of
economic boom.

To maintain the pace of consumption and investment
growth Poland switched from being a country which shunned
debt, to becoming a major international borrower.

It all started with the granting of Soviet consumer credits
amounting to over 250 million dollars (including 100 million
dollars in hard currency) to put out the social fires after
December 1970. "We have to realize," wrote a prominent
publicist, Rakowski, "that, as from this moment, we are living
on credit."(161)

And so they were. Credit played a crucial part in
Poland's development strategy over the next five years. This
strategy was based on the following assumption: imports of
consumer goods obtained on credit, mainly from the West,
would help to establish market equilibrium. The large-scale

imports, again largely on credit, of technologically advanced
Western facilities, would greatly boost the productive capacity
of the Polish economy. As a result Polish industry and agriculture would, within a relatively short period, not only be
able to satisfy domestic demands, but would also increase
exports sufficiently to repay most of the original debts in
turn.

Poland's creditworthiness was first class at the time,
since Gierek's predecessor left very few outstanding loans to
be serviced. Furthermore, Poland's good material base, her
raw materials, cheap labor and the high technological level
which she would be able to attain as a result of modernization
were the reasons for continued Western willingness to extend
credits and go on cooperating with Warsaw. The climate of
detente made this cooperation relatively easy and Gierek's
active diplomacy in this area yielded impressive results. To
speed up this process, many large enterprises were allowed to
borrow hard currency and purchase facilities from the West
provided they repaid these loans by their export earnings.

Here are just a few examples to illustrate Gierek's
achievements in obtaining credit facilities. In 1975 Bonn
granted a credit of 1,000 million deutsche marks. Polish
imports from West Germany trebled between 1970 and 1972, and
doubled again in 1973. Washington contributed 1,300 million
dollars credit from various sources and agreed to increase
Polish-American trade from 700 million dollars annually to 2,000
million by the end of the decade. France opened various
credit lines amounting to 1,800 million dollars. In Polish-
British relations the Massey-Ferguson-Perkins co-production
agreement was worth Ł155 million; the British-built VPC
complex in Poland secured a loan of 265 million dollars and the
Export Credits Department had negotiated approximately Ł72
million worth of credits. The Polish-Belgian protocol in 1975
provided for Belgian imports of Polish coal at a rate of 0.5
hundred million tons per year in exchange for credit of 7,000
million Belgian francs. Austria advanced a credit of 3,000
million Austrian shillings and Spain of 185 million dollars. By
the end of 1975 Polish indebtedness to the West exceeded 8,000
million dollars.

To finance the rush of trade and modernization, Poland
has therefore been dipping even deeper into the barrel of
available Western credits. At one time, in 1975, the Western
estimates put the limits of Poland's creditworthiness at another
500 million dollars. But Western bankers observed(162) at the
same time that Warsaw had important raw material resources to
stake against additional borrowings and that its terms of trade
had improved appreciably in 1974. It was these reserves
which enabled Finance Minister Kisiel to assure the Chase
Manhatten Bank that Poland would continue to borrow from the
West "as long as we can." The limits of indebtedness should

be the value of exports, the Poles argued, and servicing the debts should not exceed 25 percent of that figure. Polish debt servicing was estimated in 1975 to be about 13.5 percent of its foreign debt. Since few of the debts have a grace period longer than five years and many have had less, repayment on the initial low-interest debts has already started(163), and the deadlines for the `later debts, which usually carried a significantly higher rate of interest, will come up during the five-year plan 1976-1980.

By contrast with the flow of foreign currency into Poland from the West, one of the problematic features of trade with the East was the absence of a fully convertible currency. This has led to a complex system of "tied trade exchanges" within Comecon - trade agreements by which imports of a certain commodity must be replaced by exports of a generally similar commodity. Complicating this procedure still further was the stipulation that "hard-currency products," that is, goods which by virtue of quality or demand could be sold on hard-currency markets, must be repaid with goods equally salable on Western markets, or else be paid for in hard currency itself.

After the substantial shift of Polish trade toward the West, Comecon's participation in Poland's world trade was diminished. In 1970 the Comecon countries commanded 62 percent of Poland's total trade, but the figure fell to only 47 percent in 1974. Throughout this period Poland's balance of payments within Comecon has improved significantly and with Bulgaria and the Soviet Union, Warsaw even enjoys a surplus. Because of the barter-type system within Comecon this surplus could not be transferred to balance the trade deficit with other countries.

One of the methods developed to ensure a balanced flow of imports and exports within Comecon are specialization and cooperation agreements in 1971-1974. Polish industry specialized in the production of metal working machines, ships and nautical equipment, machinery for agriculture, building, oil and gas industries, paper machines and complete installations for the production of sulphuric, nitric and phosphoric acids. Poland also took part in more than 150 bilateral agreements.

The increased prices for Comecon raw materials and particularly for Soviet raw materials made the call for transferable ruble convertibility and the agreements on the extraction and processing of raw materials all the more significant. Specially crucial was Soviet oil. Its price, revised early in 1975, was set on a sliding price scale linked to world prices and was due to achieve the level of world prices by 1978. In 1974 the Soviet Union supplied only 85 percent of all Polish oil requirements(164) and therefore deliveries from other, mostly Arab, countries amounted to three million tons, at full world prices. A year later Poland was already paying eight dollars per barrel for Soviet oil and in the long term the Soviet Union would supply only two-thirds of the country's oil needs, leaving about five million tons to be found elsewhere.(165) In 1975, Soviet oil prices rose on the average by 131 percent and raw material prices by 52 percent. To assist the other Comecon members in their trade with the Soviet Union the prices of agricultural goods from Eastern Europe, including Poland, were increased by an average of 28 percent, those of consumer products by 19 percent, and capital equipment by 15 percent. But it has been estimated that these price increases will help cover approximately only one-third of Eastern Europe's higher Soviet oil bill.(166) These increases will have to be made up for by increased "tied trade exchanges," which for Poland mean higher exports of coal, sulphur, copper and other raw materials to the Soviet Union instead of the Western hard-currency markets.

One of the conditions of Soviet raw material deliveries to Comecon countries including Poland is that the latter coinvest in extraction and production facilities of these commodities, to be repaid by Moscow through the deliveries of commodities over an extended period of time. The most important of these projects were the Orenburg and Polock pipeline projects.(167) In the Orenburg project six East European countries will each construct separate sections of the 2,750-kilometer-long pipeline which will carry natural gas from Orenburg in the southern Ural Mountains to the border of the Soviet Union. The Polock venture is a bilateral project, and the pipeline will transmit crude oil the 907 kilometers from Polock in Russia to Poland. As payment for its investments, Poland will be ensured deliveries of 2.8 million cubic meters of natural gas and one million tons of crude oil for 20 years. But Poland had also to contribute manpower needed for its part of construction - some 7,000 highly skilled workers, and adequate services for them as well. Given the increased prices for Soviet oil, the charge that the required pipeline investments constituted double payment for the same product, gained in stature.

There is, moreover, no security even in these arrangements. Several experts have predicted that by 1980 the Soviet Union itself may well face an energy gap that will compel it to import large amounts of crude oil and natural gas. Therefore, the future expansion of Soviet energy supplies may not grow as rapidly as demand, thus provoking sharp competition between domestic and foreign consumers for these resources. In this competition the economic profitability of energy exports to Eastern Europe, as opposed to exports to hard-currency areas, will be a critical variable influencing Soviet calculations of the optimum level of such exports. The Soviet Union is exporting crude oil to hard-currency countries and has a strong incentive to increase them. Poland's growing energy gap and the Soviet Union's unwillingness or inability to fill it completely have forced the country to turn increasingly to nonsocialist sources of energy supplies, particularly in the Middle East. That is also why there was growing Polish interest in Norway's offshore oil and in the Adriatic pipeline, a joint project by Yugoslavia, Czechoslovakia and Hungary which represented the most ambitious attempt so far to bring Middle Eastern oil to the region. British Petroleum has a contract with Poland to supply three million tons of oil annually over ten years, which was about 20 percent of Poland's consumption in 1975. But the oil bill is going to rise heavily. The prospect is not entirely bleak since Poland could call on exports of other raw materials, but even with their increased prices the gap will be extremely difficult, if not impossible, to fill.

The Soviet Union is Poland's largest trading partner, claiming one-third of Poland's world trade and one-half of its trade with socialist countries. All the imported coal in the Soviet Union comes from Poland. Every fifth ship is produced in Polish shipyards. Half of Poland's production of building equipment, road construction materials and machinery, and delivery vans is purchased by Moscow. In return the Soviet Union provides raw materials and some technology on which the Polish economy greatly depends. Forty-two percent of all Polish raw materials imports are of Soviet origin including 80 percent energy fuels and iron ore, 60 percent cotton, 55 percent nonferrous metals, and 45 percent asbestos.(168) For reasons already discussed Soviet terms of trade have improved well ahead of Poland's. Another indication of the close links is the fact that 11,000 Soviet specialists have spent time in Poland and twice that number of their Polish colleagues have been trained in the Soviet Union. Altogether nearly 400 organizations in 37 different branches of the economy were involved.

Total trade value has risen considerably and in 1974 amounted to 15,692 million exchange zlotys and the balance of payments, as is common in Comecon trade, was basically stable. In terms of Poland's world trade, exchanges between Warsaw and Moscow have increased rather more slowly than those with the West. After Kosygin's visit to Poland in August 1975, it was agreed that the turnover between the two countries would rise 50 percent over the first half of the decade and reciprocal deliveries of machinery and equipment were to be doubled. The Soviet economy is an essential partner for Poland and it is natural that their trade should expand. But if the reason for this expansion is primarily raw material prices, the fact that these prices should be on a par with present world costs by the late seventies and possibly higher thereafter, is a disturbing one.

Soviet grain deliveries have also presented problems. In 1975 the Soviet Union was unable to supply Poland with the amount of grain Warsaw had contracted for. This was presumably due to the poor Soviet grain harvest but it was the first known instance of a Soviet cancellation of contracted deliveries to a Comecon ally.(169) Since Polish grain yields were approximately two million tons less than expected in 1975, Warsaw had to seek some three million tons of grain elsewhere, mainly in the United States.

And lastly, there is a problem with the many Polish-Soviet industrial cooperation agreements. Very often the Soviet Union will buy one new Polish machine for "testing only" and then reject the offer of industrial cooperation in production of this machine. They will simply reproduce the same machine themselves.

While the Polish leadership never tired of proclaiming their support for Comecon, the facts of their trade with the West seemed to go against the grain of their apparent sincerity. Indeed, an important reason given by the Poles for the new trend was that they wished to modernize their industries in order to improve the quality of their exports to the Soviet Union and the rest of the communist world. The Poles were leaning over backward to dispel any notion that their trade with the West was designed to make them less dependent on Russia. But the uses to which this trade has been applied and the influences that it has exerted in the past five years raised the question of whether Warsaw actually planned not only increased trade but a structurally different political-economic system as well.

More interesting was the prognosis which sprang from the past five years of relations with the West. Gierek began the new policy of importing modernization in order to raise the standard of living. While the short-term solution of this problem was the import capital and consumer goods from the West, the long-term prospect called for intensive investment in those sectors of the Polish economy that would both serve the growing consumer-orientated society and foster Polish trade throughout the world. The result was a strong concentration on these areas of the Polish economy that would be of most use to Poland in its further drive to integrate itself into the international division of labor, such as the raw materials industries, machine building, construction, and shipping industries. The influx of Western credits and goods has also had the positive effect of fostering a transformation of the Polish economy from one of a basically anti-import character to a more pro-export stand. Those areas where Polish production was not as efficient as elsewhere should be covered by additional imports from the countries which excel in these products.

Besides, there was also some psychological advantage in such a change. The credits granted Poland were indirect votes of Western confidence that the Polish economy was a good business risk. But these decisions were probably also influenced by Poland's able foreign-trade officials and the generally efficient, businesslike impression they were said to make. This image was probably best personified by Gierek who himself has the pragmatic touch that appeals to Western businessmen and politicians.

Economic Management: Dilution of Reforms

There was clearly a conflict between more centralization and decentralization, between pushing forward with a pragmatic, economic, managerial approach and the apprehension that at some level, at one time or another, the leading role of the Party could be eroded in the economic field.

Immediately after December 1970, the new leadership made economic management reforms an integral part of its economic recovery program. It publicly stated that it would not be deflected from its chosen course by the opposition of dogmatic elements within the Party apparatus nor within the state and economic bureaucracy. Most of the economists and specialists I have met in Poland were fascinated by the Hungarian experiment which, according to some of them, however admirable, could not be transplanted into the entirely different Polish conditions. Some others were impressed by the Yugoslav model. On the whole, in 1971, the tendency was to look everywhere, to select adaptable experiences from abroad and to devise in the future "a specific Polish Model."

But in fact nothing much happened except for some experiments, most of them haphazard, some of them reversed in due course. The new concept of management was worked out by a party-government commission. Its task was clear: to strengthen central planning and at the same time the management of large industrial concerns through linking several enterprises in one group, the so-called "WOGs," also at times referred to as "initiating industrial and commercial units."

All this boiled down to careful and hesitant experiments. In March 1971, the government broadened the powers of the directors of key industrial enterprises in the spheres of planning, foreign trade, technological progress, employment, wages, and prices.

The new system, proposed by the commission, was introduced as a pilot scheme on January 1, 1973 and by the end of the year, it embraced 25 large industrial concerns consisting of several enterprises (WOGs), covering 20 percent of the country's total industrial capacity. By the beginning of September 1974, 46 such industrial organizations(170) were working under the new system, embracing over 40 percent of the total industrial production. The principles of this experimental minidecentralization were designed to strengthen central planning but simultaneously to give greater independence to economic units, mainly in investment policies, management of wage funds correlated with efficiency, cost effectiveness with profit as a crucial factor. In essence, the new system attempted to relate wages and salaries not only to quantitative output but also to profitable economic management of an enterprise. The new system did not go as far as the Yugoslav model where wages were dependent entirely on the profitability of the enterprise.

Some central control continued to be maintained over wages by means of a wage fund. Enterprises were expected to be able to work out how large the fund should be and therefore the size of the payments above centrally decreed minima, and where the extra money should come from. The purpose of the new system of minidecentralization was to encourage both management and labor. If all went well the labor force would benefit because wages were to be related to the net output of an enterprise, while managers would profit because their remuneration in bonuses was to be based on the net profit of the unit in question.

After the first year the huge new concerns proved more responsive to the market, selling more than other factories, and showing a much faster increase in productivity. In 1973, they increased their productivity by 11.6 percent while in the rest of the industry productivity rose by only 9.2 percent. In 1974 when many more huge concerns were included in the experiment(171), the results were even more impressive with the percentages being 15.7 percent and 12.3 percent, respectively.

However, before the new system could prove itself entirely, the authorities decided in 1975 to amend it. A turnover tax on all exports was introduced as that any surplus profits gained, particularly in view of increasing Western inflation, could be transferred to the state budget in order to compensate for the lower profit when the same goods were sold on the domestic market. Further, it was decided to tax all surplus income obtained as a result of the marketing of the so-called novelties retailed at prices that, by implication, were recognized to be excessive; to analyze and relate government subsidies to turnover tax so that by using effective economic instruments, the former could be reduced and the latter increased. Moreover, there was to be introduced the practice of using up surpluses to finance each factory's own nonproductive and social profits in order to finance its own and cooperative investments, and to pay off, whenever possible, any debts and loans accumulated.

This legislation obviously limited the WOGs' independence. This was explained away by the objective difficulties of the internal market supply situation, by the problems that foreign trade was starting to pose, and by the need, in view of the country's rising indebtedness, to control the rate of invest-

ment, which seemed to have gotten out of hand. Gierek
himself hinted at these difficulties when he admitted that even
if extenuating circumstances were taken into account the
quality of production did not as yet reflect the high level of
technology introduced in the seventies. He was very emphatic
in saying that if the Polish economic priorities, as laid down
by the Party, were to be met, only those managerial initiatives
would be tolerated that absolutely conformed to the agreed
national plan. Such conformity could only be exacted by the
central authorities; therefore, this was another turnabout in
the system of economic management, towards recentralization.
As one diplomat put it to me in Warsaw, coal and agricultural
goods might help the country in the short run the way they
had helped in the past, but this would not do much to establish export markets in the West. The reforms initiated and
experimented in WOGs were essential for Poland to establish
herself in industrial export markets. Otherwise the whole
economic edifice might collapse for want of firm yet flexible
foundations.

This went beyond the question of the frequently unnecessary investment-spending sprees which some managers
embarked on. These could have been stopped by proper
economic adjustments. The underlying reason for the managerial reversal was political. It can serve as an example of
the destructive influence of the political system on economic
processes.(172) The reversal in 1975 was dictated chiefly by
apprehension that the reform might possibly put some limits to
the autocracy and high-handedness of the political authorities.
It goes without saying that economic reform cannot be considered as the panacea for all economic difficulties, but even
within these limits to continue with it would doubtless be very
beneficial.

ECONOMIC   DYNAMISM   AND   POLITICAL   RETRENCHMENT

In his first year of office Gierek showed himself to be both
aware of and responsive to the concerns of three main con-
stituents: the population, possible contenders for power within
the Party, and Poland's eastern neighbor. Indeed his performance, mixing conciliation with firmness, seemed in part an
attempt to reach compromise solutions that would resolve immediate popular grievances, preempt the position held by
domestic advocates of a different policy, and convince the
Soviet Union that the situation was well under control.

That Gierek had achieved differing degrees of success in
each of these endeavors was an indication of the divergent
demands and expectations with which he was confronted. He
undoubtedly achieved one thing: by a mixture of immediate

material improvements and long-term unorthodox economic policies of dynamic development on the one hand, and promises for political reforms including suggestions of restructuring channels of communication and participation on the other, he made it appear in a remarkably short time, that the country had emerged from its political and psychological trauma. No effort was spared to associate the leadership with Polish history, tradition and Polish national interest, and to remind people that whatever they might think of communism, it had at least brought them a materially better life and 30 years of peace and security. But, as one American observer suggested, although the national eye retained its glint of skepticism, however its general expression seemed chastened rather than defeated.(173) The skepticism was understandable, since a number of slogans and promises of early 1971 bore a remarkable similarity to those of 1956 which remained unfulfilled. This "action replay" therefore evoked less belief and enthusiasm.

The December events brought sharply to the surface the most substantial problem of the relationship between rulers and ruled. At the initiative of two prominent Polish publicists, Rakowski and Toeplitz, in a booklet "Poland's Number One Problem"(174) some of the most distinguished journalists and intellectuals expressed their own personal views.

A well known journalist, Gornicki, wrote: "....material improvement does not contribute to a real improvement in the social situation of an individual if it is not accompanied by an extension of individual group freedoms."

Rakowski argued: "The guiding idea of basic changes in existing structural methods of management and governing must be the absolute liberation of people from the stratjacket which we put on ourselves during the years of practice in building socialism."

Poland taught the communist leaders of other countries that people would no longer put up with inefficient and irresponsible rule. They would stand up for their rights. If changes of Party leadership and government were not to be forced by strikes and by riots in which innocent people were killed, the lesson was that other ways had to be found in which the people would be able to influence official policy.

One can assume that Gierek came to the same conclusion. But because of external pressures and recent experiences in the socialist bloc, and partly because of his own firm belief in the principle of the "leading role" of the Party, he was determined to reestablish its control, while simultaneously satisfying the economic demands of the people and introducing his own style of dialogue and consultation based mainly on his personality and his human and direct approach to the people.

From the very beginning Gierek did not take into account any structural political reforms of the existing institutions which had proved inefficient as channels of communication between rulers and ruled. He had promised reforms in an effort to depoliticize existing tension. But Gierek is a man with a mind of his own. He is not a seeker after abstract truth, but above all, a seeker after efficiency. That was, perhaps, why he did subordinate doctrine to pragmatism in the economy, but was not prepared to do the same in the political field even within the existing system.

Gierek also had to face slightly less pressure from below than Gomulka did in 1956. This factor strengthened his ability to define the dynamics of the "renewal" process and to keep it strictly within limits defined by himself and by the Party. The failure of other groups in society, particularly the intellectuals and students, to make common cause with the workers in 1970 (in contrast to 1956), made Gierek's task that much easier. In 1956, Poland both contributed to and drew from the general atmosphere of ferment and relaxation or collapse of controls throughout Eastern Europe. Given the repudiation of the myth that had held communists together, the scope for reform appeared endless, and a more justified definition of intrabloc relationship possible. In contrast, for any politician coming to power after August 1968, the limitations imposed on reforms were well defined, while the idea of divergent roads to communism had been largely subordinated to the conservative concept of "the defense of common social achievements," in other words, to the Brezhnev doctrine.

As the new regime matured and Gierek's position within the Party consolidated, it became quite clear very soon that the drastic and beneficial economic changes were not to be followed by the fulfillment of promises of political reforms. The leadership evinced an understandable caution about tampering with the stability it had created mostly through the economic measures. Anything which carried political implications was played down or simply forgotten. It would have been out of character and perhaps politically dangerous if the leadership had seen fit to let its political control rest on a precarious and shifting balance of interests. Despite the mood of economic pragmatism, the Party could hardly have been content with the prospect that its authority and political power would have to reckon with semi-autonomous influences of various social groups and organizations, or with the continued need to placate extraneous demands which possessed an independent political force of their own. In other words, regardless of its tacit recognition of the need to come to terms with political dissatisfaction, which was the result of the country's more pressing inequities and problems, and while avoiding confrontation, the leadership moved rapidly and convincingly to consolidate its political control, to reestablish and interpret the leading role of the Party in unbending terms, and to eliminate actual or potential pockets of autonomy outside the Party. The political structures were deemed sound; the only thing to be done was to make them work better. But a steam engine cannot change its nature. No matter how many improvements you make it still remains a steam engine, and woefully ill-suited to the needs of the twentieth century.

However, and this was also part of his strategy, Gierek was firmly convinced that once the economic situation improved, as it did, there would be no need for any political structural changes. Toward the end of 1975 if anything was clear in Poland, it was that enlightened, pragmatic policies, or the leadership's response to popular aspirations, must not be confused with the liberalization of political authority and control. All this maintained stability for as long as the standards of living were rising. When economic constraints not only slowed down progress but also forced upon the country an austerity program, the demands for political structural reforms and for greater freedom grew stronger every day. Gierek failed to take into account, and perhaps to fully understand, that economic progress and political reforms are indissolubly linked in people's minds.

Nevertheless, Poland still remained the freest country in the Eastern bloc; only Hungary was even partially comparable. Poles talked absolutely freely, sparing nothing and nobody. Millions of Poles go abroad, and not only to socialist countries. In contrast with the Soviet Union, a traveler can easily move around the country - by car, for instance - and go anywhere. While the censorship of correspondence to and from abroad remains it is rather haphazard and not very regular.

What is perhaps most striking is the indomitable spirit of feeling free whatever controls there are and whatever restrictions exist; small wonder that whenever average Russians or Bulgarians -or for that matter, Czechs or Slovaks - visit to Poland, they suddenly find themselves in a different world. Some of them are envious. All of them are either shocked or fascinated by the climate of intellectual alertness and the spirit of nonconformism.

5 Foreign Policy: 1971-1977

In a world which exists by the balance of
Antagonisms, the respective merit of the
Conservator or the Innovator must ever
remain debatable.

Thomas Carlyle in "On Boswell's
Life of Johnson"

Poland's geographical place in Europe between Germany and
Russia - or, strategically speaking, between the Soviet Union,
the Soviet fleet in the Baltic, and the Soviet divisions in East
Germany, Czechoslovakia and in Poland itself - would suggest
that the country has a limited list of options in her foreign
policy.

During the interwar years and in the postwar period
Poland had tried out many options, most of them more or less
unsuccessfully, mainly because of external reasons. But as
the Nestor of Polish scientists, Professor Kotarbinski put it:
"Poland is a large fly, not a small elephant." The dust had
hardly settled after the 1970 crisis and the leadership change
when an active, outward-looking foreign policy was established.

Under Gierek's leadership foreign policy, toward the West
in particular, assumed a new sense of movement. This was
the result of several interrelated factors(1). First, the
December 1970 Warsaw treaty with West Germany and the other
agreements that have marked the process of East-West detente
have provided Poland with a new room for maneuver in foreign
affairs as the earlier threats to territorial changes and the
consequent need for strong reliance on the Soviet Union have
receded. The Polish Western frontier has become secure.
Poland's political debtors' status within the Warsaw Pact and

above all in its relations with the Soviet Union has also been
mitigated.(2)   Poland's security has finally ceased to be
dependent on Moscow, and her foreign policy has thus blos-
somed into the art of expanding the possible.

Second, foreign policy has been reconstructed to serve
the needs of an ambitious program of domestic economic development and of a change of direction in foreign trade.   The
opening to the West has become a necessity.   Third, the
leadership was fully aware that the nation inclines culturally
toward the West and toward political contact with Western
countries, and therefore no Polish government could hope to
achieve any degree of national legitimacy without an active
Western policy.   In the accelerated pace of East-West contacts
in general, Poland has become more active than her socialist
allies except the Soviet Union, and to a lesser extent Rumania.
Finally, Polish foreign policy has acquired to some extent an
independence that has required Poland to be more vigorous
and significant not only in East-West relations, but within the
Soviet orbit as well.

It would be difficult to overplay the significance of the
Warsaw Treaty of 1970.   After its ratification one commentator
wrote: "Today the independent Polish State lies beyond the
reach of direct outside danger.   Its territorial and political
shape is not only guaranteed by the alliance with the Soviet
Union, but has now finally been approved by potential ad-
versaries.   We have reached the point of maximum strategic
advantage."(3)   The new guarantees of the national existence
represented by the treaty and the prospect of an emerging
equilibrium in Europe constituted a turning point that, while
holding to the fulcrum of the Soviet alliance, provided new
opportunities for an independent momentum in Polish foreign
policy.   "We can," wrote another commentator "look around
throughout Europe with the feelings of a man who has finished
laying the foundations and can now build the house."

Poland's view of her own security moved from the narrow
objective of obtaining recognition of the Western frontier
toward broader, more comprehensive considerations of security.
At the same time this approach has strengthened Poland's
position within the communist bloc; she became more assertive
in the pursuit of her own interests.

In the twilight of Gomulka's rule, during the summer of
1970, Poland's place in the Warsaw Pact and Europe as a whole
became the open topic of a most unusual and provocative
discussion in the newspapers.   The well-known sociologist,
Professor Szczepanski, put it in a nutshell by stating: "The
future of every state depends on its contribution to some
international community, on the role it plays in a group of
states....The mere fact that we exist guarantees nothing."   It
was candidly acknowledged that the lessening of tension would
differentiate the states of the Warsaw Pact(4), whose political

and economic interests were not identical. With the "shifting of forces within the blocs" and in a world of superpowers, the burden of securing and extending national interests would fall on Polish shoulders and here it was the country's internal performance that would have the determining effect in limiting or enhancing its international importance in both East and West.

In the circumstances, only two options remained for Polish foreign policy; the Soviet-Polish alliance as a cornerstone of Poland's position in the world accompanied by close links with most socialist states, and the reassertion of Polish national interests within a wider European framework. A consequence of the latter was the strong determination to advocate (with Soviet support) the idea of a European conference on security and cooperation (CSCE). The two options were strictly inter-related. It was strongly argued(5) all the time that the country has genuine interests in both East and West, but that the effectiveness of this on the Western side of the equation would depend on Poland's strength, vitality, economic progress and her influence in the East. It was suggested by some Polish officials and journalists that it was precisely because of the trusting relations established with Moscow that Poland could follow a more national policy.

In the first option, a fundamental Polish nightmare transcending communist or contemporary dimensions was always present. What happens if Russia and Germany decide to bury the hatchet? The shadow of a possible Rapallo (Soviet-German pact in the twenties), although not always realistic, loomed heavily. When in 1964 Krushchev announced his intention to seek better relations with West Germany, an "iron triangle" between Poland, East Germany and Czechoslovakia emerged due to misgivings about any normalization of Soviet relations with Bonn. When again in 1968 Soviet diplomats started long and partly secret talks with West Germany, Gomulka, a year later, in May, made a volte-face proposing a bilateral treaty recog-nizing the Western frontier. The proposal was interpreted by some as anticipating Soviet moves toward detente which in their effect might have compromised Polish interests. It showed that an effective Polish foreign policy had to con-centrate on influencing the development in the West and not simply on defending the frontier of socialism on the Elbe. Conditions for diplomatic relations had improved. Instead of de facto recognition of East Germany there was only renuncia-tion of Bonn's claim to speak for all Germans. The defensive solidarity with East Germany was thus greatly modified. During the post-1970 period of difficulties in normalizing Polish-West German relations Warsaw tried its best to secure Soviet support for its demands. And finally, as I was told by a high official in Warsaw, when the two "big brothers", i.e., the two superpowers, talk to each other and have increasingly frequent direct "hush-hush contacts" Poland must feel uneasy in case they do a deal at the expense of Polish interests. The first option, reliance on a powerful neighbor, was certainly still in force, but it was being reassessed on the basis of a more realistic view of Soviet superpower interests in the modern world and not so much on ideological grounds.

The second parallel option of reasserting, with Soviet approval, national interests in a European context, was simply dictated by the realities of Poland's past history and of her present geopolitical situation. A nation which paid such a price for independence knows the value of peace, and the search for peace by the Poles must be active, not passive. The successive occupations and wars on Polish soil have taught this lesson well. The alternative then was to seek a broader peace, a strong European framework for the solution of local problems. Poles genuinely expected a much larger margin of maneuver within such a framework and saw the nation's security in a broader sense in a new balance of East-West interests and influence. If a new European equilibrium is to emerge, based less on force and the paralytic tension of antagonistic positions, the country, in the eyes of one of its leading commentators, Wojna, will be of key importance as a "stabilizing element in Europe," because of its unique position in the Warsaw Pact:(6) "Thanks to our geographical location, to our economic and military strength, we represent the second most powerful nation in the socialist camp."

The most effective outlet for Poland's stabilizing influence was thought to be in an expanding network of bilateral ties in which the defense of mutual interests would serve as a stabilizing factor in European politics. This policy was seen as marrying European security to Polish national interests including the development of ties with the West and including what was described to me in Warsaw as the Europeanization of Poland. The expansion of Poland's contacts with the different Western countries enhanced Poland's position in the Soviet Union. The greater Warsaw's influence in Paris, Bonn or Washington(7), the stronger its voice in Moscow. The Poles could then carry more weight in the formulation of the common policy of the communist bloc.

But the prospects of achieving more international signif- icance were to be governed in large measure by the inter- dependent factors of domestic political stability and economic progress. This was certainly conditioned by the close rela- tions with the Soviet Union as well as by Poland's internal development plans, the search for credits and technology on which they depended and a successful process of detente that would ensure the political conditions for securing the latter.

Yet with all these aspirations there remained a healthy
sense of proportion. Poland realized that it would be unrealistic to act as a go-between in East-West relations. But it
assumed that although the major powers in this world possess
enough megatons to involve everyone in a holocaust, without
the participation of medium-sized states, they could not
straighten out the world's problems and turn toward constructive cooperation.(8)

This policy was in order as long as detente developed.
But in 1975-1977 the buildup of Soviet forces threatened the
equilibrium both in Europe and on a global scale. The issue
of human rights created a serious obstacle to the progress of
detente which found itself in a fluid state with many floating
question marks, particularly in the West. While Polish national
interests might flourish in the climate of decreasing tensions,
the possibility of retrenchment on both sides and particularly
in the East, where a tightening of the screw of uniformity was
in progress, might endanger the aspirations of the Poles and
make it very difficult, if not impossible, for them to harvest
the fruits of East-West rapprochement. Poland was trying
hard to achieve results commensurate with its own national
interests, but absolute loyalty to the Soviet Union remains one
of the imperatives of Polish policy.

Here Moscow has a problem. Stability in Poland must be
maintained at all costs. But this stability depends to a great
extent on still closer economic cooperation between Poland and
the Western countries, thus pushing Poland further toward the
West, both economically and in terms of friendly relations.
This fact is welcomed by an overwhelming majority of Poles,
but it also pulls Poland away from Comecon and its efforts
toward integration, of which the Soviet Union is the most
ardent champion. But the Soviet Union is itself playing the
game of economic and political detente with the West, and it
would be difficult for her to stop her ally doing just that,
particularly since, from the point of view of Soviet interests,
what is at stake is the most sensitive region in Eastern
Europe.

THE SOVIET CORNERSTONE

At the eighth Central Committee plenum in February 1971,
Gierek testified to the "truth" by stating: "Poland can de-
velop only as a socialist state, inseparably united with the
Soviet Union, and with our neighbors and allies."(9)

The attitude of Moscow in all this was obviously crucial
and the Polish leadership has shown itself to be sensitive to
Soviet superpower political interests. Gierek has proceeded
cautiously, coordinating most of his major initiatives with the

Soviet leadership. After assuming power he traveled to the
Soviet Union on no less than six occasions up to November
1971. And he has, occasionally, displayed a deference to the
Soviet Union and the Soviet Communist party that equalled if it
did not exceed that shown by his predecessor.

However, Gierek's attitude also reflected his awareness of
the dynamics of political power in Eastern Europe and of Soviet
concern that the renewal in Poland should proceed along
clearly defined lines. He strongly sought to convince Moscow
that, although certain aspects of Polish policy might diverge
from the Soviet experience, he was a firm internationalist,
most loyal, and, perhaps as important, the only man who could
ensure the stability of Poland that Moscow needed so badly.
Throughout that year he had to tread warily, with the
memories of Czechoslovak events still fresh, particularly when
the initial Soviet interest in a return to stability in Poland
soon turned into concern lest reforms should overstep their
basic political and ideological limits.

Meanwhile the Warsaw treaty removed the reasons for the
convergence of the nation's and of the regime's interests when
both were faced by the specter of German revanchism. Given
the nationalist and strongly anti-Russian feelings of the
people, the border issue was a useful trump card to check
certain tendencies. Obviously such a trump card was like a
nuclear weapon: its mere presence was a formidable fact, but
its use, a rare occurrence. Still, the Soviet guarantee of the
western borders had a power which all Poles realized and
appreciated. But when the new borders were recognized by
West Germany and the other powers, the threat of German
revanchism became groundless, and the primary purpose of the
Soviet-Polish alliance was undermined. However, the Poles
recognized that in their geopolitical situation cooperation and
friendship with the Soviet Union had to remain the cornerstone
of Polish foreign policy. Obviously, the "Czechoslovak
bogey," based on the "Brezhnev doctrine," could provide
another such trump card, but it was not a trump card that
Gierek wanted to play all the time. Besides, for the people at
large, it was the nation's position within the bloc and in the
world that really counted. Because of these sentiments and
convictions any Party leader had to present himself to the
people as a "realistic nationalist." His strong position in
Moscow was, therefore, considered an asset, but at the same
time anyone who had an ambition to be a leader had to
demonstrate some measure of independence; it seemed that
after coming to power Gierek was striving to acquire such an
image.

Polish-Soviet relations became more businesslike and
transformed into a nominally equal partnership. While they
remained the cornerstone of Polish policy, the face of the
stone has been changing slowly but surely. Poland aspired to

and, finally in 1973-1974, achieved the number-two position
within the Soviet bloc. A high official in Warsaw summarized
it by saying that this is a "marriage of convenience" which
must be rational and not based on "sentimental or emotional
reasons"; it should be based on mutual understanding and
far-reaching cooperation in all fields which must be strengthened all the time.

As suggested to me in Warsaw by all my sources,
including official ones, there were several reasons for
achieving the status of "number two." Territorially, militarily,
and in economic potential Poland was the largest and strongest
country in the bloc next to the Soviet Union. It first
launched the idea of the CSCE, although this was initiated
some years earlier in Moscow. The geopolitical situation of the
country has predestined her to play an important part.
Poland formed part of the European cultural heritage and could
now make full use of her traditional historical and cultural
links with the West, after many years when she had been
forced to forget these links. Poland had a chance to rejoin
the West European cultural stream, and could, in the atmosphere of detente, present to the West a more genuine face
than Moscow or any other East European country. For the
Soviet Union stability in Poland was the key to stability in the
whole East European bloc, and Gierek held this key. The
Polish Party was able, so far, to deal with her internal problems without outright or even indirect Soviet intervention.
And, finally, a lot of fingers were being crossed in Moscow in
the hope that Poland, in her own way of building socialism and
with her close links with the West, would have something to
show the world.

The new Polish leaders were in a better position than
their predecessors to put their relations with the Russians on
a more equal footing. Gierek found it easier to get along with
Brezhnev; the two men belonged to the same postrevolutionary
communist generation. They both liked the language of
practical administrators. As a partner and negotiator Gierek
has been much more acceptable than Gomulka ever was, mainly
because the Polish leader talked in realistic, practical terms,
arguing pros and cons, using facts and hard evidence to
prove his points.

As a result of the country's upgraded status in the
Soviet bloc, Poland in 1973-1974 had excellent relations with
the Soviet Union; they were "better than at any time before,"
an official told me. Speaking of detente, he said, "We are
closest to Brezhnev and what we say does count in Moscow."
Whenever there were secret talks between the two superpowers, Warsaw became uneasy and therefore jumped on
Brezhnev's bandwagon to be as close as possible to one
superpower and firmly to establish her number-two position in
the European socialist bloc. As another journalist told me, one

has to realize that the renaissance of communism, which was now more or less a dead duck, could only come from Russia, and it was impossible for Poland to overstep certain limits unless and until there was a "Gierek" in charge in the Soviet Union. A joke circulating at the time in Warsaw illustrated what he meant: "Communism is the glorious victory of ideology over common sense."

The new upgraded status gave Poland some privileges in terms of direct accessibility to Moscow and in coinfluencing the policies within the bloc. But it also imposed new and stronger obligations. Whenever Moscow needed firm support for its policy Warsaw had to be in the front rank. These were inter-related factors. When Brezhnev visited Warsaw in 1973, the effects of Poland's swing toward the West were becoming obvious and the reception Brezhnev received was characterized by nothing short of Sovietomania. The saturated atmosphere of pro-Soviet praise in the Polish media became stifling. The people, for the most part, certainly resented this, but at the time Brezhnev himself faced sharp conflict within the Soviet PB and CC in view of his detente policy and was able to argue that he had the fullest possible support of his allies. Brezhnev's expression of support for Gierek was also extremely warm. It created the impression(10) that each man was trying to assure the other that their mutual loyalty remained intact, no matter what certain policies might seem to indicate.

One must not forget, by the way, that for an average Russian anybody beyond the Soviet Western frontiers is an imperialist. If, in the Soviet propaganda, the Moscow leadership conducts a policy of detente with the West, and is helping the Poles, Czechs, and Hungarians economically, to an average Russian this is an aid given to the imperialist camp.

By 1975 the mood had changed again in Moscow-Warsaw relations. By then Gierek had been skillfully exploiting the political detente between East and West. When Kosygin visited Poland in August, official statements and press commentaries were careful to emphasize the equality of relations between the two countries and stressed the partnership. While some observers saw in this meeting a Soviet attempt to increase its influence in Warsaw, the fact remained that there had been some very hard bargaining in the economic negotiations which had not gone entirely the Soviet way. Kosygin, for instance, had suggested that the West German credits only just granted to Poland be invested in the Soviet Union in comprehensive Comecon projects. This was flatly refused.

In 1975, when Gierek came back from Moscow, he dis-closed some of his troubles before a restricted gathering of journalists. The Russians, said Gierek, had refused to partici-pate in Polish investment projects in the Lublin region where huge coal deposits had been found, and, therefore he in turn

had refused to supply the Russians with electrical energy to
be produced in this region. "If they don't give us help,"
announced Gierek, "we won't give them anything." Obviously
the story was not confined to the 60 journalists present. Some
less informed people promptly saw in Gierek an independent
leader who could stand up to the Russians. Those better
informed drew a different conclusion, namely, that Gierek's
position in Moscow had to be pretty strong if he had allowed
himself to criticize the Russians in front of the press. This
double impression was precisely what Gierek had intended.

Regardless of how much stronger Poland's position had
become in the Soviet bloc, Moscow was forever uneasy and
watchful. Kosygin suddenly arrived in Warsaw in August 1975
immediately after the Helsinki summit. Then Gierek went on
an unexpected one-day trip to Moscow after President Giscard
d'Estaing had left Poland. Both with Giscard d'Estaing in
Warsaw and Chancellor Schmidt in Helsinki, Gierek had
displayed self-assurance and a willingness to make politically
ticklish compromises. There was certainly much more than just
a timely coincidence between these important steps in Polish
policy and the ensuing discussion with Moscow.

Strong anti-Russian sentiments in Poland remained, even
among the Party functionaries. However temperate, these
often bordered on disdain and in themselves were rather
dangerous since they tended to disregard not only the position
of the Soviet Union as a superpower but also any real
achievements the Russians have made. However, politically
minded people not only appreciated Poland's position relative to
the Soviet Union but also saw some advantages in expanding
trade on the huge Soviet market.

POLAND AND THE SOCIALIST COMMONWEALTH

Very soon, in 1971, three undeniable facts appeared on the
surface. The political and economic interests of the socialist
countries were not identical. Poland's membership in the
community of these countries would not in itself guarantee
participation in the scientific-technological revolution. Real
economic integration within the Comecon remained a distant
goal rather than a fact. Gierek proceeded, therefore, with an
attempt at reinvigorating relations with at least some Comecon
countries. One of the most interesting developments was the
marked improvement in relations with East Germany in 1972
(see section, "East Germany: Toward Integration," in this
chapter).

One of the main problems for Poland was integration, or
the lack of it, in Comecon. Economists, journalists and
officials I talked to in Warsaw were in complete agreement that

no real integration within Comecon was possible without far-reaching economic reforms and their coordination. There were two groups of Comecon members: the Soviet Union, Rumania and Bulgaria on the one side with their centralized economic power and the quantitative criterion in production; on the other side were Hungary, Poland and Czechoslovakia whose economies had become more or less decentralized with in-clinations toward giving some play to market forces. It followed, therefore, that the mechanisms of cooperation in Comecon remained in sharp contrast with the mechanisms of economic policies in Budapest, Warsaw and even Prague.

Then there remained unanswered the fundamental ques-tion: What would integration mean in practical terms? The Rumanians were hostile because they feared that it would in-crease the dependence of the smaller countries on the Soviet Union. The Hungarians and the Poles argued that integration also meant integration of the Soviet Union with all the other countries. Consequently the smaller countries would be in a much stronger position at multilateral negotiations and agree-ments than with bilateral agreements. In the latter each country was on its own, faced by the Soviet giant.

In the circumstances, my sources maintained in Warsaw, no cooperation or even dialogue between the Comecon and the EEC was practicable. A nonintegrated region cannot negotiate with one already highly integrated. Besides which, Comecon was not institutionalized, as was the Common Market. All sources agreed that it was unrealistic to expect full European economic cooperation or, at a later stage, an integration with either the United States or the Soviet Union as integral parts of such an economic organism. The outlook instead was for full businesslike cooperation between an economically integrated Europe and two already integrated economic giants - the United States and the Soviet Union. With America included as a member, the Common Market could not have achieved such hopeful integration, an economist in Warsaw told me. The basic disadvantage of the Comecon was the Soviet Union's membership in it, which made genuine integration extremely difficult, if not impossible.

Except for the "special relationship" between Warsaw and East Berlin, not much love was lost in relations between Warsaw and other Warsaw Pact countries, save for the traditional friendship with Hungary. Another exception was Yugoslavia which was not strictly speaking a member of the so-called socialist commonwealth. In fact, Poland and Yugoslavia enjoyed very healthy economic cooperation. Tito's visit in 1972 was followed by Gierek's journey to Yugoslavia and another subsequent visit by Tito to Warsaw. Gierek was undoubtedly the first East European leader, apart perhaps from Ceausescu, who could bring himself to praise Yugoslavia's peculiar brand of socialism without a qualm.(11) Tito himself described Yugoslav-Polish relations as the model for co-operation among all states. In this he reflected the growing warmth and friendship between the two countries since Gierek came to power in 1970. The good relations between the two countries may also be attributed to the fact that under Gierek Poland had become one of the most flexible and relaxed communist states in Eastern Europe.

WEST GERMANY: TOWARD RECONCILIATION

From the very outset the new Polish leadership made it clear that they planned to continue along the course started by Gomulka in 1969, aimed at a reconciliation with West Germany within the general climate of detente in Europe. But it was made equally clear that no full normalization of relations was possible before the ratification of the Warsaw Treaty.(12) The Poles were certainly disappointed that the Warsaw Treaty had been signed only after the Bonn-Moscow agreement. For historical reasons and because of their experiences during the war they claimed priority. The problem of recognition of the frontiers was well advanced in Polish-West German negotiations when it was accepted in the Moscow-Bonn Treaty.

Since 1971 Poland had continued its conciliatory policy toward West Germany. During the bitter debate in Bonn over the ratification of the Warsaw treaty the Poles acted with considerable restraint; the press did not conceal its apprehension, but its tone was very moderate. When in May 1972 the treaty was eventually ratified by Bonn the exchange of ambassadors followed in November. The Polish Party PB stated(13) officially that it was only and exclusively the text of the treaty which was binding for Poland. Polish media either ignored or dismissed the Bundestag declaration which held that the treaties do not prejudice the ultimate settlement of German boundaries at the peace conference. A significant difference in the Polish and Soviet stand appeared on that occasion. While Moscow accepted the Bundestag resolution, Poland made it clear many times on official levels that it regarded the territorial settlement as final. This was an interesting reaction in view of the active role played by the Soviet ambassador in Bonn in the inter-Party consulations about the declaration.

During the first visit by a Polish foreign minister to Bonn, in September 1972, Olszowski explored with Brandt and Foreign Minister Scheel a broad range of possibilities for expanding cooperation between the two countries. The breakthrough in relations was hailed by a noted Polish commentator, Malcuzynski, as a step "opening new prospects and even a new chapter in the postwar history of Europe." The revision of textbooks by a Polish-West German commission progressed satisfactorily. Bonn paid out ₺40 million as indemnity for pseudo-medical experiments in Hitler's concentration camps. But Polish Prime Minister Jaroszewicz listed several conditions for the normalization of relations, including full normalization of Bonn's relations with all other socialist countries, the abolition of the German citizenship law based on the assumed existence of Germany's 1937 borders, an elimination of "revisionist organizations," and cautioned against "ideological subversion" in cultural cooperation.(14)

The fact that Gierek went on an official visit to Bonn six years after Herr Brandt came to sign the treaty in Warsaw reflected the difficulties which continued to plague Polish-West German relations. Contacts between the two countries were being maintained at all levels including that of foreign ministers, and both sides implied that goodwill existed to solve existing problems. The Germans for their part insisted on priority for the "humanitarian problem"; in other words they pressed for an assurance that Polish citizens of German origin who wished to emigrate to West Germany would be allowed to do so. According to the West German Red Cross more than 280,000 people were involved. Although Poland had not agreed to write anything on the subject into the 1970 treaty, Warsaw did agree to speed up the procedure dealing with applications for emigration in the so-called "information document.

In London in April 1974, Polish Foreign Minister Olszowski had described the German figure of 280,000 as "most fantastic," and confirmed that between 1970 and February 1974 a further 51,000 "resettlers" left Poland and that there were no more than between 60,000 to 80,000 persons of German origin still left in the country. He also accused the Bonn government of making an iunctim between the reunification of families and economic questions. Even among those 60,000 to 80,000 people still left in Poland there were, I was told in Warsaw, too many "Volkswagen Deutsche" who wanted to leave for purely economic reasons.

On the question of credits, Bonn offer Poland 1,000 million deutsch marks, while the Poles asked for much more. Warsaw also put forward a claim for compensation for about 180,000 former concentration camp inmates still alive in Poland. This was, according to the Poles, a problem of considerable moral and political importance; the Polish foreign minister described it as being "at the root of the conflict between Bonn and Warsaw. We will not withdraw these claims."

By early 1975, relations had sunk to a distressingly bitter nadir, with Warsaw's self-righteous protests and Bonn's legal objections equally missing the core of their bilateral problems. It became evident, though, that neither side was keen on a total and lasting freeze in relations. Bonn, interested in settling accounts with Poland and restoring peace with one of the Ostpolitik's most important participants, indicated a willingness to compromise. The pressure on Poland to accept this out-stretched hand was great. The Party congress was looming large on the political calendar in Warsaw, and a continuing feud with Bonn would have marred the image of international cooperation and domestic success the Party hoped to project. But perhaps the most important factor was that Gierek and the new West German Chancellor Schmidt found a common language. Both had a similar pragmatic approach to pressing problems.

Toward the end of the final Helsinki conference in July 1975, those two, during an all-night session, hammered out a solution of the problems in three agreements. These had finally broken the impasse that had strained bilateral relations for years. The Polish side agreed to allow 125,000 ethnic Germans to emigrate over the next four years. The West Germans granted credits of 1,000 million deustch marks to be repaid over 20 years, after a five-year period of grace, and a lump payment to Poles who had made social security payments to the Third Reich during World War II.

The agreements met with criticism in Bonn and were uneasily received in Poland. The fact that Poland hesitated two weeks before mentioning the details in its official media indicated the gamble Gierek took to make this important compromise. It was easy enough for the West German opposition parties to pick holes in the agreements. What about the other thousands of Germans who were said to want to leave Poland? Did not all the government leaders who had attended the Helsinki conference pledge themselves, and without financial incentives, to promoting freer movement? Had not Poland received enough compensation by getting former German territories? The West Germans have tended to overlook the importance of the Polish concession on the ethnic German issue; among Poland's German minority there was an unusually high proportion of skilled workers in key industrial jobs. To lose all these in a short period would have serious effects on an already deeply troubled Polish economy. Both sides made concessions and neither side was overjoyed about them; yet both sides realized that as the West German newspaper Die Zeit wrote: "No other road leads toward the future."

It was questionable whether Poland's allies would see the agreement as fully acceptable. Apart from the manpower problem in Poland itself, the agreement made less Polish manpower available for East Germany but more resettlers free to emigrate to West Germany which was an ironic twist not lost on East Berlin. Bonn's growing influence in the German question must also have caused ill feeling within the East German Communist party. And the Polish example of "people for money" exerted pressure on Czechoslovakia to settle its German problem in kind. Finally, Gierek had failed to obtain specific compensation for war victims. But he was able to argue that his

tough tactics had brought considerable results and that the
way was now open for considerably increased economic
cooperation which Poland badly needed.

The Bundestag ratified all three agreements without
difficulty. The difficulties arose in the Bundesrat where the
opposition had a majority. And here the opposition insisted on
asking what would happen to - according to their estimate -
155,000 Germans who would still be left in Poland after the
others had been allowed out by 1980. To meet this objection
West German Foreign Minister Genscher drew up a letter to
Polish Foreign Minister Olszowski, and asked him to confirm its
contents. After days of relentless negotiation the Polish side
accepted the text. The key passage said that after 1980
"further exit permits can be issued" to ethnic Germans. The
key word was "can." The Christian Democratic Union said
that this was far too weak and announced that they would vote
against the government unless the word was changed to "will."
Another negotiating marathon followed until late at night before
the final voting. Bonn was told that Warsaw had accepted the
amendment, and this enabled the opposition to deliver a unanimous vote in favor of the treaties amid sighs of relief which
were as loud on their side as on the government's side.(15)

Gierek's visit to Bonn in June 1976 finally set the seal on
postwar Polish-West German reconciliation and was quite rightly
described as a milestone in postwar European history. Indeed,
the West Germans did their best to make the Polish leader feel
welcome. Chancellor Schmidt dismissed cliche perceptions of
hereditary hostility between the Germans and the Poles although the past had not always been harmonious: "As
Germans we do not want to and we cannot wash out our hands
in innocence. There is no forgetting. There may be
forgiveness, but this is up to the judgment of those who have
suffered."(16) He added, however, that he was not afraid to
recall that "innocent Germans have suffered for the guilt of
others." Gierek in his speech referred to the "periods of good
and bad neighborliness." But he stressed the merits of the
two coalition parties and emphasized that the Poles knew how
to appreciate other political groups, the working class
organizations, and the Evangelical Church.

Apart from the fourteen economic cooperation contracts,
the two leaders signed a joint declaration of intent to normalize
fully and develop mutual relations. The two sides also agreed
that their foreign ministers should meet annually for talks on
bilateral and international affairs and in particular on the
securing of peace and security in Europe. They also
agreed(17) that there should be increased contacts between the
young people of Poland and West Germany, and that some
forum should be created for regular meetings between the two
countries' politicians, scientists, businessmen, and journalists.

From Warsaw's point of view some important problems of economic cooperation were solved. The Poles could hardly afford to turn aside further potential West German aid and technology for very long. As I was told in Warsaw, Bonn was economically in a very strong position in Poland and her participation in some Polish investments was indispensable. The Poles were used to West German technology and were generally satisfied with the equipment and services provided. But the Party leaders and the people at large were worried that the Germans might become much too strong a partner, which, as I was told, would be undesirable, both for Poland and the Soviet bloc. Warsaw, despite all the advantages of Polish-West German cooperation, did not want to become too economically dependent on Bonn.

The reconciliation was not an easy proposition. The older generation, who had lived through the horrors of the Nazi occupation and also with the bitter taste left by the protracted debate on the ratification of the Gierek-Schmidt agreements, was still suspicious. The younger generation, on the other hand, was free of any constraints and apprehensions. They regarded the West Germans as much Europeans and normal people as themselves. After what had passed between Poland and Germany since the thirties there could be no room for euphoria in their relations. But there was some truth in the view of the London Times that something like a "special relationship" between the two countries has now been achieved. This was based partly on the gradual recognition by the Polish leadership that the democratic West German state desired friendly and mutually beneficial relations with Poland, whose present frontiers it accepted. Warsaw also evidently saw the friendly links with Bonn and her economic aid as a strengthening of its own relative independence and economic weight within the Soviet bloc.

EAST GERMANY: TOWARD INTEGRATION

However politically and economically important a qualified reconciliation with West Germany had been, it was only a part, although the more important part, of Poland's overall German policy. The triangle of relations of Warsaw-Bonn-East Berlin had to be firmly established. When, after Gierek came to power, Poland was keen to move its negotiations with Bonn out of the doldrums, a consolidation of the Warsaw-East Berlin side of the triangle was judged by Gierek as a means of providing a fresh impetus. An event of great political and economic significance was the opening in January 1972 of the East German-Polish border to unrestricted bilateral tourist traffic without passports and customs control. Sixteen million people traveled in both directions during the year and, as the weekly, Polityka, wrote: "This was a dynamic basis for a real political, economic and social integration." After a year or two the Polish authorities had to limit the amount of currency available to the huge numbers of Poles who entered East Germany in search of cheap consumer goods and who thereby disrupted the carefully planned economies of both countries.

But the crowning event was the Gierek-Honecken meeting in June 1973 in East Berlin. The visit was given unprecedented coverage by the news media in both countries and, as one of the papers wrote, the splendor and accompanying atmosphere accorded to Gierek(18) could only be compared with the recent visit of Brezhnev to East Berlin. It opened the way for the creation of a politically and, most important, economically integrated microregion in Comecon. Of Poland's 141 co-production agreements with other Soviet bloc states no less than 82 were with East Germany. Bilateral trade was to double by 1980, and nearly one-third of it was to be accounted for by goods produced by an agreed division of labor and in industrial cooperative ventures. In a joint political document, which has never marked the bilateral ties between other Warsaw pact states, both leaders stressed the importance each country attached to the support of the other's international position. In one particularly important passage both sides emphasized the "strict and consistent implementation" of bilateral agreements concluded with Bonn acknowledging existing borders, guaranteeing territorial integrity and the four-power Berlin agreement. It also pledged that both states would "firmly counteract any possible attempts to undermine the existing political and territorial realities in Europe."(19) This was an expression of the conviction of both sides that a common position was as important in maintaining the status quo as it was in achieving its recognition. As Gierek himself commented: "There exists between our countries a coincidence of interests and a political interdependence." Both countries' future diplomatic position toward Bonn depended upon uncompromising support for each other's interests and goals. This was one of the factors distinguishing Polish-East German ties from those between some other allied states.

But the will and perhaps the need to tighten relations also reflected the perceptions of national interests in a period where the dynamic Soviet Westpolitik had engendered not only a more fluid international setting, but also set an example for the Soviet allies on the extension and protection of national interests. From the purely Polish point of view there were other, perhaps more important, reasons. The Poles, except for the leaders in official utterances, had never distinguished between "bad" West Germans and "good" East Germans. But, even with the formalized division of Germany, many Poles, including the leaders, remained apprehensive at even the

faintest suggestion of any distant German reunification, and
lost no opportunity to counterbalance the East-West German
rapprochement with a close Warsaw-East Berlin link. Even in
the atmosphere of detente most political journalists and some
Party officials I have met in Warsaw were apprehensive that
the two Germanies might get too close together for comfort.

The fear of some sort of reunification loomed heavily and
the Poles were particularly uneasy when Brezhnev talked to
Nixon or Ford because, as they stressed to me, you never
know what those two might decide above our heads. They
thought that the Soviet Union supported Polish efforts to
"integrate" with East Germany as fully as humanly possible.
But as some politicians explained to me, this is purely a serious attempt at complete Polish-East German integration to
counterbalance the potential danger of German reunification.

Even the "Finlandization" of both Germanies was too
dangerous. One commentator said: "Honecker facing Schmidt
is afraid and therefore plays the Polish game instead." The
intra-German historical, traditional, cultural and economic links
are dangerous because, apart from anything else, they are
much stronger than in other divided countries. East Germany
must, therefore, depend entirely on the East and first of all
on Poland. There was a double-edged danger here, according
to one well-informed source. East Germans were fully aware
that they would never achieve on their own a status in the
world even slightly comparable to that of West Germany.
Bonn's potential would grow and so would her attraction for
East Germans. On the other hand, the trouble was that some
materialistically minded, consumer-oriented West Germans might
be attracted by the "Prussian traditions" alive in East Berlin,
such as the military uniform, soldiers marching in goose-step -
a symbol perhaps, but a symbol of discipline and uniformity.
The same source said quite clearly: "A unified Germany, even
communist-orientated, could become a China in Europe."

To summarize, therefore, reconciliation with Bonn tied to
"integration" with East Berlin has not only strengthened Poland's position in both countries but has also made it easier
for Poland to conduct her own slightly more independent
German policy under the Soviet umbrella.

OPENING TO THE WEST: AN EXERCISE IN COUNTERBALANCE

A slight opening of the windows to the West already began
under Gomulka, but never before had Polish Western policy
acquired such a dimension as during Gierek's years. The
Polish leader himself went to Paris, Brussels, Stockholm,
Helsinki, Bonn, and Washington. In 1972 alone the Polish
foreign minister paid fourteen visits abroad, seven of them to

the most important Western capitals and then over the years he
visited the West several times and held long consultations. The
prime minister traveled extensively in south, north and west
European countries. Political consultations at the foreign
minister level have been established with almost all Western
capitals. Foreign policy was regarded by the leadership as an
important means of achieving strategic and economic aims,
particularly in the West. Poland as the first ally of the Soviet
Union and the second largest socialist country in Europe
played the European and American card with the dual objective
of paving the way for a European security conference and for
easier access to the Western technology.

The most dramatic change took place in Polish-American
relations. The distinctly cold climate which prevailed in the
latter Gomulka years gave way first to businesslike contacts
and then to mutual efforts at cooperation not devoid of cordial-
ity. Washington's response to Warsaw's overtures was both
positive and swift. Three American presidents have visited
Poland: Richard Nixon in May 1972; Gerald Ford in July 1975;
and Jimmy Carter in 1977.

When Nixon stopped in Warsaw on his way back from his
first summit in Moscow, the official reception accorded to him
was in every respect proper, but not demonstrative. He was
compensated for that, however, by a tumultuous welcome from
the crowds which gathered for a wreath-laying ceremony at the
tomb of the unknown soldier in Victory Square in Warsaw.
This was the first-ever visit by an American president to
Poland and it gave the public a chance to demonstrate the
traditional Polish affection and respect for America. Crowds of
men, women and children, of all ages and conditions, turned
out to see Nixon. The youngsters climbed trees, walls and
lamp posts for a glimpse of him. People chanted: "Nixon!
Nixon!" and "Long live Nixon!" in Polish. They cheered and
shouted and clapped as the presidential car inched its way out
of Victory Square after the ceremony.

The atmosphere of this brief visit was clearly marked by
the optimistic afterglow of the Moscow summit(20). The Poles
were hoping that they might be among the first in Eastern
Europe to reap some of the concrete benefits which were
expected to flow from the new era of East-West cooperation.
After the Nixon-Gierek talks both sides, in a joint communique, noted some differences of views, particularly on Vietnam, but agreed on a mutual reduction of armed forces and
armaments, primarily in central Europe, and on full-scale
economic cooperation. Nixon welcomed the Warsaw-Bonn treaty, including its border provisions, endorsing thereby the
Polish view that the recognition of the Western frontier was
final.(21) At the farewell banquet he stressed his hope that
he expected Poland to be an important participant in the forthcoming negotiations on Europe. There was no doubt that the

visit enhanced the prestige of Gierek both at home and abroad. Poles had every reason to be delighted with the visit and there was evident pride in the comments of officials and in the press commentaries.

This outburst of national pride was laced with a measure of concern that Poland might have appeared to have moved too close to the United States in the eyes of its communist allies, and especially in Moscow's. As a Polish commentator told me in Warsaw, both Prague and East Berlin voiced some objections in Moscow, mostly because they were jealous that "Nixon might have allocated sacks of dollars to Poland." Several editorials were quick to point out that although the visit opened a new chapter in the relations between Poland and the United States, the way to it was paved by the results of "historical Moscow agreements."

By the time Gierek went as the first leader of a Warsaw Pact country to meet the new president, Gerald Ford, in Washington, the "American connection," both political and economic, was well established. In addition, Gierek was the first Polish leader ever to pay an official visit to the United States, which was especially significant for the Polish government in terms of international prestige and progress of detente. The key purpose of the visit was to prolong Poland's economic boom with America's help(22), which obviously would require a further cash flow of American credits, technology and know-how, plus a more receptive American market for Polish goods.

Gierek was very warmly welcomed in Washington and on October 10, 1974 both leaders signed two policy documents establishing the framework of political and economic relations between their two countries for many years to come. For the first time each country was taking a serious interest in the other's markets. In political terms, both leaders agreed(23) on a statement of principles of friendly relations and cooperation, expressed mutual goodwill and mutual trust to work toward a strengthening of European security and provided a wide-ranging framework of further dynamic developments in economic cooperation, including new American credits.

From Gierek's discussions with American political and business leaders, and in his speech before the United Nations, a picture emerged of the self-confident leader of an important European state. Although he was careful to remind his American hosts of Poland's alliance with the Soviet Union, Gierek displayed a perceptive knowledge and use of the Western art of public relations. In an interview with Time magazine, for instance, while responding to a question about the free movement of people and information, he confirmed that Poland fully supported this in all but a few special cases. "For example," he explained, "what would happen if several thousand streakers decided to come to Warsaw and run naked there? That

would be an insult to our morality. I am not sure that the
Catholic faithful in Poland, of whom there are a great number,
would not beat these people up." He also highly praised the
church in Poland (see section, "The Church: A key force in
the country" in Chapter 4). It was statements like these that
moved several American commentators to characterize Gierek as
"an outgoing, highly practical, political animal, who might have
done all right in American politics had his parents moved
across the Atlantic." It was only a statement of the obvious
when, during Gierek's visit, the Washington Post commented
that the Polish leader, by broadening economic ties with the
United States "risks importing inflation and increasing dependence on a political adversary, but he is evidently figuring
that the advantages more than compensate for that."(24)

Here the paper touched on the key issue, the underlying - although never publicly expressed - trend in Warsaw's
"American connection." It was absolutely necessary for Poland
to jump on the bandwagon of one superpower, i.e., the Soviet
Union, particularly in the dynamic period of Russian Westpolitik, but it was still better to have at least one finger in
the other pie, so to speak. The growing dependence of the
Polish economy on economic cooperation with America provided
a useful counterweight to the overriding Polish-Soviet economic
links. Friendly political ties with Washington, particularly
after the obstacle of Vietnam had disappeared, were seen as
capable of providing a useful counterbalance to the unavoidable
and necessary political links in the Polish-Soviet alliance. This
might have been the unexpressed hope of Polish policy makers.
The only hints of this possible policy came in two remarks
made to me in Warsaw by a high official and by an expert on
international affairs. There must be a limit, said one, to the
reduction of American influence in Western Europe. The other
maintained that "for the sake of detente the American military
presence must be maintained in Europe at all costs." As a
comparatively young and very intelligent man put it to me in
Warsaw: "If the American presence in Europe provides an
umbrella for you, at least part of this umbrella covers us as
well. In any conflict we in Poland and the people in Germany
will be in the forefront and will feel the first tremendous
impact." The thinking of an average, politically minded Pole
ran like this: There must not be any conventional conflict in
Europe because of the tremendous striking power of West
Germany. But, at the same time, in the Soviet nuclear strategy the first strike would be against West Germany and NATO
strategists have accepted that the first nuclear strike in a
conflict in Europe would be against Poland. Consequently, in
the present balance of terror Poland and West Germany have a
chance of surviving in the sense that a deterrent will save
them from obliteration. The deterrent was the American military presence in Western Europe.

There was great satisfaction in Warsaw when, in July 1975, President Ford returned Gierek's visit and came to Warsaw to be greeted by a quarter of a million flag-waving, cheering curbside bystanders. It was strongly stressed in Poland that both leaders began to implement the principles formulated in the CSCE document and it was of symbolic significance that both of them left immediately after their talks for the Helsinki conference.

The Polish "presence" in Washington, the buildup in relations with other NATO allies, particularly Britain, France and Italy, the Polish Nordpolitik with Scandinavian countries, could also serve another purpose. Although from the Polish point of view the West German-Polish relationship was of central importance for maintaining European balance and for the security of the continent, too much economic dependence on Bonn and too close political ties with both West and East Germany had to be counterbalanced, as most politically minded Poles told me, by much wider and closer relations with West Germany's partners in both the Common Market and NATO. The underlying fear of West German domination in Western Europe remained almost unchanged. In all Polish official statements the order of priorities in friendly relations with countries other than the socialist ones always put France first, followed by Scandinavian countries, and then all the rest, including Britain, Italy and Belgium. But, in fact, the most important European partners for Poland were Britain and France. And the most important criterion was whether Poland was treated as a national entity, a medium-sized power with whom one had to deal, or as an appendage to Soviet-West European accommodation.

The drive for an enlarged role for Poland made necessary a critical appraisal of any questioning in the West or in the East of Poland's ability to fulfill this role. The most common criticism(25) concerned West European integration and the EEC, whose further development Poland feared could result in a mutilated Europe. This opposition was fully in keeping with the Soviet position, of course, but the motivation differed. For Moscow an integrated Western Europe complicated the exercise of political influence in that area; for Poland it threatened relegation to a permanent position on its periphery. The stronger the signs of West European integration, the more difficult it became for Poland to be "independent" both politically and economically in Europe. Moreover, in some Polish eyes, Western European integration strengthened the system of blocs by increasing similar pressures in the East. What Poles wanted to avoid at any cost was to have Moscow speaking on behalf of all her allies in coming to some sort of terms with the Common Market. Hence, the many Polish semi-official contacts with the Brussels Commission and the insistence on bilateral agreements with EEC members. In this approach Warsaw found a favorable response among EEC members, particularly in Britain and in France.

Franco-Polish relations have enjoyed a long historical tradition. Admiration of all things French was widespread in prewar Poland. After the war Poles liked to think of France as a member of the Western bloc(26), yet a country with an outward-looking policy of bridge building toward the East, as a mirror image of themselves. After all, de Gaulle was the first to recognize Polish western frontiers. Moreover, France favored a looser model of West European cooperation while West Germany has stressed the importance of supranational authority and closer integration up to, and including, the limits of national sovereignty. Secondly, a Western Europe in which France played a strong national, even chauvinistic role, would provide a counterweight to the West German influence for a more closely knit West European community.

When Gierek visited Paris in 1972 he was described and treated as "the number-one Pole." A special relationship between Poland and France was initiated. President Pompidou singled out Poland as the most important country in Eastern Europe, after the Soviet Union. Several economic agreements were signed, but a separate declaration of friendship described the relationship between the two countries as a model of relations between a socialist country loyal to her alliance and a capitalist country which refused to abandon her friends. Gierek acknowledged the existence of the enlarged Common Market as an irreversible fact of life, but there remained considerable apprehension in Poland about the consequences of her trade with the EEC countries. When, in 1975, Giscard d'Estaing chose Poland for his first presidential visit in Eastern Europe, the Polish press excelled itself in repaying the compliment. The warm welcome given the French president during his stay in Poland, against strong objections from French communists, was evidence that Gierek had different goals in mind than the French Communist party and different means to those ends. The narrower considerations of the French Communist party were disregarded in favor of the broader interests of the Polish communist state. The emphasis throughout the talks was political rather than economic. Giscard d'Estaing spoke repeatedly of the progress made by Poland under Gierek and had warm words for the Polish leader himself. He praised(27), his "personal contribution" to what he called "the transformation of Poland." A joint communique noted an atmosphere of "confidence and friendship." Giscard d'Estaing repeatedly emphasized the importance of Franco-Polish relations as a model for states with differing social systems, and said that this model was proof that Europe was "not condemned to division and confrontation, but can organize itself for exchanges and dialogue." Gierek responded by describing France as the first Western nation to espouse the

cause of detente, an assertion which some Western nations will
find debatable, but which presumably pleased the French.

The Poles were particularly pleased when in October 1976
Giscard d'Estaing arrived in Warsaw for a purely informal
working weekend visit. He spent two days with Gierek at the
latter's hunting lodge in the Carpathians. And in the subsequent communique published in Warsaw it became clear that
Poland, according to Giscard D'Estaing(28), could be important
for the French president's new European policy of an "opening
toward the East." Gierek was offered in exchange not only
material aid, vital at a time of serious economic difficulties,
but also political support. He was the first East European
leader with whom Giscard d'Estaing ever held a "working
session" of this type without a fixed agenda or the usual
ceremonial trimmings. This was so much more important for
Warsaw because it happened at a time when clear strains had
appeared in Franco-Soviet relations on human rights.

Britain, of course, had initiated an Ostpolitik well before
de Gaulle talked about it. But when London was involved in
everlasting negotiations with the Common Market and was
looking for its new role in the world, Britain paid much less
attention to Eastern Europe than the Poles would have liked
the British to do. There had been strong links of friendly
and cordial cooperation between Poland and Britain during the
war and these bonds of friendship and comradeship-in-arms
survived very strongly after the war and to a great extent
have changed the attitude of an average Pole from being a
Francophile to becoming an Anglophile. In my conversations in
Poland everybody I met complained about the absence of a
British "political presence" in East Europe for many years
past, which has been "painfully felt."

Although Poles were rather apprehensive about the economic consequences for them if Britain joined the Common
Market, nevertheless there was a strong trend of opinion that
if Britain joined the EEC the political chances of stability in
Europe would be tremendous. "We need Britain in Europe as a
stabilizing factor with her pragmatism and traditions in diplomacy," said one well-known commentator on international affairs. Poles were always looking for a counterbalance to the
West German economic, political and military preeminence in the
European community; they were hoping that with Britain in the
Common Market, a possible strengthening of the British-French
entente cordiale could provide an excellent and firm counterweight to Bonn's economic and financial domination, particularly with British technological potential and know-how.

Political contacts have been becoming more frequent and
more fruitful. Warsaw was looking toward Britain for support
in continuing the CSCE negotiations and in the Vienna Mutual
Balanced Force Reduction (MBFR) talks, for support of compensation payments for Nazi concentration camp victims which

Poland was claiming from West Germany, and for more close and regular political links. Shortly after his visit to Poland in 1973 Julian Amery, then minister of state at the British Foreign Office, agreed that Britain and Poland might have a special role to play at the Geneva-Helsinki negotiations as medium- or small-sized countries - Britain within the Atlantic Alliance and Poland within the Warsaw Pact. Polish Foreign Minister Olszowski's visit to London in April 1974 provided an opportunity to measure the temperature of East-West relations in the new situation created by the change of government in London. Callaghan, then foreign secretary, stated in the House of Commons that the Labor government intended to develop bilateral relations with East Europe "to the limit that each case will allow." Anglo-Polish relations did not appear to be marked by any outstanding difficulties. The Polish minister visualized Britain within the community as a spokesman for better relations with the socialist countries while hoping that the British government would help to dismantle the barriers which limited Polish exports to Common Market countries.(29)

This was followed by Callaghan's visit to Poland in 1975 and the Polish prime minister's visit to London in 1976. The emphasis at these meetings was on widening and deepening economic relations and cooperation. At one time in 1974 Poland was the biggest customer for British goods in Eastern Europe, bigger even than the Soviet Union. It always remained the second biggest trade partner for Britain in the eastern half of Europe.

By 1975-1976 closer political ties with regular consultations at many levels, including the foreign minister level, were well established. As Callaghan, by then prime minister put it:

> We are closely linked, Poland and ourselves, by long traditions of friendship and those traditional ties, combined with our present-day shared interests, with the possibility of our expertise and experience to be linked with that of Poland, give us a chance to make our bilateral relations a model for the development of relations between countries within the Eastern and Western halves of Europe.(30)

In a further warming up of the climate of British-Polish relations, the two unofficial visits by the Duke of Edinburgh to Poland and the first official royal visit to Warsaw and Krakow by Princess Alexandra have certainly contributed very much.

The importance of Poland's Nordpolitik, the opening toward Scandinavian countries, was made explicit by the Polish foreign minister when he said that cooperation with Scandinavia was the third main plank of his country's foreign policy(31),

the other two being the alliance with the Soviet Union and
economic and industrial cooperation with France.

But there was much more to it than just the overall
priorities mentioned by Olszowski. The link with the north
was Gierek's idea expressed in his speech at the United Nations in 1974 of "building a bridge across the Baltic." He
himself had gone to Helsinki and Stockholm, but the Polish
prime minister and other ministers had traveled extensively not
only to those two countries but also to Denmark and Norway
with many return visits from top statesmen of these countries
to Warsaw. Here again was a publicly unexpressed attempt to
create a counterbalance among NATO and the neutral countries
to West Germany's economic assistance and cooperation. Of the
five countries with which Polish trade grew most rapidly, three
were Scandinavian - Denmark, Finland and Sweden - who,
along with West Germany were Poland's main Baltic neighbors
and easily accessible from Gdansk, whose port had been greatly expanded.

Poland took the lead in formulating a Baltic convention
that limited the multilateral use of resources and provided for
the environmental protection of the sea. All the Baltic states,
including East Germany, have signed the convention. Close
relations with Norway have an added significance in view of
the fact that because of the discovery of oil the country will
become by 1980 one of the top ten producers of crude oil and
Poland was looking for alternative sources of energy. In
Polish-Finnish relations, economic considerations apart, the
fact that Finland was playing host to the Helsinki conference
added an important political element. At least as important for
Poland was the Swedish support for the CSCE and the special
contribution that the neutral could make to the solution of
outstanding problems.

Yet Poland's Nordpolitik could find itself in murky waters
in view of the growing Soviet interest in Scandinavia, which
seemed to be increasingly concentrated on the strategic possibilities of the Oslo-administered island of Spitzbergen. Moreover, the Danes were rightly annoyed by the frequent and too
close interest taken by the Soviet air force in Danish shores
and installations. The Norwegians were already concerned
about Soviet designs on Spitzbergen and the strong concentration of troops off the Kola peninsula, the Soviet territory
nearest to Norwegian soil. Closer Polish relations with Norway
and some other Scandinavian countries could put Warsaw in a
ticklish position if Moscow should ever attempt to shift the
moving balance of power. The most recent Swedish differences
with Moscow over security issues, the Baltic oil, and the
problems of political asylum for Soviet refugees in Sweden
added to the delicate situation in which Poland found herself in
her Nordpolitik.

The Polish opening to the West, which also covered the Benelux countries, Italy, Austria and Japan, has raised some questions and caused some apprehension. Many politically minded people in Poland, including some journalists and economic experts, were markedly apprehensive about the state of the Western democracies and appeared concerned lest the inflationary crisis should pave the way toward authoritarian rule, either of the Right or of the Left. Somewhat ironically they were also concerned about the growing left-wing forces, particularly in France and Italy. They were worried about the economic state of Britain and even of further developments in West Germany. This underlined the extent to which the Poles continued to look westward with admiration, and to regard the revival of Western democracy as a matter of vital importance to themselves. They were hoping that backward-looking hard-headed extremists in both the East and the West would be kept under control.

There was certainly no shortage of such hard-headed dogmatists in the East. Already in 1972 Trybuna Ludu reminded its readers that detente strengthened the ideological war in a worldwide confrontation between socialism and "imperialism." An article in an army monthly(32) warned that the new international climate might well be exploited by the West to penetrate the socialist countries with its own ideology and admitted that the new pattern of Poland's international relations might affect the political climate in the country and lead "us to lower our guard and fall into the temptation of extending compromise from politics to ideology." But, obviously, what the Party feared as a threat of ideological penetration was welcomed as an attraction by the people at large. Certainly the Party warnings did nothing to mobilize national sentiment.(33) On the contrary, the national sentiment flourished in the climate of closer ties with the West which were after all traditional in Polish history.

In the West, Poland's westward drive was summed up by the London Times in a question: "How far is Poland running her own foreign policy, and how far is she controlled by Moscow?" Undoubtedly Gierek was stressing Soviet policy objectives at all times. But he himself was simultaneously looking at Moscow's Westpolitik in terms of Soviet power interests and not of ideology. Within this context, while trying to avoid any antagonism between Warsaw and Moscow, he made every effort to assert Polish national interests whenever possible and whenever they were not in open conflict with overall Soviet policies. He even tried to pursue Polish interests when they were slightly at variance with some of the Soviet aspirations. Poland's presence in the West and the country's accessibility to Western businessmen, tourists and even information, might well have disarmed some people in the West in their suspicions about the real Soviet objectives in detente. But it

should not be difficult for the Western policy makers to differentiate between what was really and exclusively in Poland's
interests and what represented a strictly Soviet line.

THE CHINESE FACTOR

Gierek has radically changed Gomulka's policies toward China.
No more ridiculous efforts were made to mediate between Moscow and Peking nor to influence one side or the other. While
not going nearly as far as Ceausescu, Gierek tried to maintain
calm. and qualified objectivity. The first official visit to
Peking for many years by the Polish minister of shipping was
very much played up by the officials I met in Warsaw.
    The situation changed when President Nixon went to
Peking. On the first day of the American visit, Gierek round-
ly condemned Chinese anti-Soviet policies as extremely harmful
and expressed the hope that the Chinese people would throw
out the present leadership.
    According to representatives of the Polish establishment
whom I met in Warsaw, Chinese policies were against Polish
interests for several reasons. Peking was against the Helsinki
conference. The Chinese were emphasizing the Soviet military
threat. They were undermining the principle of inviolability of
frontiers by their anti-Soviet frontier claims. They were
trying to build a cordon sanitaire around Russia in Asia, and
were becoming too friendly with the Americans. Finally, they
were flirting with the Christian Democratic Union - Christian
Social Union (CDU-CSU) opposition in West Germany. Moreover, China's military potential might all too quickly and
dangerously be developed with the help of Japanese technology
and economic cooperation at a time when Soviet-Japanese relations were at a low ebb. On the whole, as one prominent
journalist argued with me: "We are facing a paradoxical situation in which the Chinese, by their policies and attitudes, are
forcing the pace of Europeanization of the Soviet Union; they
force the Russians to try to work within a truly European
framework and to emerge slowly from their Byzantine past and
attitudes."
    The man-in-the-street did not underestimate the possibil-
ity of a Sino-Soviet confrontation, but the main point most
people made was that the Chinese were the only ones claiming
that the Soviet military buildup was directed not so much
against themselves as against Western Europe. In this context, cuts in military budgets, particularly in Britain, but also
in some other Western countries, were described to me as
sheer madness. People I spoke to favorably accepted the
Chinese support for a strengthening of the Common Market and
the NATO alliance, because, in the minds of average Poles,

this was the only counterbalance to the overwhelming Soviet power and the ultimate aims which the Soviet leaders, perhaps not Brezhnev, but his successors, might want to achieve.

LOOKING TOWARD EUROCOMMUNISM

When in the autumn of 1976 I discussed in Warsaw the European Communist parties conference in East Berlin and the problem of Eurocommunism, one professional man, highly intelligent, and a member of the Party told me: "The meeting in East Berlin was important because the statements, particularly by Western communists, could be very helpful to us. Almost like the sound of liberation." The varying interpretations of what really happened in East Berlin, he continued, provided strong evidence of pluralism, a definite split within the communist movement and the third challenge to Soviet hegemony following the examples of Yugoslavia and China: "One can talk about the influence on the Polish situation of Italian communists, but the impact, so far, has only been felt on the first transmission belt and not on the whole huge combine. This is a hopeful, positive and even most promising sign. If I or anybody else were to express controversial views, nobody in the Party could call me a revisionist. The answer is very simple. After all, the 'fraternal' leader Berlinguer says the same."

Many other politically thinking Poles, including Catholic politicians and very many journalists, were overjoyed by the appearance of Eurocommunism on the horizon. This, from their point of view, might in due course have a substantial influence on the situation in Poland. But as almost everyone stressed, one can never know whether the Italian or the French communists, or for that matter the Spanish communists, would, once in power, ever step down if defeated in an election.

When Western European communists came to East Berlin in June 1976 and said openly that the Soviet Union is no longer any sort of model for them, when they talked about the pluralism, democratic elections and the abolition of the dictatorship of the proletariat, then only slightly revised versions of these speeches were reprinted in Polish papers.

There were certain people inside the ruling establishment who pinned quiet hopes on the Italian example and knew that they had no hope of legitimacy until they brought their system closer to the traditions of central and Western Europe. On the other hand, according to non-Party sources, the reason why Moscow had stopped short of formally severing all relations with West European Communist parties and excluding them from the movement, might be that the Russians were still hoping that in the long run these parties would serve its interests by weakening the Western alliance...as well they might.

More dangerous from the Polish leadership's point of view was the fact that among young people, both of communist leanings and those who do not want to have anything to do with communist ideology, the Eurocommunism idea became very attractive. Their line of thinking was very simple: if we have to live in a communist-ruled state, better the solutions suggested by Eurocommunists than the archaic and anachronistic methods applied by the existing Party apparatus.

HELSINKI: HOPES AND APPREHENSIONS

For the Poles wedged between East and West, detente, the relaxation of tension, had a real meaning in terms of increased leeway for self-development of all kinds in the national interest. Hence Poland has been a prime mover in the CSCE.

The geopolitical factor was strictly limiting any reasonable independence in Polish foreign policy, a high Polish official in Warsaw told me in 1971. But these limits fade to a great extent in an atmosphere of detente in Europe. Poland is very firmly locked in between these limits whenever international tension increases, but in a climate of dialogue and cooperation between East and West, Poland might be able to play her part as a "bridge," suggesting and even to some extent influencing the decisions to be taken.

The tightening of the ideological screw imposed by Moscow in preparation for Helsinki, especially after the signing of the final act, was grudgingly accepted by Poland and implemented in practice in many bilateral agreements on ideological issues between Warsaw and other socialist capitals. It was also implemented to some extent and with some qualifications in certain areas of internal policies.

In Polish eyes the detente process must be irreversible since any retrogression would be catastrophic for Poland and for other countries. Unofficially, I was told in Warsaw that the detente process was fraught with many dangers, such as: the danger of a superpowers confrontation in the Middle East and Africa; the Chinese threat, which, however, should not be exaggerated; the unification of Germany, possible though nobody wanted it save the Germans; and the danger of growing nationalism in some parts of Western Europe and certainly in the East European states as well as growing problems with nationalities in the Soviet Union. And finally, the detente process, according to a journalist and a Party member I met in Warsaw, was fraught with dangers because of the global build-up of the Soviet armed forces.

The Poles, both some leaders and the people at large, were certainly very happy with the conclusion of the Helsinki conference and with the results achieved. It was explained to me that whatever the official interpretation of the Helsinki declarations might be, the fact remained that for instance the principle of noninterference in internal affairs of other countries eliminated the "Brezhnev doctrine" of limited sovereignty and therefore (theoretically) excluded military intervention by one socialist state in another socialist state. Most politically minded Poles also saw the "final act" of Helsinki as a document which would not endorse Soviet hegemony over Eastern Europe, and left, unfortunately for the Poles, the possibility of the change of frontiers by peaceful means. It did not sanction government control over the movement of people and information.

In Poland the Helsinki agreement has frequently been invoked, particularly in 1975-1977, on behalf of human rights. It has had a powerful effect as a generator of dicussion, a point of reference, a political and moral yardstick. It has firmly established itself(34) in the vocabulary of East-West relations. Poland has had a better record in the fulfillment of the Helsinki declaration than any other East European country, save perhaps Hungary. She has certainly made giant strides in the direction of economic cooperation with the West. But she has also made good progress in implementing "basket three," in easing regulations and contacts for foreign firms which operate in Poland, and in speeding up visas and similar measures. Poles argued, and rightly so, that their record in freedom of speech, of travel, and of exchanges, was outstandingly good in comparison with other East European countries. This still applied in 1977 despite the often heavy administrative pressure which was put on the dissenters.

For the average Pole, the danger of Helsinki has always been of an illusory success. But, thanks to the human rights controversy, such a flight from reality was no longer possible.

6 From Boom to Reality: December 1975

Few countries in either East or West have undergone such a profound transformation as Poland in 1971-1975. The workers' riots of 1970 swept into power a vigorous administration which modernized the economy and brought a rapid rise in living standards. But, as the leadership prepared for the seventh Party congress in December 1975, it faced some unpleasant decisions about how to correct the severe imbalance in domestic economy and foreign trade which was the price of progress. What happened in and after 1970 became part of East European history and it would be hard to overstress this moment in Poland's postwar years so profoundly did it affect everything in the everyday life of the people, in both internal and external policy. The phrase "Poland 1970" still reverberates around the whole of Eastern Europe as a reminder that people will only put up with so much.(1)

The seventh Party congress had a special significance. It marked the end of the first five years of Gierek's rule. And it also marked the end of the most prosperous five-year period in Poland's postwar history. The leadership embarked on a pragmatic policy of industrial modernization, funded mostly by Western credits, and founded largely on Western technology.

In the Palace of Culture Party members listened in December 1975 to Brezhnev praising Gierek's achievements and giving him his full support. The emphasis put on the consolidation of the Party's position in Poland was a special sign of support for Gierek - with a sort of warning, however, that socialist transformation must achieve a final victory not only in industry but also in agriculture.

Poland approached the congress in an atmosphere of apprehension and questioning.(2) There was great unease about whether the boom could really last. Had Poland not overreached itself? Would the Soviet Union continue to look benignly on Poland as she reached out to the West for trade and investment? Would the West bail Poland out of its 10,000 million dollars in foreign debts by buying more of its products? Would there be enough meat to supply both Western exports and Warsaw? The question about meat did symbolize the country's dilemma. Poles like meat, and as meat eaters were at the top of the world league. Its availability was a measure of the country's progress. But it was also one of Poland's most popular exports, and satisfying both markets abroad and at home was one of the major political challenges facing Gierek when he entered the next five-year period.

Both Gierek and Jaroszewicz realized that the economy was already in danger of overheating. The boom of the last few years had to give way to a more frugal rate of growth and automatically a period of some austerity. There had been many other problems in the last few years and some of these converged upon the Party at a most unpropitious time. As the Polish economy began its upward swing the international economy started on a downward slide. Poland could not develop a closer relationship with Western markets without coming closer to Western inflation as well. Then the domestic market shortages in 1975 led to disturbances and there were clear warnings to a leadership that was itself a product of such unrest.

Because of the serious problems which emerged from the boom strategy, a definite change of course was declared at the Party congress. In a rough draft of the new five-year plan which by the end of 1975 had not yet been fully worked out, real incomes were scheduled to rise by 18 percent (compared with 40.2 percent in 1971-1975); investments by 40 percent (against 90 percent); industrial production, with an emphasis on consumer goods and coal, by 48 to 50 percent (against 73 percent); and agricultural production by 16 percent (against 27 percent). The unpopular and politically dangerous decision to review basic food prices, frozen since 1971, was postponed until 1976.

Gierek outlined two major problems(3) to be solved in the 1976-1980 period. First, the production of market goods and services would have to be substantially increased. Second, export production would have to develop quickly to permit the continuation of an active policy in foreign trade. He warned, however, that in the modernized and reconstructed branches of industry, production increase should be based exclusively on an increase in labor productivity. In the new policy on incomes, Gierek's message to the Polish people could be summed up as, "You never had it so good, but you will have to work harder and more efficiently if improvement is to be maintained."

As Jaroszewicz stressed there was also the problem of the price of imported raw materials.(4) For example, in the second half of the 1971-1975 period, average prices of imports from capitalist countries increased as follows: grains by about 140 percent, cotton by 40 percent, wool by almost 30 percent, oil by over 200 percent, steel products by 130 percent, and paper by about 100 percent.

With all these difficulties, however, the emphasis on a socialist transformation of agriculture remained. Jaroszewicz announced that by 1980 socialized agriculture should increase its holdings from 20 percent to over 30 percent of the total area of arable land, i.e., by about two million hectares. This came as a significant surprise. One of the most important concessions of 1956 was to let the private peasants keep the land they had acquired when the collectives disintegrated, and the private sector had remained predominant in agriculture ever since. Although Gomulka spoke of the gradual socialist transformation of agriculture, he did little to foster its realization, and it was only after Gierek came to power that the program began to be implemented.

According to Western experts the new five-year draft plan could be regarded as the second stage in a ten-year over-all strategy.(5) From being a country where public spending, wages and industrial expansion were allowed to go ahead with temporary disregard for the balance of payments, Poland in the new five-year plan became deeply concerned with its foreign debts, with raising production and efficiency and in saving as much as possible whenever possible.

This shift came as a matter of some urgency because of the complications created for the balance of payments by the world economic crisis. The plan, of course, was overshadowed by nagging political problems which were to test Gierek's abilities, his nerve and stamina, the more so since investment cycles had been delayed and a number of plants for which the most modern technological know-how had been imported from the West were slow in coming into production. Gierek's dilemma was sharpened on the one hand by the need to keep up labor morale to sustain economic growth and on the other by servicing and partly repaying foreign debts.

The generous wage policy of the previous five-year plan had created a serious problem for the new five-year plan. Justified as it was on political grounds, wages heavily out-stripped both the growth in industrial production and the supply of consumer goods (particularly food and especially meat) to a damaging extent.(6) The new five-year plan aimed, therefore, to restore equilibrium by holding back the growth in wages to less than half the previous level while keeping industrial production and deliveries to the consumer market as high as possible.

The three main aims of foreign trade strategy were outlined in the new five-year plan as: 1) to achieve balanced trade by 1980; 2) to raise the share of manufactured goods in total exports; and 3) to increase the share of foreign trade in the national product and bring Polish participation in world markets up to a level compatible with its own size.   In 1975 Poland accounted for 2.5 percent of world production, but only 1.5 percent of world trade.

For a leadership dependent on working-class support, the decision to call a halt to the economic boom and replace it with the prospect of an earned material improvement was a politically dangerous one.   But the change was vital for the maintenance of the economic performance on which support was based.   It was evident from the tone of the speeches at the congress that the emphasis was now on maintaining and expanding what had already been achieved rather than taking bold new steps forward.

In the ideological section of his opening speech, Gierek implied that the transformation of a dictatorship of the proletariat into an all-national state, embodying the will and interest of the entire nation was well on its way to conclusion. The only yardsticks by which a citizen could be measured were "his work and his ideological and moral attitude" Gierek said. The inclusion of "ideological" criterion was a far cry from what he had said earlier in September 1971 (see Chapter 3).

Practical proposals took precedence over ideological formulations in the resolutions of the sixth congress, whereas the resolutions of the seventh congress showed an opposite tendency.   The comparison between these two congresses provides a rough measure of how far Gierek had gone with his plans to strengthen the leading role of the Party and to carry on with the socialization of Polish society.   After the riots of December 1970, the political situation called for a straightforward, pragmatic style.   This Gierek was able to provide, and it was reflected in the resolutions of the sixth congress.   But while the new Party leader saw the value of an infinitely more flexible approach to the economic problems he did not go so far as to see his power base lying anywhere but within the Party. Therefore, while responding to popular pressure for a higher standard of living, he also set out to strengthen the leading role of the Party through an increased emphasis on ideology and Party control.

It was only in his closing speech to the congress that Gierek resembled the leader he was in 1971.   There was not an hour or a day to lose in getting on with the job.   Once again Gierek coupled an appeal for greater productivity and higher standards of workmanship with a characteristic reference to the unity, patriotism and social sense of Poles as a source of future inspiration.

7 The Growing Social Tension: 1975-June 1976

The economic medicine, however necessary, prescribed by the leadership in a vague form at the Party congress, coupled with the uncertainty about the prices of basic foods, was, for the people, very hard to swallow. It is difficult to accept a halt of constantly rising expectations in any circumstances. It was infinitely more difficult in the climate of an ideological offensive, deliberately intensified by the Party, once it became clear that the enlightened, pragmatic, economic policies of the previous five years were not to be confused with or construed as the dispersal of political authority and control.

The Party pressed on with its long-term program of "socialization of society." At the beginning of 1976 the government's policies and various measures had alienated different social groups up and down the country.

Already in 1971 the leadership announced that it intended to revise the constitution of 1952 in view of the social, economic and political changes that had taken place since then. After well over four and a half years the Party disclosed its intention to proceed with the revision when they published in September the guidelines for the 1975 congress. One passage stressed that the leading role of the Party must be confirmed in the constitution. The rights of citizens were to be inseparably linked with the fulfilling of their duties to the state. And PB member Babiuch recommended that the constitution had to reflect Poland's "unshakeable fraternal bond with the Soviet Union."(1)

Poland's great constitutional debate began. There had been a flurry of vigorous protests from various representatives of public opinion. The most substantial opposition came from the church in two memoranda sent to the authorities in December 1975 and in January 1976.(2) The Episcopate opposed the codification of the leading role of the Communist party, the

244

linking of civic rights with citizens' duties, and the inclusion into the basic country's law of "unshakeable bonds with the Soviet Union." They also listed those principles which, in the opinion of the church, and of the Catholic community as a whole, should be incorporated in the constitution. These should include such internationally acknowledged human rights as free elections, free trade unions, and independent law courts. Particularly worrying for the church was the formula linking citizens' rights with the fulfillment of their duties, since this offered an excuse to deny full rights to citizens who, for religious or other reasons, were judged to be neglecting their political duties.

On December 5, 1975, before the beginning of the Party congress, 59 distinguished intellectuals, in a memorandum sent to the Council of State(3), demanded that the constitution should guarantee: freedom of conscience and religion, freedom to work, freedom of expression and information, and freedom of scholarly pursuits and learning. "These fundamental freedoms," said the memorandum, "are not compatible with the official recognition of the leading role of only one Party within the state. Such recognition by the constitution would confer upon that Party the character of a state agency, beyond the control of public opinion." The signatories were, of course, fully aware of the de facto role of the Party and of its monopoly of power. In another move 12 law experts of the Polish Academy of Sciences(4), in a letter addressed to the CC, saw the inclusion of the clause concerning the "unshakeable bonds with the Soviet Union" into the basic law of the country as constituting legalized limitation of Poland's sovereignty. In a letter(5) addressed to the Sejm, 300 academics and students said they regarded the proposed constitutional amendments as being incompatible with the Helsinki spirit. The former education minister under Gomulka, Bienkowski, who was expelled from the party in 1969, stated in an unpublished letter to the Party paper, Trybuna Ludu, that the introduction of the leading role of the Party into the constitution would amount to a "retreat to pre-democratic and feudal traditions."

The Party acted swiftly to preserve the procedural niceties. A drafting commission under the chairmanship of the head of state, Professor Jablonski, met for the first time on January 7, 1976 and within two weeks the chairman was able to present the revised draft amendments to the session of the CC. The first version of the revised amendments was published by official media on January 24, which again, since the Sejm was scheduled to vote them on February 10, left barely 17 days for the consultation with the people so strongly emphasized in all official statements.

After the publication of the revised amendments, several writers, actors, academic and legal personalities lodged a strong protest with the drafting commission. In a sermon in

Warsaw Cardinal Wyszynski(6) went openly into the attack. He
deplored the proposed amendments that would link a citizen's
rights to the fulfillment of his duty to the state, saying: "The
state should protect the rights of the citizens. A citizen
never loses his rights, even if he does not fulfill his duties to
the state." In an apparent reference to Gierek the primate
suggested that no one genius can assure a state's greatness
or its future - this lay in the hands of the nation as a whole.
He then bluntly stated that the Polish government should consider national realities and interests, and not undertake international obligations that would harm the nation's culture and
its economic sovereignty. In conclusion the cardinal warned
that if the authorities persisted in their attempts to destroy
the national culture and the church it would result in a dramatic slowdown of the country's ambitious economic development. Although obviously voicing the feelings of the church,
many of the issues Wyszynski raised were of great concern to
broad sections of Polish society who had hoped that Poland
under Gierek might see a gradual broadening of civic freedom
to complement the leadership's dynamic economic drive. A
prominent CC member described to me the official constitutional
exercise as "provocative."

Although none of these petitions, protests and memoranda
were ever explicitly acknowledged, let alone answered, nor
were the objections either published or openly discussed,
nevertheless they did much to bring about modifications of the
amendments. Gierek, who has always been markedly sensitive
to national feelings and aspirations, seemed to have been
caught off balance by the extent of the opposition. The Party
responded by claiming that hundreds of thousands of citizens
had spontaneously offered the authorities their support.

But an authoritative admission of dissent came from Professor Jablonski, the chairman of the drafting commission,
who, in his presentation to the Sejm of the final text of the
amendments on February 10, admitted that these were not
totally endorsed by the population. He distinguished between
"an insignificant fraction" of chronic malcontents, who took the
opportunity to manifest their hostility to socialism and a "somewhat bigger group" of those who had deliberately "misinterpreted the intentions" of the authors of the amendments.
Obviously this remark referred to the signatories of petitions
to the Sejm, and especially to the protests voiced by the
Episcopate. In Jablonski's opinion it was not possible for such
suggestions to "contain anything constructive" but he did
acknowledge their usefulness, because they pointed out the
need for more explicit formulations.

In fact, the final draft passed by the Sejm on February 10, 1976 was twice revised in comparison with the
original Party proposals. Poland was now a "socialist state"
but the name had not been changed and remained as the Polish

People's Republic. The Party no longer appeared as the sole
"leading force in the state" but as the leading force in "the
construction of socialism" in alliance with the two other Sejm
parties. That "unshakeable fraternal bond" with the Soviet
Union disappeared from the final text. A clause in the original proposal that would have made citizens' rights dependent
on fulfillment of duties towards the state disappeared as well.
There was no mention that citizens would be denied their civic
rights if they did not comply with these duties. Of particular
significance was the removal from the constitution of two of its
1952 clauses providing for legal sanctions in case of "abuse of
the right of conscience and religion," by engaging in action
harmful to state interests and in cases of "sabotage, subversion or other threats to public property." This was another
concession to the petitions which pointed out the danger of a
further restriction of civic rights for dissenters in cases where
the expression of opposing views would be regarded as "harmful to state interests."

But the affair of the constitution did not end in the Sejm
division lobby. In an article published in the Osservatore
Romano by the Archbishop of Krakow, Cardinal Wojtyla, who
was regarded as one of the more prominent figures of the
Catholic Church in Europe, stressed that believers in Poland
were still being treated as second-class citizens. As long as
one single social group, no matter how well deserving, he
wrote, was able to force upon the whole nation an ideology
that runs counter to the convictions of the majority and as
long as in an eminently Catholic country atheism was imposed
as the "foundation of national life," the situation could hardly
be deemed satisfactory.

In a letter to the Speaker of the Sejm, 92 students protested against the enshrinement of the Party as a leading
political force:

> This has nothing to do with democracy or even
> with a socialist democracy. According to its statutes
> the Party is atheistic and therefore its institutional-
> ization endangers the freedom of religion and
> practically abolishes equal rights for believers - the
> overwhelming majority of the people.

In a pastoral letter read in all Polish churches(7) in April, the
Episcopate reiterated the church's opposition to the amendments and in a defiant tone came out in defense of those
citizens who answered the appeal of the drafting commission
and expressed their misgivings through legal channels. In
spite of the legal character of their action, some of the petitioners had recently been subjected to official repression.

The letter confirmed some of the facts which were general
knowledge in the country at the time. Newspapers and period-

icals were no longer able to print the names nor the works of
some of the signatories. Books planned by authors involved in
the protest were removed from publishers' printing schedules
and a number of contracts were cancelled. The effects of the
ban were acutely felt by some artists working for radio and
television who were all dismissed. Tape recordings made by
them were wiped clean.(8)

The repressive measures against intellectuals were confirmed in an open letter addressed to the "Honorable Comrade
First Secretary" by Professor Edward Lipinski at the end of
April and published in full by the Paris newspaper Le Nouvel
Observateur. Professor Lipinski, at that time almost 92 years
old, was perhaps Poland's most famous economist, for 62 years
a militant socialist and still a Party member. In his letter he
recalled the memorandum on the constitution signed by 59
intellectuals and wrote:

> No one doubts that the alliance with the Soviet
> Union has become a political necessity....We would
> like to be good neighbors and form relations based
> on mutual trust. That is impossible until Polish
> policy toward the Soviet Union is purged of all
> traces of servility. That will not be feasible until
> the Soviet Union has the courage to openly admit
> the "errors" she had committed against Poland. In
> the present circumstances, imposing a love of the
> Soviet state on us and introducing it into our
> constitution, demonstrates a total incomprehension
> of human psychology....Ours is a system which
> destroys its critics, a system not answerable to any
> form of social control, which has no respect for
> fundamental civil liberties. It is a system in which
> every change of the ruling group is preceded by
> the spilling of blood....A government imposed by a
> minority has an in-built tendency toward totali-
> tarianism....That is why we need a legal opposition,
> with the rights of freedom of association and as-
> sembly guaranteed by the constitution....Socialism
> cannot be the result of a decree. It is born, and
> can only be born, in the free activity of free
> men....It is imperative to make fundamental changes
> or, at the very least, to make a clear start on them.
> Unless we do so, we will no longer be able to avoid
> a tragedy which could take the form of violent
> revolt, or of a return to Stalinist methods."

Lipinski's open letter to Gierek was an epitaph on the
constitutional issue which had provoked the first real political
controversy during Gierek's five years as Party leader. To
some it might seem immaterial as to what was in the Polish

constitution. Like the parliament, the constitutions of East
European countries are subject to the dictates of the ruling
Communist party. But at the same time the constitution is the
basic law of the land, and in Poland the historical traditions of
the state and of the constitution were taken very seriously
indeed. After the voting in the Sejm, Party officials maintained that the amendments did no more than to codify what
had long been the salient features of Poland's domestic and
foreign policy. But for the average Pole acceptance of
political realities was one thing, but to codify them into the
basic law was another and quite unacceptable proposal.

Poland had, in fact, lagged well behind the other East
European countries in the redrafting of its constitution. What
the amendments were supposed to do was merely to bring her
into line with the other communist states. But even so, while
essentials were maintained in the Polish constitution, the
formulations were considerably toned down. Thus the constitutional amendments, although toned down, were still declared
unacceptable by the church and many other social groups for
two basic reasons. First, in an overwhelmingly Catholic country an atheistic Party could not have the leading role.
Second, the mention of the cooperation and friendship with the
Soviet Union, however politically necessary, and formulated in
strikingly dry words, was regarded as a legal limitation of
Poland's sovereignty.

What the whole exercise had shown was that wide sections
of public opinion were alert, unfrightened and sufficiently
powerful to bring about small but significant changes in government policy. It has also shown that the government,
while certainly dismayed and even shocked at encountering so
much sensitivity and distrust among people it had ardently
wooed for five years, felt calm enough to engage in a certain
amount of genuine consultation and then to admit openly that it
had modified parts of the draft in response to many opposed
reactions. But the modest changes(9) came too late to restore
belief in the government's dedication to the Polish interests.
In the short term Gierek might have managed to save the day
with a virtuoso piece of last-minute political maneuvering. But
the initial, uncharacteristically clumsy handling of the problem
almost certainly damaged the Polish leader's popularity. In
terms of Polish domestic politics, the growing controversy over
the constitution proved to be something of a turning point in
Gierek's Poland.

Some other highly unpopular measures also contributed to
the growing social tension in the country. On May 20, 1976, a
new bill provided for the private land which the owner did not
personally farm to be confiscated and taken over by the state
land fund. The legislation made it clear that the land taken
over would be incorporated predominantly into the collective
sector, and the "gradual socialization of agriculture" would

thus be accelerated. On December 31, 1975 the state land fund had at its disposal well over 920,000 hectares of appropriated or bought-up land which, as two prominent economists told me, remained fallow because the socialized sector did not have enough equipment or money to cultivate it.

The legislation was deeply resented by the individual farmers and the church immediately took up their defense, urging the authorities to stem the unhealthy and disastrous mass migration of rural youth into the cities, to stop the wholesale confiscation or purchase of the so-called "uneconomic farms." "We are defending the rights of private peasants," a member of the primate's secretariat told me, "and in the church-peasant relationship there is not much the state can do without the Episcopate's support." The confiscation of private farms was stopped for all practical purposes in the middle of 1976.

On April 28, 1976, the three separate organizations - the Socialist Youth Union, the Socialist Rural Youth Union, and the Socialist Military Youth Union ceased to exist and were merged into the Polish Socialist Youth Union (see section, "The Young Generation: The Future of the Nation?" in Chapter 4). The essence of your life will be to build a developed socialist society in Poland," said Gierek.(10) After nearly 20 years of a considerable degree of organizational pluralism, young people in Poland were forced back into a mammoth organization, which in its form and contents was very similar to the Soviet Komsomol and to the Association of Polish Youth discredited in 1956. A prominent publicist described it to me in Warsaw as a "provocative Gleichschaltung" of youth.

Under strong pressure from the Episcopate the final implementation of the educational reforms (see sections, "Educational Reform," in Chapter 4) was postponed by the government until 1978. But, in the meantime, the preference of school authorities for Party workers to teach in the new schools and the fact that about half of all parishes had already introduced the new system, moved Cardinal Wyszynski to condemn the state's "political struggle against the church" (May 2, 1976). He most strongly opposed the attempt to replace religion with a sort of "temporal laicism that is a vulgar, psychic and spiritual laziness." "Here we have a source of conflict," a member of the primate's secretariat told me, "in which no compromise is possible for us."

One of the more complex anomalies of the Polish political scene is its intricate network of lay Catholic groups and politicians. These represent some organized form of non-socialist public opinion within the country, and range from the traditional Catholic laymen of the Znak group to the strongly progovernment and firmly Party-associated Pax organization. Its leader, Piasecki, chief of the prewar small fascist Falanga group, formed Pax in 1945, after a long talk with Colonel

Serov of Soviet intelligence. Piasecki, condemned to death by
a Soviet court(11), was released from prison by Serov.   In
between are groupings which express various views of allegiance to the Episcopate, interest in aggiornamento (in other
words, in the implementation of the decisions of the Second
Vatican Council), and commitment to social reform.   It became
clear, at the beginning of 1976, that one part of an overall
government policy was to undermine the most independent
Catholic organizations.

The Catholic Sejm deputies club, Znak, was born in the
great days after October 1956.   During the 20 years of their
political activities, the Znak deputies were in most cases the
only ones in the Sejm who attacked, or even criticized, some
of the government's proposals and legislation.

The first signs of a split appeared at the beginning of
1976 when one of the Znak members, Lubienski, had a long
interview with Gierek without informing the leader of the
group, Professor Stomma.

The 1976 debate over the proposed constitutional amendments led to a deepening of the split.   The Stomma-led
traditional Znak group opposed the amendments and wanted all
Znak members to sign a statement supporting the Episcopate's
criticisms of the amendments.   But three members, including
Lubienski, refused.   In the actual voting in the Sejm, Stomma
was the only deputy to abstain, although it had been agreed
beforehand by all the members of Znak that they would abstain
as a group. While Lubienski officially played the main role in
the Znak splinter group, the real force behind him and the
split was another Znak deputy, Zablocki.   Stomma's name
failed to appear on the list of candidates for the 1976 March
Sejm elections and all the Znak's seats in the new Sejm went to
the Lubienski-Zablocki faction.   This group insisted on
retaining the name Znak for the new and entirely different
body of Catholic deputies, despite strong opposition from the
former Znak representatives and the majority of politically
active Catholic opinion.(12)   After the Sejm election, the Party
paper, Trybuna Ludu, stressed, significantly, that Znak would
continue its work in parliament under the same name, although
under a different leadership and in a greatly modified constellation of members.

Outlining the new Znak's programmatic principles at the
first session of the Sejm in March, Zablocki said that the
"common program of the Front of National Unity would remain
the main criterion of Znak's work."   This was a declaration of
far-reaching loyalty which left little doubt that the new Znak
would be much more amenable from the Party point of view
than the former independent group.

By transforming the Znak club the authorities hoped to
weaken the "only center of rightists' social forces" as described in 1974 by the PB member Szydlak.   The leadership

has always been unwilling to risk a frontal confrontation with the church and therefore the authorities have chosen to attack some of the church's main outlets. Cardinal Wyszynski made it clear that any attack on Catholic intellectual circles would be seen as a direct attack on the church itself.(13)

II

The Fulcrum of Poland's Fate

8 One Friday in June 1976

> Who is not prepared today
> will be less so tomorrow.
>
> Ovid

The Party congress in December 1975 marked the end of the unprecedented most prosperous period in Poland's postwar history. To give the country this strong push forward, Gierek had deliberately ignored the cost, calculating that once the economy had achieved a certain momentum it could start paying its bills automatically. The turning point arrived at a time when Gierek's success had generated a revolution in people's rising expectations. After five years of efforts to establish a personal dialogue with the people of dynamic economic growth and endeavors to simultaneously develop heavy industry and a consumer society, Gierek ran up against the constraints of economic reality.

A belated attempt to get the economy back on the rails by a package of price increases in June provoked massive workers' protests and forced the government to capitulate within 24 hours, for the third time in six years. The June crisis had been preceded by growing social unrest in Poland which showed how much importance the people had attached to an agreement on political consultations which, they believed, the country's leadership had finally concluded with them after decades of authoritarian rule. Polish society insisted that the leadership acknowledge the real political meaning of its pledge and that this be put into practice. As one highly placed CC member told me, the June decision was the last straw, with political measures which were regarded by the people as either unnecessary and provocative, or, at best, misjudged and misconceived.

255

After coming to power in the wake of the violent food price riots which had toppled his predecessor, Gierek was acutely conscious of the need to formulate such policy changes well in advance; the 1970 price rises which toppled Gomulka had been ill conceived and ill prepared. Gierek had realized then that what Poland needed was not just a new economic policy to quell the immediate source of discontent but also a new style of government.

What went wrong then? Basic food prices had remained constant since February 15, 1971 - largely for political rather than economic reasons. For all his caution Gierek knew that price increases would have to be introduced sooner or later. The only question was how this should be done...and it was on this issue that serious mistakes were made. The first official hint of impending price increases came at the Party congress in December 1975 when Gierek warned that "...the structure of basic food prices would be analyzed in 1976 by the government which, after 'consulting on the problem with the working people would submit appropriate proposals."(1)

On March 21, 1976, at a Sejm session the prime minister envisaged future changes in the price structure which would adapt market supply to economic potential while simultaneously giving another commitment not to decrease living standards.

Those were the only two official warnings, except that according to Deputy Premier Jagielski, in an interview with the West German weekly, Stern, the price increase problem "was discussed and an opinion poll in the Party was conducted, although on a limited basis." Otherwise possible price increases became a taboo in the mass media, which merely mentioned the cost of the freeze in basic food prices and cautiously hinted at the need to restructure prices. But all the while the Party line ceaselessly peddled by the media had been the propaganda of success. The focus on Poland's economic progress and the country's growing international stature, both genuine enough, had been allowed to obscure Poland's difficulties. The press extolled the brilliant successes of the regime, churning out statistics on the rising standard of living and smugly assuring people that socialism would protect them from the economic recession and inflation of the Western world. In the days immediately preceding Friday, June 24 some Party activists in the 160 largest enterprises had indeed been consulted by the Party leadership. And then came the crunch, and with it a period of contradictions, hesitations, inertia and diffidence.

9 Events Speak for Themselves: June 1976-March 1977

Wednesday, June 23

At a session of the politburo of the Central Committee strong differences of opinions emerge less about the need to increase prices, than about the manner and the range of the operation. Gierek, Szydlak, Jaruzelski and Wrzaszczyk argue against the proposed package. But finally they submit both to the arguments and to the decision of the majority under the peculiarly communist device of "democratic centralism." Minister of Defense, General Jaruzelski warns that the army will not intervene if there are any disturbances.

Thursday, June 24

The leadership "consults" 46 of the highest Party echelons and some directors of the largest industrial enterprises. On the hot line to Gierek all but one of the 49 first secretaries of the VPCs assure him that the working people fully accept the proposed increases.

Meanwhile, the Sejm in session has exhausted the only two items on its agenda by lunchtime. Radio Warsaw does not explain what brings the deputies back into the chamber after lunch but reports the speaker's announcement that the Sejm presidium has received a letter from the prime minister and the additional item on the agenda reads: "The Motion of the Council of Ministers on the subject of a proposal to make certain changes in the structure of retail prices and the principles on which the nation is to be compensated for the effects of these changes."(1)

With Gierek listening from his seat in the chamber, Prime Minister Jaroszewicz announces the following price increases to take effect from Sunday, June 27: a) food prices between 30 percent and 100 percent including meat (69 percent), poultry, butter, sugar (100 percent); b) payments to the peasants for their deliveries of agricultural products by between 12 percent

257

and 50 percent; and c) the cost of vital agricultural production means and services by 20-45 percent.

To compensate for the proposed price increases, the government announces wage supplements ranging between 280 zlotys in the lower income bracket to 600 zlotys for the highest salaried staff, as well as some increased allowances for each child, nonworking mothers and student grants.

In introducing the package Jaroszewicz refers to the "lively discussion and national debate" which had supposedly taken place before the Sejm session. PB and CC member Babiuch, accepting the proposals on behalf of all the parliamentary parties, recommends that they be presented for consultation with representatives of factory employees, institutions and parishes and the results of these discussions be reported back to the Sejm. The consultations are scheduled to take place the next day, Friday, June 25, and parliament will discuss and vote on the proposals on Saturday, June 26. From other passages in Jaroszewicz' and Babiuch's speeches it becomes clear that the discussions the prime minister mentioned were actually conducted with economic experts.

The official PAP communique on the Sejm session says that by announcing the price increases in advance the government has expressed its confidence in society and its faith in "civil discipline." The government(2) is confident that the people will not betray this trust.

Friday, June 25

This morning the busy clamor of factories is missing; machines are idle, work benches empty. The country had erupted with well-organized and mostly calm strikes and sit-ins in at least 130 of the nation's largest factories. Strike committees suddenly appear on the surface and remain in telephone communication with many other factories. The simultaneous timing of strikes was almost perfect.

At the Ursus tractor factory just outside Warsaw the group of workers march to the administration building, where attempts by the manager and the secretary of the Party organization to calm the situation end in a scuffle. The workers ask for a consultation with the highest Party authorities but this is rejected by the management. Security men circulate among the workers and mark those who are most outspoken with a phosphorizing paint which is invisible during the day but clearly detectable in the evening.

Five thousand tractor workers now march to the railway lines outside Warsaw and sit down on the tracks, stopping local trains into the Polish capital. The Paris-Warsaw express is trapped as rails are ripped up while metal barriers and wooden sleepers are slung across the track. The overhead electric power supply is cut off. As passengers leave the train, strikers insist the express will not be released until the government drops the price increases or at least reduces the

size of the rises. Militia cars block the road half a mile from
the factory gates, but train passengers walk around the road
blocks and join the strikers. Workers stand on an embankment
overlooking a solid line of halted trains which disappear
around the bend. They demand that the price rises be reduced. To quote one man: "Wages have been pruned down
enough. The average increase is 60 percent on basic things
we buy. We just want prices put back. Maybe we can just
agree on a maximum 10 percent rise." And another striker:
"The whole of Poland is out on strike today."

Plock, northwest of Warsaw

A giant petrol-chemical complex stands here, the site of a
vital link between gas pipelines from the Soviet Union to East
Germany and elsewhere in Poland. Over 20 workers are on
strike in the transport and maintenance department. The
whole plant will come out on strike within the next 24 hours.
Demonstrations take place in the city streets.

Radom, a manufacturing town southwest of Warsaw

The workers on the early shift at the General Walter
weapons and ordnance factory come out on strike. The Walter
plants has, until now, counted as a politically most reliable
enterprise. The workers form themselves into a column,
carrying red flags, singing the Polish national anthem and the
Internationale. They are joined by workers from other plants,
by housewives and large numbers of pupils from local schools.
The majority of the strikers are young people.

The demonstrators make their way to the local Party
headquarters, where the Radom Party first secretary refuses
to talk to them. The workers want him to forward a resolution
to Gierek in which they demand the cancellation of the price
rises and ask for improvements in conditions in the more
neglected factories. So far the demonstrations are orderly and
well organized. The first secretary's deputy attempts to
negotiate with the demonstrators. During the exchanges a
woman carrying a small child shouts that she earns 2,200
zlotys a month and that this is not enough to feed the child,
then asks the secretary how much he earns. His sarcastic
reply is that if the woman was so concerned for her child she
should not have brought it to the demonstration. At that the
furious woman throws herself at him. A worker in overalls
exclaims that he only gets one set of working clothes a year
despite his right to four sets, then challenges: "How much did
the Party secretary's shoes cost?" When the official refuses to
reply, the answer is hurled back in his face: "Six thousand
zlotys!" At that point a voice in the crowd suggests that the
secretary should have his expensive clothes taken off him and
this is duly done. The Party secretary flees into the Party
building with just his underwear.

The crowd has been thrown into an ugly mood by these
exchanges and now storms the Party headquarters. The gate

is smashed with a tractor and once inside the demonstrators
are even more infuriated to find the building well stocked with
various luxury foods. Furnishings are destroyed, files thrown
out the windows and the whole place set on fire by a crowd
shouting: "Down with the traitor's Party and down with price
rises." Many workers burn their Party membership cards.

Early in the afternoon the second shift, as well as a
number of hooligans, join the demonstrators. Destruction of
private property and some other public buildings, together
with shop looting, now begins in earnest. The demonstrators
spread through the town. Firemen are prevented from ex-
tinguishing the deliberately started fires and barricades are
erected around the town. Petrol is pumped from a tanker
along the whole high street and set alight as a measure against
the militia. Security police reinforcements from elite units in
Warsaw arrive by helicopters and counterattack. Although no
firearms are used a street battle takes place in which the
security police use special riot truncheons against the rioters
who have armed themselves with, among other weapons,
butcher's knives. The battle lasts from noon until midnight
and the situation is eventually brought under control only by
the use of tear gas. During these events the demonstrators
are filmed from helicopters to try to identify the participants.
Later, according to official sources, two people died and 75
were injured that day.

As of noon in Plock emergency courts martial begin
handing out sentences of up to ten years imprisonment to
strikers and hooligans.

Shipyards at Gdansk and Gdynia are fully on strike.
The strike committee in Gdansk has closed all the gates leading
to the shipyards, and members of the committee on watch at
the gates send back home all those workers they knew could
provoke disturbances. The strike is absolutely orderly and
calm.

The General Swierczewski tool factory workers in Warsaw
go on strike. Works stoppages also occur at the Zeran car
plant where the Polish Fiat is produced and at the Warynski
crane plant.

The workers in many other places come out on strike,
including two factories in Nowy Targ, a truck factory at
Starachowice, in Pruszcz Gdanski, Elblag, Szczecin (one of the
big ports on the Baltic Sea) and in the Lodz textile mills.
Again all the strikes are well organized, extremely well timed
and orderly. Everywhere the workers have made sure that
everything is left in working order, but refuse to work until
the price increases are withdrawn....

All these disturbances and strikes are not mentioned by
Warsaw media, which still push the line on "consultations."
Meanwhile, reports from the regions are pouring in to the CC

headquarters. Later during the day a delegation of women textile workers from Lodz appears in the CC building in Warsaw and is assured by Gierek that the price increases would indeed be withdrawn.

Shortly after 2000 hours Prime Minister Jaroszewicz, visibly shaken, addresses the nation on radio and television. He has asked parliament to withdraw the government's draft of price increases since consultations had been had with workers on the issue and many proposals and remarks which merit thorough examination had been made. "In this situation" the government thinks it necessary to restudy the whole problem again and this will take several months. The decision is "yet another confirmation of the democratic principles by which the Party and the government guide themselves in their social policy" and it is hoped that this step "dictated by the highest interests of the nation would be accepted with a sense of responsibility and in an atmosphere of hard and disciplined work."(3) The short statement lasts under three minutes and contains no reference to the strikes and protests which were now the unpalatable reality of "this situation."

In the words of a retired senior government official: "The mood has gone dangerously sour." Or as a young, smiling Ursus factory worker puts it when learning of the backdown: "Now we know how to push them back."

Saturday, June 26

During the night militia and security police, who yesterday behaved with by and large reasonable restraint, now begin mopping up demonstrators and strikers. "Now they'll have a chance to get their own back!" says a Party official. In Radom, 2,000 workers and hooligans are arrested and all immediately dismissed from work. Most of the Radom demonstrators are sent to prisons outside the city. Within hours local administrative tribunals sentence minor offenders to fines and imprisonment. In a number of cases the principle of collective responsibility is applied to justify the sentence imposed. The official argument is that the defendants took part in a public gathering, the participants of which committed acts of violent assault.

In the Ursus tractor factory well over 120 workers are arrested and many more dismissed; 50 offenders are fined or sentenced to imprisonment by administrative tribunals.

Ninety-three persons in Radom and 45 at Ursus declare that they have been beaten up and their families have seen the traces of maltreatment. Those arrested are passed through so-called "health paths," i.e., forced to run militia gauntlets while they are beaten by truncheons. In many instances fines and dismissal from work imposed by local administrative tribunals are objected to by militia as being too mild, whereupon the cases are instantly reviewed and harsher punishments of two to three months inprisonment, often combined with fines,

are meted out. Dismissals take place in most other strike-
bound factories and the number of dismissed strikers ranges
from 20-600, the biggest being in the Gdansk shipyards and in
the Zeran motor car plant.

The situation now appears to be returning to normal.
People are out doing their weekend shopping as usual and
workers report back to work. Here and there the withdrawal
of price increases is celebrated with bonfires.

The Sejm session scheduled to approve the rises has been
postponed indefinitely.

Radio Warsaw announces that the withdrawal of price
rises, after consultations with the workers and the population,
constitutes a great victory for socialist democracy. Indeed the
mass media insists that democratic consultations with the
workers in their factories were held on Friday. The strikes
and other disturbances are blamed on "irresponsible elements"
and "adventurers masquerading as workers."(4)

Sunday June 27 - Monday, June 28

The Party apparatus now applies the old discredited
prescription of carefully organized mass meetings which will
automatically condemn the strikers and demonstrators, express
confidence in the leadership and support the idea of price
changes. According to official claims, between 50,000 and
200,000 people take part in each of the rallies organized by
the Party all over the country.

At a rally of Warsaw citizens, the Warsaw Party first
secretary, Kepa, admits that there have been disorders in
Plock, complete stoppages in some Warsaw factories, and partial
ones elsewhere. A resolution passed(5) by the meeting con-
demns the action of those workers who downed tools in an
attempt to disrupt the dialogue the Party had initiated with the
people. The rally is being held at the Warsaw stadium which
has a seating capacity of 80,000 yet is - according to Radio
Warsaw - attended by 120,000. A West German television
correspondent points a camera toward large empty sections of
the stadium and records that the crowd consists of a selected
audience, all those present having been equipped with special
recognition tags.

The PAP reports the conviction which prevails "that it is
indispensable to restructure the prices and that the decision to
examine thoroughly the results of the social consultation that
has enriched the proposal with valuable comments and other
proposals from the working class was a correct one." The
press takes a tough line on the damage done, denouncing it as
the work of an "irresponsible minority." Demands for "severe
conclusions" to be drawn in regard to the rioters are voiced.

The official image of mature, level-headed workers in
their factories discussing the price rises while an irresponsible
handful of hooligans take to the streets does not go down well
with the country's workers. Radio Warsaw concedes that

"businesslike debate and sensible argument are sometimes joined by emotion." There are hints that communication between the authorities and the workers is not all that could be desired. One paper, <u>Slowo Powszechne</u>, while condemning the riots points out that "an increasingly enlightened society needs to have full access to rational argument and this is not merely a mechanical process." Perhaps predictably, messages of support for Gierek and the Party leadership fill at least three pages of most Party papers over the coming four days.

All the organized rallies are fully covered by PAP reporters. Each of them is instructed to prepare two reports. The first one, circulated to all mass media, is supposed to describe in glowing terms the mass attendance at the meetings, the enthusiasm and the warm support for Gierek and the whole Party leadership. The second, confidential report, typed by selected PAP secretaries in locked rooms, and destined for the eyes of the organizational department of the CC, describes what actually happened at the rallies. These accounts register who said what, note all the complaints and accusations, and report the instances when so-called resolutions were not voted or passed by the meetings, but simply prepared by the Party secretary and handed over to the PAP reporter.

On Monday, five special administrative tribunals take over in those towns where riots occurred. Each of them pronounces some 700 sentences a day. By July 4 it will have been estimated that some 5,000 persons were sentenced - usually to three months prison plus 5,000 zlotys fines.

Tuesday, June 29

In an open letter to the speaker of the Sejm, eleven intellectuals praise the government for withdrawing the price legislation in the face of workers' unrest and avoiding the bloodshed which occurred in similar situations in Poznan in 1956 and at the Baltic ports in 1970. The events of the last few days, says the letter, indicated that under the present system the only way in which the real views of the citizens emerge were in the form of dangerous outbursts of social dissatisfaction. This kind of system could not be continued without risking an incalculable catastrophe. The letter adds: "The establishment of a real workers' representation has become an urgent issue. The trade unions did not fulfill this role during the latest events thus proving that they are fictitious." To remedy this situation nationwide discussions must be more authentic and a "broadening of democratic liberties" including a free press and the right of free association must be allowed.

Gierek, who since the Sejm session on Thursday, June 24 has remained completely in the background, arrives in East Berlin for the long-delayed conference of European Communist parties. Almost immediately he has "a friendly meeting" with Brezhnev and also with Husak, general secretary of the

Czechoslovak Communist party. The internal situation of
Poland is discussed, and both leaders as well as the leaders of
the Bulgarian and Yugoslav Communist parties want to hear
from Gierek what had truly happened, and why.

Wednesday, June 30

In the first official version of the events in Radom on
June 25 the mayor of the city, Karwicki, maintains that a
group of Walter factory workers went into the streets, where
they were joined by "parasitic, hooligan, criminal and antisocialist elements." It was in this "well-chosen" company,
says the mayor, that the group had terrorized the personnel
of other factories and set fire to the Party committee headquarters. "Drunken hooligans and hysterical women ran the
show, the mayor complains. Seventy-five militia men were
wounded, and two participants in the riots were dead -
"crushed by their own cronies with a trailer used for building
a barricade." The militia detained, on the same day, a
number of "active participants" in the incidents, some of whom
had already been sentenced by administrative organs.(6)

In Plock, a press conference for foreign journalists is
held. The managing director is present and the secretary of
the Party organization is in the chair. One of the journalists
asks the Party secretary for details of the strike and demonstrations in Plock on June 25. The secretary, looking clearly
apprehensive, turns in desperation to the managing director.
"My God. What shall I tell them? How many details can I
disclose?"

In the Ursus tractor factory outside Warsaw which was
strike bound on June 25, a production meeting is held. It is
disclosed that out of 15,000 workers only 1,200 stayed behind
to man essential equipment during the massive strike. Referring to the price increases, the meeting report says: "We take
the view that each action of this kind must be shored up by
the necessary economic analysis which should be presented to
the people and must be preceded by preparatory political
work...."

One participant in the meeting maintains that "these
things would not have happened if our shop floor activists had
talked to people beforehand and if they had found time for the
people." In striving to improve communication with the
workers, the first secretary of the Basic Party Organization
(BPO) states: "We must teach everyone respect for others and
courage to tell the truth. What is most valuable at our Party
conferences is the fact that we are learning to say 'no,' 'not
like this,' 'you are wrong,' and 'your work is no good and we,
the workers, have to pay for it.'"(7) In short, the plant
committee at Ursus admits a complete breakdown in communication between the Party and workers.

A comment in the Warsaw daily, Zycie Warszawy emphasizes that the civic consultation on the price proposals had

turned into a "genuinely creative, honest, economic dialogue" which was "proof of the democratic principles that guide the Party in its social policies."

Friday, July 2

After a week's absence from the public scene in Poland Gierek faces the workers once again at a mass rally in the Silesian industrial city of Katowice. He calls on the Poles to join in what he terms open, honest and sincere discussions aimed at finding the solution to the national problem of food prices. After the setback of price increases, Gierek has significantly, chosen to mount what might be termed a counteroffensive from the secure base of his own home constituency. He tells the rally that the government will reintroduce the "unavoidable" price increases only after it has consulted "patiently and tenaciously" with the people, seeking solutions which will unite the Polish community. He does not concede the point that the workers definitely felt they had not been consulted, but his urgent pleas for a democratic dialogue suggest that past experience had left something to be desired.

Obviously very moved, Gierek refers to the disturbances as painful and important. Significantly he stresses that patriotic consciousness, political maturity and civic discipline should constitute the basis of national life and would create an atmosphere in which "no one, no outside interference, would ever be able to disturb Poles when they were discussing national issues among themselves." In discussing the strikes Gierek tries to isolate the strikers and protesters from the great majority of workers who had participated in "responsible and serious discussions." Noticeably lacking, however, are any references to hooligans, rioting or looting. This emphasis, which prevailed in the initial reactions to the strikes, has all but disappeared from the broad lines of official comment.

Monday, July 5

Prime Minister Jaroszewicz warns that the present structure of prices has become a barrier to further development, but the Party remains determined to maintain a high rate of development. The solution, therefore, is price increases which the Party will undertake only after an exchange of views and opinions with society. This exchange, he claims, has now yielded its results. Price levels would first be raised successively in separate groups of goods and then on a small scale each year so that further high increases following years of frozen prices would be avoided.

Draft proposals, according to Jaroszewicz, will be drawn up on the basis of consultations so far and these will be submitted to the Sejm committee for further discussion. The Sejm text(8) will be submitted for discussions in factories and institutions, and after a nationwide discussion the government will take a stand on the motions put forward during the consultations and present the issue at the plenary session of the Sejm.

Tuesday, July 13

With the caution of those once bitten the leadership begins its second attempt to raise the prices of some basic foodstuffs. Speaking at the session of the politburo of the Central Committee Jaroszewicz reports that the government, after consultations with the workers, had decided that the prices of meat, meat products and poultry only should be raised in 1976 by about 35 percent (69 percent in the original package) and this would not come into effect until the government's proposals were examined by the appropriate Sejm committee and discussed with the workers. Other food prices, Jaroszewicz promises, will remain unchanged in 1976, but will be "examined in the years ahead."

In a related development the Council of Ministers announces a rise in payments by the state to farmers for their agricultural products (between 19.2 and 45 percent) and in retail prices for agricultural production essentials, such as fodder, seeds, machinery and building materials (between 25 and 45 percent). The increases are to become effective next day, July 14. Procurement prices thus rise 19.2-45 percent. But at the same time farmers will have to pay 25-45 percent more for their production essentials. As compensation, however, the Council of Ministers announces that banks will allow for remission of part of the credits taken out by farmers for building projects. The farmers were satisfied with the original proposals in the June package and the danger exists that they could withhold or reduce deliveries if the promises made to them on June 24 were not kept.

By raising procurement payments before meat prices and far in advance of other price increases the government has actually accepted increased economic burdens for the sake of political calm. This represents a partial concession toward economic reality and a further bow in the direction of the people. In putting forward the revised proposals so soon, however, the authorities are presumably hoping to dissuade the nation from rubbing salt in wounds which, until three weeks ago, had been dormant since the 1970 riots which brought Gierek to power. Now the official reaction to the June upheaval is taking its hesitant course.

REPRESSIONS AND HESITATIONS

With the beginning of July, the official reaction to the protests and strikes moved from the stage-managed mass rallies to trials of individual workers who had participated in the demonstrations. The trials, together with wholesale dismissals and several bitter complaints about militia brutality both during the investigations and in the prisons, provided one of the main topics on the internal Polish political scene during successive months. According to the European Trade Union Confederation in Brussels(9), 6,000 workers were arrested during and after the June troubles and some 20,000 lost their jobs.

The trials played down the political aspects of the strikes. Because of scanty media coverage, however, it was difficult to distinguish the various crimes allegedly committed by the accused. It often remained unclear who was sentenced for committing specific offenses under the penal code and who was imprisoned merely for participating in strikes or peaceful demonstrations in factories or in the streets. The PAP reports on court proceedings only covered one of four known Radom trials together with the Ursus trial and two appeals dealt with by the supreme court.

The authorities reissued directives to the managements of large enterprises saying that workers who refused to work could be dismissed, not for political reasons, but for breach of contract. However, under the pressure of public opinion, some workers were reinstated although in lower graded and worse paid jobs. Moreover, a number of those sentenced have since been quietly released or their sentences suspended. The hesitation and indecision of the authorities as to how best to proceed was quite clear.

Some facts, however, based on official information and on eye-witness accounts can be established. On July 19 in Radom six men accused of "taking a particularly active part in street riots, attacks on militia and plundering public property" were sentenced to prison terms of between four to ten years. On subsequent appeal the supreme court upheld the nine- and ten-year sentences on two of the defendants. Three others had their sentences reduced or suspended, and the last defendant was set free pending retrial. A source inside the courtroom later quoted the prosecutor as saying that nearly all the defendants were "genuine representatives of the working class and not hostile elements, but they were overcome with a passion to destroy."

On July 20 seven workers from the Ursus tractor factory, charged with destroying railroad tracks, derailing a locomotive and threatening its engineer, received sentences of three to five years. These were commuted by the supreme court to suspended one-year sentences. The prosecutor did not proceed on the possible charge of sabotage for which the maximum penalty is death.

About three weeks before the Warsaw trial the text of a letter signed by 67 Radom workers complained to the public prosecutor about militia torture. "Every one of us," the letter said, "was forced to crawl through a double row of police officers armed with truncheons who beat and kicked us till we were unconscious." A similar complaint drawn up by 17 families of workers injured by the militia was also circulated in Warsaw.

On July 29 the official government spokesman, Minister Janiurek, speaking to foreign journalists stressed that although there would be no action against the majority of those workers who had protested, further trials were planned against "a certain number of delinquents." The 53 persons already tried, he added, were brought before normal courts of law, not special courts set up immediately after the disturbances – thus contradicting the mayor of Radom who on June 30 stated that several dozen workers were convicted immediately by special administrative tribunals. The announcement that 53 persons had been sentenced thus far came as a surprise since only two trials had been reported and only 13 convictions made public. It left, therefore, 40 unaccounted for by the media.

While reports were coming from all over the country about hundreds of trials of individual demonstrators, three other workers of the Ursus plant, accused in the Warsaw court on December 29 of tearing up railway tracks near their factory were sentenced to prison terms of one to three years. All three claimed that they had been badly treated after being arrested. One of the three, Marek Majewski, claimed that his jaw had been broken in two places during interrogation. His trial had to be postponed because he had to be sent to the hospital to have his jaw operated on.

Further repressive measures included disciplinary transfers of workers from their jobs to other distant factories and unexpected call-ups for three-months military service.

On November 19 the government spokesman Janiurek complained to foreign correspondents about distorting reports on life in Poland in Western mass media, and of "lie-studded" articles in the Western press and maintained that 74 persons, mainly from Radom, were now being held in penitentiaries – all of them guilty of criminal offenses. He added that upon the recommendation of the Council of State, a certain number of persons have been released from prison. When queried by a correspondent about the militia reprisals, Janiurek said that he felt the militia had behaved correctly although he did not deny the essence of the charges. He could "officially and authoritatively" state that nobody was punished for striking, but he admitted that dismissals were possible. As to the extent of the June protests, Janiurek emphasized that on June 25 "less than 0.5 percent of all workers and employees in the whole of Poland went on strike."(10)

In this atmosphere of repressive reaction – some of it sporadic at local levels, some more massive – tension grew and the kaleidoscope of significant events further unrolled each day.

July 16

In a letter to the prime minister the Episcopate protests against the harsh punishments inflicted on workers and calls for an end to "interrogations, arrests and investigations" of those involved in the rioting while condemning the excesses of a "few antisocial elements." The government is wrong, says the Episcopate, to blame the workers when the protests were due to a miscalculation by those in high places, and to faulty information supplied to the authorities by the government-controlled trade unions. Moreover, the authorities acted unconstitutionally by dismissing some workers and then offering them less well paid jobs far from their homes, only because they protested to protect themselves and their families from excessive price increases imposed by the authorities through miscalculation.

In an appeal to the first secretary of the Italian Communist Party, Berlinguer, Jacek Kuron, a historian and one of the leaders of radical leftist dissent, describes in detail the events of June, including the massive reprisals against the strikers and innocent bystanders, and concludes:

> The blame for all this lies with the system which does not allow the workers any means of expressing their opinions. To hold workers, demonstrators, morally and legally responsible for damage that has actually been caused by the system is a vendetta by men who during their 30 years in power have learned nothing and understood nothing....(11)

July 20

In an almost instant reaction, the Italian communist Party secretariat in a note to the Polish Party CC complains that there had been a lack of information about the trials and reiterates their belief that "it must be possible in socialist countries to resolve social conflicts without serious disturbances through a continuous search for active collaboration by the workers.(12)

Meanwhile, Gierek assures Party activists from major industrial enterprises that no "instant decisions" would be made on meat prices. The consultation process, though longer and slower, will be followed because it "takes better account, not only of political and economic reasons, but also of psychological and emotional factors that are extremely important in the life of every community."

July 23

Another letter appears, this time in the Paris paper, Le Nouvel Observateur, addressed to American, British, French and West German intellectuals – to all those "who have defended the persecuted people of Chile and Spain, Czechoslovakia and the Soviet Union." In it 13 Polish intellectuals protest against sentences in the Ursus and Radom trials and argue that to prevent dramatic upheavals in the future it would be necessary to return to the workers the rights which were theirs and not to use repression. The appeal ends: "Help the imprisoned Polish workers."

August 16
Sugar rationing is introduced.

August 18
A number of Party members in Radom, the scene of the most serious riots in June, are expelled from the Party, because they remained "passive" during the disturbances, and apparently never attended the Party meetings.

August 26
Cardinal Wyszynski speaking to 200,000 pilgrims in Czestochowa on the six hundredth anniversary of the shrine of the Black Madonna warns:

> If we want greater efficiency from our people - an indispensable factor in rebuilding the economy - then let us endeavor to liberate ourselves from the imposed policy of atheism. The atheistic campaign not only slows down the economic and social transformation of the country, but whips up mistrust against the authorities even when they make sensible and necessary decisions. There is no other force but the church which can unite the whole nation in tragic circumstances.

September 3
In his second face-to-face meeting with workers since the June events, this time in Mielec, Gierek promises(13) no early respite and implies that the situation would get worse before it could improve. The country had suffered a third bad harvest this year which would mean massive grain imports of over seven million tons in 1976. To seek proper solutions, Gierek envisages the creation of five commissions made up of government and CC representatives, and various experts and workers. They will have "at least a year" to come up with their findings in the following economic areas: 1) working out the guiding principles on price policy of food articles, including meat products; 2) activization of market production; 3) investigation into the agricultural and food economy reserves; 4) a draft program of savings in the national economy; and 5) draft suggestions for the implementation of a housing policy. Upward revisions of food prices, to be accompanied by necessary wage adjustments, are inevitable, but they will take time to work out. In the meantime the decision to form the commissions means that all food prices, including meat (which, it was proposed in July, should go up

in price by 35 percent) will be frozen for at least another year.

As so often in the past, Gierek appeals several times to Polish patriotism. He cuts down ideological allusions to the barest minimum and mentions the Soviet Union only once when referring to the source of most of Poland's raw materials. On another familiar theme, Gierek stresses, rather defensively, the need for yet closer consultations between rulers and ruled. He does not mention the June disturbances or the trials nor does he blame any individuals or groups for the mistakes which had been made.

Deliberately Gierek chooses to answer the question from one of the workers about relations with the church and the faithful. Answering at considerable length and carefully associating the politboro, Central Committee, and the supreme state authorities with his view, Gierek replies that there is no conflict between the state and the church with the exception of a very few members of the clergy. Though Poles differ in their attitudes to religion, the Party thought it essential to recognize mutual tolerance as the principle of relations between people of differing opinions. He said: "There is a large area of fruitful cooperation between the church and state in the efforts to achieve important national objectives." Gierek's answer to the question of state-church relations is remarkably positive considering the open criticism of government policy by the Episcopate and Cardinal Wyszynski only a few days earlier.

Ecclesiastical sources close to the Episcopate recall that quite recently the minister in charge of the Office for Religious Denominations, Kakol, referred to the church as a "living corpse which has to be defeated." Gierek's statement, according to these sources, shows the inherent weakness of the position of the state which is trying to rally support from all quarters.

September 9

Two centers of power hold meetings today.

In Czestochowa the Episcopate conference ponders over the deplorable state of the nation.

In Warsaw the CC plenum finally discusses the country's problems two and a half months after the June events. Gierek announces that the 1976-1980 five-year plan will be reviewed(14) and some investments shifted from industry to agriculture, though priority will be given to the "socialist sector" of agriculture. Those individual peasants who follow the state's policies on farm modernization and specialization, as well as those entering into and fulfilling their contractual obligations can also count on state support. Even a retirement pension scheme is being considered for them.

Gierek confirms what he has already said in his Mielec speech, namely that all Poland's economic problems will be referred to five special commissions. Their recommendations

will be put to a national party conference, which is not expected to take place before the autumn of 1977. All food
prices, including meat, would remain frozen until the commissions' recommendations are accepted. Gierek still describes
the original package as a "proposal" subject to consultations
and amendments, whereas, had it not been for the outburst of
June 25 it would have become operative two days later. The
withdrawal, says Gierek, shows "the Party's flexibility, which
enables it to correct its own policy on the basis of the
opinions of the working people."

By referring for discussion issues which brought such
strong reactions in June, Gierek tries once again to show that
he is not one to ride roughshod over the sensibilities of the
population. The image of Gierek as a leader prepared to listen
to the grievances of the ordinary workers and their families is
projected anew.

The authorities now adopt a series of measures to reduce
electricity and coal consumption. Starting in the autumn, cuts
will be applied to less essential industries, agricultural and
some municipal facilities. During winter, power supplies to
houses and shops will be greatly reduced. One reason given
is that power generators "need overhauling."

September 10

"In present circumstances, peace and order in the country are vital," appeals the communique published after the
Episcopate's conference in Czestochowa. The communique
maintains that:(15)

> The authority of the state should fully respect
> civic rights, conduct a real dialogue with society,
> and take account of society's wants in arriving at
> decisions which affect the whole nation. The
> plenary conference, therefore asks the state author-
> ities to stop all repression of workers involved in
> the antigovernment protests. Those workers who
> have been dismissed must be reinstated and their
> social and professional positions restored. They
> should receive compensation for their losses, while
> those sentenced should be amnestied.
>
> As the current economic situation of Poland is
> difficult, all citizens are duty-bound to contribute to
> its improvement. That is why the conference ap-
> peals to society as a whole to increase its efforts
> and solid work, and even to make sacrifices for the
> common good and the preservation of social order.

The balance maintained in this communique indicated the
Episcopate's desire to calm the domestic situation and help both
Party and people to find a way of resolving the nation's dif-
ficulties. It is also a masterful political stroke on the Epis-

copate's part to clothe its first public call for amnesty and reinstatement in a balanced call for sacrifices from all sides for Poland's sake. Almost all the national newspapers publish part of the bishop's appeal (something unknown in postwar Poland) in an endeavor to substantiate Gierek's claim that there are no conflicts between church and state. But the call for amnesty and the appeal to respect human rights are omitted from media reports on the conference. This selectivity serves to heighten rather than lessen the very tension the Party leader has denied.

September 19

An episcopal letter read in all churches singles out man's rights to correct information and the right to practice his faith in private and in public in complete freedom:(16)

> Unfortunately, in our country, press censorship does not allow us to print in Catholic weeklies the full text of documents from the Apostolic See, nor the Polish Episcopate, nor from individual bishops. We cannot, therefore, remain silent if fundamental human rights, including the right to religious freedom, are not fully respected, if radio, television and the theater are used to praise materialistic attitudes and the laicism of life, while access to these media is completely denied to the church."

This is a strongly worded reminder to the government that the church will continue to raise issues on which it feels it has a duty to speak out despite the generally more conciliatory atmosphere now prevalent in church-state relations.

September 21

The PB appoints chairmen of the Party-government commissions which are to examine the country's economic problems. The commissions are partly a device for gaining time and partly a means of seeking new ways of approaching price rises which cannot be postponed indefinitely.

September 22

The Sejm accepts the decisions of the last CC plenum as a government program, "fully supported" by Gierek, who took part in government discussions.

Jaroszewicz summarized the country's food problems(17) as having been caused by three bad harvests, by the rapid rise in wages with consequent demand outstripping supply, and by the food price freeze which had hampered the regulation of the market and strained the country's resources to provide huge government subsidies in holding down prices. On the other hand, inflation and recession in the West had prevented any increase in Polish exports - so vital in paying off the accumulated foreign debts used to build up and modernize industry.

Jaroszewicz also returns to the subject of the June price increases and to the sensitive problem of consultations. This part of the statement is particularly significant in view of the fact that, for all practical purposes, the nation was expected to participate in consultations spread over the whole of a single Friday. As Jaroszewicz admits: "We did not have at our disposal an evaluation of the whole spectrum of attitudes; we did not know whether the concept of a radical reconstruction of prices at a stroke had been generally approved by society."

September 23

Fourteen Polish intellectuals, whose number rises within a few weeks to 23, form the Committee for the Defense of Workers (CDW) to provide a legal, financial, and medical aid to workers who have allegedly been subjected to repression and "physical terror" because of their part in the June 25 demonstrations. The signatories demand amnesty for all jailed workers and reinstatement of those who had been fired. Families subjected to persecution are called upon to provide the committee with all the relevant information and courageous people in every enterprise are urged to collect money for the group's work.

The CDW in a letter to the Speaker of the Sejm, Gucwa, informs him of its existence and attaches the text of an "appeal to the nation and to the authorities of the Polish People's Republic." The letter is promptly returned by Gucwa together with the appeal, "the text of which cannot be submitted for discussion owing to its contents and its formal and legal aspects." Undeterred, the CDW starts issuing information bulletins and communiques. The editorial in their first bulletin says "Our aim is to break the state's monopoly of information imposed by censorship in our country." The bulletin is designed to be a chronicle of repressive acts carried out against Polish citizens. In fact, it is a record of the strikes and disturbances which occurred in Poland during June and of the trials which followed. It also amounts to a typewritten "self-help manual" of advice on how to deal with official repression through entirely legal means, using the proper legal channels.

September 25

The CDW releases an "appeal to the nation and to the authorities of the Polish People's Republic" which reads in part:

> The workers' protest against exorbitant price increases expressed the feeling of the whole nation. Brutal repression followed. The repressive measures broke the law. Courts passed their verdicts without adequate evidence. The labor code was infringed. For the first time in many years physical terror was applied during arrest and investigations. The whole

of society must take responsibility since the workers
acted in the interests of the nation. The repressive
measures against the workers completely disregard
the most basic rights of man guaranteed under
international law and also in the Polish constitution.
The CDW demands amnesty for all those sentenced
and arrested and reinstatement of those dismissed.
The committee is in full solidarity with these
demands which were voiced by the communique of
Polish Episcopate's conference of September 9, and
appeals to the whole of society to support these
demands.

September 26
    In two sermons in Warsaw churches the primate of Poland
sets the record straight on church-state relations. Rejecting
Gierek's statement in Mielec that there was no longer any
conflict of substance between the authorities and the church,
Wyszynski stresses that the church is concerned about several
specific problems: "It is the clergy's duty to defend the
workers' interests against hasty and ill-considered government
measures...it was painful that workers should have to struggle
for their rights against a workers' government." The other
main problem, according to the cardinal, is the authorities'
atheistic policy, in particular their attempts to prevent
children from receiving religious education.
    This outspoken criticism of the Polish authorities and
Wyszynski's frank comments provide a strong contrast to the
church's cautious and discreet attitude immediately after the
June unrest. The church had then evidently judged the
situation to be grave and refrained from any public comment
which might exacerbate the tension. Now the church very
responsibly seeks to minimize the danger of another major
upheaval, while at the same time making it quite clear to the
authorities that repressive measures could only worsen the
situation.
September 27
    The Committee for the Defense of Workers makes public
the announcement of its existence.

COMMITTEE FOR THE DEFENSE OF WORKERS

The idea for this committee was born in the corridors of the
court house at Radom in July 1976, where 18 relatives of
accused workers were found to be in need of money, legal
advice and personal support. Money was collected - first for
specific cases and then more generally. Lawyers were found
and advice offered. But, adhering strictly to legal provisions,

the committee was publicly and openly set up in the middle of September, and has since then been known in Poland as the KOR. It was initially formed by a handful of people. Widespread support came within a few weeks, not only from the workers, victims of repressive measures, but also from the students, and significantly, from the Catholic Church.

The committee formulated four main objectives: 1) financial, legal, medical aid and moral support for imprisoned workers and their families; 2) amnesty for all workers arrested and sentenced; 3) reinstatement of workers dismissed for taking part in strikes; and 4) official investigations by a special Sejm commission of alleged militia brutality - less during the actual demonstrations on June 25 than immediately afterward during interrogations and investigations and in the prisons. The CDW proclaimed that it functions openly and is ready to disband when these objectives are achieved and when institutions such as trade unions, social security, etc., assume their responsibilities. Until then, however, the CDW feels that its duty to the people, who by their generosity have proved their solidarity with the committee, is to continue its efforts. The CDW, therefore, did not regard itself as a permanent organization.

As of September 29, 1976 the committee started issuing news bulletins and communiques. Observers were sent to attend the trials of the strikers in order to document the prosecution charges, the defendants' testimonies, and the legality of the proceedings. The committee made public in its communiques the information gathered at these trials as well as new information it had received about the June protests and official measures taken against the workers and the committee members since then. Careful reading of these communiques leaves no doubt that the committee's facts were checked and rechecked and that credibility of information was, for the authors, of paramount importance. At the end of January 1977, with the help of priests in various parishes and university students in Warsaw and Krakow and donations from abroad the CDW had collected more than two million zlotys (over Ⱡ37,000 at the tourist exchange rate), to aid persecuted workers and their families. Over 400 workers had been given aid. The communiques and news bulletins issued by the CDW included full names, addresses and telephone numbers of all CDW members.

The CDW was paradoxically enough an "unorganized" organization, unique in Eastern Europe, led by intellectuals from various walks of life - writers, actors, artists, literary critics, students, priests, historians, and economists - some of them expelled from the Party a long time ago. The most prominent members of the Committee were already well-known figures on the Polish political scene, engaged in the struggle for human rights and in various protests against Party and

government measures for several years past. Professor
Edward Lipinski is a world-renowned economist, a left-wing
socialist in his youth and a member of the Polish United
Workers party. It would be hard to overestimate Jerzy
Andrzejewski's outstanding place in Polish cultural life or his
well-deserved fame abroad where over a hundred of his works
have been translated into other languages. Jacek Kuron, a
dissident Marxist of a Trotskyite persuasion was arrested and
imprisoned several times in the past. Jan Jozef Lipski, a
renowned literary critic and essayist, served in the noncommunist underground Home Army during the war. On the whole
the Committee felt that real reforms cannot emerge from within
a Party which was dominated by technocrats and opportunists.
Nor can the CDW claim any potential allies in the higher
echelons of the Party. For this reason they saw no purpose
in trying to overthrow the present leadership. Their aim was
to exert pressure for specific and limited concessions.
Speaking in a program on BBC Radio 4 a member of the committee, the young writer Stanislaw Baranczak summarized the
aims and the activities of the committee when he said:

> We are not a political party and we do not have
> any political program. My aim is to fight the
> enormous lie which is our everyday reality. We are
> full of wrong ideas, of falsifications, of faked books,
> faked words - and the reprisals which took place in
> our country are only a part of this whole atmosphere
> of our life....The opposition in Poland claims to be
> trying to contribute to the country's well-being by
> pressing the government and the Party to live up to
> the socialist ideas they profess.(18)

The reaction of the authorities to the CDW was, at first,
both cautious and prudent. But in time, particularly since the
committee was declared illegal by the government spokesman on
November 19, there were signs of increasing pressure and
intimidation. Contrary to an earlier declaration that only
intellectual methods of persuasion would be adopted against the
CDW the authorities seemed to be concentrating on the intimidation of individual members, no doubt hoping that the
dissenters would lose heart or grow weary of the struggle.
The militia and security police, who may not always have been
under full central control, harassed individual members, frequently hauling them in for interrogation and threats, detain-
ing some of them in police stations overnight, diverting their
telephone calls and depriving some of them of passports.
During militia searches of committee members' apartments,
the money collected to aid the workers and their families,
documents, letters, typewriters were all confiscated. The
Polish post office had been ordered to seize and turn over to

public funds all monies sent to the committee. Eight members of the CDW who had turned up at the court in Radom to attend the trial of a worker were pushed around and pelted with eggs in the corridors of the court house and then sur- rounded by about 20 unidentified men who kicked and pushed them. The militia seemed to have timed their intervention to coincide with the disappearance of the assailants. On oc- casions the militia broke up meetings of the committee held in private homes and detained all the participants overnight for interrogation, strongly stressing that their meeting was illegal.

There were also some quite childish interventions by the security police. When a Western correspondent was in the house of a member of the committee the telephone suddenly rang. After a brief conversation the man turned to the correspondent and explained that it was the daily reminder of how many days he had left before he too would be dealt with. That evening he was down to 77 days.

In another countermeasure, forged bulletins and com- muniques to counteract the committee's official news bulletins were circulated by the security police. These warned the committee members that the committee had been infiltrated and that nobody henceforth could be trusted. A well-known device used in the past after many other incidents of protests was also applied. People who had signed petitions and open letters were subsequently blacklisted, barred from appearing on the radio or television or from publishing articles and books.

Despite all these measures, no committee member has been imprisoned. Some have been allowed to travel to the West where they have spoken in support of their cause, and have subsequently been allowed to return to Poland. There were no serious attempts to silence them or deport them, and no vociferous slander campaign was launched on the sort of scale, for instance, that the Czech authorities conducted against the authors of "Charter 77." Thus the government considered the committee and its activities illegal but apparently felt that it would have more to lose if it pressed serious charges against its members. This reluctance represented a prudent approach, at least until the middle of 1977.

The political attack on the committee was also rather subdued, not always convincingly argued and quite often paradoxically expressed. Gierek described the CDW as an "ally" of the opponents of the normalization of relations be- tween Poland and West Germany. On another occasion, he also described them as a handful of people who had learned nothing during the last two decades and with whom "we have to deal again today." According to the Warsaw daily, Zycie Warszawy, the CDW represented "a terrible chaos and a mixture of ideas such as utopianism, Trotskyism, social democratic odds and ends, Zionism, and a bit of Christian democracy." There were also occasional antisemitic accents, reminiscent of 1968. A

distinguished Polish commentator, speaking in a program on
BBC Radio 4, put it more subtly when he said that sometimes
there appear irresponsible actions by different small groups of
society. But many of them are very far away from the main
stream of everyday Polish life. On the other hand Jaroszewicz,
interviewed in the British newspaper, Financial Times, mentioned the committee, "which is supposed to defend the rights
of the workers" and added, "we can only laugh at them." It
is an either-or situation. Either the CDW is an illegal organization, as government spokesmen had declared, and
logically it should be stamped out by proper legal procedure,
in which case there was nothing for Jaroszewicz to laugh at;
or it was just an insignificant handful of people "far removed
from the mainstream of everyday Polish life", i.e., just a
nuisance which happens in any society and any system. In
that case, why the militia harassment? Why the official
political statements linking this handful of people with one or
another antisocialist stream either in the country or abroad?

There are partial answers to these queries, some of them
provided by the authorities themselves. The committee included the hard core of men whose political opinions varied
from extreme radical views to what might be termed moderate-
left within the communist system. But the important
phenomenon is that all these people had joined together in a
unique effort to defend workers against measures taken by a
workers' government. The name of the committee, including
the words "Defense of the Workers" was a challenge to the
Party itself. That much was admitted by the government
spokesman, Janiurek, when he said on November 19 that the
Polish workers did not need to be defended from the Polish
government, if only because it is a workers' government.

The Polish authorities, as their reactions suggest, were
evidently disturbed by the emergence of this organized support by intellectuals for working-class grievances. The
inclusion of workers' demands within an intellectual platform
was perhaps the fruit of reflection on the failure of intellectual
protest in 1968 and the success of workers' protests in 1970-
1971. Such a move did constitute a potential threat to a
leadership which had decided to call a halt to the economic
boom, to try to stem a flood of rising expectations, and to
restrict what many workers had come to regard as their fundamental rights, namely, a steady improvement in living
standards.(19) Moreover the regime was perturbed by a
flurry of protests from distinguished French, American,
German and Swiss intellectuals and from French and all-
European workers' organizations.

Perhaps more important, the committee gained in Poland
the support not only of students but of the powerful Catholic
Church. Church-CDW relations were not a model of unanimity.
The two groups shared a common concern for the jailed work-

ers and the general question of liberties in Poland. But the
CDW opinions and programs were far more overtly political
than the program of the church. For the intellectuals the
church's support of their efforts was crucial because without it
they would represent too small a group to make the authorities
grant political concessions. The church(20), however, was
careful to maintain a certain distance from the intellectuals, in
order to avoid the impression that the bishops were engaging
in overtly political activities. There was no doubt that the
Episcopate shared the CDW opinion about the militia brutality
charges. But consistent with its image as protector of both
the faith and the nation, the church was wary of becoming too
closely associated with groups it felt did not enjoy the same
relationship with the people, no matter how sympathetic some
of their views. Nonetheless, however small their number, the
committee represented one of the factors in the convergence of
various oppositional trends in Poland.

Meanwhile the country was still waiting for some effective
measures designed to overcome the economic difficulties and to
decrease still further the existing political and social tension.
October 10

In its second communique the CDW notes that 73 workers
have been sentenced in Radom and that the total number of
workers sacked is about 1,000. Detailed information is
provided about the beating of defendants, attempts to intimidate their families, and the financial needs of those discriminated against. In official letters, the CDW calls on the
chairman of the Polish Red Cross, the secretary general of the
Committee for Social Assistance, chairman of the Children's
Friends Society, and the minister of health and welfare to
provide material and medical assistance to the families of these
victims of discrimination.
October 12

Wladyslaw Bienkowski, once an influential member of the
Gomulka leadership, in an appeal circulated in Warsaw (subsequently published by the Paris newspaper, Le Monde)
charges (21) the authorities with using torture to extract
admissions of alleged guilt from the accused workers: "These
attempts to reintroduce methods into our country that bear the
hallmark of the occupation, and of the practices of Stalin,
Beria, and the Polish security apparatus in the fifties, must
provoke in everyone a feeling of disgust and grave danger.
They must also be considered symptoms of the decay of the
organs of the state."
October 14

In Katowice Gierek defends the changes in the constitution and, referring to the principle of consultation claims:
"Today, more than ever, decisions on the problems of the
state belong to the Polish working people, to the whole
nation." Gierek accuses domestic allies of foreign reactionaries

of intensifying their activities when the Party and the state had to deal with obstacles and difficulties. In an obvious reference to the CDW he warns:

> Depending on the situation and the group they wish to address, these people cloth themselves in the garb of spokesmen of democracy, of defenders of national sovereignty and of the economic and social rights of the working people. It is in Poland's best interests that we shall resolutely rebuff every attempt to distort our democracy and abuse its blessings by this sowing of fear and anarchy.(22)

In a clear effort to improve his image, tarnished by the June events, Gierek maintains his crowded schedule of meetings and speeches in various places and industrial enterprises. There were 16 such meetings between September 10 and October 14.

October 29

Speaking in the Sejm, Prosecutor-General Czubinski insists that 78 persons are still in prison but that nobody has been punished because of any acts committed at his place of work or while on strike. He states that in September the Council of State had praised the activities of the militia and courts and found these to have been "just and proper." The Council of State also recommended to the authorities and courts an "understanding treatment" of those participants in riots who were workers and had no police records.

October 30

In their third communique released in Warsaw the CDW takes meticulous care to produce information pertaining to "verified cases only." This preoccupation with credibility is best illustrated by the following passage: "We have data concerning 11 deaths in Radom, probably in connection with the incidents on June 25. However, only four cases have thus far been fully confirmed."

A fake CDW communique No. 3 forged by the security police announces the resignation from the committee of Professor Lipinski, who immediately disowns this statement, adding that he considers the work of the committee to be necessary and calls on the authorities to halt the "mass repression" of workers.

November 4

Eight hundred and eighty-nine workers of the Ursus tractor plant ask Gierek in a letter to reinstate those dismissed "as it is indispensable in view of the country's difficult situation, the tense atmosphere in the plant, and difficulties in the fulfillment of production targets caused by the lack of those experienced workers who were dismissed." The letter continues:

The union proved themselves incapable of expressing even a weak protest against the repressive measures of the authorities and have let themselves be made into active participants in the repressions. Thus, the workers must secure protection of their interests with their own hands. The spontaneous reemergence of forms of "communal defense" is the first step toward the creation of authentic representation of the working people.

November 5
In Moscow Gierek secures Brezhnev's political support and some Soviet economic assistance as well as the Soviet leader's approval of plans for dealing with the situation in Poland.

November 16
The CDW sends a motion to the Sejm calling for the appointment of a special commission of deputies to investigate charges of militia torture and brutality against workers who took part in the June demonstrations. In justification of the motion the CDW produces a long list of acts of violence and abuse by both the militia and the courts based on thorough examination by the committee of 96 cases of detention on or after June 25 in Radom and 94 cases in Ursus.(23)

November 17
The government introduces coal rationing.

PAP admits that coal rationing is causing discontent and exasperation, all the more so since Poland is the fourth biggest world producer of coal and the second largest exporter after the United States. The authorities attribute their energy crisis to industrial expansion, transport bottlenecks and to the increase in the sale of electric household appliances.

November 19
The Polish bishops plead on behalf of workers who had lost their jobs or were jailed after the June riots, and complain that their earlier appeals for an amnesty had been ignored. The Episcopate also announces that it would start collecting funds for the families of dismissed workers.(24)

Government spokesman, Janiurek, declares the CDW an illegal organization under a prewar law of 1932.

November 21
Cardinal Wyszynski, in a sermon in Warsaw, appeals indirectly to Poland's leaders: "The world needs rulers with a heart but all powers are mortally ill if they lack love, life and mercy. If someone wants the honest truth and justice, he must build on mercy and peace."

November 23
In what appears to be the most spectacular roundup to date, the militia breaks up a meeting of the CDW in a private home and detains 14 of its members. The Polish agency, Interpress, states that "nobody has been arrested." In a

sense Interpress is right, since those arrested are actually
detained for the purpose of having their identities checked,
being seen as people who had taken part in what the militia
considers to be an "illegal gathering." They are soon
released.

This is the first such action against the CDW as a whole.
Previously, individual members had been questioned and
threatened while other people associated with the committee had
been taken to the police station for several hours.

November 24

In Moscow, Dr. Andrei Sakharov, the human-rights
campaigner and Nobel Peace Prize winner, publicly lends his
support to the CDW.

November 25

In a document circulated in Warsaw, Jacek Kuron, a
radical dissenter and historian, writes that since, in the
present circumstances of economic and political tensions in
Poland the authorities are virtually paralyzed, the political
opposition should take responsibility for the fate of the
country, and work out a plan of action. He defines "the
opposition" as any individual or any group of people convinced
that the present crisis has its roots in the communist political
and economic system. He himself believes in pluralism understood as tolerance of varying political thoughts and convictions. Only under such conditions, in his opinion, can a political compromise be achieved.

The prevailing totalitarian system isolates the authorities
from the population and, in effect, deprives the Polish nation
of its sovereignty. Kuron clearly states that full Polish
sovereignty would be an unrealistic aim in the present geopolitical situation of the country. But he insists that idealistic
aims should be spelled out because they are important for
retaining and strengthening national identity. His main argument against a totalitarian system is that it does not solve
social crises but indeed renders a lasting solution of such
crises virtually impossible to achieve. The authorities must be
confronted with organized action. Therefore, he argues,
people should organize themselves on a local or professional
level and these small groups should preserve a general solidarity. The authorities would then, as Kuron sees it, have an
opportunity to start a meaningful dialogue with the people.

November 28

The state is waging a hateful and brutal campaign against
religion, says an episcopal letter read in all Polish churches.
"One can constantly feel a secret conspiracy against God."
The letter lists a number of complaints and accusations: some
professions and particularly managerial posts are almost exclusively reserved for nonbelievers; building laws and
regulations are used to prevent the erection of new churches;
an atheistic campaign is conducted in schools, universities and

summer camps where young people are prevented from attending religious services and catechism classes; clerics in seminaries are threatened with military service contrary to state-church agreement; university students are blackmailed and interrogated by the authorities in an effort to deprive them of their religious rights; and mass media, theater and films are exploited for spreading atheism, pornography, and blasphemy.

The pastoral letter reminds those government officials engaged in the persecution of religion that they are maintained in office by taxes paid by the victims of their persecutions. It also reminds the government that, in the last resort, antireligious propaganda is detrimental to the government's social and economic policies because it causes anxiety as well as distrust in the country's leadership, and "embittered people do not work well."(25)

This is the Episcopate's full answer to Gierek's claim in Mielec that there is no conflict between state and church in Poland and at the same time represents the price to be paid by the leadership for the church's support granted in the critical days of June and September 1976.

November 30

In a letter circulated among Western correspondents in Warsaw, students and other groups, Polish intellectuals belonging to the CDW urge the people to petition to government for an investigation of June events.

December 1

At the CC plenum Gierek announces some changes in economic policy described as "economic maneuver." The main objective of the 1977 economic plan is to improve domestic market supplies; he discloses that the import of eight million tons of grain and fodder will cost hundreds of millions of dollars. Besides affording adequate supplies these imports should be used to rebuild the country's livestock population. The second major task facing the economy was the shift in investment emphasis from capital to consumer goods. Domestic supplies of consumer goods should increase by about 60 percent as against the original 40 percent. Agricultural production, instead of rising by the foreseen 15-16 percent will increase by only 13-15 percent. The projected growth in exports will be about 12 percent yearly, a drop of 7 percent compared to the period 1971-1975. The projected fall in imports is, however, even greater. This shows Warsaw's continued determination to bring the balance of payments under tighter control. A lowering of the ration between investments and overall national income is the third goal. Investments accounted for about 32 percent of national income in 1975 and are expected to be down to 27 percent in 1977.

That economic difficulties had produced certain political problems is admitted by Gierek. In a clear reference to the workers who took part in strikes last summer, he blames various Party organizations for having failed to influence industrial workers. His emphasis on the importance of the Party and state activists is the signal for a strengthening of the Party's leading role at all levels of administration.

Propaganda efforts are particularly necessary when, according to Gierek, reactionary forces in West Germany would welcome disorder in Poland, are seeking allies there, and nurture dreams of returning "to our Polish soil." This is a rather surprising statement, reviving the old West German specter after years of normal and fruitful relations between Warsaw and Bonn. In a clear reference to the opposition among intellectuals and workers, he continues:

> Only a small group of persons of old bourgeois political orientation and incorrigible revisionists are responsible for the attempts to create discord in Poland. They poison national debates with their demagoguery, and try to attack the basis of our sociopolitical system and international policy. These people are in fact raising their hands against the fatherland.

December 2

At 1600 hours Warsaw Radio reports that a two-day plenary meeting of the CC is ending and a Sejm session beginning. The economic plans for 1976-1980 and for 1977, unanimously approved by the CC are passed on to the Sejm, which in turn sends them to committees for detailed analysis and evaluation (see Chapter 13).

December 4

Sixty-five workers appeal from prison to the government to set up a Sejm commission to investigate charges of brutality against the security police and prison wardens.(26)

December 6

In his sharpest attack to date on the authorities' handling of last June's riots, Cardinal Wyszynski, in a sermon in St. John's Cathedral in Warsaw accuses the militia of having used brutal methods against the strikers and claims to have a list of over 30 jailed Ursus workers of whom only four had not been beaten or led through the so-called "health path" or police gauntlet. The persecuted workers and their families must be helped: "We must give up expensive luxuries in our homes. This will be transforming money into the spirit of Christian love."

This sermon represents another slow, but steady escalation of the church-state dispute over the striking workers. Church leaders had already been active behind the scenes, pleading for amnesty and for greater consideration of workers' demands. When discreet diplomacy failed to achieve what the

Episcopate desired, however, public pronouncements were made. And when these had only limited success, the call for believers to contribute to workers aid programs in their parishes went out. Now Cardinal Wyszynski is publicly declaring his support for these actions and calls for sacrifices from the congregation.

At the trade unions congress in Warsaw Gierek continues his drive to improve communications between the leadership and the workers and suggests that the trade unions and the Council of Ministers should meet at least once a year to discuss the key problems of social policy and working conditions. The unions, he says, are strong and important links in socialist democracy and it is important for them to be familiar with opinions and moods, and to take up in good time the problems with which the workforce lives and resolve them efficiently. Kruczek, chairman of CCTU merely emphasizes the need for increased grass-roots activity within the unions: "Such activity makes it possible to detect conflicts or dissatisfaction among the workers in time and resolve them effectively."

Gierek also announces the increases by 16 percent in minimum wages from May 1977 as well as in old-age and disability pensions.

December 8

The Party proposes that farmers who bequeath their holdings intact to their children should be rewarded with a state pension. At the moment such pensions are only available to farmers who give their land to the state.

December 13

For the first time Trybuna Ludu, the main CC paper, admits the existence of the CDW and links "anticommunist hysteria in the Federal Republic of Germany" with "the active although small group of opponents of socialism in Poland whose activity objectively harms the interests of the state and the nation." Their harmful activities are listed as: preparation of information for foreign propaganda centers, winning the "naive trust of some outstanding Western intellectuals," publishing typewritten information bulletins and communiques, giving interviews to the Western press and television, writing letters addressed to the leadership of Communist parties in the West, and declaring that they are motivated by concern about the problems of the Polish nation, about its future. The article admits(27) that the CDW managed to activate a certain number of university students in Warsaw and that this is an abuse of the confidence of these young people in the same degree as it is an abuse of the confidence of public opinion in the West.

December 16

In the Paris newspaper Le Monde CDW member Michnik looks for ways and means of improving the situation in Poland. Trade unions should become independent representatives of the workers. The alternative is totalitarianism and further bloody clashes. Catholics must have the right to participate fully in public life as Cardinal Wyszynski has said. Although it is for the moment unrealistic to ask for a complete abolition of censorship, it should be possible to devise a reasonable law for the press. The mass media, even censored, should provide simple political information.

Party leaders must give up their insane hope of eradicating pluralism among young people. The students in particular must be given the legal right to create independent scholarly circles, research clubs, etc. While appealing to the "democratic opposition" to keep in mind the limits of possible reforms, Michnik appeals to the Party leader to realize at long last that they are digging their own graves when they decide to resort to reprisals against rebellious workers and students.

December 18

Prime Minister Jaroszewicz announces an increase in the import of consumer goods and full implementation of the program for developing trades and services also in the private sector.

December 21

Twenty-eight prominent professors, including members of Polish Academy of Sciences ask for a parliamentary commission to investigate the strikes and demonstrations last June as well as the legal proceedings and other reprisals which followed. After references to the suppression of information about the earlier interventions on behalf of workers by both the church and the CDW, the professors write: "Only an objective and detailed investigation of this affair by an authoritative body such as a parliamentary commission, followed by the publication of its conclusions will stop the rising tide of discontent...."(28)

January 3, 1977

The CDW issues a statement in which it charges that terror and lawlessness have reigned in Radom since June, and that the blame lies, not only with the local authorities but above all with the prosecutor-general's office, which had been receiving complaints about beatings and brutality from Radom workers since the beginning of September. The CDW again calls on the Sejm to investigate allegations of militia brutality.

January 5

In a Sejm committee, Prosecutor-General Czubinski refers to a score of letters, including the collective ones, in which charges were made about the militia using impermissible methods against persons suspected of disturbing the peace in Radom and Ursus. The investigation conducted by the prosecutor-general's office proved the baselessness of these charges, says Czubinski.

Czubinski's statement meets with immediate reaction. One hundred and seventy-two prominent intellectuals in an open letter sent to a number of Sejm deputies stress the urgency of setting up a commission to investigate the militia abuses and tortures which are the talk of the country.(29)

The 172 are soon joined by 271 more petitioners mostly from Gdansk, including students, scientific workers and professors of Gdansk University and the Medical Academy. Separate letters are sent by Warsaw intellectuals, residents of Lodz, the country's textile center, and by clergymen of the southeastern diocese of Przemysl.

There are also some individual letters addressed to Gierek. In one of them a former air force colonel writes: "In a situation reminiscent of the one that existed during predecessor's time, the Party leadership has rapidly lost touch with reality, creating an abyss between society and the authorities." This is precisely the situation which Gierek set himself to remedy when he came to power.

January 16

The CDW complains that the Party organization of the Radoskor shoe factory in Radom had put pressure on the workers to sign a petition demanding the expulsion of CDW members from Poland. Similar efforts were made at a metallurgical complex in Zielona Gora in western Poland, but only 160 of 5,000 workers at the two factories had signed the petition.(30)

January 21

The Office for Religious Denominations issues a decree cutting off funds from the Catholic Intelligentsia Clubs (CIC). These clubs, formed shortly after October 1956, are independent lay Catholic discussion forums in Warsaw and other cities and have several thousand members. Their activities are financed from the profits of the Libella, a chemical and cosmetics firm of which they own most of the shares. These funds are now being transferred to a splinter group founded in October 1976 which is politically more amenable to the Party: the Polish Catholic Intelligentsia Club (PCIC).

The CIC leaders in Warsaw link this move with the Party's policy of trying to cut the links between Catholic groups close to the Episcopate and what are termed "liberal democratic circles" i.e., the nationwide dissent movement. Many members of the CIC are very close to the CDW. The Episcopate firmly states that any attack on CIC independence would be viewed as a hostile act directed against the church.

At the plenary session of the CC Gierek makes a special effort to reassure private farmers. He departs from his usual emphasis on the importance of the socialist transformation of agriculture and instead assures the private farmers of permanent support and all the guarantees and prospects for development.

January 22

Gierek tells Iwaszkiewicz, chairman of the Polish Writers

Union, that there may be an amnesty for jailed workers, conditional, however, on the suspension of protests and attacks against the authorities. He also indicates that there would be no repression of writers who had demanded a parliamentary investigation of alleged militia brutality against workers.

February 1

Despite expectations and fears the annual meeting of the Warsaw branch of the Polish Writers Union is rather calm, although not devoid of sharp criticism of the official cultural policy, and of censorship in particular. Although a number of CDW members, as well as some of the 172 signatories of a petition for a parliamentary enquiry into police brutality are present, there is no stir from the floor, the attitude being one of "wait and see and let us not let ourselves be provoked."

Twenty-two members of the CDW sign a brief message of solidarity with human rights campaigners in Czechoslovakia ("Charter 77").

February 3

At the rally in the Ursus tractor factory, where demonstrators had ripped up railway tracks last June, Gierek announces that he has recommended to the Council of State clemency toward those sentenced for the disturbances.

Referring to the opposition within the country Gierek says: "There are opponents of Poland and socialism who have been trying to exploit for their own purposes the disturbances of public order which occured in June, which put us all to shame." The militia had to intervene, but only when hopes of settling the situation by other means had failed. They had no firearms and had acted with moderation and common sense, though they were subjected to brutal attacks. In other words, Gierek makes it clear that the leadership is still not prepared to concede to popular pressures for an investigation into the brutality charges by a Sejm commission:

> We were all seriously affected by the drama of the June events....A fundamental conclusion which emerged from last year's experience is that...we must learn democracy and the art of making joint decisions on common issues. We shall perfect social democracy and in particular...the constitutional principle of consultation....A refusal to discuss proposals, and to take issues into the street strikes a blow at democracy. Whoever uses violence to oppose consultations is summoning the enemies of socialist Poland to take part in our affairs and harms the motherland....(31)

In other words, he expresses the hope that workers' power will in the future be used more constructively, in democratic debate, and to secure higher productivity.

Then Gierek discloses that on September 1 he submitted a request to the Council of State that wider use should be made of the right of clemency for those convicted who have shown contrition and who undertake not to embark on a path of crime again. Gierek began this particular passage in his speech with the words, "As you probably know...." The fact is that at no time have the Polish media reported on Gierek's approach to the Council of State.

The Council of State accepts Gierek's recommendation to avail itself of its prerogative, namely, the right of pardon.
February 5

In a comprehensive statement the CDW welcomes the decision of the Council of State to implement clemency but lists several objections and new charges. It regrets that the Council of State, by accepting the report of the prosecutor-general and the minister of justice on the activities of their subordinate officers, have, by implication, sanctioned militia brutality and obvious abuse of the administration of justice. Making applications for clemency dependent upon the penitence of those convicted is humiliating to the imprisoned workers and excludes from any form of pardon those who defend workers' interests and their own human dignity. Excluded also, according to the CDW are those who do not admit their guilt, and those beaten up and degraded.

The CDW further complains that during the meeting with the few hundred Party activists at the Ursus tractor plant, Gierek did not take a stand on a letter from 1,100 workers at the same plant demanding reemployment of all those dismissed in connection with the June events. Such dismissals were a "mass phenomenon" in the whole country. The CDW statement concludes with the following demands:

1)   reemployment in work corresponding to their qualifications of all those dismissed;
2)   unconditional amnesty for all accused and imprisoned;
3)   making public the whole extent of the repressions;
4)   disclosing the names of, and punishing the persons guilty of, violations of law, and the torturing and beating of workers; and
5)   creation of a special parliamentary commission that would impartially investigate these burning problems which have so aroused social anxiety.

"When these demands are met, the CDW will lose its raison d'etre," the statement concludes.
February 11

The CDW sends to the Sejm and to Warsaw newspapers a report on the June disturbances in Radom drawn up at the request of the committee by its member Miroslaw Chojecki, a chemist and former employee of the Institute of Nuclear Research. It is evident that the CDW does not diminish its efforts to unearth the whole truth, thus, in a way, making itself a substitute for a parliamentary commission. According to the report, compiled from interviews with 200 witnesses: "Rumors among the population were circulating about 17 citizens killed during the riots in Radom, but it was impossible to establish the exact number; it was probably less than 17." Quite important was the charge that Tadeusz Ziembicki, whose family had been officially informed that he had died when a trailer overturned during the riots, was in fact in jail some time after the riots on June 25. Chojecki states in the report that he, himself, was arrested by the militia without any explanation after he had asked to see Ziembicki's death certificate.

February 16

Trybuna Ludu singles out those who left Poland for the West after March 1968 and are now conducting a campaign against Poland. It is these "renegades and deserters who are the promoters of the tactics adopted by today's organizers of letters and petitions." The operations of these people, allegedly acting in the interests of the working class, play into the hands of cold war centers abroad. What is particularly disquieting is the fact that not for the first time the people now acting in the CDW and taking part in other protests and petitions are linked with the events in March 1968 when, for the first time in Polish history, antisemitism became official government policy.

These references to 1968 worry many intellectuals. As a prominent Polish sociologist told me: "When the chips are down this is a system that puts too much faith in the militia and Party bureaucracy."

February 17

The CDW repeats its appeal for an amnesty of all workers reporting that, thus far, 965 persons have sent letters to the Sejm demanding special parliamentary investigation of charges of militia brutality. Later 1,000 students from Warsaw and Lublin (in eastern Poland) joined in the appeal.

10 The Economic Necessity

By June 1976 the economic reasons for increasing prices were both compelling and urgent. But the need for it did not come suddenly out of the blue. Several factors, accumulating since 1974, clearly indicated that Poland's boom would have to be reduced, even perhaps stopped and austerity measures introduced. The new affluence since Gierek took over was inadequately based and had been bought on credits. Because the immediate trigger of the events in December 1970 had been Gomulka's pre-Christmas food price rises (much lower than the ones in June 1976), one of Gierek's first acts in 1971 was to freeze basic food prices at the pre-rise level. But what was intended as a temporary expedient dictated by a political crisis was soon transformed, by the workers, into a status quo which lasted until June 1976. Gierek found it extremely difficult to overcome the widespread resistance to any real increases in the price of basic commodities, and his price policy has all along been one of procrastination because he needed a contented workforce for the success of his dynamic industrial expansion policies.(1)

But he was backing himself into a corner and only sweeping measures would get him out. In order to keep prices at their frozen levels the state was paying out a fast-growing volume of subsidies amounting to ₺2,000 million in 1975.(2) When bread became cheaper than fodder, farmers fed it to their animals.

The position was complicated by two bad agricultural years in 1974 and 1975, and by the drought in 1976. These effects combined to reduce supplies of every type of food from fruit to meat, and resulted in long lines at the shops, widespread dissatisfaction, and an officially admitted widespread black market. The lines began forming outside butchers' shops as early as three a.m. and some housewives were lucky to get what was left, if anything, by nine a.m. On the legal free market, operated by private and cooperative farmers, prices soared, and suppliers quite naturally channeled more of their products in that direction at the expense of the state shops where the shelves became even more bare than before (see Chapter 6). The subsidies, of course, cushioned people against the real cost of home-grown agricultural produce and against the cost of largely hard-currency imports of grain (about 7.5 million tons in 1976). Poland, traditionally an exporter of agricultural produce for hard currency, began to run up a deficit on her agricultural trade.

The problem of consumption structure was a direct result of the freeze on basic food products. The rapid real wage growth was principally a consequence of the leadership's fundamental reluctance to take a firm stand against managers' frequently indiscriminate use of the wage fund to satisfy workers' rising expectations in an officially generated climate of prosperity. One direct result was a growth in purchasing power by one-third - double the planned figure. Too much money was chasing too few goods. Low-income families spent 55 percent of their income on food and those with higher incomes about 28 percent. In terms of meat consumption in various forms, Poland was certainly at the top of the world league with 70 kilograms per annum per head of population. Much of the dramatic rise in average buying power was spent on food since prices were relatively low and became even lower, comparatively speaking, with each wage increase. This in turn put special pressure on the food section, and par-ticularly the meat sector of the market which again led to recurring shortages. The rapid increase in the rate of meat production was mainly based on the growing size of expensive grain and fodder imports.(3) That so much of the higher consumer demand fell on basic foodstuffs was in part also due to the inadequate supply of durable consumer goods. The waiting time for a refrigerator or washing machine was, in 1976, about six months and more often than not the quality was unacceptable to the increasingly selective Polish consumer. This imbalance between demand and supply produced a serious suppressed inflation.

According to a popular saying in Warsaw, it was no good being on first-name terms and having drinks with ministers and highly placed Party officials or managers any more. The most important friend one could have was the butcher - not only because you can get all the meat you want under the counter, but also because you can obtain virtually anything you need through his good offices. A young journalist who badly needed a washing machine for his family and would have to wait six months for delivery went to his friend the butcher and asked for help. "It's all right," said the butcher, "but this will cost you an extra 500 zlotys. Not for me, mind you, because we are friends, but for the girl who will arrange this." The butcher rang the girl in a department store and simply said that Mr. X will call within an hour to pay with a proper "bonus" for a washing machine. As a result the washing machine was delivered to the young journalist's home the same evening. One of the bitterest jokes making the rounds in Warsaw was about a man who walked into a butcher's shop and asked whether there was any pork. "No," said the assistant. "Any beef?" "No." "Any veal?" "No." As the disappointed man left the assistant said to his colleague: "What a good memory he's got!"

By a curious twist of economics Poland had to spend more foreign currency on grain purchases abroad in order to earn more foreign currency for her products. Because of the poor harvests in 1974 and 1975 Polish authorities were forced to buy grain abroad to feed its animal population, whose meat was one of the country's successful export items. The Soviet Union failed to fulfill its contractual obligations to Poland. In November 1975 the American secretary of agriculture negotiated a long-term agreement in Warsaw which provided for Polish purchases of 2.5 million tons of grain annually over the next five years. At the time of the agreement this represented a deal of about 300 million dollars on credit. In 1975 alone[4] Polish imports of grain, mostly from the West, exceeded 24 percent of that year's domestic grain production.

Poland's dependence on imported goods presented considerable problems. Gierek's boom was fed on Western credits. The West's share in the total Polish foreign trade exceeded 50 percent, and its share in total Polish imports rose from 25 percent to just over 50 percent. This opening toward the West, not only for grain but mostly for technology and credits, was one of the characteristics of the Gierek economic outlook and acted as an important catalyst for Polish domestic development. Many new plants were being equipped with the most modern Western machinery and most advanced Western technological know-how, but all this put Poland deeply in debt to the West, to an extent estimated by EEC in 1976 at 10 billion dollars. Western bankers[5] have calculated Poland's trade deficit with the West at 2.5 billion dollars in 1975. No wonder, therefore, that doubts have been growing in 1975 how to service the foreign debts. The problem had been aggrevated by the worsening terms of foreign trade. Western recession had made this more difficult by diminishing the market for Polish exports, while inflation in the West had increased the price of Western imports by something like 2,000 million dollars. At the same time the Soviet Union had also increased the price of oil by 131 percent and the price of raw materials, including grain, by 52 percent.[6]

The Western recession had exacerbated fundamental domestic production problems in export performance. Although production grew considerably, Polish industry failed to supply sufficient quantities of the high-quality manufactured goods acceptable on the Western market which were to pay for both servicing and, in due course, repayment of foreign debts. Instead, a great share of the burden fell on such traditional export sectors as fuel and food at a time when food in particular came under intense pressure from domestic demand. Moreover, investment went out of control and sucked in more imports.

The oil price problem created, as it did everywhere, additional difficulties. With the increase in price of Soviet oil, the cost of Polish imports of Soviet oil will rise in the present five-year period. The original Polish-Soviet contracts for 1976-1980 oil deliveries provided for about 50 percent of Poland's oil needs by 1980. In 1975 the Soviet Union supplied only two-thirds of the country's long-term oil needs(7), leaving about five million tons to be found elsewhere - in Arab countries and in Iran. A plan to cut Poland's refineries expansion program and give added emphasis to coal will help reduce the bill for oil imports. But since Poland will be paying nearly twice as much for relatively less Soviet oil, there will still be a need for substantial imports from the West. (see section, "Foreign Trade: The Instrument of Growth," in Chapter 4).

In the circumstances the emphasis was on agricultural self-sufficiency, a goal proclaimed for many years past, which the leadership had admitted would be difficult to achieve. Price increases were considered necessary in order, as Deputy Premier Jagielski had said to "base the entire food economy sector on economic cost calculations to a much greater extent than before." They were supposed to help foot the bill for the increase in payments to farmers for their products. These were necessary, planners felt, to encourage higher production, particularly in view of the fact that some increases in 1975 had not produced the expected results in the output of meat and meat products. Besides, Polish farmers had grown more dependent on grain imported from the West, and the inflationary character of its prices pushed up the cost of Polish agricultural production.

Another area in need of investment was the mechanization of agriculture, which was some ten years behind Rumania and Bulgaria, 15 years behind Czechoslovakia and West Germany up to 20 years behind such Western countries as France and Italy. Moreover, it was the socialized sector of agriculture which was being heavily favored in the distribution of agricultural machinery (see section, "Agriculture: Socialized or Private?" in Chapter 4). In any case, even if agricultural production did expand, the expansion would be insufficient to meet the demands of both the export and the domestic market. Over half of Poland's meat products went abroad.

Then there was also the very disquieting question upper-most in the mind of the average private farmer: When and how would socialization of agriculture be introduced? The answer from the authorities was always misleading and always confused. The countryside thus reacted with a wait-and-see attitude, and in the meantime, slaughtered animals to meet wholly local needs, not only in the peasants' own villages but also to help other villages where perhaps cattle and pigs were scarce.

Warsaw had also been under pressure to raise food prices, both from the East and the West. In the eyes of Comecon, the Polish economy could not be considered to be in good order. About 80 percent of the country's agriculture was in private hands, trade was roughly balanced between East and West, indebtedness was still on the rise, and prices were uneconomically low. The standard of living in Poland was much higher than in the Soviet Union. From the Comecon side it was argued that Poland must bring its domestic prices more into line with those prevailing in the other East European countries.

Equally, Poland's extensive trade dealings with the West may have exerted pressure on the domestic price situation. The attitude of Poland's now well-stretched list of creditors became worrying. Although at the time the country's credit rating was good, nevertheless Western bankers had been speculating about Poland's credit ceiling for over a year before June 1976. Western credits had hitherto been there for the asking as far as Poland was concerned.

11 Who Rules the Country?

THE POLITICAL MISJUDGMENT

There were two schools of thought about how to introduce the price increases. One school suggested that there should have been a gradual increase in certain prices or even small comprehensive increases in most prices from 1973 onward - a Hungarian pattern - of announcing regular bit-by-bit small price increases many months in advance, and accepting the cost of inevitable speculative hoarding as preferable to bloody demonstrations. The other school saw this solution as dangerous because it would have amounted to a constant nagging at people. Throwing consumer psychology to the winds, they argued that there must be one comprehensive, massive package which would deal with the existing problems and difficulties once and for all over the next five years; any attempt to prepare the Poles for the price changes by announcing them well in advance would only have driven food under the counter and led to hoarding.

In the event, the second school of thought won the day. The economists and managers who backed this approach had long been advocating price rises in one package and at one stroke. They found allies at the top of the Party among people who not only believed in a shock treatment, but for whom Gierek's liberal economic policies were, if not abhorrent, certainly unacceptable, both in the long term and in view of the Comecon overall policies. In the event the "shock treatment" produced a shock all right, but opposite to the one intended. Everything that the authors wanted to avoid, like hoarding or withholding of deliveries by farmers, did occur, together with mass strikes and demonstrations.

The sweeping measures failed and it really marked a bitter setback for one of the few countries of the Soviet bloc that showed the makings of a genuine relationship between the government and the people. The June operation was described to me in Warsaw by young economists as really a devaluation of the zloty. Because of mass strikes, the losses in production value were twice as high as anything which could have been financially gained over the whole year by the price increases. In the process Gierek has lost much good will, his popularity has been dented and his political judgment called into question. This was so much more depressing, disquieting and surprising since Gierek had proved in the past his economic ability, had tried very hard to keep abreast of public and particularly workers' opinions, and proved to be a very clever and skillful political operator. But the Party apparatus, lulled by procrastinations, failed to make careful preparation, and again, as in 1970, lost contact with the feelings of the people and either did not bother assessing their reactions or embarked on an exercise of disinformation. There was shock at the magnitude of the increases and astonishment that Gierek could so misjudge the popular mood.

ASSESSMENT ON THE SPOT

I went to Poland late in September 1976 and discussed the June crisis with many prominent journalists, intellectuals, Party and government officials, students and ordinary people. All agreed that the price increases were an economic necessity, but argued that they were, nevertheless, unnecessarily high, and should have been introduced gradually over two to three years after December 1970.

Everybody strongly condemned the mass media which had thrived on their "propaganda of success" line without a hint of the economic difficulties and the approaching end of the boom. Lukaszewicz, CC secretary in charge of mass media was blamed by all. Catastrophic, shameful, blatantly stupid, were the more moderate words used to describe the behavior of the press which, as a prominent journalist told me, must bear "a tremendous responsibility for what happened." After all that, in September, at a long briefing session with top editors in the CC Lukaszewicz issued another world-shaking directive: "Success generates difficulties, and difficulties generate success." This was to be the "new" line.

There was no doubt in anybody's mind that the strikes were massive and the workers' solidarity was as unprecedented as in 1970. "It was frightening," a high Party official told me, "it was spontaneous, but I would not rule out the existence of interfactory communications and organizations." Even if there were no underground strike committees then they certainly exist now. A member of the politburo of the Central Committee wondered: "What is all the fuss about? After all, only 70,000 workers went on strike, a mere one percent of the entire work force." But he did not answer the question from a journalist, "Why, therefore, did you capitulate in the face of protest from only one percent of the people?"

The angry mass reaction of the workers came as no surprise to anyone except the Party itself, I was told. The authorities had no contact with the people and no idea what they thought. "The Party apparatus," a professor active in politics told me, "is frustrated, rebellious and dissatisfied."

Everyone I talked to, argued that for at least three months after the June riots nobody in the Party knew how to deal with the situation. The net result was chaos, many contradictory statements, and measures which only added to the general confusion. On the whole the Party went on to the defensive as did Gierek himself. The only thing they were able to do was to apply totally unjustified repressive measures against the strikers.

There was no alternative for the Party and the government but to capitulate, if, as I was told by everyone, another December 1970 situation was to be avoided. According to one editor: "A capital error was committed, since there were no consultations." A well-known commentator said: "Capitulation was a courageous step and not a sign of weakness. One can fight with a bayonet but one cannot sit on it." An economist and journalist made no bones about the facts of life: "On Friday, June 25, the sovereignty of the government did not exist and the question remained: "Who really rules the country?"

Many of the more prominent representatives of the establishment and also most of the ordinary people I met were sure that the events in June 1976 were incomparably more important politically than the upheaval in December 1970 and could have more far-reaching consequences. This time, not only economic difficulties but also the critical political question of consultation and communication pushed into the public arena the whole problem of reform of the political structure within the existing system.

During my many visits to Poland I frequently met and talked to a highly intellectual, very well informed, politically mature communist with much more than a "human face." After over 30 years of life in People's Poland, here are some of the thoughts he expressed to me after the June events in 1976:

> We are living now through not so much a crisis of concepts as through a crisis of structures. June was the last straw after many other measures which have directly affected all the people in an unnecessary and painful way....

The environment changes and so do the people. New generations are growing. They seek something new and better. Everything is changing around us in Poland but the Party has not changed and has no intention of changing. There is absolutely no control of the Party. Absolute power makes you drunk.

The party is in a state of inertia at present and, at the same time, has the feeling of power. There is a buoyant atmosphere of self-satisfaction and self-congratulation with the various successes until a blow comes. Such a blow came that Friday in June. And, unfortunately, in this system, it is difficult to imagine that any basic and necessary reforms could ever be introduced without gallons of blood being spilled once more.

The June Friday was incomparably more important politically than December 1970. And that is why what is now needed is post-December type of dynamic leap forward within the leadership and this time in the field of structural reforms. There is no doubt that Gierek was shocked by the reaction of the people and by the mass protests. His reply to the nation was: "Here I am, the man who in the last five years has given you so much, and done so much but you are ungrateful, you are no good." He was a broken man and still remains on the defensive. From June to October no significant action has been taken. Institutionalized channels of consultation and communication still do not exist.

The only real partner we have at present is...Cardinal Wyszynski. He writes memoranda, he speaks publicly on what should be done and could be done, he modified the decisions of the Party or proposed legislation. Right now he is playing a game with the Party, but, of course, in time he will submit his bill. And we will have to pay it as best we can.

What is the use of my telling you what I feel and what many other people like me feel? If all of us like-minded people could gather together in the largest square in Warsaw, tomorrow, it would overflow. But what's the use? There is no access to the people who matter, no way of convincing them of what could and should be done, even within the limitations we are living in and in the present situation....There is such an atmosphere of hopelessness and unwillingness to even try to break down this brick wall that people relapse into a resigned frustration and say quite cynically: "Let's just let things go on as they are."

What we need at present is a "Gierek's autumn"
not in the sense of fading him out but in terms of
an offensive. Real reforms are needed, with the
proviso that all the promises, including political
ones, will be kept. But Gierek is a prisoner both of
the political structures of the Party, and of the
situation itself. I am deeply pessimistic and I cannot
see any light at the end of the tunnel....

The Party does not realize, or perhaps does not
want to understand, that the Soviet Union will
tolerate quite a lot as the price of stability in
Poland. Inertia reigns supreme in the Party and
people are frustrated and tense as they have not
been for many years past.

This examination of the conscience coming from a comparatively
young communist speaks for itself. After over 30 years of
"socialist" Poland this man's view is one of hopelessness and
cynicism. But he himself, along with many others who similarly assess the situation, though occasionally less pessimistically,
seemed determined to improve the system occasionally less
pessimistically, seemed determined to improve the system either
by moderate or radical means in a way in which the final
outcome might change the face of socialism as it is now
practiced in Poland.

12 After June: Confusion

> It is always the best policy to speak
> the truth, unless of course you are an
> exceptionally good liar.
>
> J.K. Jerome in "Idler," February 1892

The June events shook the Party to its very roots. After the miscalculations, the mishandling, the breakdown in communication between ruled and rulers, and a gross failure in political judgment came confusion and uncertainty. The pressures that persuaded the leadership to introduce higher prices had intensified in the past three months leading up to June, but the subsequent humiliating backdown had diminished the leadership's authority to deal with the unresolved problems.

At first the mass media, true to past form, argued that, in the wake of peaceful and constructive consultations, people understood the need for price increases, that these were disturbed by only a handful of individuals including hooligans, and that at the mass rallies hundreds of thousands of people supported the Party leadership and its policies. No commentator, however, explained why - if only a handful of people disturbed the constructive consultations, if the people genuinely understood the need for price increases and indeed supported government policies enthusiastically - the government had withdrawn the package.

Only when Party leaders themselves admitted that not enough prior consultation had taken place between the Party and the people, did the mass media take up the problem of consultation. But even so nobody admitted that in many places the workers' delegations wanted to discuss the issues on

June 25 but that their demand for consultation was rejected. No one mentioned the fact that in some plants and institutions the time allotted for "consultations" did not exceed 30 minutes. Mass rallies in support of the Party further illustrated the inconsistency. If so many workers supported the government's policies why did the government react so quickly to the "scattered incidents" of protest? And if the workers supported the government policies and at the same time rejected price increases, how would the government ever be able to raise prices against the will of these hundreds of thousands of supporters now rallying to its side? The mere fact that workers went on strike was proof that attempts to win voluntary support for price increases had failed. In a sense, therefore, when the trials of workers began, they were being tried for a failure which the government itself had admitted.(1)

There was also considerable confusion in the leadership's presentation of the whole exercise. Three versions of the "truth" appeared. In the first version the decision to increase prices was presented quite suddenly as a "proposal" at the Sejm session after, according to the officials, having been prepared in the best possible way, and after "consultation with the workers." The proposal was scheduled to become operative within three days. This was rejected by the workers on June 25. Then came the second version: "Yes, the reforms were only proposed; we started consultations and then some hooligans destroyed this process but we will propose a second price reform after consultations which will take a few months." And finally, the third version appeared: "The situation is rather more complicated and therefore five special commissions will work on it and report, after further extensive consultations, in a year or so."

Hesitation was quite apparent in subsequent decisions. At first the whole package was unconditionally withdrawn. Then, it was suggested that the price of meat should be increased while other food prices would remain stable. Very shortly the increased procurement payments to peasants included in the original package were restored. This concession increased food production costs, but these would not be passed on to the consumer and the government would have to absorb them somehow. Another month passed and five commissions were formed to study the whole economic scene, and, in the meantime, all food prices, including meat and meat products were to remain frozen for at least another year.

The extension of the freeze, politically designed to buy time and to placate an infuriated people, was a half-measure and not a cure. It merely delayed the inevitable. The state subsidies had to rise because of the higher prices paid to the peasants for their products, but also because of another bad harvest in 1976 which was bound to increase the cost of food production. The envisaged import of another eight million tons of grain and fodder was bound to aggravate Poland's balance-of-payments difficulties which were already serious.

After his return from Moscow in December Gierek again revised some of the previously revised targets in an already much more moderate 1976-1980 five-year plan (see Chapter 9). What emerged from various official statements on the whole economic issue after June was the impression that the leadership was still not entirely sure what course it planned to take. Praise was directed at both continued dynamic development and at the decrease in investment without any clear indication of how these two lines were to converge.

These inconsistencies in Party policy, which pointed toward a degree of indecision and hesitation, were explained to me by three well-informed and reliable journalists and economists. There were within the Party three factions each favoring a different course. One supported the present strategy of economic expansion but modified and moderated to take account of the current difficulties. These modifications would include a cutback in expensive imports, a reduction of the growth rate in industrial investment and an all-out export drive. The second faction was in favor of a much harder line, advocating domestic austerity - a siege economy of sorts - combined with a much more Comecon-oriented economic policy, much more integration within the Comecon price and investment structures. This would mean a very difficult belt-tightening exercise which could have jeopardized Gierek's political and economic opening to the West. The third, and the smallest faction, favored liberalization of economic management, quoting the Yugoslav example. It would promote workers' councils, much more decentralization and an attempt to reduce social tensions by encouraging genuine consultations between rulers and ruled.

The third solution would hardly have been acceptable to the Russians and they would have instinctively preferred the second approach. But there must also have been the realization in Moscow that such a policy would run the risk of antagonizing the Polish population. Continued rising standards of living was the price that the Poles now demanded of their leaders. Not only did Gierek have to try to pay this price but Moscow must have hoped that he would succeed. On balance it was clear that the first course prevailed and the government was trying to carry on much as before with some comparatively minor adjustments. This meant that Giereks' precarious balancing act would go on. In slowing down economic expansion, Gierek might have been trying to make Poland's economy appear more orthodox in Comecon terms and, at the same time, by putting more substance into Party-people consultations, he might have been trying to secure popular acceptance of future tougher economic policies. The change was vital for the maintenance of that very economic performance on which popular support was based.

A joke circulating in Poland illustrates in paradoxical terms Gierek's dilemma: Gierek and Brezhnev were traveling together from Moscow to the Crimea by train. After an hour or so of conversation they felt hungry. Gierek took out of his briefcase a piece of fresh bread, plenty of butter, ham, sausage and other delicacies. He had been eating heartily, when, after a while, Brezhnev took out from his briefcase some hard, dark brown bread, sprinkled some salt on it and started to eat. Gierek looked amazed at the leader of the Soviet Party and said: "My dear Leonid, you really do represent the leading Party in the world. You are always ahead of us by at least five years."

It was one of those ironies in this whole situation that a government which claims to represent the workers could be so out of touch with the workers. Why? A distinguished sociologist and a member of the Polish Academy of Sciences, Professor Strzelecki, believed that the government's political "tutorship" is all very well for children but not for adults: "I am not against political influence on the economy but I would like to have more countervailing powers, which do not at present exist. Under the cover of unity there are so many divergent views and if they cannot be expressed openly we have such consequences as we have had in June."

By the capitulation in June Gierek had, in fact, granted workers the power to veto government policy by direct action as well as through formal consultations. The June events and the upheaval of December 1970 demonstrated that, particularly in Poland, but also potentially in all the communist states, one of the social forces capable autonomously of exerting decisive influence on the political power situation, are the workers when roused. June also reaffirmed that the issues which galvanize the working class to such a pitch of protest are bread-and-butter issues and the need for proper, efficient channels of communication between rulers and ruled.

The immediate measure which triggered off the upheaval was, of course the staggering package of price increases. Yet people had been expecting some prices to rise gradually. The economic realities would have been understood by the workers had these been properly explained to them. But what provoked the trouble was the manner of the operation itself. First of all it was accompanied by complicated and badly explained compensatory wage increases which were meant to offset the burden of the food-price increase but which, in fact, gave more to the richer than to the poorer. As people told me: "We all have equal stomachs." Moreover, the price increases came after the army and the police had received quite substantial pay increases. It came on top of the widespread feeling that the elites were getting too much and that differentials were being upset.(2)

Second, there was the shock of having been misinformed.
The consultations promised by Gierek had been, as one British
expert on East European affairs wrote in the London <u>Times</u>:
"...in part a sham, in part based on wrong information about
the extent of the increases, and in part vitiated by the Party
merely talking to itself and giving itself wrong answers about
the mood of the people." The people became suspicious and
would not talk to Party officials. The result was a serious
misjudgment of the public mood, of the possible public reactions.

For years the mass media had been stressing the brilliant
successes of the leadership's economic policies and assuring
people that the economic chaos which reigned supreme in the
Western world could never happen in a socialist country. And
then, almost overnight, came the news that the situation was
so serious that the increase in food prices had to average
about 70 percent and, therefore, Poland was indeed exposed to
world trends. The people, therefore, felt cheated and
humiliated.

The secret trials by secret courts and open trials of both
hooligans and striking workers had considerably increased
tension again after it had abated initially when the price
package was withdrawn. But it was one thing to arrest and
sentence hooligans and vandals who were breaking the law,
and it was another matter to take repressive measures against
workers merely because they had demonstrated and gone on
strike, particularly when these measures included massive
arrests, large-scale dismissals, and the most flagrant violations
of human rights, including police brutality.

The general message which emerged from the trials, which
were publicized in the mass media, seemed to be that while the
government was prepared to respond to the wishes of the
people, the expression of these wishes must be contained
within the law. The leadership can bend policies but not
ordinary laws designed to stop people from, for instance,
tearing up railway lines. This was reasonable but it left at
least two questions open. First, it was a mistake to exclude
all Western journalists from the "open" trials and to order a
very scant reporting by the national media. Obviously the
government wanted the minimum of publicity in order not to
provoke further outbursts. But, second, if it wanted to
convince people that the law was taking its ordinary course,
then justice had to be seen to be done and should have allowed ordinary reporting of the proceedings. Secrecy breeds
suspicion. The people's prickly suspicion of anything which
the Party was trying to do, the impatience with continuing
material shortages, and a consciousness of their own power
remained.

As one British observer put it toward the end of 1976,
Poland appeared rather like a ship which had run aground.

Some of its officers and crew were desperately trying to re-float it, but some were either not doing so or seemed unable to do so very well for both internal and external reasons. The passengers lining the decks were not even bothering to conceal their indifference to the sailor's efforts, while now and again the crew hurled abuse at the passengers for their lack of public-spiritedness. And the great ship remained stranded.

13 New Measures: Who is Leading Whom?

> And when we think we lead
> we most are led.
>
> George, Lord Byron in "Two Foscari"

After almost five months of confusion, contradictory reactions to the June events, uncertainty and diffidence, the Party had partly overcome the inertia within its body politic. Gierek, his image unavoidably tarnished but still in charge, had to thread carefully between conflicting trends in the Party and widespread dissent in the country.

Consultations with the Soviet leaders in Moscow (November 1976) came first since the Polish leadership needed economic and political support to help it weather the difficult winter months ahead. Privately, Soviet officials did not hide their anxiety about the situation in Poland, and saw no other way out but to give Gierek 90 percent of what he asked for. He did not get a reduction in the level of Polish investments in the Soviet Union, nor did he secure a short-term freeze on the prices paid for Soviet oil. But he did obtain Soviet deliveries of one million tons of grain and other foodstuffs and supplies, on credit and of some machinery, above the established quotas. Poland would sell to the Soviet Union industrial equipment, worth 1,000 million rubles. Poland's contribution to Comecon and economic assistance to Cuba and some African countries were reduced.

However, there was a political sting attached to this economic assistance. The joint declaration(1) emphasized "a new stage in the mutual relations," fuller economic integration and the pledge: "The staunch defense and consolidation of the achievements of socialism are the internationalist duty of the socialist state," a phrase hinting at the "Brezhnev doctrine" used to justify the invasion of Czechoslovakia in 1968.

This political price had to be paid, particularly since the Soviet leaders have always been keen - like little children - to have everybody praising them and assuring them of un-shakeable friendship. But, paradoxically, the 1976-1977 in-ternal situation in Poland and strong Polish economic links with the West on which the economy had become dependent might well have strengthened Gierek's position in Moscow. With an overwhelmingly Catholic country which he had to rule and with private peasantry, Gierek was able to argue that if he were not allowed to do things his own way there could be a repetition of the 1970 and 1976 upheavals. Polish internal policies had, therefore, to develop more freely although within certain limits. The most glaring of these was the clearly ex-pressed opposition movement, which might provide a dangerous example for other East European countries. The Soviet leaders are on the other hand hard political realists, and they know that serious trouble in Poland would threaten not only Gierek's regime, but also vital Soviet interests in maintaining stability in Eastern Europe.

After his return from Moscow Gierek announced the "economic maneuver" in investments (see Chapter 9) and in the clear shift of emphasis on the importance of private farmers once again showed his pragmatism.

At the February 1977 CC plenum Gierek assured them that not only was Party policy on individual farms permanent and that these farms had all the guarantees and prospects for development, but also that they would be able to buy ad-ditional land - as much as they desire, provided they could increase production. There would be no difficulties, said Gierek, anywhere at local levels, which, hitherto, had made it impossible for most farmers to purchase additional land. He also announced an old-age pension scheme for all farmers irrespective of whether they turned their farm over to the state or left it to their children.

This policy shift acknowledged the private, hereditary principle and had two aims. First, to prevent the further fragmentation of small farms. Second, to ensure that farms stayed in the hands of people with agricultural experience. Although the measure ran counter to communist ideology the Party believed it would make private farming more efficient. They also decided once again that they cannot bully the farmers into producing more. They must cajole them into doing so.

The new legislation introduced in December 1976 offered both incentives and stability to the private sector in services. Gierek flatteringly referred to private enterprise as the third sector of the national economy after industry and agriculture. It will now be included in the national plan. The services will

increase by 70 percent; some will even be trebled. Financial
measures provided for the tax-free threshold to be raised and
many other tax allowances. The private sector will have
guaranteed access to tools and equipment withdrawn from the
socialized sector.

These concessions could be regarded as progressive in
view of the in-built, doctrinaire resistance to any attempt to
favor the private enterprise, strangled until now by various
punitive measures. In the opinion of some economists, I met,
a "mix" between state and private enterprise was not only
acceptable but financially rewarding. They would like somehow
to get out of the straight-jacket of socialized economy - the
costly state capitalist system, with its imposed bureaucratic
inefficiency and thousands of contradictory directives.

In efforts to rectify the economic situation the leadership
turned, therefore, for help to private enterprise, both in
agriculture and in the service industry. At the same time, in
January 1977, at various meetings of administrators and
experts two problems were thrashed out. The unwarranted
increase in the wages had to be stopped, warned Jaroszewicz(2)
because it demoralized people who benefited from this regardless of their performance. Wages had to be related to productivity instead of being linked to the cost of living.

Furthermore, Jaroszewicz bluntly coupled his call for
better performance with indications of the possibility of dismissals to deal with the "incorrigibles." He came out very
strongly against those pockets of resistance among demoralized
bureaucrats and obdurate "neo-Stalinists" who, in silent
protest, had been patiently marking time.(3) The leadership
seemed to be trying at the beginning of 1977 to restrain,
contain, and if possible, intimidate dissenters at large while
seeking to reduce the discontent that brought them support.

The most difficult problem proved to be the consultations.
After June Gierek seemed to be aware once more of the need
for fuller, more credible information both upward to the
leadership and downward to the people. Warnings about the
dire consequences of the lack of such information could be
heard. These were encouraging signs but they had been
heard before - it was, on a smaller scale, a repeat performance of the period after December 1970 - and in the end
the monolithic system had always closed in and reasserted
itself.

In his Katowice speech (see Chapter 9) Gierek said that
every citizen had the "right" to take a stand on various issues
submitted for consultation. A detailed scrutiny of press
articles and public pronouncements by Party leaders made it
possible to conclude that: 1) the principle of consultation had
not been abandoned; 2) no structural changes were envisaged
in connection with it; 3) the process remained the responsibility of existing "representative bodies" (so many times com-

pletely discredited in the past); 4) the time allowed for consultations had to be extended; and 5) the process of consultation remained the main instrument of the Party's ideological activity and therefore overall control of the Party in
this process had to be reestablished.

The "great debate" about consultations and participation
produced in actual measures, in 1976, something which was a
far cry from what the people regarded as a basic dilemma: the
new, real, institutionalized channels which would transform the
fundamental relationship between rulers and ruled. Five
commissions had been established (see Chapter 9) to study all
aspects of socioeconomic developments. The main reason was
to fill for a year the void created by the necessity which had
prompted the government to decide not to decide anything. In
the meantime Gierek tried hard to instill once again more life
into local Party organizations and insisted on their having
contacts with the people, and subsequently on a two-way
information and consultation. He tried to do this a number of
times before without much success, as it had been proved in
June. But Gierek, always the pragmatic politician, fully
realized that the church, the intellectuals, the workers and
the CDW had put the question of democratic liberties on the
agenda and, therefore, he left his long-term options open. He
drew a blueprint for increasing Party influence, but left some
of the details blank.

A new frontline team emerged in December 1976. Olszowski left his job as foreign minister, rejoined the SCC and
took over the responsibility for socioeconomic development.
Known as a tough talker who could be firm with subordinates
and not exactly a "liberal," he was assigned the difficult task
of conceding to society only enough power to give a semblance
of sharing in decision making, but not enough to endanger the
leading role of the Party. Olszowski, who was never strictly
speaking a Gierek man, now seemed to have replaced Szydlak
as number two in the Party and many become a counterweight
to him. Karkoszka (removed as first secretary of the VPC in
Gdansk after December 1970 riots) became another secretary of
the CC.

In addition to Szydlak (who lost all his Party posts) and
was appointed deputy premier, two others became deputy
premiers: an economist, Professor Secomski, and Kepa, who
thereby lost his position as first secretary in the Warsaw Party
organization. A well-known hard-liner he was one of five PB
members critical of Gierek's policies. Wojtaszek, former ambassador in Paris, became foreign minister.

Observers in Warsaw regarded these appointments as a
follow-up to the removal of higher Party officials who lost
prestige as a result of the June events. Although no rival to
Gierek could be spotted on Warsaw's political horizon it could
indeed be argued that the changes appeared rather to be the

product of a tug-of-war between Gierek and his most trusted people on the one side and groupings far from close to him on the other.

14 Gierek: Prisoner of the System

Most people I spoke to in September 1976 thought that Gierek had lost some of his popularity, at least for the time being, but that he remained "the only leader we have." "He has become a prisoner of the system, and of the situation," said a well-known journalist. According to ecclesiastical sources close to the Episcopate, Gierek was deeply apprehensive but rightly said that everything depended on what "we decide ourselves and what we ourselves can work out."

At the very beginning, he rather cleverly remained on the sidelines and then went on the defensive and was trying to gain time. He did not really know what was going on outside Warsaw. This, it was felt, was mainly because the Party apparatus as a whole had no real contact with the people. As in the past two years people still insisted that Gierek was one thing and the Party another. The Party organization was like a heavy stone chained to the legs of the man who wanted to go forward and meet the demands of the people.

There was evidence to prove that during the June crisis Kepa, the chief of the Warsaw Party organization and some others, tried to take over if possible. But after the Party leader's speeches in Katowice and Mielec, and particularly after his return from Moscow they realized that there was no chance of anybody displacing Gierek. This was because there were no people, apart from Gierek, who could get the country out of its mess. Inevitably tarnished, he remained in the circumstances the most popular figure and the Party's greatest asset. People refused to pay the clumsily prepared bill for the affluence of the Gierek era, but they feared that any change of Party leader would be for the worse.

The situation, the editor of a Warsaw daily paper told me, reminded him of that famous film, The Towering Inferno. In a huge, multistory hotel there was a fire somewhere. At first the source of the fire could not be found. But when the source had been located it was difficult to approach the fire because it was much too hot and by then threatened to get out of control. An economist, also given to analogies, who described himself as reasonably optimistic about the future said, "We are traveling in a car through a tunnel, but the steering wheel is desynchronized and the vehicle hits the walls of the tunnel every now and then. The point is not to knock oneself against the wall too hard."

Everybody agreed that the problem of consensus socialism remained unsolved. At first sight it seemed quite paradoxical, because no communist leader in the history of the communist movement has done so much as Gierek to try to get across to the people over the heads of the Party organizations and local administration, the message of the new style of government by dialogue between rulers and ruled. Later he tried as hard as ever to encourage the members of the middle apparatus to do the same. In most cases this was totally unsuccessful.

Why, then, the June upheaval? The answer would seem to be that there had been no essential change in the system and the structure of consultation. Hence the greater the disappointment after Gierek's promising start. There was no revitalization of the workers' councils, of the workers' self-government, of the trade unions, the issues which have played such an important part in the first upheaval in 1956 and then in December 1970 (see section, "The Workers: Their Strength and Their Pressure," in Chapter 4). There had been no devolution of decision to workers' self-government as, for instance, in Yugoslavia. The Communist Party, with its ruling bureaucracy and tame trade unions, remained the essential instrument of consultation and it had failed. During the last five years up to 1976, the public-relations nature of Gierek's meetings with ordinary people came to the fore, while hopes of their marking the beginning of a greater devolution of power to the people have receded into the background. This was only one symptom of the clear line drawn by the Party between the opening up of channels for consultative access to policy makers, and devolution of real decision making, influence and power. The first was seen by some Party leaders as a desirable trend, and the second as something which must be resisted.

For five years Gierek's economic policies led to something approaching a Polish economic miracle. It was a decision in the spirit of what used to be called "goulash communism," a philosophy which was summed up by the late Nikita Krushchev in his memoirs in the words: "Most people still measure their own freedom, or lack of it, in terms of how much meat, how many potatoes, or what kind of boots can they get for one rouble...." For five years this formula worked splendidly in Poland, before the goulash began to run out. For such expansionist policies tend to lead communist countries, as well as capitalist countries, into debt. And that, of course, is always the crunch for any regime when growing expectations meet with disappointments. It was at this stage that the consultations which Gierek had tried so hard to set up broke down and did so for a quite simple reason. Consultation was always one-way. It was "we" the Party authorities who took the decisions, consulting "them," the workers. And "they," the workers, had no independent legitimate channels through which they could influence the decision already taken, and therefore they did so by strikes and demonstrations which led to illegal excesses by means of which they were highly successful in forcing the government to capitulate. Logically, therefore, something had to be done to avoid similar upheavals in the future. But nobody could say how this could be done. The principle of the leading role of the Party made answers to this question impossible. Some prominent people rather pessimistically maintained that no real reforms could be introduced without another, perhaps bloody, intervention on the streets.

Some of the reasons for Gierek's misjudgment of public mood and his faulty political assessment seem to be apparent. The internal debate at the highest Party echelons over when and how to move on prices had gone on too long, aggravating the economic situation and exacerbating simmering political tensions. Although Gierek had to be convinced about the need for a staggering comprehensive package, he probably thought that after he had done so much for the country people would accept this shock treatment and would understand it. He had not allowed the mass media to be as open as he was himself at some meetings. The language in which the authorities addressed the people through the media was dead, uniformative, and an invitation to skepticism and indifference. Consequently the leadership has misread the people's attitude. The consultation was conducted on an extremely limited scale within the Party and, therefore, with the wrong people, although nationwide consultations had been promised. Party activists, in the way of the Party faithful, told the leadership what it wanted to hear rather than what it needed to know.(1)

This, of course, still does not explain Gierek's own wrong diagnosis. Some years earlier he began rushing round the country talking personally with the workers with the best of intentions. But the system began to reassert itself. When I visited two factories in 1971 and then in 1973 I was told that before 1970 they had painted only one side of the machines when Gomulka paid a visit because his itinerary was so carefully prepared. When Gierek came they had to paint all the machines because they did not know where he would go. By 1976 they again only painted one side. Gierek's visits had become more formalized. He was now meeting selected people like Party activists and official delegations.

A large part of the blame must be apportioned to the provincial Party apparatus, on which Gierek seemed to think he could rely. Some provincial Party bosses either tried to wreck Gierek's more liberal policies, or they simply did not report truly and conscientiously what was going on in their particular regions for fear of being blamed for the existing situation and subsequently for fear of losing their jobs.

The Party apparatus was severely shaken and purged by Gierek himself after 1970, more than once, because of stagnation and complete indifference reigning during the last years of Gomulka's leadership. But by now it had regained control and because it runs the information system which reports on its own work it passes out more good news than bad. Some Party organizations did not really bother to inform the leadership, but merely bolstered their own successes for fear of tarnishing their own good image. Others would not tell the truth, either from fear, or so as not to damage their own vested interests. Even if sometimes, very occasionally, some bitter truth found its way into the report, the relevant copy did not necessarily reach Gierek since it ran against official statistical data and contrary to the climate of the propaganda of success. It simply remained in the drawer of a CC secretary.

An amusing incident occurred when, during one of his provincial tours, Gierek was scheduled to visit a village and have tea with one of the private farmers. The local Party organization wanted to do everything possible to make the farm look prosperous and therefore the local state farm sent the farmer five cows to graze on his grassland. Unfortunately, Gierek could not come. The farmer sent the cows back to the state farm and simultaneously sent a registered letter to the first secretary of the Party in Warsaw including an invoice for the fodder which the state farm cows had eaten on his private grassland.

Another source of information for the Party secretariat was certainly the political police. Two versions of this aspect were circulating in Warsaw at the end of 1976. Either the political police had sent thorough factual reports which were disregarded by the CC or the political police had misinformed headquarters. In both cases they were to be blamed.

Finally, the Party and perhaps even Gierek himself probably believed their own propaganda of success and underestimated the disenchantment resulting from the government's inability to satisfy the revolution of rising political and economic expectations. All this was the more surprising in that Gierek must have been acutely aware that the workers had tasted power in bringing down Gomulka in 1970 when he tried to raise prices. Gierek realized that the same power could be turned against him if he did not win their confidence. Nowhere else in Eastern Europe(2) have the workers rediscovered their muscle and the power to force the government to retreat or even to change the government and the Party leadership.

The problems confronting the authorities were more difficult in 1976 in the short term than those which had faced the Party in December 1970. Then there was an alternative leader available whose expansionist economic policies promised to pacify popular demands for an end to austerity. There were no such easy options now. Economically it had become difficult for Gierek to satisfy the demand for a higher standard of living, but politically it was dangerous for him not to go on trying.

The political problem, therefore, went much deeper and had much wider implications. In the past the church, the peasants, the workers, the students, and the intellectuals had defended their individual interests in their separate ways at separate times. They always tended to see their grievances against the authorities as existing in different compartments. Only in the first heady days of October 1956 did the aspirations of some workers, of students and intellectuals, even of some more reasonable and forward-looking Party members, coalesce for a short period. But very shortly thereafter the workers, the intellectuals, and the church tended to try and defend their own positions without paying too much regard to their common interest. In March 1968 student demonstrators and intellectuals received no help from the workers. In 1970 the striking workers received no support from students or intellectuals. The church had always supported the oppressed, but tended to claim sole custody of the nation's heritage. The church, particularly, which had struggled under communism to maintain the faith among its own flock had, in recent years, broadened its moral concern to insist on every citizen's social and civil rights.

If the authorities believed in June that they enjoyed more popular confidence than they in fact did, they should have been warned by a number of reactions from the people to various recent government policies which had alienated different elements of Polish society (see Chapter 7), and united them in opposition.

The June events provided another show of unity of all classes. The workers were not left alone in their protests. They were helped by the students and the intellectuals and the church stepped in more strongly than at any time in the past few years. The CDW, created for the purpose of defending the workers against the "workers' government," provided more evidence of some degree of cooperation between industrial workers and intellectuals. These were only the most important signs of growing discontent and social tension.

The June events, as a prominent journalist told me in Warsaw, also proved that the working class was not the only powerful factor in Polish life. The church was still more

powerful. It now became stronger than ever. The church
intervened in and modified the Party decisions. The church's
support was sought by the Party and it was given under strict
conditions and in certain dangerous circumstances, as for
instance, in September 1976, when the Episcopate appealed for
moderation among the faithful but also demanded moderation
and respect for the people from the authorities. Was this
cooperation? Not exactly, but nearly so. The church was
following policies of urging moderation on both sides. Nevertheless it was not hesitating to raise forcefully those matters
with the government on which it felt it had a moral duty to
speak.

What had become indisputably clear after June was that
for the first time in many years, a real feeling of solidarity
existed among all sections of Polish society. By its measures
at the end of 1975 and in 1976 the Party has managed to unite
against itself the church, workers and peasants, students and
intellectuals in what could be described as a widespread civil
rights movement. At stake was the fundamental relationship
between rulers and ruled in a country governed by the Communist party. The movement, clearly in opposition to the
imperatives limiting the present mechanisms of dialogue, consultation and participation, was much more widespread and
went much deeper in its public expression than in any other
East European country. It was dangerous because, with one
or two insignificant exceptions, it did not demand the overthrow of the system, but strongly insisted on far-reaching
changes and improvements imposed by the people and, what is
even more dangerous, the strict observance of civil rights and
liberties as guaranteed by the constitution. In other words
the Party did not possess a monopoly of wisdom; therefore
there had to be new, institutionalized mechanisms for consultation and participation. It was not an easy proposition.
The Party in its methods remained well behind the dynamic
economic progress, its natural exigencies, the changing
political climate, and the people's rising aspirations and
demands.

The repetition of disappointments played a significant part
in cementing this widespread opposition movement. Reformed,
and to some extent in a communist context, liberal national
communism failed to consolidate after 1956. A students and
intellectuals' revolt demanding more freedom and an end to
censorship failed in 1968. Now the technocratic solution with a
dynamic economic development had also been found wanting, at
any rate to the extent of producing neither continuous material
prosperity nor a revival of national spirit to which it advocated hope. As of October 1956 the people's expectations
and hopes were too high, but there was nonetheless a very
important difference. The revolution of rising expectations
was fully justified during the first two, or even three, years

of Gierek's leadership. Prosperity grew, the economy was developing dynamically and at first the average person did not notice that some promises of political reforms had disappeared into thin air. But when people began to realize that politically and even economically something was going terribly wrong, the Party did not explain that the boom had to stop, that a policy of retrenchment was necessary because of external objective reasons and did not admit that bad management had played a significant part.

The developments in Poland have been watched with fascination by some and with deep apprehension by others in neighboring countries and no doubt with profound alarm in Moscow, not only because the Communist party had lost control over the country for a considerable time, but also because the demands of the mass opposition movement went against the traditional principle of the leading role of the Party. In other words, if there was going to be a real participation by the people, the Party's political overlordship had to be toned down at least, if not transformed.

This might prove to be dangerously infectious in other East European countries. The Russians, of course, will go quite a long way to avoid Polish-Soviet confrontation while slapping down briskly any weaker dissent in other neighboring countries so that the Polish infection will not spread; the repression of the signatories of "Charter 77" in Czechoslovakia has provided only one example. But in Poland, a grudging half-tolerance of the opposition by the Party actually existed in 1977 because it was too strong to be put down by a quick campaign of suppression.(3) In fact, the situation remained precarious and the atmosphere nervous. A leading dissenter told a British correspondent on a visit to Warsaw: "The regime is sitting on a powder keg." Yet the authorities and the opposition had at least one thing in common - the desire to avoid another explosion. Each had the power to destroy the other but the cost would be disastrous for all. The result was a restrained confrontation in which almost everyone was displaying a degree of caution and realism quite unusual in Polish politics.

15 Playing for Time: 1977-March 1979

> You can only govern men by serving them. The rule is without exception.
>
> V. Cousin

TENSION GROWS AGAIN: 1977

Those who, at the end of 1976, had hoped for a push forward by Gierek, were deeply disappointed in 1977. After some initial concessions (see Who is leading whom? Chapter 13) Party policy, if there was one, became erratic. Some, often conflicting, decisions were taken quite at random. The leadership gave every indication of being unsure of its next step.

Between February and April 1977 Gierek seemed confident that the post-June 1976 tensions had been essentially reduced and that the time for new policy initiatives within the context of "socialist democracy" had come. While official policy reflected the regime's sensitivity to Western coverage of Polish internal affairs, Gierek maintained an attitude of qualified tolerance toward opposition groups outside the Party and of their increasing influence. For over a month there was almost no harassment of CDW members. At one of his journalist briefings in February, Gierek praised the church for its constructive attitude in pointing out to the Poles the gravity of their economic problems and urging them to work hard to overcome them.

A PB resolution called for more matter-of-fact constructive press criticism and an "expansion of the range of information supplied to society." The press began printing sharper criticisms of economic inefficiency and the weekly,

Polityka, expanded on Gierek's proposals for socialist democracy, i.e., much wider consultations, increased responsibility at all levels, etc. In March, two controversial films,
The Marble Man by world-famous director Wajda and Camouflage
directed by Zanussi, were released for public screening, the
former by a decision of Gierek himself, against a dissenting
majority in the PB. Wajda's film was a bold attempt to
demythologize the Stalinist era and it attacked one of the most
sacrosanct taboos of those times: the cult of the so-called
"heroes of socialist labor," The Stakhanovite movement which
Wajda exposes as not only inhuman but also ludicrous. He
shows how fear of uncovering the past still persists in
present-day Poland. The film is full of innuendos and
allusions to most recent events.

It seemed then as if Party policy was developing in the
direction of a cautious and well-controlled openness, even
liberalization. But at the CC plenum in April, Gierek had to
face dissent in the top Party ranks. Two views appeared.
One group, privately known as the "Hammers" because of their
crude methods, advocated repression. Another group known
as the "Sickles" favored a policy of reform. They argued that
the authorities had been taken by surprise in June 1976. The
remedy lay in freer information and independent channels for
expressing people's grievances - in other words, a "mini"
repeat performance of post-December 1970 days.

At the plenum several speakers attacked Wajda's film and,
by implication, Gierek's too-liberal treatment of protest and
opposition. Szczepanski, the radio and television chief, was
advocating a reversal of the new policy when recent ideological
communist meetings in Sofia and Prague seemed to point toward
a harder line on human rights.

At the plenum, Gierek attacked those "opponents" of
Poland and socialism who were trying to create confusion in
the country and who "find few allies" in Poland. All "class
enemies", he announced, "both at home and abroad must be
unmasked and will be opposed by all available means." This
was Gierek's answer to the surge of criticism of his policies
within the Party. At the same time, he promised to "deepen
socialist democracy," particularly guarantees of workers'
co-management of their enterprises, of their regions and of the
country.(1)

Ten days later, at the national conference of local Party
secretaries, he appealed for unity and enlarged on the need to
consult the whole people, attacking some Party functionaries
who had failed in their duty. He also warned those higher up
in the Party that they must observe the principles of "democratic centralism," in other words, they should not disregard
Party decisions.(2) This meeting, the first of its kind during
Gierek's rule, and coming so soon after a CC plenum where
divergent opinions emerged and some of his policies were

criticized, seemed to suggest that the party leader was seeking support in the mass of Party organizations.

In April and May the hard-liners within the Party had grown in influence, though they were still far from being able to press their policies on Gierek; but compared with the relative lack of opposition to him during most of his time in power, this was a significant development.

Almost immediately after the CC plenum some CDW members were detained and then released again. Two committee meetings were broken up by the militia. Adam Michnik, a dissenter historian, who had returned to Poland after several months stay in Western Europe, was branded a "political renegade" and Leszek Kolakowski, now teaching in Oxford, was called a "communist hater."(3) Official criticism tried to link Polish dissenters with West German "revanchists," accusing them of collaborating with "right-wing" West German expellees' organizations.

The Party press itself strongly attacked Wajda's film. A scapegoat was offered to Party "Hammers" in the person of the deputy minister of culture, Wojtczak who was replaced by a "strong-man," Wilhelmi, a former editor of the weekly, Kultura, and then director of all television cultural programs. One of his first acts was to withdraw The Marble Man, which had been highly praised by the Italian and French communist press, from public screening and to prevent its distribution abroad. In an interview with the Paris paper, Le Point, Wajda insisted that young Poles had the right to know about the past exploits of their fathers and they would succeed "in getting at the truth." It was, he said, "a reasonable hope for a nation that has for so long been thirsting for the truth."(4)

While more repressive measures against the CDW continued, some workers, both strikers and those sentenced for criminal offenses after June 1976, were quietly released. According to official sources only five workers remained in prison.(5) Two CDW members, Kuron and Lipski, were officially warned that they were suspected of maintaining illegal contacts with foreign organizations said to damage Poland's interests. This opened a way toward legal action. While releasing the workers and reinstating those dismissed, the leadership was effectively chipping away at the CDW foundations and their declared aims.

But the widespread demand for an inquiry into militia brutality against the workers remained unanswered. This was one of the leadership's major blunders, I was told by a Party journalist. The Party was in a rather difficult position. If there had been excesses by the security police, the tricky question of the extent to which the Party controls the security forces might prove embarrassing.

The hard-liners' backlash became quite clear when an open letter to Gierek was suddenly circulated, signed by some

800 so-called workers, mostly Party activists, demanding an even harsher line both internally and externally.(6) Ominously, Deputy Premier and former PB member Szlachcic who had been removed from Party positions saw the Soviet ambassador in Warsaw before the letter circulated.

In May tension increased once again. On May 7 a Krakow university student, Stanislaw Pyjas, was found dead in a house in which he had neither friends nor relatives. He was one of six students, all supporters of the CDW, who had filed a complaint with the Krakow prosecutor's office about anonymous death threats they had received. He was also one of the organizers at Krakow university of a petition for an inquiry into militia brutality after June 1976. Thousands of students attended a requiem mass for Pyjas in Krakow and then marched with black banners to the house where his body had been found. That evening (May 15) an estimated 5,000 students staged a candlelight procession through the city. As they gathered around the royal castle, a student read a manifesto describing Pyjas' death as murder and demanding an inquiry and the punishment of those responsible. The establishment of a Students Solidarity Committee was announced as an "authentic and independent student representation" to replace the official Socialist Union of Polish Students (see Chapter 7). Requiem masses were also held in Warsaw and Lodz. The authorities claimed that Pyjas' death was caused by a fall while under the influence of alcohol. It was only in September that the prosecutor's office officially described Pyjas' death as a "tragic accident," stressing the lack of any evidence to support suspicions of a criminal action and therefore discontinued proceedings.(7) But doubts remained in the minds of well-informed journalists I met in Warsaw.

The events in Krakow brought to the surface the problem of student activism. The organizers of the street demonstrations maintained a calm and dignified mood; the demonstrators and the authorities both avoided an open clash. Although students formed a large part of the CDW supporters, they have generally played second fiddle to the more prominent intellectuals. Now they emerged as yet another social group pressing for reform. In an official declaration the Students Solidarity Committee stated that the official Socialist Union of Polish Students had cooperated with the security services and therefore no longer represented the students.

The ferment among the students had already become clear at the Socialist Union of Polish Students congress in April, when the minister of higher education, Kaliski, warned students against sterile arguments about freedom and civic rights.(8) Even the press admitted that the impact of the organization on students' masses "left very much to be desired."(9)

   Meanwhile, the CDW itself was undergoing a transformation, while claiming a 1,000-strong network of active helpers
in the country. Already in March some tensions were exposed
between the social democrats and younger, more radical, members. The former were given the original CDW duties of
helping workers and families; the latter, including Kuron,
though not led by him, were inclined to form their own more
permanent dissenters' movement. After the Krakow events the
CDW announced the setting up of an intervention bureau to
collect and publicize information on official violation of human
rights, and a social self-defense fund to support those who
had lost their jobs because of their connections with the CDW.
The statement warned that only "the activity of the whole of
society can resist acts of repression and slow down the
dangerous process of unpunished violations of human and civil
rights." This constituted a significant redefinition of the
CDW's original scope and purpose (see section, "Committee for
the Defense of Workers" in Chapter 9). Thus any official
strategy based on fulfilling the CDW original demands in order
to speed its dissolution was seriously undermined. The CDW
communiques continued to be published and the group also
helped in printing and distributing the underground literary
magazine Register (Zapis), which published those works of
Polish writers banned by the censors.

   Independently from the CDW another dissenters' group informed late in March, the Movement for the Defense of Civil
and Human Rights (known as ROPCiO) was growing in
influence. Whereas most CDW members are Marxists of
different colors, no indication of any Marxist leanings could be
found in the other group. The new movement started
circulating another unofficial publication called Opinion
(Opinia).

   Simultaneously, various conceptual, individual programs of
what should constitute "democratic opposition" continued to
appear (see Chapter 9). In a new controversial article,
published abroad(10), the historian Adam Michnik, a CDW
member, maintained that there was no hope of change from
above and further argued in an essay entitled "The New
Evolutionism" that society should press the Party to make
changes. The workers' realization of their own power is the
crucial condition of the new evolutionism, wrote Michnik, but
two other social forces have an important part to play. One is
the church, because of its central position in Polish life and
the fact that it "affirms a nonconformist and dignified attitude
and stimulates the aspirations for greater civil liberties."
Another is a pragmatic school within the Party. The latter
are, according to Michnik, not necessarily democrats but they
"have reason to think that a compromise with the forces
struggling for political pluralism can be more effective than
brutal repression."

This turning toward the church (not for the first time) as a protector of civil liberties was a significant development coming from a Marxist intellectual; it opened the door to further informal coalitions of interests between the two groups.

At the same time the church once more took up the issue of civil rights. In May, thousands of young people, mostly students, thronged the streets of Krakow led by their bishops during the celebrations in homage to St. Stanislaw. When Cardinal Wojtyla spoke in the open air in defense of civil rights and against repressive measures a military turbojet plane circled above the square in a childish effort to make him inaudible. This was greeted by a derisory laughter from the crowd and by applause when the cardinal made a joke about the "uninvited guest."(11) The primate in a sermon in Czestochowa strongly condemned detention of people for their views; it was the duty of believers to see that those who hold views different from the official ones were not persecuted and imprisoned.(12) This was the first time that the cardinal had made even an indirect reference to the persecution by the regime of the CDW. In fact he warned the authorities that the church would oppose not only religious repression but political repression as well and that they could not continue to rely on the church as a stabilizing force in society and yet constantly ignore its demands.

The various oppositional trends began to coalesce once more. The connection between the CDW and the Krakow students, the stand of the church coupled with the possibility that similar demonstrations could develop elsewhere, was apparently the last straw for the authorities. In the middle of May, eleven CDW members, including Kuron, Michnik, and Lipski, were arrested and charged with maintaining connections with foreign organizations allegedly hostile to Poland, i.e., Radio Free Europe and the Paris-based emigre monthly, Kultura.(13) This was on a prosecutor's warrant and provided for three months' investigative detention. East Germany was meanwhile urging Gierek to deport the CDW members, but he rejected the suggestion out of hand.

This desperate step seemed to indicate that the hard-line opponents of Gierek's more flexible policies within the Party were still well entrenched. The arrests produced a spate of individual and mass protests and petitions demanding the immediate release of all those arrested. The Italian and French Communist parties strongly condemned the measures. On May 19 Cardinal Wyszynski said in a sermon in Warsaw that:

A man should not be thought irritating when he speaks out about his rights as a human person. Sometimes people request their rights in a drastic and impatient way, because they feel the noose

326   FLASHPOINT POLAND

tightening around their necks.... How can a nation
live when basic human rights are not being observed?.... It would then be not a nation but a
mass of dummies without a soul, and with soulless
beings neither the nation nor the state would be able
to achieve their tasks.(14)

This was the strongest of a whole series of sermons which
the cardinal has delivered on the subject of human rights. He
warned the authorities not to condemn the actions of young
people, who run "a social temperature," but rather try to
understand them.

At the end of May, eight people, including editors and
intellectuals, began a hunger strike in a chapel of St. Martin's
church in Warsaw in protest against the arrest of CDW
members. They were soon joined by six other people. After
one week the strike ended peacefully. The authorities did not
interfere. The head of state, Professor Jablonski, admitted
for the first time that the influence of the CDW was neither as
small nor as unimportant as the mass media had often
maintained, when he spoke about a handful of those bitterest
enemies of Poland who had succeeded in leading many Poles
astray.

The hunger strike represented a new and dramatic tactic
in the conflict between the intellectuals and the leadership.
The strikers showed that there was a second line of protesters
to sustain the cause if the first line should be arrested, and
the authorities were probably not much interested in finding
out whether there might be a third line as well. Another
significant factor emerged. The strikers' appeal for the
immediate release of the arrested CDW members was handed
over to the Council of State by Mazowiecki, editor of the
independent Catholic monthly Link (Wiez), a fact which in itself established a connection between intellectuals in the CDW
and some of the Catholic lay community. A common platform
uniting Marxist and non-Marxist, including Catholic intellectuals, emerged in 1977.

Polish media mounted an unprecedented week-long
campaign against Western reporting of recent events in Poland,
described as a "hue and cry" of anti-Polish propaganda.
Tension rose at the beginning of June to an uncomfortably
high pitch, particularly since economic performance did not
improve as was hoped for. Gierek faced a situation that was
as complex as it was unpredictable. The church, even more
strongly than before, regarded as its duty the active
engagement of its office in the human rights campaign, and to
extend the scope of its public activity beyond purely spiritual
matters. As one Western correspondent put it: the church is
again taking up its historic role as the "paramount factor
molding the national identity of the Poles."(15) In pastoral

letters and sermons between April and May the Episcopate decried the prevailing "favoritism on political grounds" and the banning of Catholics from responsible positions as a "striking example of man's exploitation by man"; attacked attempts to force atheist ideology on society, particularly on youth; and reaffirmed that government-Vatican contacts had to be complemented by parallel negotiations between the government and the Episcopate.(16)

Meanwhile Gierek had to decide what to do with the arrested CDW members. If he resorted to more repressive measures, his regime was not only likely to be singled out for criticism at the Belgrade (CSCE review) conference, but its standing in the country would suffer still further. Most people knew that the overt activities of the CDW had nothing to do with any outside bodies, but were deeply rooted in Poland's internal developments. The CDW arrests were an obvious political blunder. Even the more conservative Party leaders must have feared a position in which the excesses of the security police might get out of hand.

Finally, the Party had still not changed its ways. It retained the ingrained mistrust and fear of public opinion, linked with an arrogant belief among many activists that they knew best. Gierek's conservative opponents argued that the freedom to complain, to publish controversial articles in the press, to tolerate intellectual dissent and a real participation in decision making, were all concessions portending political conflict and an open defiance of the Party's leading role.(17) They were afraid of a pre-1956 revolutionary atmosphere (see Introduction) particularly since the demands from below were very similar to and often identical with those of 1956 and 1970 even if the economic and environmental circumstances have changed substantially in the meantime.

In June the harsh policies were abandoned. Cardinal Wyszynski warned: "We fear anything that might be a violation of human rights today, as this might give birth to new unrest tomorrow."(18) Under strong pressure from intellectuals and mass petitions, Jan Jozef Lipski and another CDW member were released from prison on health grounds, and no charges were made against them.

At the Sejm session on June 30, without condemning anybody, Gierek said that "conditions have been created for the actual implementation of human rights...."(19)

But Gierek also made three further points: the issue of human rights was "our internal affair"; the communists would be entitled to a say on the issue; and he strongly rejected any "politicizing activity alien and unnecessary to us which disturbs the so much needed atmosphere of confidence and social peace and sows confusion in people's minds." We are going to act, he promised, "in our own Polish way." This was a frank enough speech, but somehow no real decisions were ever taken, and this at a time when the Poles have emerged as people who wanted to be treated as average Europeans, to be trusted by their rulers, to be heard, to take a share in deciding about their country. One of the many paradoxes of Polish life was the fact that the government, with enormous centralized power ostensibly at its disposal, found itself unable to solve the country's growing economic, social and political problems.

And the Party had only itself to blame. As the writer Andrzej Kijowski said at a meeting in June: "A mendacious world has arisen.... And that is its main fault, its basic, structural fault."

Gierek seemed to have prevailed, to some extent, over the hard-liners at the top of the Party, to whom it must have become clear that further repression would only exacerbate the situation. The Party leader had to come up with a new and credible policy, but he was still bound to come up against a feeling of deja vu either among the people or from a less flexible faction within the Party. Thus Gierek's main problem remained. As Harold Macmillan, the former British prime minister once succinctly put it: the job of the leader is to change angles into curves.

In July came the amnesty decree. All the arrested CDW members were released well before the three-month period of their investigative detention elapsed; so were the remaining five workers sentenced to up to 9 years imprisonment for disturbances in June 1976 although they were not covered by the amnesty decree. This was agreed to at the church's request in confidential exchanges with the government. The move has certainly shown a realism on the part of the leadership and at the same time implied a recognition of the importance of oppositional groups. Apart from the strong pressure of public opinion, the releases were an act of faith by Gierek, a silent appeal to the dissenters to show restraint in return for their freedom and tolerance. It was also a recognition of facts; since the end of July the ridiculous press campaign against dissenters was switched off completely. Besides, further repression including possible trials would have embarrassed the Poles at the Belgrade conference, and offered Western Eurocommunists a convenient platform for further strong attacks on repressive methods in East European parties.

At a press conference one of the leaders of the CDW just released from prison, Kuron, called the decision "an act of political realism" and thanked all who had helped to bring about their release singling out the church in particular and the movement for the Defense of Human Rights (ROPCiO).(20)

But the more or less loosely organized oppositional groups pressing for human rights grew constantly and represented all political attitudes from, in Western terms, radical Left to radical and nationalist Right (see section, "The Anatomy of Opposition: 1977-1979," in this Chapter).

Both a highly placed Party member and a Catholic intellectual described these oppositional groups to me in 1978 as a movement for the reclamation of civil and human rights, within the constitution. It fills the political vacuum created by outdated Party methods. This is an unconventional opposition, a Catholic politician told me in 1977, which runs parallel to the conventional opposition represented by the Catholic press (except PAX), by genuine Catholic politicians and quite often by some articles in the press, particularly in the weekly, Polityka, which enlivened the otherwise conformist and boring media, with some outstanding and controversial assessments.

Gierek's soft line was dictated by a tricky political situation, and by mounting economic difficulties. In a pastoral letter in September, Cardinal Wyszynski(21) strongly attacked for the second time the communist-controlled mass media for carrying "the persistent propaganda of a godless ideology and the cult of a robot man." The media, he said, were used "to consolidate total dictatorship, to employ coercion, to spread lies and to justify the violation of the basic human rights." The letter reminded the authorities that the media were being paid for by the overwhelmingly Catholic nation, and appealed to the people to oppose publications and programs which offended faith and good morals. The letter requested the authorities to make it possible for the church to broadcast holy mass on radio and television.

In October, Cardinal Wyszynski(22) appealed to the authorities to show more understanding for the basic, everyday needs of the people in the area of food supplies because: "There is no other sector which can show such an accumulation of degradation and humiliation...."

The cardinal knew what he was talking about. He had, himself, before issuing the pastoral letter, stood in a line dressed in an ordinary priest's black robe, chatting unrecognized to people and listening to their complaints. When he was finally recognized, the people, forgetting the meat, gathered around him kissing his cardinal's ring. In his pastoral letter the primate once again took up the defense of "victims of ideological reforms" who were often left, he said, without a livelihood because of their convictions. And he hit harshly at the reform of education:

> It is impermissible to be silent when the nation's culture, its literature and art, its Christian morality and the links between Poland and the Roman Church, the spiritual forces brought to Poland are being pushed right into the background in the plan for the education of the young generation.

Here again specifically Polish paradoxes emerged. At the time of the cardinal's strictures the authorities in an obvious gesture of reconciliation, suddenly granted permits for the building of 18 new churches in the Warsaw area alone.

The Party paper, <u>Trybuna Ludu</u>, accused Polish film makers, including such famous directors as Wajda, Zanussi and Kawalerowicz, of concentrating on "marginal problems," of not "creating a realistic, credible hero of our days."(23) Yet at the same time such films as <u>The Marble Man</u> and <u>Camouflage</u>, previously withdrawn began to reappear in some local, obscure cinemas. And in November the rage of Warsaw was the film <u>Death of a President</u>, directed by Kawalerowicz. This was a story of the assassination in 1922 of the first elected president of Poland, Narutowicz, by a fascist fanatic. What was dangerous in the film, as some Party members told me, was that it faithfully portrayed the events of the day with a real parliament and various political parties often in sharp conflict, with mass demonstrations against the new president and the government and with the police trying halfheartedly to keep order without shooting. Great political figures and leaders of the political parties were beautifully portrayed by actors. Marshal Pilsudski, the victor in the 1920 Polish-Bolshevik war, the first head of the reborn Polish state, and a Polish prewar national hero - however badly he was judged by history and his contemporaries for his later methods of ruling the country after the coup d'etat in 1926 - dominated the film as an outstanding personality and leader.

Polish television began to screen a series of dramatized features on Poland's recent history, with the dialogue and texts based strictly on official documents and speeches. In the episodes entitled <u>Before the Storm</u> covering the last months of peace in 1939, prewar Polish Foreign Minister Beck appeared almost as a national hero, magnificently played by a well-known actor. Excerpts of his famous Sejm speech in May 1939 in which he rejected Hitler's demands were dramatized. Then Polish viewers heard Beck explaining to Neville Chamberlain why Poland would not allow Soviet troops on Polish territory as demanded by Moscow in the 1939 British-French-Soviet negotiations. Quoting from official documents, Beck said on television that if the Nazis attacked Poland they would take away her independence which she would regain in the war with British help. But if the Soviet armies marched into Poland they would impose Marxism, and that "would rob Poland of her soul." The script of these series, written by CC secretary Frelek and Party historian Kowalski, was reprinted without any ommissions.

This return to the recent past in the second half of 1977 was most significant. Those who saw the film came out of cinemas, as I was told, yearning for those distant days of freedom with all the inherent dangers. The historical television series brought up facts which were certainly not to the liking of the Soviet comrades. For many years past (although

not during Gierek's era) the prewar Polish leaders, including
Pilsudski and Beck were constantly condemned as reactionaries
who had brought about Poland's defeat in September 1939 and
as Soviet haters who cooperated with Nazi Germany. This
reappraisal of the recent past coincided with Gierek's renewed
emphasis on national unity, patriotism and with his constant
subtle playing on Polish nationalism.

But the economic situation was worrying. Recession in
the West, another poor harvest, no reserves of skilled labor,
the arthritis of central direction and communist "un-enterprise"
proved to be a daunting combination. The food supply, particularly of meat, deteriorated even further. In the middle of
the year, Jaroszewicz went as far as a communist leader can
go to unadulterated pessimism when he admitted that the
supplies of meat were lower than in the previous year, despite
huge imports of food worth 450 million dollars.(24) At the
June CC plenum on housing(25) it was admitted that the
housing shortage had jumped by half a million units between
1970 and 1975 and at the end of 1976 almost two million people
were waiting for homes, some for fifteen years.(26) The poor
harvest, due to prolonged rains and a shortage of spare parts
for agricultural machinery, would, according to Jaroszewicz in
August, make it hard to maintain food supplies in 1978-1979,
even if in the second half of 1977 meat supplies were kept at
the same level as in 1976, when severe shortages occurred.(27)
Total agricultural production in 1976 dropped by 0.8 percent
in comparison with 1975 when it was already 2.4 percent down
on 1974.

At the very beginning of October, production stoppages
took place in six mines in Silesia and in some textile mills.
The miners refused to go down the pits until they were firmly
reassured that meat supplies would be immediately available.
The stoppages, all lasting up to one hour, all occurred simultaneously after telephone consultations between the mines.
Within a few hours army trucks brought more than enough
meat to the affected areas, and supplies also improved for a
day or two in Warsaw. Gierek rushed to Katowice and had a
face-to-face question-and-answer session with some miners but
this was only scantily reported in the press. The Ursus
tractor plant near Warsaw, which had been so crucial in June
1976, remained a hotbed of unrest. The management was so
frightened of the workers that it made incentive payments
automatically, whether earned or not. When Gierek went to
Paris, one of his aides rushed to a factory in Lodz to prevent
a strike by workers protesting against a pay cut.

Poles have once again become cynical about the economic
system. More blatantly than anywhere else in Eastern Europe
they have learned once more, as they had to in the pre-Gierek
era, to look after their own interests. Two jokes illustrate the
situation:

Question: "Why are Poland and America exactly the same?"

Answer: "Because in neither can you buy anything with zlotys."

This pointed clearly to the shortage of available goods. And another Warsaw joke: "The average Pole earns 4,000 zlotys a month, spends 7,000 and saves the rest." Here the inflationary increase in prices quietly introduced by various enterprises came to the surface; the "second economy" was booming and working efficiently. The peasant sold meat on the free market or to his selected customers at their homes rather than to the state. Many officials became artisans, plumbers, carpenters, mechanics after office hours doing private jobs and using materials and tools pilfered from state-owned factories and garages. The authorities were reluctant to interfere since this would irritate people, and instead were trying to compete with this unconventional private enterprise. A network of so-called "express shops" and commercial shops has been created, in which you could get meat and other foodstuffs for higher prices without waiting in line. Finally in November the government permitted private individuals to lease and run state shops (except those selling meat, alcohol, jewellery and some others) and take home the profits in return for a fixed payment to the state.(28) So here was another paradox, since the "socialist" economic system turned for efficiency and rescue to private enterprise, which it was hoped would be able to stock the shops better, to sell both state and privately produced goods more efficiently and to cut down the bureaucratic distribution structure. It was estimated that the measure would cover 60 percent of all Polish shops. By the end of 1976 most of the garages and 95 percent of taxis were privately owned.

Gierek's report on the state of economy at the CC plenum at the beginning of October was frank to a degree rare in a communist state.(29) He admitted that the "economic maneuver" did not work properly. Of course, rising world prices, deterioration in the terms of trade with capitalist countries and a poor harvest all contributed to the difficulties. He admitted that the increased prices of Polish exports did not compensate for the increased expenditure on raw materials imported from abroad, and for the first time the word "internal inflation" appeared in an official report. The investment front he said was still too wide, the necessary regrouping had not been carried out; efforts had therefore to be made to speed up the commissioning of unfinished projects and not to start new ones. Only 31 of 92 particularly important projects were completed in 1976.(30)

Barely has a Party leader concentrated so much, almost exclusively, on criticizing deficiencies in practically all fields of economic life. He blamed the Party organizations, the state administration, the social organizations, the trade unions, the workers' self-government, for their "unsatisfactory efficiency and discipline in the implementation of the plan," for their sluggishness and resistance to changes, and their failure to carry out Party recommendations. It was, to some extent, a repeat performance echoing his statements after December 1970 and June 1976. Once again, the Party was right, the structures and organizational framework were sound. Only the methods of working and the attitude of the people in the apparatus had failed. And again he almost desperately appealed to the whole nation for trust, discipline and honest work, strongly condemning the widespread speculation, corruption and favoritism.

At the follow-up Sejm session, Jaroszewicz(31) admitted that the meat supply still failed to meet the demand and the considerable decline in the number of livestock had to be made up by the import of 130,000 tons of meat. He promised a much stricter control of prices and emphasized that wages had to be linked to productivity. The Sejm passed the bill introducing the promised pension scheme (see Chapter 13) and other social benefits for all individual farmers, "aligning their social rights with the rights of workers in the socialized economy." But to encourage them to deliver more to the state and to increase their holdings, the size of the pension would be linked to the value of production sold to the state.

What was not disclosed in the media about this soul-searching at the CC plenum was that provincial Party secretaries had pressed hard for something to be done immediately in supplying the market with foodstuffs, since the situation was becoming desperate. It was also significant that CC secretary, Olszowski, responsible for the economy had prepared much more drastic documents for the plenum but did not speak. All the sources I talked to in November 1977 regarded the leadership's performance as disappointing. There was not much hope in it for the frustrated and impatient people.

Faced with the unpredictable internal situation the leadership tried to maintain as wide international contacts as possible. Between them, Gierek and Jaroszewicz met all the leaders of the East European bloc to reassure them again, as in 1971, about developments in Poland. East Germany was singled out for special attention. A new friendship treaty(32) signed by Gierek in East Berlin included a significant addition to the 1967 wording. The definition of present frontiers in Europe was not only "inviolable," but also "unalterable" even by peaceful means. Bonn regarded this clause as contrary to the Helsinki agreement. The treaty also contained a pledge to regard any attack on either of the countries by any state or group of states as an attack on the treaty partner. A high official told me in Warsaw that this defense clause was included at the insistence of the Soviet Union. What Moscow wanted was that if any member country of the Warsaw Pact decides to withdraw from the military alliance (as is theoretically possible), the bilateral treaties would remind other member countries of "their obligations."

In an effort to enhance his personal position by demonstrating his international prestige and anxious to raise foreign loans and increase Polish exports, Gierek continued to maintain a wide opening to the West. He went to Paris and to Rome. The joint Polish-French declaration signed by him and President Giscard d'Estaing reaffirmed that a respect for human rights and basic freedoms constituted one of the main principles of relations between states.(33) Already in 1976 France had jumped to second place as Poland's biggest trading partner in the West and during his visit more economic agreements were signed. Willy Brandt the chairman of the West German Socialist Party (SPD), Chancellor Schmidt, the King of the Belgians, and the Shah of Persia all visited Poland. In December, President Carter came to Poland, the only communist-ruled country during his worldwide tour. Poland was still regarded in the West as an acceptable financial risk with its modernized industry which had yet to give its full return, and as the richest Comecon country, except the Soviet Union, in energy and raw materials.

STATE OF THE NATION AS SEEN IN WARSAW: OCTOBER 1977

"There is no conceptual program of structural reforms, no clear-cut policy: we are drifting helplessly along, hoping for the best," said a CC member in Poland when I was discussing the current situation. The time was long overdue for some sense of purpose, some confidence to be restored to the nation. The people must feel that they are really participating in managing the country. Most of them no longer believed that the present team was able to get the nation out of its difficulties. The credibility gap widened, and Gierek's credit was diminishing substantially. While many people still did not doubt his intentions, they saw him as a prisoner of the system and of the Party.

The Party has failed miserably. For months they tried to maintain the myth that those who criticized and opposed were just a handful of "enemies of socialism," while the nation as a whole stands firmly behind the Party and its nonexistent program. If that were the case then there would be many millions of "enemies" since the opposition was so widespread. In fact what the people resent is the outdated authoritarian style of the Party, representing a tiny minority. There may be no labor and prison camps, secret police terror and whole-

sale executions, a prominent Party journalist told me, but the
basic tenets of Stalinist mechanisms of power are nevertheless
still in operation. Every one of us, he said, is born with a
little dormant Schweinhund somewhere deep inside. The
trouble is that there are so many insomniacs among Party
leaders and activists.

The Party has certainly one ability: to destabilize.
Gierek's 1971 program contributed toward stabilization but the
Party successfully managed to destabilize the situation after a
few years while the only stabilizing force in the country
remained the church.

The central problem is the hard-core bureaucrats who
still tend to ignore or even wreck central Party policies (see
section, "First Six Months: Reactions to Change," in Chapter
3). The overwhelming majority of over two million Party
members has nothing to do with its ideological premises. They
have joined to further their careers, since there is no chance
for them to take over any responsible posts even with the best
possible qualifications, if they are not Party members. Hence
the cynicism, opportunism and a "dual" image of most Party
members.

Despite some strenuous efforts, Gierek was unable to
change radically the attitudes of the apparatus. The old-
fashioned system prevailed. The Sejm is "of course, the most
powerful state organ in the land...without any power except
paying daily subsistence to its members," said one of my
sources. The independence of trade unions remains taboo,
said another.

The Party leader looks a mentally exhausted man, without
the drive and dynamism one was used to expect from him.
Somehow he does not seem to understand why his most successful administration of the Silesian region could not have
been transplanted on to a national scale. He seems to think
that the absence of repressive measures and the degree of
political moderation, which he has shown in the second half of
1977, constitute the apex of any liberalization. "Is he
grasping the fact that the roots of the frustration, the
cynicism, the impatience and of the accumulating tension have
for some time now been psychological and political?" asked a
distinguished journalist.

The undercurrent of factional opposition at the top
against Gierek's more flexible economic and political moves
remains only slightly subdued, some politicians told me. Huge
overmanning in the modernized plants and administrative apparatus (and therefore hidden unemployment), the poison of
mediocrity in the administration and management of the
economy, threaten the system. "How on earth is it," a Party
economist asked me, "that after 30 years of socialism they
[The Party] still haven't come up with an efficient economic
system? Rakowski's ideas of decentralization and incentives for

efficiency, published in the weekly, <u>Polityka</u>, were, for instance, strongly attacked by other regime media as dangerous
revisionism. Moreover, many Party leaders are trying to grab
as much as they can while the going is good: a second car, a
second house, a second television set, etc. The Party establishment is transforming itself into a separate and isolated
bourgeois class.

Finally, there is a new and dangerous threat to the
outmoded Party stance: the impact of Eurocommunism not only
on the intelligentsia, but also within the Party, particularly on
younger members. In September the Party press harshly
condemned the statements by the Spanish communist leader,
Carrillo. Political pluralism, as advocated by Eurocommunists
was "undoubtedly progressive and suits the interests of the
working class," but only in a capitalist society. Poland and
other "socialist" countries have already made their choice of
political forms. "Pluralistic institutionalization of differences of
political platforms" would be a "step backward" and is therefore unacceptable since it would "institutionalize opposition to
the policy of the Party" and inevitably "lead to a confrontation
of political systems".(34) This only confirmed that what the
people, including some Party activists, wanted was a political
pluralism which would modernize the existing system - a fact
that the Party is afraid and unwilling to admit. This situation
coincided with strong opposition pressure from outside the
Party.

Another myth stubbornly projected, I was told, is that of
"collective responsibility." Nobody will admit that he was
responsible for blunders, for militia brutality after June 1976.
Everybody will meekly defend himself with timeworn excuses:
"I was obeying orders, and implementing 'collective decisions'",
which, of course, was rubbish, a prominent Party politician
told me. You cannot pinpoint the guilty ones. There are only
the scapegoats, frequently innocent. Gierek's greatest mistake
after June 1976 was that he did not immediately and candidly
admit that Party policy and methods were basically wrong.
When I argued that no politician anywhere would do that, the
answer was: "Schmidt or Callaghan would not hesitate to admit
mistakes to some extent at least, but they do not 'order the
people' to accept their Party as a 'leading' force in the
nation." This is the crux of the matter.

Few people believed toward the end of 1977 that changing
the present leadership would solve anything. Some would
argue that the alternative to Gierek is not a liberal Dubcek
but a hard-liner like Husak in Czechoslovakia. The others
recall that Dubcek appeared in Prague almost an unknown from
nowhere. Many more would say that there is nobody in the
present leadership who could gain at least a minimum of
credibility and confidence, or has a standing comparable to
that of even a dwarfed Gierek. Apart from personal qualities

his endurance comes from a tacit agreement of Poles, Russians and Westerners alike that he is still the best man in sight to face up to Poland's troubles, however disappointed and tired he may be and whatever mistakes he has made in the last two years or so. His best hope is that recovery in the West will make the going easier and that he will be able to reap the benefits of the huge investments made in the past six years.

Two points were forcefully stressed by almost everyone. First, there is a desperate need to restore the truth about both past and present. The media, except for a short period in 1956 and to a lesser extent in December 1970, are still falsifying the picture, remaining either "mute through malice" or by adjusting facts to fit the Party line. A caricature emerges, because the media are controlled and directed by a handful of stubborn CC bureaucrats, who think they know better but underestimate the real feeling of the nation, and treat people as idiots who have to be taught what "the truth" is, thereby displaying a frightening ignorance of the psychology of Poles. They have achieved one thing. The journalistic profession is regarded by the people as a well-paid, reliable Party prostitute, I was told by several journalists, who admitted they are "ashamed" to be in the profession. All this enrages the people, who remain fully aware of what is going on, who travel abroad by the millions and have, fortunately, access to both internal and mostly external reliable sources of information.

Second, even well-meaning Party leaders are often in the dark. The information from below is mostly false and concocted to please the leaders either because the provincial Party bosses do not make an effort to learn what the people really think or disregard their aspirations. Even if the information is true and the assessment realistic it is killed or distorted by the central apparatus before it reaches the leadership. These people and the Party overlords of the media have learned nothing over the last 30 years, to quote Gierek in another context. Only if you see sharp criticisms in the press or rejection of some Party decisions before they are implemented and not several years later can you say that some basic changes are coming, one politician told me.

Political change must follow social and economic changes. The leadership needs more than a reliance on the passive acceptance of the system by a nation once more disillusioned. To do nothing or just to tinker with the country's need for political modernization is the clear way to court disaster.

CHURCH-STATE SUMMITS: OCTOBER 1977-JANUARY 1978

In these circumstances the single most important political event of the year was the two-hour "summit" meeting between Gierek and Cardinal Wyszynski on October 29 in the Sejm building. The official communique said(35) that Gierek had exchanged views with the primate on "the most important problems of the nation and the church which are of great significance for the unity of Poles in the work of shaping the prosperity of People's Poland." The communique was broadcast in all radio and television news bulletins as the leading headline from 1800 on Saturday, October 29 until 2330 on Sunday, October 30. This in itself was without precedent by any news standards and certainly unique in the Eastern bloc. It proved the paramount importance Gierek attached to the meeting and his obvious desire that as many people as possible should be aware of it; even if no details of the discussions were disclosed.

The meeting itself had been on the cards for some time, but the timing was significant and came at Gierek's request. The next day he was going to Moscow, ostensibly for the October Revolution anniversary celebrations but mainly to have some exhaustive talks with Brezhnev. Then at the end of November he traveled to Rome and had an audience with the pope. October 29 was the first day the cardinal reassumed his full functions after two abdominal operations and a joke made the rounds in Warsaw that Gierek and Jaroszewicz had paid for a mass to pray for the cardinal's health. The meeting was the primate's first with Gierek.

I had an opportunity in Warsaw to discuss the significance of the meeting with people both close to the Party leadership and the Episcopate. The two most powerful men in Poland were talking openly, honestly and were deeply concerned about the state of the country. The Party leader was in a weaker position, with mounting economic, social and political problems to contend with. The primate, as always, was speaking on behalf of the nation, since the nation and the church are an indivisible entity. Gierek, I was told, had asked the cardinal and the whole church for help, to calm the troubled waters on the economic front and to slow down the mounting political opposition. The situation had become so serious that any minor incident could have far-reaching nationwide consequences. "We are administering the country," a highly placed Party member told me, "but the cardinal is ruling the nation and the people's souls. He has much greater influence than we could ever hope to have, since he is talking to the nation in terms of 'timeless national values' which appeal to ordinary people." "Even the most dogmatic communists have realized by now that the church is here to stay indeed it will be here forever," as Gierek once said privately. "It would be a catastrophe," a CC member told me, "if there were no powerful church in Poland."

This was not the first time that Gierek had sought the church's support but perhaps never quite so urgently. The church, on the other hand, has always acted at times of acute internal difficulties as a stabilizing force in society anxious to avert any explosive situations.

The operative word in the communique was the "unity" of the nation. The situation in the country was discussed at length and the primate outlined the church's position, based mainly on pastoral letters drawn in March and June 1977. The main issues were: full respect for human rights, guaranteed by the constitution; discrimination against believers in more responsible positions; the atheistic ideological offensive; the church's access to the media and co-participation in the reform of education; badly needed permits for building new churches; freedom of religious instruction; and the church's legal status. The primate, I was told, pointed out that some promises had been made in the past and not much has happened since. No details were discussed at this stage but some promises were made by Gierek. Both leaders were reported to agree that the nation must patiently brace itself to overcome the present difficulties, but according to church sources, justice to all people must not only be done, but be seen to be done.

For the Party leader's prestige this was a vitally important meeting. Here he engaged in consultation at the highest level trying to show that he has the interests of the nation as a whole at heart. It was a welcome sign of political realism, since he was discussing the situation with the man representing the most powerful church in Eastern Europe, which at all times acted on behalf of the nation and in defense of its interests. For the primate, always fully aware of the church's influence and its historic place in Poland, the meeting confirmed that the Party had to accept the realities of life if there was to be peace and calm; Poland could not be ruled effectively while the authorities ignored the demands of the nation and the church. Both men were fully aware of the limitations originating in the existing system. But both the church and the people were not convinced that the limits of freedom of political maneuver had been fully reached by the Party. The Soviet leaders would probably be prepared to pay much higher prices for the internal stabilization in Poland. And the church holds the "stabilizing key" - at a price, of course.

The fact that the leader of the communist, and therefore, by definition, atheist Party had asked for help from, and the cooperation of, the church requires no comment. It is just a most telling paradox of life in Poland. Speaking in a sermon a few days later, Cardinal Wyszynski emphasized that in "especially difficult situations the bishops and the primate must clearly see the demands of Polish raison d'etat."(36)

The meeting paved the way for Gierek's historic audience with the pope (December 1, 1977). This was the first ever such meeting by a top Polish communist leader, and in the course of it he offered cooperation and tolerance stressing "the patriotic unity of the nation as imperative." In turn the pope assured Gierek that the church stood ready to cooperate, but not without conditions, namely, "a climate marked by recognition of the mission of the church in the modern reality of the country." The pope then listed demands familiar from the countless complaints made by the Polish Episcopate. The church's contribution would be more effective if: "...other conditions, favorable to the high moral level of society, starting from the education and upbringing of youth in schools and state institutions up to the environmental conditions and socioeconomic situation of the country become equally better." The pope expressed the wish that difficulties in this field ought to be promptly and satisfactorily overcome.

Gierek did not seem even to hint at a readiness to study such demands, at least not in his public statements. At the same time the official media were attempting to create euphoria among people by presenting the moves as a major meeting of minds between state and church, a sign that an end had arrived to the fundamental conflict between the two and that their relations had normalized.

At this point both the Episcopate and the primate stepped in. The government was strongly denounced(37) in a pastoral letter read on December 4 for promoting declining moral standards and for its attempts to alienate the younger generation from the church. The Episcopate's further communique on December 16 made it clear that "cooperation for the good of the nation requires a lasting foundation." While favoring further talks along the road to full normalization, the bishops demanded full respect for the basic rights of all citizens, including the right to state their opinions on society and public life openly. They listed all the church's often repeated complaints and demands including the creation of an independent Catholic student organization. But the cornerstone of normalization had to be recognition of the legal status of the church (as before the war) and a corresponding bilateral agreement. This new basic condition was strongly underlined by the primate in his Epiphany sermon on January 6, 1978 and was publicly raised for the first time now(38), since no true revival was deemed possible without the engagement of a church fully endowed with appropriate means and working facilities. Cardinal Wyszynski also asked for the reestablishment of traditional Christian associations, the setting up of an independent Catholic press, permission to print religious information, and the right to educate the young in the spirit of Christian and national traditions.

The tone of all these statements clearly demonstrated that the Church refused to be swept up in the media-inspired euphoria. Gierek's remarks that no conflict existed in church-state relations were being denied and contradicted by the church. There are conflicts, the Episcopate was saying, and until they are settled to the church's satisfaction then its contribution to surmounting the nation's crisis would be impaired. The partnership and cooperation suggested by the state had to be genuine and not just a propaganda exercise. One of the partners could not be expected to bear the full share of the burden if it were crippled in its functioning; nor, for that matter could the people, to whom the church would ultimately appeal.

THE ANATOMY OF OPPOSITION: 1977-1979

The various oppositional groups active since 1977 (except the CDW which was formed in 1976) should be seen in the wider context of pressures from such powerful forces as the church, the workers, and the peasants. Poland is a workers' state in which the idea of workers' grass-roots power supported by the church is a scenario dreaded by the Party bureaucracy.

The more or less loosely organized oppositional groups have grown constantly. The CDW transformed itself into the Social Self-Defense Committee in 1977 (known as KSS/KOR). It was henceforth to concentrate on fighting against and assisting the victims of political, religious and racial repression. Its base lies to a great extent among Marxist intellectuals and not too many students, some of whom belong to the radical Left. In comparison with other groups the CDW is smaller but with well-organized cells. It is more vocal and better known in the West than any of its counterparts, because it has its equally vocal spokesmen in some West European capitals. But by 1979 the CDW could not be regarded as the main opposition group, despite its remarkable record in 1976-1977 (see Chapter 9).

The Human Rights Defense Movement (known as ROPCiO) was born in March 1977 and since then has built up a nation-wide network of consultation points and claims to have well over 1,500 activists. It was regarded by many of my sources as at least, if not more, influential than the KSS/KOR. Non-Marxist, and almost devoid of Party members ROPCiO approximates to a politically centerist or slightly right-of-center representation. By 1979 a very small splinter group left the organization and tried to act independently.

A third group, the Polish League for Independence (known as PPN), the most intellectual and intelligent group has remained conspiratorial in the style of the Polish wartime

resistance. It is a Western-style social democratic movement
with some nationalist members. In October 1977 a fourth
group emerged known as the Democratic Movement. While not
strictly a separate organization it is one which purports to
represent people of kindred minds no matter what their organizational or political connection. Its political manifesto was
signed by 110 intellectuals, students, workers, academicians
including some KSS/KOR members, and politically reflected the
ideas of the former Polish Socialist party.

The Students Solidarity Committee, known as the SKS
(see first section, "Tension Grows Again: 1977" in this
chapter) and represented in all university cities, grew in
stature, firmly opposing the official mass youth organization.
By 1979 a loosely knit movement of young Poland began to take
shape on the Baltic coast. In 1977 SKS initiated the so-called
"flying university" - a series of academic courses initially held
in private homes designed to offset the "socialist" biased
curricula of state high schools. In January 1978 over 60
scholars and intellectuals publicly formed an unofficial
Education Courses Society (known as TKN) which took over
this venture and was strongly supported by the church.
During the 1977-1978 academic year 120 lectures were held and
were attended by 30-100 students per class. The new
academic year for these courses started in November 1978.
This time teaching also took place in some churches, including
five in Krakow which Cardinal Wojtyla (before he became pope)
made available, for full-year courses in history, literature,
philosophy and social sciences.

In 1978 the Independent Team for Scientific Cooperation
sprang up and grouped together young scientists pledged to
undertake "independent research" in various fields, without
any ideological or political interference. Discussion clubs in
private homes, organized mainly by ROPCiO, SKS, and
KSS/KOR, mushroomed and attracted students and young
workers. Exclusively workers' discussion clubs appeared in
some industrial centers.

Two other unofficial organizations sprang up in 1978. In
the regions of Silesia and the Baltic coast, local committees of
free trade unions to defend workers' rights, were formed in
opposition to the official discredited unions. Finally the
farmers too decided to speak out. By October 1978 over
480,000 farmers refused to pay old-age pension contributions
(see Chapter 13) which they deemed too high and unjustly
calculated, organized strikes in milk deliveries and formed
farmers' defense committees in several villages. The farmers
also complained that they were not consulted about the implications of the pension scheme and bypassed in agricultural
policy decisions. This Gierek promised to correct immediately.
But by the end of the year a loosely limbed national farmers'
self-defense committee began to take shape. With the country-

side thus also touched by protest, dissent now extended into
virtually every segment of society. Finally in 1979 Believers'
Self-Defense Committees were formed in some parishes - to
press authorities to build new and repair old churches and
chapels.

All the main opposition groups publish unofficial and,
hence, uncensored regular and irregular papers and
documents, which include the addresses and telephone numbers
of their editorial offices and of their most prominent members.
When I was in Warsaw in January 1979, it was estimated that
85 such publications appear and enjoy a circulation of over
300,000 copies. Some of them are printed, others mimeo-
graphed or photostated. Among the regular publications are
the Information Bulletin (Biuletyn Informacyjny) of KSS/KOR;
The Voice (Glos) representing the Democratic Movement;
Opinion (Opinia) published by ROPCiO; and documents and
appeals by PPN. Some publications are oriented toward particular groups of society such as young people: Brother (a
loose translation of Bratniak, the title is derived from the
prewar students fraternal aid organization's publication) supported by ROPCiO; Index (Indeks), an independent student
publication; and Encounters (Spotkania), edited by young
Catholic students. Similarly, there are at least two regular
papers for the workers: The Worker (Robotnik), edited mostly
by KSS/KOR; and Progress (Postep), published jointly by
intellectuals and workers. The best literary quarterly is The
Pulse (Puls), followed by Register (Zapis), both printing
works by Polish writers banned by the censor. Some local
irregular papers appear in particular cities as for example the
Lodz Chronicle (Kronika Lodzka), and also in a number of
industrial enterprises.

Most of these publications started in 1977 but some new
ones became available in 1978 like The Farmer (Gospodarz)
which addresses itself to peasants; Criticism (Krytyka), an
irregular political quarterly; and The Road (Droga). These
are but a few titles from the whole spectrum of informative and
programmatic publications now available in Poland. An independent publishing house, Nowa, prints books by distinguished Polish writers banned by official censors.

The major groups of this widespread human rights movement - a movement unique in Eastern Europe in its strength
and influence - understand that the difficulties between and
among them represent a potential danger to unified action and
the existence of the movement itself. They quite successfully
aim, therefore, at: maximum agreement in their respective
programmatic pronouncements; a "concensus area" in the
rectification of commonly agreed upon injustices and grievances; and the creation of a widespread system of links among
as many individual groups as possible. Finally, except for the
PPN which remains anonymous, all other organizations are

public and open and insist on the legality of their existence as
based on Polish laws and conventions on human rights sub-
scribed to by the government.(39)

A close scrutiny of most of the unofficial publications
freely available in Poland provides an outline of the "democratic opposition's" short-term aims, some of them successfully
achieved. In the forefront is the human rights issue and the
opposition's task lies in monitoring observance of the former
by the authorities, publicizing both inside the country and
abroad any violations of these rights and finally the securing
of legal and financial aid to those deprived of their rights.
The second opposition aim is to break the state's monopoly of
information. This is not only by the publishing activity outlined above but also by a strong campaign against censorship
and by the generation of a social and political impetus to have
it weakened in practice. In November 1977 KSS/KOR publicized a 700-page volume of the most ridiculous and childish
censorship directives which had been made available by a
Krakow censor who escaped to the West. A full "anthology" of
these documents was also published in London. (see section,
"Mass Media: The Instrument of the Party" in Chapter 4).
But, at the same time the unofficial publications keep people
informed about events in Poland and abroad, fighting against
ignorance and for an informed public opinion. It is this fight
which has been so dramatically supplemented by creating
independent teaching, study and educational facilities. Encouragement is given by the unofficial literary magazines to
creative, artistic activity. The Pulse hammered out its
message in precise terms:

> Lack of freedom of speech and criticism
> paralyzes the development of culture and destroys
> its wealth and variety. Enforced silence, or the
> forced expression of ideas contrary to personal
> conviction destroys the sense of personal dignity of
> man and of the writer. When the possibility of the
> public expression of thought and free discussion
> disappear, the inclination and desire to think in
> general also disappear.(40)

The third opposition aim is to introduce a genuine system of
political and social pluralism outside the official power structure since the Party refuses even to tone down its so-called
"leading" role. This means the voluntary establishment of
independent social institutions representing a wide spectrum of
views, yet linked together by the basic identity of their
general goals. Finally there is what might be termed the
"constant activism" of society. In October 1978 KSS/KOR
called on people to challenge official decisions at public meetings on all issues. Independent, organized, effective public

action was needed to counter growing disorganization and
stagnation. The public would achieve their rights not by
powerless despair, but by firm, conscious and dignified
demands.(41)

The net result of these oppositional activities is the
appearance on the scene of alternative culture, alternative
education and alternative information. There is a feverish
activity beyond the dead mass of the outward facade, away
from the exasperating culture of the zealous journalists,
obedient writers and "socially committed" singers. There are
literary meetings in private houses; satirical songs and poems
are born; and discussions, exhibitions and theatrical performances are organized. All this without the approval of the
authorities, who have tried so hard until now to monopolize
men's minds. A new society has arisen.

As for the long-term aims of the opposition two left-wing
KSS/KOR dissenters circulated their own individual programs.
Michnik is in favor of evolution which will extend civil liberties
and guarantee a respect for human rights (see Chapter 9).
Kuron (also of KSS/KOR) wants Poland to achieve a status
similar to that of Finland: a parliamentary democracy with
limited independence in foreign policy where it touches directly
upon Soviet interests.(42) The PPN, on the other hand
presented a comprehensive program of a complete reconstruction of the system, including:

> ...genuine national sovereignty (the Soviet
> Union must admit past wrongs and agree to place
> bilateral relations on a footing of equality); full
> participation of all in governing of the country; full
> respect for human rights; multiparty democracy; free
> development of learning and national culture;
> freedom of movement and of exchange of thought and
> information with the world.

Some of these concepts are politically unrealistic in the present
circumstances, although the opposition, with more or less
emphasis seems to understand limitations imposed by Poland's
geopolitical situation. They appear united and determined to
press on with their aggressive, yet gradualistic tactics in
support of short-term objectives. They do not press for a
return to the capitalist system, but the fashionable slogan now
is "social democracy Western-style," with a proper readjust-
ment and especially a far-reaching reduction in the power of
the Communist party. They advocate in various degrees of
emphasis a drastic reform of the existing system, and more or
less accepted pluralism, but they are, as yet, and with some
exceptions, not willing to compete for power with the Party.
They share the authorities' concern about economic difficulties
but insist on a drastic reappraisal of economic policies. In-

numerable programmatic, conceptual articles and essays appear
regularly in the "democratic opposition's" publications. Some
of them outline the vision of a future truly democratic Poland
and specify gradual steps which could lead to this ultimate
aim.   Most of them are realistic in geopolitical terms but there
are also exceptions which go beyond "the art of the possible"
in present circumstances.   Many articles and reports, with
contributions from distinguished and well-known experts, deal
with outstanding problems in many areas which have not been
solved in the last 35 years and affect, to say the least, painfully the everyday life of its citizens in the country.   They
discuss such issues as, for instance, violation of human rights
by state authorities and security services; church-state
relations; economic reforms and priorities; the state of agriculture; health service; education; atheistic indoctrination; the
role of intelligentsia; the attitudes of workers; censorship; and
cultural policies.

The movement has of course been the subject of continuing and selective police harassment: detention of prominent
dissenters for a day or two; house searches; confiscation of
documents and equipment (which, nevertheless, often reappear
mysteriously a few days later, originating sometimes from
official institutions); and the closure of meetings, "flying
university" lectures or satirical theater performances by the
police.   There have been cases of intimidation, persecutions
for "criminal offenses," and imprisonment, but mostly these
have been inflicted on the organizers of free-trade union cells.
In contrast - in communist terms - to the tolerance of intellectual and student dissent, the workers are firmly warned
against any attempts at self-organization.   On the other hand,
the official weekly, Polityka, printed two stories by a prominent young dissenter and its editor, Rakowski, has said on
German television that some of the dissenters' ideas are shared
by people like himself.(43)

The opposition movement has not only survived, but has
flourished, creating new alternatives to those frustrated by
the established and inert power structure.   It has done so
because its enjoys the tacit approval of the masses of unpredictable workers and, by now, militant peasants.   But
perhaps the most important factor is the church, which indirectly defends the dissenters and supports some of their
initiatives.   The church sees as its duty not the changing of
regimes but registering its presence in any political constellation, ensuring full respect for human rights and complete
freedom to carry on its mission.   The Party simply cannot
afford to rule the country against the church.   The civil peace
in Poland is too tentative and too fragile to be disturbed.   To
make a frontal attack on the opposition movement would be to
run a grave risk indeed.

PROCRASTINATION AND QUALIFIED TOLERANCE:
1978-MARCH 1979

Whatever concessions the leadership made to various segments
of society during 1976-1977 they have been largely a reflection
of the Party's periodic operational breakdowns and policy
failures rather than possible alterations of the system. With a
margin of maneuver seriously reduced by economic recession,
growing opposition and political frustration, the leadership
appeared in 1978 to be clearly hesitant about making important
decisions, lest a faulty move were to precipitate an increase in
tension. Gierek's team responded with expedients designed to
avoid trouble, procrastinating in the hope that new investments would at last be coming on stream. The policy, therefore, was to sit out the current problems while preserving
political continuity, and de-dramatizing existing conflicts.
     The economic maneuver (see Chapter 9) failed to bring
the hoped for results. The leadership overestimated the speed
with which the shift of investments to consumer goods could be
carried out and underestimated both the strength of regional
vested interests as well as of the resistance to change in some
local Party ranks. The cut in investments was somewhat
indiscriminate, slowed down investment projects and delayed
production by interrupting the supply of parts and materials.
The relative rigidity of a system that does not allow for the
introduction of flexible modern management methods to match
the imported technology or permit science and research the
margins of freedom it needs if it is to play the productive role
it should have, all contributed greatly to the difficulties.
Moreover, the chain of command in the economy and government was so extended and the decision process so slow and
unresponsive that these two effects often combined to produce
built-in obsolescence in many industrial capital-intensive
projects, which in turn had an impact on Poland's competi-
tiveness abroad and affected the domestic supply. In some of
the factories which were not completed on time, expensive and
sophisticated Western equipment stood unused, outdoors, exposed to the weather. Several such instances were quoted to
me in January 1979.
     Procrastination rather than initiative was the hallmark of
Gierek's report at the national Party conference in January
1978 although the Party's intention to continue the "economic
maneuver" until the effects of the next five-year plan came
through loud and clear. The conference itself was interesting
not so much for what it achieved, but for what it failed to
achieve. The five study commissions, created in 1976
produced no solutions (see Chapter 9 and Chapter 13). "We
have not come up with any definitive solutions," said CC
secretary Lukaszewicz.(44) The commission on prices failed to

reach a decision and so subsidies will continue. In 1978 these exceeded by 61 percent, the figure for 1975. Nevertheless, some prices will be allowed to push upward gradually. State-owned so-called commercial shops offer meat at higher, realistic prices. Prices are also raised indirectly by such familiar expedients as phasing out cheaper goods and introducing newer, more expensive lines. Jaroszewicz warned that despite a 2.2 percent increase in meat supplies in 1978 there would not be any noticeable improvement. Imports of Western grain worth 1,000 million dollars amounted to nine million tons in the agricultural year 1977-1978.

In March the CC plenum once again increased investments in agriculture and later the procurement prices paid to peasants for their produce were increased, though supplies still did not improve. Farmers were selling almost 50 percent of their produce on the free uncontrolled market. The agricultural production dropped by 3.6 percent in 1977, if the increase in the number of animals is discounted. Despite Gierek's reassurances to private farmers in 1977 (see Chapter 13), a strong suspicion remained about the leadership's apparently irrevocable commitment to "socialize" agriculture. The socialized sector now controlled 32 percent of agricultural land (20 percent in 1976) and in 1977 only 70,000 hectares of land were sold to individual farmers with very limited allocation of tractors.

In May, Gierek criticized economic managers for granting excessive wage increases and has warned the workers that if their work was unsatisfactory they face the prospect of wage reductions. This was likely to be unpopular among the workers who were already deeply dissatisfied because of chronic shortages on the market. Managers too resented the measures since wage bonuses provided them with the principal means of attracting labor and boosting productivity.

In November the Party leader predicted further economic difficulties and tough austerity measures in the coming years. He blamed Western recession and discrimination against Poland's trade and supplies shortages. He warned, however, that there was a need for greater discipline among the workforce. The planned economic targets for 1977 were not fulfilled. Progressing domestic inflation which has been estimated by Western observers at nine percent started to erode some of the hard-won improvements in living standards. But, because of the chronic shortages of meat, housing and consumer goods, too much money was still chasing too few goods.

At the CC plenum on December 13, 1978, Gierek frankly admitted that there were persistent problems which could only be solved in 1979 by far-reaching austerity measures. These would include freezing the growth of real wages to only 1.5-2.0 percent, putting a ceiling on industrial investment and a curtailment of administrative expenses. Over 30,000 ad-

ministrative workers were to be transferred to production.
The main emphasis remained on development of food production, housing and consumer goods, together with a wide-
ranging program of savings in energy and other available
resources. The latter has already come into force and has
included substantial power cuts in 3,000 large industrial plants
and also for some nonindustrial users. The measures reflected
the government's determination to avoid a repetition of the
1977 power breakdowns which resulted in 800,000 dollars'
worth loss of production.

The main accent at the plenum was on basically conservative socioeconomic strategies and on repeated appeals for
social cooperation in the task of revitalizing the country. The
general tone of Gierek's statement appeared defensive, with
emphasis on justification of current policies, rather than
changes or modifications.

By February 1979, Poland's Western debt had risen to
over 15 billion dollars and was on the increase despite an
improvement in the trade deficit and the switch of imports
from West to East; imports from the West decreased and the
ratio of trade with socialist countries in the total Polish trade
turnover increased from about 50 percent to 56 percent. The
main factor here was closer economic cooperation than in the
past nine years though this was not yet that economic integration with the Soviet Union, agreed upon in two Gierek-
Brezhnev meetings in April and August. Gierek described this
"cooperation" as of "fundamental importance" to which
Brezhnev is "personally" devoting much consideration. It
involves long-term economic cooperation and numerous co-
production ventures based on specialization in both countries,
and on planning coordination. It came at a time when Poland
has a huge deficit with the Soviet Union and, apart from
grain, further hard currency has had to be spent in Western
markets to supplement oil shortages which the Soviet Union is
unable to cover. At the same time drastically increased prices
of those Soviet raw materials which Poland has to import,
particularly oil, cannot be balanced by Polish exports to the
Soviet Union. It could be argued that this trend toward a
form of economic integration is the price Gierek has to pay for
his marginal freedom of maneuver in internal politics, even if
one accepts that the Soviet Union is a huge market which
might be attractive.

The deteriorating economic situation has brought to the
surface again, in a sharper form, the latent political tensions
in the Party and in the establishment as a whole. In January
in an open letter to Gierek, 14 former Party personalities and
intellectuals who had been involved in more liberal policies in
October 1956, and who included the former first CC secretary
Ochab (associated in an informal, private grouping known
popularly as the "Red Sofa" Club) strongly criticized Gierek's

style of rule and his policies as undemocratic. They spoke of
the crisis of conscience in Poland and called for a real dialogue
and democratic discussion between the government and the
people. The leading role of the Party, as practiced now, had
to be radically changed and the Party itself reformed. Reply-
ing indirectly to these suggestions and to the demands of the
opposition movement outside the Party, Gierek spoke about the
"fight against those who are checking our socialist development" taking place "amid a class struggle." But mentioning
the "political confrontations" he tried to dissociate himself from
"administrative" or judicial measures.

Already in January at the Party conference many
speakers concentrated on more discipline at the factory-floor
level. In September, Polityka published a letter from six
industrial managers who put the blame for the existing difficulties on slack labor discipline and absenteeism. While
accepting that the working class is the leading group of the
nation, they pointed out that such a position implies "greater
responsibilities and not greater privileges or the absence of
punishment." These people must be shaken up and the
managers called for a tightening up on discipline and even for
the creation of a "pool of unemployed."

Polityka opened its columns to debate and an avalanche of
letters followed. The suggestions ranged from demands to
expand the private sector of the economy and allowing the
profit motive free play to an insistence that Party organizations and trade unions should be absolutely independent of the
management. Polityka was distressed to find that there was
less interest in liberalization than in much stricter discipline.
Ironically, as in Gomulka's era, managers seemed to be
yearning for a return to hard-line economic thinking of the
late sixties, for the right to dismiss lazy or unneeded workers
and even some workers themselves said that a pool of unemployed would have a salutary effect. Politically this means
that if anyone were to make a bid for power from within the
Party such a person would be tempted to rally support with a
fairly tough policy of order and discipline; a policy which
might alleviate the symptoms but which would hardly cure the
disease.

Even General Moczar, the former ousted leader of an
authoritarian and nationalistic faction in the Party (see
section, "The Party: The Power and the Weakness," in
Chapter 4) suddenly reappeared attacking political leaders for
tolerating fraudulent statistical reports and calling for a purge
of dishonest and incapable managers.

On the other side of the coin was the workers' alienation
not only on purely economic grounds, but, as some of them
explained to me in 1979, because of bad management and
inefficient organization of work. One of their main pre-
occupations was the perennial problem of the continuing non-

existence of any independent channels of participation in decision making despite many promises. The government decreed in August 1978 that workers' self-government conferences (an old discredited form [see section, "The Workers: Their Strength and Their Pressure" in Chapter 4]) would be set up in all enterprises and that one-third of their composition (presumably the workers' council) were to be workers elected directly by the personnel. But, as Zycie Warszawy(45) admitted, there is now an overall erosion and dismantling of these conferences. They are ignored and their power reduced to mere rubber stamping of decisions taken earlier.

Towards the end of 1978 the inter-Party divisiveness became even more apparent and not only in the area of management and economic policies. In December Gierek insisted(46) that the Party maintain close contact and continuity with its "heroic past" and communist revolutionary traditions. For the first time since 1970 he paid an unusual but highly significant tribute to some former Stalinists of the fifties like Bierut and Minc and to anti-Stalinists like Gomulka and Rapacki. This may have been an answer to those hard-liners in the Party who accuse the present leadership of deradicalization in what was supposed to be a radical social transformation of the country. At the CC December plenum one of the VPC first secretaries, applauded loudly by about a third of participants, indirectly accused Gierek of tolerance and moderation, and of forming a "privileged elite"; he demanded harsh policies both in the economic field and against the opposition. Gierek interrupted the plenum debate, convened the politburo and having secured their support only then rejected the charges and demands, while simultaneously appealing for national unity and support. He indirectly admitted that such unity has yet to be achieved. Even before that, Polityka warned the hard-liners that they may create "a climate of fear, which leads to further conflicts and forces the sharpening of repressions; this is the way of no return."

Then in November 1978 an officially sanctioned "conversatorium" of some 100 intellectuals who met to discuss current socioeconomic problems and ways of solving them took place in Warsaw. The participants represented a diversified spectrum of opinions. They included some CC members (such as Rakowski and Gierek's adviser Zawadzki), Catholic politicians connected with the oppositional groups, Catholic writers, prominent scientists, artists, economists, Party members, and non-Party people. It was hoped that this discussion club might emerge in time as an unofficial think-tank, which could provide the Party leadership with advice on formulating policies. Their second meeting was scheduled for the end of December but never materialized. The spirited discussion was recorded on tape and presented to some CC departments, but the delegates were told by the annoyed Party "apparatchiks"

that no such forum could be accepted without the "leading"
role of the Party firmly established. This came from a group
of hard-liners who were tentatively identified with leaders such
as Olszowski, Lukaszewicz and Szczepanksi. A CC member
who attended the original meeting explained that Party officials
have no time for such discussions, since they were too pre-
occupied with the current crisis and besides, "there are already too many such platforms." So much for an attempt at
some new form of participation!

The problem of the structure of state power, as it exists
today, was analyzed in January 1979 in Polityka by Professor
Wiatr, a long-standing Party member, and established political
scientist who is on the best of terms with some members of the
establishment. Political power, he wrote, must be strong, just
and wise:

> The strength is based on a proper mixture of
> centralization and decentralization...it must not be
> measured by a multiplication of orders and/or
> prohibitions....A strong power leads and maintains a
> vision of future generations....It must be founded
> on authority at the roots of which is the confidence
> of the ruled for the rulers....
>
> The just power applies the principle of equal
> treatment under the law for both the leaders and the
> led....Only a just power could count on the full
> civic involvement of all those who are led.
>
> One can lead wisely only when one is openly
> prepared for regular comparison of one's own ideas
> with the knowledge and experience of others....One
> can govern wisely only when one consults different,
> alternative viewpoints...before making a final
> decision, and only when one allows the supporters of
> different options to present their opinions...by
> creating mechanisms which would make these com-
> parisons easier and surer....

Wiatr's argument did not seem to be directed at Gierek personally but it was a comprehensive criticism of the current
power framework and a veiled call for its modification; and
after all Gierek, although pressed by hard-liners, was in
charge. Polityka, in which the article was published, is
closely identified with the more dynamic and liberal tendencies
in the Party. It seemed to indicate that the spirit of political
contest might extend to some members of the Party establishment elite. The article was certainly against the progressing stabilization, even stagnation, of the existing institutional framework of decision making.

In 1978 even some Party-approved organizations manifested not for the first time their desire for more autonomy, if

not full freedom of action. The spirit of dissent appeared strongly at the Polish Writers Union congress in April and was preceded by a long controversy about cultural policy, particularly the issue of censorship following Tejchma's "resignation" as minister of culture. He is certainly one of the more liberal and brilliant PB members. A more liberal faction in the Party has been arguing for greater freedom of expression and maintained that if the media had been allowed to reflect popular discontent the June 1976 upheaval might have been avoided. In February 1978, just before the journalists' congress, the government decided to give the press greater access to official information and even granted some latitude in reporting workers' discontent. Deputy Minister of Culture Wilhelmi (who later died in an airplane crash) admitted that censorship restrictions might be excessive.

In a lively debate at the writers' congress one writer (Braun) strongly attacked "censorship which threatened the future of Polish culture ... and ... the harassment of students attending 'flying university' lectures." Another Catholic intellectual writer, Wozniakowski, called for an end to the illegal repression of people for their nonconformist views and claimed that censorship pushed Catholic culture into a ghetto.(47) Still another writer listed over 30 books which were held up by the censor not because of their contents but because the author was in disfavor. A resolution called for censorship and other administrative interference to be clearly defined. Party CC secretary Lukaszewicz, in charge of ideology and culture appeared to be on the defensive. While advocating "creative criticism" which does not coincide with that "emanating from foreign centers hostile to socialism" he promised to create a kind of appeals tribunal for censorship grievances. Even more fascinating was the fact that, for the first time, the Party negotiated with nonconformist writers on the composition of the union's board. As a result four dissenters (connected with oppositional groups) were elected and the ratio was 10:9 in favor of rebellious and nonconformist writers.

In November, Wajda, that gifted and controversial film director, was elected chairman of the Polish Film Makers Association. While this organization has no power of decision making, the choice of Wajda and the fact that at least half of the new board members are nonconformists suggests that even there a strong pressure group has emerged, challenging the Party's cultural policy.

In this climate of overall dissent and contention the church remained the bastion of "loyal" and subtle opposition (see section, "Church-State Summits: October 1977 - January 1978" in this chapter). It became clear at the beginning of 1978 that the government had tried to obtain the church's cooperation at a minimal cost to itself despite some concessions.

(Indeed the primate was now being described by Kakol, the minister in charge of the Office of Religious Denominations, as "an eminent Polish patriot." The syllabus of the new schools [see section, "Educational Reform," in Chapter 4] was slightly changed in line with the church's demands and the whole reform considerably slowed down mainly for technical reasons. Rakowski, writing in Polityka, elaborated on the need for the church's cooperation in maintaining peace and order but was vague on what the church could hope for in return. However, by abjuring "primitive atheism" and "vulgar materialism" and by emphasizing the prospects for a "successful dialogue" he admitted that the church-state equation had two sides. Yet at the same time (April 29) Kakol, in a letter to the primate, accused the church of engaging in a political struggle, and implied that this was holding up the improvement in mutual relations. Cardinal Wyszynski not only strongly denied the charges (June 10) and supported the "flying university" but also criticized the growing influence and interference by the political police in all spheres of life.

The bishops meanwhile reiterated that normalization could not be achieved without the recognition by the authorities of the legal status of the church for which, as Archbishop Poggi reported in the Vatican, after his return from Poland in June, the government "was not yet ready." But the Episcopate maintained its pressure. Once again, in March, they gave tacit support for the unofficial academic courses and raised the problem of the way the nation was being forced into a mono-lithic, materialistic and secular mold that was utterly alien to the Polish spirit.

> The restriction of science and research, as well as artistic and religious activity, through state censorship was to be regretted....The church would accordingly support those initiatives which strove to manifest the culture, the products of human spirit, and the history of the nation in an authentic form, because the nation had a right to objective truth about itself....(48)

On September 17, 1978 the Episcopate demanded the abolition of state censorship, which, "...has always been a weapon of totalitarian regimes...." Censorship was an institution that crippled the cultural and religious life of the entire nation, and misinformed the people. Millions of believers were being deprived of expression by the limited printing of religious instruction books and journals, and the state's refusal to allow the church access to radio and television. The official media had instead been "given over to the service of an ideology aimed at bringing up men without God," and were being used "to impose just one set of views and models of behavior on the

nation and to wield power over its people." The Episcopate
called on the state to allow at least one independent Catholic
daily, and to permit the mass with its sermon to be broadcast
on Sundays and holy days. Catholics should develop a critical
attitude toward state-monopolized information, to protest and to
make use of "other more reliable sources...." Harrassment of
people who have the courage to express openly their opinions
is a necessity, for "without freedom, man atrophies, and all
progress is condemned to a slow death. We demand to be
respected and to have our convictions taken in earnest."

By statements such as these, the church engaged the
Party on the most important issue of the day: the ability of a
communist system within the Soviet orbit to allow its citizens
freedom of speech, information and debate.

In a paradoxical Polish situation relations between the
primate and the authorities hardly appeared to have suffered
from the former's outspoken criticisms - mainly because of
Cardinal Wyszynski's supreme skill in subtlety and diplomacy,
and because Gierek, whom the primate described as an "honest
man," could not afford to antagonize the church. With full
official approval the primate paid an official visit to West
Germany where in discussing Polish-German relations in September he said that these should be "...future orientated
rather than always looking back to the past, although one had
to remember the past in order not to perpetuate its mistakes."
The visit was assessed by the authorities as "useful."

On the sixtieth anniversary of the Catholic University in
Lublin, Cardinal Wyszynski addressed himself to Minister Kakol
who was present and asked for an end of censorship by "simply pensioning off all the censors." Two days later, on November 12, on the thirtieth anniversary of Wyszynski's ascen-
dancy to his office, Kakol sent him congratulations and best
wishes in the name of state authorities. The primate chose to
go to Lublin to attend the less politically exposed celebration,
rather than to preach in Warsaw, as originally scheduled, at
the commemoration of the anniversary of Poland's independence. But at the end of November he celebrated a special
mass to mark the four hundredth anniversary of the Stefan
Batory University in Wilno (the prewar Polish city annexed by
the Soviet Union in 1939) and said that "...a golden thread of
Polish Catholic culture which has been preserved runs from
Lwow [another Polish city annexed by Moscow in 1939] through
Warsaw to Wilno and Krolewiec [now Kaliningrad in the Soviet
Union]."

The apex of national feeling came on the anniversary of
Polish independence which was proclaimed on November 11,
1918 and officially celebrated for the first time in postwar
Poland. This was an unmistakable repudiation of the old
Polish communist traditions, since the prewar Polish Communist
party was strongly opposed in 1918 to the independence of the

country. The Party celebrated the anniversary on November 6
when, in the Sejm, Gierek, while omitting some crucial historical facts and names of the real architects of independence
(Pilsudski, Dmowski, Paderewski), appealed for a "patriotic
unity of hearts, thoughts and actions." The Episcopate replied on November 11 with a pastoral letter which had been
drafted by Cardinal Wojtyla before he became pope, demanding
that "...conditions must be created by the authorities in which
people can fully feel themselves masters of their homeland...."
National integrity must be preserved through the full respect
and recognition of human and moral rights of all citizens.

Following a ceremonial mass in Warsaw Cathedral, several
thousands of Poles marched to the Tomb of the Unknown
Soldier in an atmosphere of a solemn commemoration of religious
and patriotic songs and recitations for the past heroes who
had died in the struggles for independence. Some speakers
appealed for respect for human rights and for truth about the
nation's history. The authorities did not intervene. In one of
Warsaw's churches the bust of Pilsudski, the victorious hero of
the Polish-Bolshevik war in 1920 was unveiled. All this
seemed to mark the leadership's new effort to unite society
around commonly recognized symbols of national past and
continuity.

16 The Pope from Poland: Has History Smiled on Poles?

On October 16 all lights were turned on Rome and on Poland. And Poland looked at herself. In this widespread spontaneous reaction we felt in ourselves an unusual upsurge of strength and hope. As if history had smiled on us.

Tadeusz Mazowiecki, one of the foremost Catholic intellectuals in Warsaw

It was probably the greatest event since Christianity first arrived in Poland over a thousand years ago.
An intellectual in Krakow,
November 1978

Karol Cardinal Wojtyla, Archbishop Metropolitan of Krakow was elected pope - the first ever from Poland, the first non-Italian for 455 years at the age of 58.(1) The election was greeted by the people with a euphoric elation and produced a massive infusion of confidence. A tidal wave of pride swept across the country, after initial disbelief and amazement. Churches were overflowing on the night of the election. For the first time and at the request of the church authorities, the whole inauguration mass in St. Peter's Square in Rome was transmitted live by Polish television. The huge power of the church was unfolding across the screens of the state network, which for so long had held it at bay. All over the country people crowded before television sets leaving streets almost deserted. There was scarcely a dry eye in all of Poland, wrote the London Times correspondent. After the transmission millions went to church in an extraordinary demonstration of religious fervor. Over 1,000 pilgrims arrived in Rome by special planes from Poland, but four dissenting intellectuals, Wojtyla's friends, were refused exit passports. The head of state, Jablonski, led the official delegation to the installation ceremony.

Wojtyla has been a poet; an actor and producer; a promising student of Polish language and literature; a fascinating orator and preacher; writer; playwright; journalist; laborer; member of a wartime conspiracy; a great outdoor man; hitchhiker, skier; tennis player; footballer; canoeist; swimmer, skater; priest (1946); brilliant theologian and a philosopher, lecturer and professor (1954-1958); bishop (1964); cardinal (1967); and finally pope. There is not much more any man could reasonably be expected to do by the time he reaches 58. Together with the primate and under him (as deputy chairman of the Bishops' Conference) Wojtyla was co-architect of the church's policy toward the state; a most prominent champion of human rights (often more outspoken than the primate himself); supporter of dissenters; a great believer in aggiornamento (implementation of decisions of the Second Vatican Council); the brain behind some of the Episcopate's pastoral letters; instrumental in drafting or supplementing some of the more important documents of the Second Vatican Council and of the Synods of Bishops; adored by young people with whom he has always been in close contact; admired by others; and feared by the authorities.

For over 30 years Wojtyla was schooled in the crucible of confrontation between the church and the communist-ruled state, between Christianity and atheism. Yet he was able to place church-state relations on the level of a civilized dialogue between opponents, rather than as a cacophony of mutual anathema, even when he insisted on the recognition of the church's legal status. He knows Marxism much better than most communists and the subtlety of his approach was to win any argument without forcing the regime into a situation from which their only escape would be the use of violence. Wojtyla recognized the importance of giving expression to Polish national feeling without allowing it to take an explosive form that could provoke a brutal reaction. His attitude was never one of political quietism, nor of supine respect for temporal power. While trying to avoid a direct interference in temporal politics he insisted that the church had to have a voice in social and economic measures. This came very close to being a political challenge to the communist leadership. He knew the real obstacles to church-state detente and knew the value of the promises of the regime and its limitations in the Soviet orbit. He would, therefore, never ask for more than he thought essential to preserve spiritual freedom and human rights. A strong man but conciliatory, open to dialogue without illusions and on the basis of reciprocity, open minded and flexible except on principles, he has always rejected compromise on essentials but accepted cooperation in practical matters.

Wojtyla's election was a shock. It created new problems for the Polish leadership. On the evening of the election the Party politburo went into an all-night session debating the significance of the event and what profile to adopt toward it. Simultaneously, CC secretary Lukaszewicz flew to Moscow. The whole country was literally covered by Wojtyla's photographs, by Polish national flags and the Vatican's white and yellow flags. After a grudging coverage in the media on the night of the election, the authorities decided to join in the general jubilation. But, to keep the general enthusiasm within sensible limits, the chief censor ordered that headlines in all papers, except the Catholic ones, be kept down to as inconspicuous a size as possible, and that photographs not exceed two regular columns in width. The Krakow Tygodnik Powszechny was refused permission to publish a special issue devoted to the pope. For about ten days the media did their best under existing circumstances. The coverage was full, with the Party papers stressing in comments that the achievements of "socialist" Poland had made the election possible. This line of comment was somehow overshadowed by apprehension as to how Wojtyla would deal with the church-state dialogue.

In their message of "heartfelt congratulations" the Polish leaders spoke of great satisfaction which filled Poland:

> For the first time in the history of the papal throne sits a son of the Polish nation building in unity and cooperation of all citizens the greatness and prosperity of its socialist country.(2)

In his reply, significantly ommitting the adjective "socialist," John Paul II wrote:

> It is my fervent desire that Poland develops both spiritually and materially in peace, justice and respect for man. In the spirit of the dialogue begun by my great predecessors....I wish, with God's assistance, also to do everything useful for the good of my beloved nation, the history of which has been linked for a thousand years with the mission and service of the Catholic Church.(3)

On October 23 the pope received in private audience the Polish head of state with whom he also discussed his proposed visit to Poland. On the same day, addressing about 5,000 of his countrymen at a special audience, the Pope confirmed that he hoped to go to Poland in May 1979 for the cermonies commemorating St. Stanislaw, his predecessor as bishop of Krakow, who in 1079 was beheaded by the then Polish King Boleslaw the Bold for opposing his authoritarian rule. And then he embraced Cardinal Wyszynski saying:

There would be no Polish pope in the Holy See,
beginning his new pontificate full of the fear of God,
but also full of confidence in Him, if it were not for
your faith, which did not retreat in the face of
imprisonment and suffering and your heroic hopes,
your boundless faith in the Mother of the Church, if
it were not for Jasna Gora and the whole period in
the history of the church in our homeland which is
linked with your service as bishop and primate.(4)

In a special statement the Polish Episcopate announced that:

The servant of the church of Krakow and of all
Poland...has been elected servant of the servants of
God. We believe that it is the achievement not only
of the Holy Spirit, but also of Holy Mary...whom the
newly elected pope loves so much, and we believe
that it is the result of the prayers of the entire
Polish people who have received this reward for
their faith and the vitality of their religion....(5)

Finally on November 23 the pope formally notified the Polish
head of state of his election, saying that the church wanted to
serve the great cause of peace and justice in the modern
world. It was the pope's conviction that "its work, consistent
with the generally adopted principles of freedom of religion,
would continue to develop in Poland...." This message was
published on the front pages of Polish newspapers. But on
the whole the news about the pope, except in some Catholic
papers, disappeared from official media after about October 25,
1978. As I was told in Warsaw, in November 1978, to some
Party leaders the giving of extensive media coverage to the
pope's inauguration ceremony was a major political blunder, or
at least something which may prove to have been the thin end
of the wedge. The censors came down heavily on Catholic
publications. The Warsaw intellectual monthly, Link (Wiez),
had about 100 censors' cuts in its December edition. In the
pope's Christmas message to the Krakow archdiocese a whole
passage about St. Stanislaw was cut out. It referred to the
martyred saint as a "patron of moral order," who "...did not
hesitate to confront the ruler when defense of the moral order
called for it....Using modern language we can see in him an
advocate of the most essential human rights, on which man's
dignity, his morality, and true freedom depends...."(6) The
full message was read in all churches but the editor of
Tygodnik Powszechny refused to print it even afterward when,
after the Vatican demarche, the authorities apologized and
withdrew the objections. Even initial cuts in Link (Wiez) were
reinstated.

When I went to Poland in November 1978 and then later in January 1979 the pride and elation at the pope's election was still there but tainted with a degree of political realism, summarized, as often in Poland, in a current joke: "God is in heaven, the Vatican is far away, and Moscow is just across the border." This attitude creates problems for both the people and the leadership. "We have gained a pope but here in Krakow we have lost a father," a girl student told me. "Cardinal Wojtyla became a symbol for us of all those trying to retain human dignity," said another. Now that he is pope a journalist explained, "I have a feeling of regained dignity – people can hold their heads high." "People really feel they can walk a little straighter," admitted an intellectual. Still, even if – at last – history "has smiled for the Poles," there is a trace of sadness behind that smile. Perhaps because, as one university professor told me, "The church is the alternative state, but unlike the (Polish) state...it works."

Wojtyla's election put Poland back on the world map more forcefully than for many years past. He not only bridges the European cleavage but also reminds the world that this cleavage is of recent origin. And so is the confrontation and/or dialogue between the church on the one side and political communism – atheism – on the other. With his intellect, breadth of culture and knowledge of the communist power structure he is also the pope – tough and ideal – not only for today but perhaps first and foremost for the post-Brezhnev era and, for that matter, for the post-Gierek era in Poland. He represents a formidable challenge to ideologies that compete for the souls of mankind. What Stalin never understood and the communists have to realize now is that given a man like Wojtyla, the Vatican does not need any divisions at all. Coming from Poland, as Wojtyla does, he draws attention to the unity of European culture, underscores the absurdity of all attempts to impose communism on ancient nations and emphasizes that Soviet presence in Eastern Europe is, to say the least, a paradoxical phenomenon.

This obvious significance of his election is one thing and the Realpolitik quite another. What it did for Poland was to enhance still further the uniquely strong position of an already powerful church. It underlined still further the resilience of Christianity as the alternative repository of a universal doctrine not based on Marxist values and traditions. The Vatican's Ostpolitik, regarded with suspicion by many Christians under communist rule, might become enriched and perhaps corrected by the new pope's experience of communism. As Cardinal Wyszynski reminded his audience on November 6, 1978: "The church had been criticized in the past as rather emotional, traditional, and nationalistic...." As a result of John Paul II's election "all those critics who had attached to our church, its bishops and its religiousness, so many various epithets – fell silent."

The election accentuated all the contradictory cross-currents of Polish politics, the trends in and the demands of, Polish society. It contributed to an extension of the level and scope of possible social pressure on the leadership to introduce changes. It has also emphasized the continuing vulnerability of the established power structure to the threat of a potential disruption. The outpouring of massive delight and confidence can scarcely fail to produce at least a qualitative change in church-state relations. The church has always played a crucial role in the nation's history and now the election of Wojtyla seems to confirm the validity and contemporary importance of this long historical experience.

The problem for the leadership, overshadowed still further by the power of a more confident church and pressed still harder by the rising expectations of the people, is how to reassert the dominant position of the Party and of the system as such. When the papal visit to Poland was proposed in October 1978(7), Deputy Foreign Minister Czyrek and Minister Kakol said it would be welcome, but, as Kakol stressed, "...the time and the date of the visit is certainly determined by circumstances which are of a bilateral and multi-aspected character." On the other hand even Arbatow, Brezhnev's adviser on American affairs suggested that the visit could be regarded as a normal step in a time of detente. Wojtyla's election might heighten the Kremlin's endemic suspicion of Poland. Soviet leaders are probably apprehensive that, as a result of the election and increased publicity for Poland's political problems, the Polish trends toward internal political and institutional pluralism could gradually infect other East European countries.

Paradoxically enough the pope from Poland strengthens the church's hand in dealings with Gierek, but it also helps him in his dealings with the Kremlin. The reason, already discussed is simple: stabilization in Poland is the key to the status quo in the Soviet East European empire. Despite some setbacks Gierek has so far managed to secure some sort of stability without using the big stick and the key to this stability is in the hands of the church, whose leaders are, in critical moments, as determined to preserve order and stability as is the Party leader. Besides, most Party leaders are Poles before they are communists and they share in the pride of their compatriots. They also feel that it is far better to have a pope in Rome whom they know and with whom they can talk, if not necessarily agree. In any case, in the triangle of the Vatican, Warsaw and the church in Poland, with growing dissent in the country, and with Moscow watching him even more closely, Gierek will need from now on more political skill than ever before. "It is a new era for us," a government official said to me in January 1979, "it is a time for joy, because the new pope is a Pole, but it is also a period of anxiety."

As for the Catholic intellectuals and politicians, one of them wrote:

> It is a significant turning point in our psy-
> chology....But in this self-reckoning there is no
> room for triumphalism. On the contrary, this his-
> torical moment imposes new obligations. We hope
> that it will not only strengthen our Catholicism, but
> that it will help us to acquire a more universalistic
> mentality and widen our perspectives....The people
> that have given a pope to the world must learn how
> to overcome their faults and ailments....They must
> show the world a religious spirit that is not only
> very much alive but binding and fruitful in everyday
> life....

As the London Times put it:

> Polish Catholics may develop broader horizons,
> becoming more conscious of their role in the world
> church and seeing their own problems universalized.
> What they do in Poland will have more relevance
> abroad and what happens beyond their borders will
> seem more relevant at home. There will be certain
> alteration of consciousness.(8)

To a very great extent, the political decisions of the leadership could be influenced by a persistent interest of the new
pope in Polish affairs, as I was told in Warsaw in 1979 particularly since the more intelligent and experienced Party
leaders seem to realize that outright Soviet intervention is
something that the Kremlin would like to avoid at almost any
price except the three well-known imperatives of the system
(see Chapter 2).

As in the past, in crisis situations, Gierek turned to the
church for help and understanding. On January 24, 1979,
Cardinal Wyszynski and Gierek met in the Sejm building for a
four-hour talk. The PAP reported that in accordance with the
decisions taken in October 1977 (see section "Church-State
Summits: October 1977-January 1978," in Chapter 15), this was
the continuation of an exchange of views on "...the most
important questions facing the nation and the Church,
questions of great importance for the proper arrangement of
relations and co-operation between the Church and the State,
for national unity in providing prosperity for Poland, and for
strengthening its position in the world."(9)

The meeting, which according to church sources, was a
discussion between "two equal, independent partners" had
considerable importance in current Polish politics. As the two
men represent the only established centers of power and

influence in the country, their relationship provides a crucial element in the process of shaping the direction of internal evolution. The primate was in a much stronger position at this meeting than in October 1977 not only because of the much more widespread and organized dissent in the country but also because he now had the pope from Poland behind him. The Party, while trying to unite the nation on the anniversary of independence failed to give a lead for ideological and political reasons, which would really make the people feel that at least on this occasion there was some common platform between rulers and ruled. It proved incapable, and some of the hard-line leaders were unwilling, to develop a pattern of adjustable response - even of a partial one to public aspirations for greater political participation and for some sort of pluralism - in the climate of severe economic difficulties.

The second Wyszynski-Gierek meeting concentrated on two issues: the proposed papal visit in May 1979 and the recognition of the church's legal status. Some groups in the Party were opposed to a visit on the nine hundredth anniversary of the death of St. Stanislaw, a politically tricky and emotive occasion, being, as it is, symbolic of the church's triumph over temporal power.

While Polish leaders continued their contacts mostly with capitalist countries (receiving among others President Giscard d'Estaing in Warsaw) the question being asked was: Would John Paul II come to Poland? When the newly appointed Archbishop Metropolitan of Krakow, Macharski (Wojtyla's junior colleague in theological seminary) returned to Warsaw at the end of December 1978, he firmly stressed that "Rome is ready to come to Poland." Obviously, millions of Poles would gather around their pope and the prestige of the church would be still further enhanced. The religious fervor would surpass anything experienced so far. For all practical purposes the Party would be nonexistent, particularly since the overwhelming majority of its members would greet the pope and take part in the commemorative mass. But - again one of the paradoxes in Poland - the visit may also strengthen Gierek's position. He will be able to show the nation that, although a Party leader, he is much more of a proud and patriotic Pole than communist. The church appeared optimistic about the outcome of the talks on this subject, otherwise the primate would not have agreed to the reference in the communique about "strengthening of Poland's position in the world." The state's refusal of permission for the pope's visit would hardly contribute to such strengthening. Significantly on Sunday, February 4, prayers were said(10) in all Polish churches for the complete freedom of religion in Poland and for the papal visit. On February 8, the Episcopate in a statement thanked John Paul II for his wish to come to his country and later a delegation of the Episcopate led by Bishop Dabrowski, the

secretary of the Episcopate, went to the Vatican to thank the
pope personally and to complain about almost nonexistent media
coverage of the pontif's activities.

The second issue discussed by the primate and the Party
leader, the recognition of the church's legal status - regarded
by Wyszynski as the cornerstone of any normalization and
possible cooperation - is as important as it is sensitive. It
would give the church, an ideological, oppositional and powerful organization, the same rights, at least, under the law as
those of for instance...the Party. Here, of course, Gierek
has to take into account some of his hard-line opponents within
the Party and, at the same time to find a way of somehow
meeting the church's demands while maintaining, at least to
some extent, the "leading" role of the Party. At the beginning of 1978 Cardinal Wyszynski had emphasized(11) that
the church did not intend to create "a state within a state";
neither did it seek political power. The church's duty, as the
erstwhile Cardinal Wojtyla confirmed, is not change nor shaping
the regimes but to be present in any political constellation and
to ensure that the church's mission could be carried out and
the human rights fully respected.

Beside the immediate importance of the meeting, it was
also significant in that it seemed to confirm an evolving
practice of periodical contacts between top church and Party
leaders. It is conceivable that such periodical contacts could
serve to bridge the gap or, at least, to facilitate an exchange
of views. Clearly, some form of mutually acceptable process of
normalization of church-state relations is needed. After the
October 1977 meeting church-state talks were resumed without
any significant results. Even cooperation becomes feasible if
the Party is ready to recognize that the church will never
compromise on principles and basic essentials.

"We are at a crossroads, even more dangerous than after
June 1956," a distinguished journalist told me in January 1979.
Only the church in Poland and the pope in Rome can help us,
he argued. The alternative to Gierek might be hard-line
dogmatism and possibly repression which, in turn, would lead
to a disaster. But, unless he were able and willing to shake
up drastically the anachronistic and obsolete Party apparatus
he would not get very far. He is a tired man not in very
good health, who is at least trying to manipulate and/or keep
on the leash some ambitious "yesteryear hard-liners." Whether
the Party likes it or not, said one noncommunist intellectual
and politician, "we have now muffled pluralism in the country
and, given no outside interference, this is an irreversible
process." Fortunately, everybody, except some Party die-
hards, fully realizes that any open confrontation might lead to
an unmitigated upheaval. What we want, he said, is a tacit
recognition of this pluralism outside the existing bureaucratic
structure based on the "mythical leading role" of the Party.

The Party must be pushed to the limits of concessions still acceptable in the existing system - limits which are far from having been reached.

POSTSCRIPT - THE POPE IN POLAND

History smiled on the Poles for the second time since October 16, 1978 when on June 2, 1979 Pope John Paul II landed in Warsaw, knelt, and kissed the ground of his native land. Poland ruled by a Communist, and by definition an atheist, Party for thirty-five years, was put firmly on the world map when what was essentially a "religious pilgrimage" was played out on world stage before the eyes of well over a thousand foreign correspondents and watched on television screens in all parts of the globe.

For nine days (June 2 - 10) of the first-ever visit by a reigning Roman Catholic pontiff to Eastern Europe, the people of Poland flooded the man they call "our own pope" with out-pourings of love and manifestations of their faith. Whenever he went - in Warsaw, in Gniezno, the cradle of Polish Christianity; in Czestochowa, with its most revered shrine of the Black Madonna; in Nowy Targ, the heart of Polish high-lands; in Wadowice, the pope's birthplace; in Krakow, John Paul's former archdiocese; in Oswiecim, the place of a Nazi concentration camp - crowds estimated overall at thirteen million stretched from horizon to horizon: young and old, students and children, workers, peasants, intellectuals, government and party employees.

After protracted negotiations, an official announcement that the papal trip would take place was made in Warsaw on March 2, and on May 7 both the episcopate and the government released special communiques on the program of the visit. Only four days before the arrival of the pope, Cardinal Wyszynski and Gierek met again on May 29 (see chapter 16). While affirming that the visit would be "an event of historical importance," both sides pointed out that "the agreement of the church and state authorities about this visit proves the vitality of the assumptions that form the foundation of cooperation between the church and the state." But serious differences in the interpretation of the essential meaning of the papal visit remained. According to Gierek, the visit would serve "the unity of Poles, the growth of Poland's international prestige," and the further successful development of relations between the state and the church. By contrast, Cardinal Wyszynski saw in the event the confirmation of a "growing conviction about the importance of the religious and moral work of the church in Poland."

John Paul's "religious pilgrimage" was for Poland a historical event of tremendous political and national significance. But many of his messages went also well beyond strictly Polish dimensions. Referring to himself time and again as "this Slav, this Pole," the Pope seemed intent on underscoring his own uniqueness. In Warsaw, and in a sense on Moscow's doorstep, the pope declared that "Christ cannot be kept out of the history of man in any part of the globe," certainly not in Poland. To understand the true history of Poland, as interpreted by the heart of Poles, he said in Czestochowa at the shrine of the Black Madonna, "We must hear the echo of the life of the whole nation in the heart of its Mother and Queen...." He thus reaffirmed the continuing, unbreakable bond between the church and the Polish nation. On other occasions the pope called for the strengthening of the spiritual unity of the whole of Europe on the basis of fundamental Christian values - "a Christian Europe," for the recognition of the essential validity of historically established links formed through the process of evangelization between Eastern and Western Europe, as well as among all Slav nations themselves. The most outspoken warning against totalitarian ideologies and the most powerful appeal for universal respect of "inalienable human rights" - and thus a challenge to the world's Marxist and other leaders - came in Oswiecim (Auschwitz), the "Golgotha of our times," as he described this former Nazi concentration camp. In another of his sermons, John Paul II, signalling his own individual approach to the church's social doctrine, stressed the dignity and Christian values of work. "Christianity and the Church," he said, "have no fear of the world of work...Christ will never approve of man being considered, or of man considering himself, merely as a means of production." This amounted to a clear rejection of the old and established dogmas of the Marxist ideological approach to social problems. In his over thirty homilies and statements, the pope spoke strongly against atheism; on the preservation of true Christian culture; on the freedom of choice of a free man and of a free nation; on the right of man to his own land; on the theme "War, never again - peace and only peace should guide us"; on the Holy See which was always ready "to manifest its openness with regard to all countries or regimes, seeking the essential good which is man's real good." Many of his remarks were regularly interrupted by stormy applause and the song "We want God, we are his subjects, we want God in our books, at school...."

In his address at the Episcopate's Conference in Czestochowa, John Paul II insisted on a dialogue with the political authorities and on a mutually acceptable platform of cooperation. "Authentic dialogue," he warned, "must respect the convictions of believers, and ensure all the rights of citizens as well as normal conditions for the activity of the

Church as a religious community to which the vast majority of Poles belong." He also stressed that "this dialogue cannot be easy because it takes place between two concepts of the world which are diametrically opposed, but it must be possible and effective if the good of individuals and the nation demands it." In his view, the normalization of relations between the church and the state "is also a practical manifestation of the fact that the state understands its mission toward society in accordance with the principle of 'subsidiarity,' that is, it wants to express the full sovereignty of the nation...." More directly stated, this meant that the legitimacy of states in Eastern Europe, and for that matter anywhere in the world, depends ultimately on their willingness to agree that they serve the people and not vice versa. Besides, the pope defined the key issues of church-state relations in a more general, European framework. In this context, church-state relations in Poland would become an aspect, perhaps even a test case, of the much larger task of creating the European Christian Community.

John Paul II met Gierek at the Belweder palace in Warsaw on June 2. The Party chief stressed the need for the unity of the Polish nation, to which the pope replied that this can only be achieved on the principle of respect for the objective rights of the nation such as "the right to freedom, to be a social and political entity and also to the formation of its own culture and civilization." The church had a vital role to play. "For that activity," he said, "the church does not desire any privileges, but only and exclusively what is essential for the accomplishment of her mission." And then, during his last Mass on Polish soil in Krakow, praying with over three million people, the pope linked the fate of the nation to the preservation of its Christian heritage and appealed: "You must be strong with the strength of faith...today more than in any other age you need this strength." Yet he was also careful not to imply that these appeals meant a challenge to established institutions and political systems: "There is no imperialism in the Church," he stressed, "only service." The real task of the church was to facilitate and support reconciliation rather than confrontation between different peoples and countries.

John Paul II's many statements have acquired a special importance of their own due in large measure to his personal appeal. Singing, laughing, chatting, and joking with young people and the old he showed that it takes more than the formal traditions of papal office to tame his spontaneity, warmth, vigour, his joy and sense of humour, his resplendent humanism. One minute he held his audiences spellbound as he lowered his voice and slowly spoke on a spiritual problem, and the next he had them laughing and applauding after one of his many asides. He displayed an uncanny flair for historical perspective, rare diplomatic skill, and an ability to preach

with subtle but clear political undertones. Without once
directly criticizing the regime, the pope dramatically effaced
its authority. Yet he never disputed the communist state's
right to exist but ignored its claimed monopoly on patriotism.
    Within the communist context, the Polish media's coverage
of the pope's visit was quite unprecedented, even if there
were special party instructions on how to minimize its impact:
three nationwide television transmissions covering also two
Masses; some other events presented on the regional television
and radio networks' official PAP reports in the press and on
radio; few press comments. But even so the coverage was
very selective and infinitely shorter than in most Western
countries. It was also miles below what the people of Poland
have expected.
    John Paul II was received by the highest Polish author-
ities with great courtesy and full honors as a head of state.
But the people who came in their millions to see him and pray
with him also showed that it would not be possible for the
government and the party to pretend nothing had happened
once he was back in Rome. The real Poland, pays reel,
emerged once more into the open and has shown its new-found
pride and sense of identity with its religion and the church,
while the country's authorities, pays legal, looked on with
either dismay or jealousy. The pope's visit considerably
enhanced the appeal of the church and immeasurably
strengthened its political weight. In the aftermath of this
"pilgrimage," the situation in Poland appeared still more con-
fusing - with strong contradictory undercurrents. The internal balance of political forces has become more disturbed.
John Paul II will now have a great role to play in building on
the results of his visit both in his own country and in the
whole of Eastern Europe.
    From Poland, John Paul II "addressed the people all over
the globe," said Cardinal Krol of Philadelphia. And the world
listened. The world's mass media and the most experienced
observers and columnists assessed the significance of the
pope's visit as worldwide. James Reston of the New York
Times described the Pontiff's meeting with his own people as
the most important summit meeting of the decade, "for it is not
the penetration of Western military power Moscow has to fear,
but the penetration of freedom and faith." The visit was
certainly the triumph of a man of whom the world at large is
now entitled to expect much wisdom. At a time when there are
few genuine leaders about, wrote the Washington Post, the
arrival of one of John Paul's caliber is a most welcome event.
If the astounding success of his pilgrimage to Poland proves
anything, it is that the power of faith is more than equal to
the power that tries to deny it.

III

Conclusion

17 Testing the Limits of the Possible

> It is easier to switch on the light,
> than to curse the darkness.
>
> Chinese proverb

"Where do you go from here?" I asked my various Polish friends in Warsaw in January 1979. That, they replied, is the 64,000-dollar question. Nobody knows the answer; yet, somebody must find ways and means of extricating the nation from its present problems.

There are many factors in Poland's situation, some of them unique in Eastern Europe, which have been discussed in this book. Above all, nowhere in Eastern Europe is there such widespread and open opposition to uniformist, however moderate, Party control in all areas of human life, and such a powerful church supported by the Vatican. Under a relative and deceptive calm, massive discontents and pressures for political reforms including some forms of pluralism continue to bubble up just below the surface, and many are on the surface.

However diffused the political and social ingredients of various social groups might be and however divergent their interests, they coalesce on two main issues: a full implementation of human rights as guaranteed by the constitution and genuine participation in decision making. However frustrated, disillusioned, cynical and impatient they may be, they are too mature and too deeply aware of geopolitical limitations to try to overthrow the system. But they certainly see a real chance of pushing the limits much further.

The involvement of the masses in the government as advocated by the leadership may mean in fact either control by

the people or just control over the people. Socialism without
social democracy is a contradiction in terms. The involvement
must therefore mean control by the people and not control over
the people. The ultimate guarantee of such a control is the
power to get rid of an unpopular government and replace it by
another, even within the existing system, provided there are
alternative, even socialist, platforms. The paradox is that the
very leadership which so effectively modernized and to some
extent humanized life now shrinks from the consequences of its
own achievements.

Poland has entered a phase of new stresses between the
Party and the people, and in economic relations between the
government and the Soviet Union.(1) The task of coping with
these stresses is made more difficult by the widening generation gap between rulers and ruled, and by the fact that
waiting in the wings is a new and unpredictable generation,
destined to take over in due course. These youngsters were
not born into the atmosphere of fear and terror of the Nazi
occupation, nor the Stalinist period. They did not live
through the upheavals of 1956, 1968 and even 1970. They
have to be formed and educated in the realities of the present
situation, and, as a Party journalist told me, the church is
the only body to do it. The task of coping with the problems
is not made easier by the uncertainty about the future leadership in Moscow. But Poland, at the crossroads of European
civilization, as the biggest and the least conformist country in
the bloc, is for the Russians the key to stabilization of their
East European empire. The Polish army might well fight any
armed outside intervention to "rescue socialism" as the Soviet
leaders would see it. The consequences would be enormously
costly, even devastating.

There is therefore room for careful probing of the limits
of the possible. The fear of breakdown in the unsatisfactory
and precarious order in Eastern Europe is still sufficiently
chilling to restrain all concerned.(2) The stresses will not
disappear by themselves. Some may indeed get worse. New
mechanisms of resolving them will have to be found: there may
be sharper conflicts between those who want to suppress and
those who want to accommodate. Economic stability, when it
comes, may encourage the leadership to deal much more
harshly with dissent and opposition. But repression would
destroy the very basis on which the present leadership came
to power. Yet without repression it is hard to see how the
opposition can be brought under control. The answer seems
to be that the civil rights movement in Poland is too strong,
more widespread than anywhere else in Eastern Europe. The
leadership cannot afford confrontation unless it is determined
to return to brutal Stalinist methods, which in Poland today
would be a disastrous act of desperation. Such a move would
also be a hopeless proposition. Demands voiced so forcefully in

Poland today are still almost identical with those voiced in 1954-1956, 1968 and in 1970, despite some short periods of repression. This only proves that although some changes have taken place for the better, Soviet interference still offends Poland's national dignity, even if the majority of people do accept the political necessity of close Polish-Soviet ties. The main reason for this lies in the conservative character of the Soviet regime(3), in the servility of the Polish media and in the fact that however much a facade this fawning before Moscow may appear, it is what the Soviet leaders, like all jealous gods, expect. But the trouble about these myths is that those who promote them must pay homage to their own lies. They are afraid to break with either the past or the ideological myths because without them where would the legitimacy to rule be.(4) All governments lie about their records but in countries where they are changed every few years, the lies do not become enshrined. Likewise, all ruling classes lie about themselves, but in free societies they cannot close the mouths of those who point to the lies.

Nobody by now can close the mouths of Poles. They have at least learned that the Pax Sovietica has been neither practical nor ethical; Moscow thinks and acts exclusively in terms of a global expansionist superpower without any ideological constraints, even though ideological arguments are used as a face-saving device. It is scarcely conceivable that the Kremlin can forever keep the lid on its kind of socialism in Poland, and for that matter in Eastern Europe.(5) Nor are further revolts out of the question. Soviet domination rests on Soviet military power and represents the last major empire in the world today. Some day it will go the way of all others.

Detente aroused a mixture of hopes among governments and people. Both desired to at least slow down the arms race and increase openings to the West. But while East European governments wanted greater international legitimacy and carefully controlled exchanges, the people hoped for more individual freedoms. The West's insistence on respect for human rights everywhere, however realistically or strongly some Western leaders are prepared to press for it, provides a strong stimulus. The basic problem touched by this issue is that at least one familiar prop of the communist regimes is weakening - external threat and revolutionary necessity involving harsher internal controls. Detente, no matter how interpreted, is bound to make them less convincing. The supposed threat now is "ideological penetration," but this is seen by the Poles as more of an attraction than a threat. Besides, Poland, being so strongly intertwined with the Western economy cannot import knowledge from Western universities, factories, laboratories and farms without importing the ideas and values at the heart of Western institutions. These constitute a continuing welcome source of

infection among the people making the country still more in-
digestible as a section of the Soviet empire.

The recession and the inflation in the West have hit
Poland painfully.   It is being called upon simultaneously to
supply more to the Soviet Union, to pay more for Soviet raw
materials, more to the West (or borrow more) to pay for capital
goods and technological know-how and more to its own consumers to meet the rising expectations - all this with managerial planning and pricing systems deeply resistant to the
necessary drastic reforms.

Polycentric communism, by now a long-established fact of
life, is a necessary component of a more pluralistic world.
Polycentrism in world communism is a condition for the very
gradual evolution of communist regimes into more cooperative
members of the international community.(6)   The birth of
Eurocommunism added a new dimension to the picture, further
reducing the already diminished "Soviet area" of communism.
The authority of Moscow can never look the same in Eastern
Europe.   The Eurocommunists are trying hard, at least in what
they promise, to prove that genuine democratic socialism in a
pluralistic society could better be realized in the West under
the American umbrella than in the East under Brezhnev's
doctrine of limited sovereignty.(7)   How far they are prepared
to reject Soviet domination once they are in power, even
shared power, is another, so far unanswered, question.   But
at present they have certainly a substantial impact not only on
average people in Poland, but also on some prominent forward-
looking Party members.   If the values of pluralistic democracy
are essential to socialism in Italy, people are saying, then why
not in Poland?

One answer could be: impossible, because we have to live
in the Soviet orbit.   Recently the leading Polish Marxist
philosopher, professor Kolakowski, now at Oxford, said at a
seminar: "The concept of nontotalitarian communism seems to
many of us like the idea of fried snowballs."   I would argue
that, even slightly fried snowballs are better than no snowballs at all.   That leading prophet of revisionism, Djilas, still
living in Belgrade, argued recently that reforms within one-
Party systems are futile and their inefficiency "incurable."
But he also maintained that events in the West and in Western
communism have already compelled the Party monopolists in the
East to be more cautious in their use of power and their
methods of repression.

Nowhere is this more true than in Poland.   The moral of
recent Polish developments seems clear.   If the Communist
party is not to keep losing contact with public opinion, it will
have to introduce in some form the principle of pluralism,
which in time means abandoning Lenin's myth of a monolithic,
all-powerful and "leading" Party, which is how the East
European Communist parties now organize themselves.   After

the June 1976 events a prominent Polish Party leader was quoted to me as saying: "I don't know what model of socialism we have to create, but it must be new and effective. Maybe even new institutions are required."

In other words, after so many years of upheavals, promises and subsequent regression, Poland is still looking for its own road, not so much toward "socialism" as seen and allowed by Moscow, but toward a specific social democracy. In a way this has already been a success story. Dynamic, lively, unsteady but mature, this country is pluralistic in political and social terms, and as such, unique in Eastern Europe.

The model of a totalitarian society evolved by Western political scientists does not apply to contemporary Poland. Squeezed between the Soviet Union and Soviet-dominated East Germany, Poles have accepted, to some extent, the limits imposed on them. People must not do certain things but they are no longer required to do many others. The Party on the one hand and the people on the other are not free to act as they please. The regime and the opposition have at least one thing in common: the desire to avoid more explosions which could be disastrous for all. The result is a restrained confrontation in which almost everyone displays a degree of caution and realism.

Theoretically, of course, a communist state should be like a beet – red throughout. Poland with its combination of a communist leadership and an almost exclusively noncommunist population is more like a radish – red outside and white within. As a result, although the Communist party has, at least nominally, monopolized power in an overwhelmingly Catholic country their political control glides helplessly over the surface of society. The Polish community has always been difficult to govern but it is still more difficult to govern against the community. The Polish leadership has perhaps, by now realized, however frightening this realization might prove to be, that they have become the center of one of the anomalies of modern times: a totalitarian (by definition) ruling party without a totalitarian state. In this they are unique in the socialist camp. And that is why Poland remains a country of paradoxes, some of them unacceptable in any other communist state.

The Poles have seen their world shattered four times in the course of three decades. But they also achieved more than they or anyone else had a right to expect in the circumstances – more successes and more still unresolved problems. The election of the pope from Poland added a new, intriguing and extremely important dimension in the context of future developments. He knows better than almost anyone else how wide a margin still remains between what exists today and the uncrossable limits of the geopolitical position of the country. In the efforts to reach these limits he is able to place on the scales the authority of the universal church.

The problem is how to transplant the polycentrism in the communist movement into pluralism inside one country without shaking dangerously the foundations of what is at present the unavoidable political order in Europe and of the Soviet super-power politics and interests. A shrewd British observer(8) has argued that one can reach the Soviet Union only over a wall and across a moat, while entrance to and exit from resilient Eastern Europe is much simpler through a crisscross of turnstiles, which East and West Europeans are now mastering. If the peoples of Eastern Europe succeed in inching their way to increased real liberties and to a greater independence (although in full and equal partnership co-operation) from Soviet rule, the Soviet Union will be directly affected and the future of Europe and of the world will become substantially brighter and freer.

For once Poland, particularly skillful in the "turnstiles" maneuvering, could show the way. In the past, I was told by many highly placed Party members, the country could take two steps forward only after Moscow had made one. Now Warsaw might be able to take its two steps forward waiting for Moscow to follow suit, because of Gierek's initial successes and in the face of growing, powerful currents pressing for reforms from below. A crisis of consultation and participation in Poland may well turn out to be a crisis of communism. And in the present situation the country shows signs of becoming a test case on the limits of freedom under a Soviet-dominated communist system.

To some extent the final word rests with Moscow. It will be an agonizing decision for the Soviet leaders whether to come to terms with the new realities of life and emerge from their schematic pattern of Byzantine, anachronistic attitudes toward a fast-changing world, including their East European allies.

Yet it is not entirely up to the Kremlin. The West's and particularly America's firm stand on human rights is of paramount importance. The "Polish" pope, the most outspoken champion of human rights has shown the way ahead. The one thing Moscow understands is strong words and power. The West should continue to exact a price both in economic and political terms from Brezhnev in return for his claim to be a peacemaker and a champion of people.(9) It should continually expose the breaking of so many of his promises, including the Helsinki agreement, and keep demanding why in the Soviet Union and elsewhere people are being persecuted for trying to hold their rulers to their pledges or are just denied their constitutional rights to do so. This will not make, as some politicians might argue, any East-West dialogue more difficult and dangerous. It will make it easier because it will be more open and honest. If this means that we must examine our own conscience so much the better.

Not only the people in Poland but also those in the West have a chance to probe the limits of the possible within the communist orbit and in other totalitarian countries. Some Western politicians would maintain that if the problem is solved with Moscow then the solution automatically applies to East Europe. Until Moscow itself becomes more liberal it will not allow more freedom to Poland, for instance, so the main pressure should be concentrated there. This argument is as out-of-date as some of the Soviet attitudes; Moscow has already had to allow unorthodox and comparatively progressive policies in Poland (whatever the imposed ideological facade), which remain taboo in the Soviet Union. This superpower giant can develop only at the slow pace dictated by its history and to accept this pace for the advance of already more advanced and politically sophisticated and mature East European countries would be a retrogression. Detente could become more mythical than it is at present. The West should concentrate on East European countries and deal with them as with sovereign states, however much their sovereignty is limited by the geopolitical factors of the world today. The Soviet leaders think in terms of imperial politics and they could go far to prevent at least the appearances of an empire from crumbling altogether. The road to a real dialogue does not (except for the arms race) lead exclusively through Moscow. Her allies, within certain limits, do not have to follow blindly the so-called "first socialist state." On the contrary, 62 years after the revolution, Russia can learn much from her European neighbors. As the British found, yesterday's revolutionary innovation is today's obsolete and dusty steam engine.

The Polish example is thus probably the most significant development in postwar history of communism and provides, despite all the difficulties, a distant light at the end of the tunnel. Realistic politics is the art of the possible; the time has come to test the limits of the possible, particularly since the truth is gloomy only to those who live by myths.

Notes

INTRODUCTION

General sources:

George Blazinski, John Paul II - A Man from Krakow (London: Weidenfeld and Nicholson, 1979); also, The Pope in Poland (Munich: Radio Free Europe Research, 1979).

1. Frank Gibney, The Frozen Revolution - Poland, a Study in Communist Decay (New York: Farrar, Strauss and Cudaly 1959).
2. R. Zimand, Propostu (Warsaw), May 1957.
3. T. Bor Komorowski, The Secret Army (London: Gollancz, 1950).
4. Christopher Seton Watson, The Cold War: its Origins from Aspects of Contemporary World History (London: Methuen & Co., 1966).
5. K. Syrop, Poland between the Hammer and the Anvil (London: Robert Hale, 1968).
6. Richard Hiscocks, Poland: Bridge for the Abyss? (London: Oxford University Press, 1963).
7. Nicholas Bethell, Gomulka: His Poland and His Communism (London: Longmans, 1969).
8. Author's own scripts and recordings of conversations with Jozef Swiatlo in Washington, September-October 1954.
9. J.F. Brown, "Hungary and Poland Twenty Years Ago," Radio Free Europe Background Report 207 (Munich), October 5, 1976.
10. William Woods, Poland: Eagle in the East (London: Andre Deutsch, 1969).

CHAPTER 1

1.   A. Ross Johnson, "Polish Perspectives Past and Present," Problems of Communism, July-August 1971; for details see also: M. Gamarnikow, "Poland Returns to Economic Reform," East Europe, November-December 1969; and Jonathan Steele, "Lessons from Gdansk," The Guardian (London), December 19, 1970.
2.   Życie Gospodarcze (Warsaw), October 4, 1970. Trybuna Ludu (Warsaw), May 13, 1971; for details see also: M. Gamarnikow, "A New Economic Approach," Problems of Communism, September-October 1972.
3.   Own conversations in Warsaw; see also A. Bromke and John W. Strong, eds., Gierek's Poland (New York: Praeger Publishers, 1973).
4.   Życie Gospodarcze (Warsaw), August 8, 1970 and June 6, 1970.
5.   Trybuna Ludu (Warsaw), September 12, 1970 and February 2, 1971.
6.   Michael Costello, "The Poles Look at Their Country and at Themselves," RFE Research, Poland 14 (Munich), September 15, 1970.
7.   Trybuna Ludu (Warsaw), February 2, 1971.
8.   Neil Asherson, "Why Poles Rebelled," The Observer (London), December 12, 1970.

CHAPTER 2

General sources:

Own conversations in Warsaw and on the Baltic coast in July, 1971; also with CC Secretary W. Krasko and many others still alive; dispatches from Reuter, AFP, and UPI, from PAP, from James Feron in The Times (London), from The Guardian (London), from The New York Times, from Le Monde (Paris), and from Svenska Dagbladet, all during December 12-31, 1970; Glos Wybrzeza (Gdansk), December 28, 1970; Zycie Literackie (Krakow), February 21, 1971; Osteuropeische Rundschau, no. 1 & 2, 1971; see also A. Ross Johnson, "The Polish Riots and Gomulka's Fall," Problems of Communism, July-August, 1971; A. Ross Johnson, "Poland: End of an Era?," Problems of Communism, January-February, 1971.

1.   PAP (Warsaw), December 12, 1970.
2.   Zycie Literackie (Krakow), February 2, 1971.
3.   Glos Wybrzeza (Gdansk), December 28, 1970.
4.   Reuter, UPI, December 14, 1970.

5.   Risto Bajalski, Polityka (Belgrade), February 23, 1971.
6.   BBC Monitoring, December 15, 1970.
7.   BBC Monitoring, December 17, 1970; see also Victor Zorza, The Guardian (London), December 18, 1970.
8.   Ibid.
9.   Glos Wybrzeza (Gdansk), December 31, 1970.
10.   Barbara Seidler, Zycie Literackie (Krakow), February 21, 1971.
11.   Kurier Szczecinski (Szczecin), December 18-19, 1970.
12.   Glos Szczecinski (Szczecin), December 19-20, 1970.
13.   BBC Monitoring, December 18, 1970.
14.   Radio Warsaw, December 20, 1970.
15.   Radio Gdansk at 17.00.
16.   Zb.A. Pelczynski, The Downfall of Gomulka from Gierek's Poland ed. A. Bromke and John W. Strong (New York: Praeger Publishers, 1973).
17.   J.F. Brown, "Earthquake Hits the Polish Leadership," RFE Research, Poland 27 (Munich), December 30, 1970.
18.   Nowe Drogi, special number, 1971, Warsaw, and A. Bromke, "A New Political Style," Problems of Communism (New York), September-October, 1971.
19.   Vincent C. Chrypinski, Political Change under Gierek from Gierek's Poland ed. A. Bromke and John W. Strong, (New York: Praeger Publishers, 1973).
20.   Text from the Primate's Press Office.

CHAPTER 3

1.   Radio Warsaw, December 31, 1970.
2.   Text from the Primate's Press Office.
3.   A. Bromke, "A New Political Style," Problems of Communism (New York), September-October, 1972.
4.   M.F. Rakowski, "Perspektywa," Polityka (Warsaw), February 13, 1971.
5.   Trybuna Ludu (Warsaw), December 24, 1970.
6.   BBC Monitoring, January 8, 1971.
7.   Reuter and UPI, January 1, 1971.
8.   Central Statistical Office (GUS), 1971 Yearbook.
9.   Trybuna Ludu (Warsaw), January 12, 1971.
10.   Ibid., December 12, 1970.
11.   Trybuna Robotnicza (Katowice), January 27, 1971, and Trybuna Mazowiecka (Warsaw Province), January 6, 1971.
12.   Trybuna Ludu (Warsaw), February 2, 1971.
13.   Franco Fabiani from Warsaw, Unita (Rome), January 12, 1971.
14.   Richard Davy, "Can Mr. Gierek Stop Poland's Powder Keg from Exploding?," The Times (London), Novem-

ber 26, 1971; A. Ross Johnson, "Polish Perspectives Past and Present," Problems of Communism (New York), July-August 1971.

15. Own conversations in Poland; for more details see also Le Monde (Paris), January 29, 1971; Charlotte Saikowski, Christian Science Monitor (Boston), February 8, 1971; K.S. Karol, New Statesman (London), February 5, 1971.

16. Glos Szczecinski (Szczecin), January, 1971.

17. Thomas Walden from Gdansk, Aftonbladed (Stockholm), January 7, 1971.

18. Transcript of original tape as recorded in Szczecin; also New Left Review (London), no. 72, March-April 1972; L'Espresso (Rome), December 19, 1971; Ewa Wacowska, "Rewolta Szczecinska i jej znaczenie," Literary Institute (Paris), 1971.

19. Radio Gdansk and Szczecin, January 25-26, 1971.

20. Vatican Radio, February 1, 1971.

21. BBC Monitoring, February 15, 1971.

22. Ibid. and Trybuna Ludu (Warsaw), February 16, 1971.

23. My interviews in Poland and Osteuropeische Rundschau, no. 3.

24. Glos Pracy, February 25-26, 1971.

25. Nowe Drogi (Warsaw), special issue, February 1971.

26. BBC Monitoring.

27. PAP (Warsaw), February 8, 1971.

28. M. Gamarnikow, "A New Economic Approach," from Problems of Communism (New York), September-October 1972; also Robert W. Dean, "Gierek's Three Years", Survey (London), Spring-Summer 1974.

29. Trybuna Ludu (Warsaw), October 14, 1971.

30. Polska lat siedmdziesiatych (Warsaw: Ksiazka i Wiedza, 1972).

31. A. Bromke, "A New Political Approach," Problems of Communism (New York), September-October 1972.

32. Zycie Warszawy (Warsaw), February 14, 1971.

33. Robert W. Dean, "Ideology and Pragmatism in Gierek's Poland," RFE Research, Poland 2 (Munich), January 21, 1974.

34. Polityka (Warsaw), February 6, 1971.

35. Trybuna Ludu (Warsaw), April 17, 1971.

36. BBC Monitoring, February 21, 1971.

37. Trybuna Ludu (Warsaw), February 20, 1971.

38. Ibid.

39. Trybuna Ludu (Warsaw), May 2, 1971.

40. My own comment broadcast in BCC output, May 1, 1971.

41. The Times editorial (London), December 21, 1970.

42. Trybuna Ludu (Warsaw), September 5, 1971.

43. Ibid.

44. Trybuna Ludu (Warsaw), September 7, 1971.

45. Polish Radio Public Opinion Research (Warsaw), November 1971.
46. AP from Warsaw, February 11, 1971.
47. Karol Malcuzynski, Prasa Polska (Warsaw), August-September 1971.
48. Prasa Polska (Warsaw), no. 11, November 1971.
49. Ibid., June 4, 1971.
50. Z.M. Fallenbuchl, The Strategy of Development and Gierek's Economic Maneuver in Gierek's Poland ed. A. Bromke and John W. Strong (New York: Praeger Publishers, 1973).
51. PAP (Warsaw), March 8, 1972.
52. Trybuna Ludu (Warsaw), February 8, 1971.

CHAPTER 4

1. Nowe Drogi (Warsaw), special number, February 1971.
2. B. Margueritte, "La Pologne do M. Gierek," Le Monde (Paris), October 21, 1971.
3. Richard Davy, The Times (London), December 21, 1970.
4. Nowe Drogi (Warsaw) special edition, February 1971.
5. Trybuna Ludu (Warsaw), February 7, 1971.
6. The Guardian (London), December 22, 1971.
7. M. Costello, "Gierek's First six months," RFE Research (Munich), June 6, 1971.
8. Thomas E. Heneghan, "Polish Trade and Polish Trends: Economic and Political," RFE Research (Munich); RAD Background Report 158 (Poland), November 13, 1975; Henry Kamm, New York Times, June 13, 1975.
9. Own conversations in Poland; also M. Costello, "Poland today: Political Prospects," Survey (London), Summer 1971.
10. Annual Register of World Events, S.V. "Poland" (London), vols. for 1971 & 1972.
11. Robert W. Dean, "The First National Party Conference," RFE Research (Munich), November 8, 1973.
12. Manuel Lucbert, "Poland under Gierek," The Guardian (London), July 12, 1975.
13. J. Turowicz, The Changing Catholicism in Poland in Gierek's Poland ed. A. Bromke and John W. Strong (New York: Praeger Publishers, 1973).
14. Alain Woodrow, "La Pologne Catholique et socialiste," Le Monde (Paris), August 15, 1975.
15. Hansjakob Stehle, "The Independent Satellite," Pall Mall (London), 1965.
16. Thomas E. Heneghan, "The Loyal Opposition," RFE Research, Background Report 45 (Poland), February 28, 1977.

17.   UPI from Warsaw, January 29, 1971.
18.   Slowo Powszechne (Warsaw), October 4, 1971.
19.   Reuter and AFP, March 30, 1972.
20.   Reuter and AFP, April 4, 1972.
21.   RFE Special from Vienna, May 30, 1977.
22.   Nowe Drogi (Warsaw), September 1971.
23.   Tygodnik Powszechny (Krakow), April 14, 1972.
24.   Reuter, June 28, 1972.
25.   PAP (Warsaw), June 28, 1972.
26.   UPI (Warsaw), June 28, 1972.
27.   La Croix (Paris), December 28, 1973.
28.   Reuter from Warsaw, January 26, 1974.
29.   Reuter (Warsaw), May 9, 1973.
30.   Text from Primate's Press Office.
31.   Reuter (Warsaw), May 22, 1973.
32.   Reuter and DPA (Warsaw), December 26, 1973.
33.   Nowe Drogi (Warsaw), May 1974.
34.   Time Magazine, October 14, 1974.
35.   Baltimore Sun, October 15, 1974.
36.   Paul Neuburg, The Guardian (London), October 30,
       1974.
37.   Documentation Catholique (Paris), no. 15, August 1976.
38.   Le Monde (Paris), August 27, 1976; Famiglia Cristiana
       (Rome), August 27, 1976.
39.   UPI (Warsaw), March 16, 1975.
40.   La Croix (Paris), April 2, 1975.
41.   A. Bromke, "A New Juncture in Poland," Problems of
       Communism (New York), September-October 1976.
42.   J. Turowicz, "Un probleme crucial: les relations entre
       l'Eglise et l'Etat," Le Monde (Paris), April 30, 1974.
43.   Trybuna Ludu (Warsaw), February 10, 1972.
44.   James Feron, New York Times March 9, 1972.
45.   Jonathan Steele from Warsaw, The Guardian (London),
       March 24, 1972.
46.   Annelise Schultze, Daily Telegraph (London), February
       29, 1972.
47.   Zycie Literackie (Krakow), March 19, 1972.
48.   Daily Telegraph (London), February 20, 1972.
49.   Reuter (Warsaw), March 20, 1976.
50.   AFP (Warsaw), December 20, 1973.
51.   Original Polish text, translated in Survey (London),
       spring edition, 1976.
52.   Le Nouvel Observateur (Paris), May 10, 1976, translated
       in Survey (London) Spring 1976.
53.   Trybuna Ludu (Warsaw), September 28, 1972.
54.   Manuel Lucbert from Vienna, Le Monde (Paris), May 5,
       1975.
55.   PAP from Warsaw, May 12, 1975.
56.   BBC Monitoring of Radio Warsaw, April 12, 1973.

57. UPI (Warsaw), October 24, 1973; for details see Ewa Celt, "Poland Reforms its School System," RFE Research Poland 19 (Munich), November 13, 1973.
58. Information Catholique Internationale (Paris), October 22, 1973.
59. Literatura (Warsaw), September 27, 1973.
60. Trybuna Ludu, (Warsaw), October 14, 1973.
61. Slowo Powszechne (Warsaw), July 8, 1976.
62. Annual Register of World Events, S.V. "Poland," vol. 1972.
63. PAP (Warsaw), August 28, 1974.
64. BBC Monitoring of Radio Gdansk, September 4, 1974.
65. Trybuna Ludu, August 27, 1974.
66. Own interviews; also, David Lascelles from Warsaw, Financial Times (London), March 30, 1974.
67. Robert W. Dean, "Gierek's Three Years," Survey, (London), Spring-Summer 1974.
68. Financial Times (London), July 1, 1976.
69. Alex Pravda, "The Polish Workers Revolt," New Statesman (London), August 8, 1973.
70. M. Costello, "Gierek's First Six Months," RFE Research (Munich), June 6, 1971.
71. Trybuna Ludu, February 25, 1971.
72. Trybuna Ludu (Warsaw), November 14, 1972.
73. RFE Research, Poland 29 (Munich), November 28, 1972.
74. RFE Research, Poland 26 (Munich), February 19, 1975.
75. Trybuna Ludu (Warsaw), November 14, 1972.
76. Reuter (Warsaw), March 8, 1971.
77. Tygodnik Powszechny (Krakow), December 5, 1971.
78. Dan Morgan, Washington Post, December 19, 1971. Bernard Margueritte, Le Monde (Paris), February 3, 1972; Jonathan Steele, The Guardian (London), February 9, 1972.
79. Jonathan Steele, The Guardian (London), February 9, 1972.
80. Prawo i Zycie (Warsaw), September 19, 1971.
81. Zycie Warszawy (Warsaw), February 14-15, 1971.
82. Trybuna Ludu (Warsaw), December 7, 1971.
83. Trybuna Ludu (Warsaw), February 6, 1971.
84. Frankfurter Allgemeine Zeitung (Frankfurt), February 8, 1972. Suddeutsche Zeitung (Munich), February 8, 1972.
85. The Times (London), February 7, 1972.
86. Tygodnik Powszechny (Krakow), February 6, 1972.
87. Georges S. Mond, The Role of Intelligentsia in Gierek's Poland. A. Bromke and John W. Strong (New York: Praeger Publishers, 1973).
88. Kultura (Warsaw), August 6, 1972.
89. Noel Clark in Vienna, "Poland and her Intellectuals," Despatch to the BBC, February 22, 1974.

90. Trybuna Ludu (Warsaw), March 3, 1972.
91. Tygodnik Powszechny (Krakow), April 8, 1973.
92. Trybuna Ludu (Warsaw), January 19, 1973.
93. Tygodnik Powszechny (Krakow), April 1, 1973.
94. Nowe Drogi Warsaw, April 1973.
95. BBC Monitoring of Radio Warsaw, December 9, 1971.
96. Ewa Celt, "Polish Theatre in Quest of a New Model," RFE Research, Poland 15 (Munich), September 3, 1973.
97. Noel Clark, despatch for the BBC from Vienna, February 22, 1974.
98. Zycie Warszawy (Warsaw), November 17, 1972.
99. Renata Hammer, "Poland: Its Writers and the Censors," Index on Censorship (London), spring 1975.
100. Trybuna Ludu (Warsaw), February 23, 1975.
101. T. Nowakowski, "The New Wave in Polish Poetry," Survey, (London), spring 1976.
102. Noel Clark in Vienna, despatch to the BBC, December 10, 1974; Reuter from Warsaw, December 9 & 11, 1974.
103. RFE special from London, October 16, 1973.
104. Michael Costello, "Poland before the sixth Party Congress," RFE Research, Poland 26 (Munich), December 3, 1971.
105. Prasa Polska (Warsaw), November 1971.
106. Nowe Drogi (Warsaw), December 1971.
107. Trybuna Ludu (Warsaw), January 26, 1973.
108. Zycie Warszawy, May 5, 1973.
109. Trybuna Ludu (Warsaw), December 14, 1972.
110. L. Labedz, The Times (London), September 27, 1977.
111. UPI from Warsaw, April 7, 1973.
112. Index on Censorship (London), spring 1975.
113. The Times editorial (London), September 27, 1977.
114. L. Labedz, The Times (London), September 9, 1977.
115. Jonathan Steele from Krakow, The Guardian (London), March 17, 1972.
116. Nowe Drogi (Warsaw), special edition, February 1971.
117. ITD (student paper), October 14, 1971.
118. Trybuna Ludu (Warsaw), July 23, 1972.
119. RFE Research Poland 30 (Munich), July 7, 1931.
120. Zycie Warszawy (Warsaw), October 22-23, 1972.
121. Trybuna Ludu (Warsaw), November 29, 1972.
122. RFE Research Poland 6, (Munich), February 9, 1973.
123. Kultura (Paris), March 1973.
124. Trybuna Ludu (Warsaw), April 12, 1973.
125. Richard Davy, The Times (London), April 1, 1977.
126. Ibid.
127. Alex Pravda, "Gierek's Poland: Five Years On," World Today (London), July 1976.
128. Financial Times (London), July 17, 1974.
129. PAP from Warsaw, October 22, 1973.

130. David Lascelles, Financial Times (London), December 5, 1975.
131. The Economist (London), November 10, 1973.
132. Statistical Yearbook, GUS (Warsaw), 1975.
133. Financial Times (London), December 5, 1975.
134. M. Gamarnikow, "A View of Poland's Current Economic Problems," RFE Research Poland 17 (Munich), November 2, 1973.
135. Financial Times (London), December 5, 1975.
136. Trybuna Ludu (Warsaw), May 11, 1972.
137. Ibid.
138. Reuter from Warsaw, June 21, 1976.
139. AFP from Warsaw, March 6, 1973. The Guardian (London), March 19, 1975.
140. Reuter from Warsaw, April 6, 1975.
141. Richard Davy, The Times (London), October 19, 1973.
142. The Times (London), July 24, 1974.
143. Financial Times (London), December 5, 1975.
144. Statistical Yearbook, GUS (Warsaw), 1976.
145. Zydie Partii (Warsaw), March 1972.
146. Financial Times (London), December 5, 1975.
147. David Lascelles, Financial Times (London), November 28, 1974.
148. Zycie Warszawy (Warsaw), October 23, 1974.
149. Trybuna Ludu (Warsaw), October 23-24, 1974.
150. Kultura (Warsaw), October 26, 1975.
151. Radio Warsaw, November 18, 1975.
152. Argumenty (Warsaw), July 20, 1975.
153. Zycie Gospodarcze, October 21 & 26, 1975.
154. Radio Warsaw, August 17, 1972.
155. Statistical Yearbook, GUS (Warsaw), 1976.
156. Radio Warsaw, April 2, 1975.
157. Radio Warsaw, January 4, 1976.
158. Statistical Yearbook, GUS (Warsaw), 1975.
159. David Lascelles, Financial Times (London), December 5, 1975.
160. David Jones, The Times (London), June 6, 1973.
161. Polityka (Warsaw), February 20, 1971.
162. Journal of Commerce (New York), May 5, 1975.
163. Financial Times (London), September 2, 1975.
164. Annual Register World Events (London), 1975.
165. PAP from Warsaw, September 28, 1975.
166. Journal of Commerce (New York), March 27, 1975.
167. Zycie Gospodarcze, (Warsaw), April 20, 1975.
168. PAP from Warsaw, July 29, 1929.
169. Reuter from Warsaw, September 15, 1975.
170. Trybuna Ludu (Warsaw), December 13, 1973.
171. Gospodarka Planowa (Warsaw), April 1975.
172. Wlodzimierz Brus, The Economics and Politics of Socialism (London: Boston, Routledge & Kegan Paul, 1973).

173. Robert W. Dean, "Ideology and Pragmatism in Gierek's Poland," RFE Research Poland 2, (Munich), January 21, 1974.
174. Polski Problem, no. 1 (Warsaw: PIW, 1972).

CHAPTER 5

1. Robert W. Dean & Robert R. King, East European Perspectives on European Security and Cooperation (New York: Praeger Publishers, 1974).
2. Kultura (Warsaw), June 25, 1972.
3. Wieslaw Gornicki, Zycie Warszawy, June 18-19, 1972.
4. J. Szczepanski, Zycie Warszawy (Warsaw), June 4, 1970.
5. Neal Asherson, "Poland's place in Europe," World Today (London), December 1969.
6. Ryszard Wojna, Zycie Warszawy (Warsaw), January 17-18, 1971.
7. Adam Bromke, Polish Foreign Policy in the 1970's from Gierek's Poland ed. A. Bromke and John W. Strong (New York: Praeger Publishers, 1973).
8. Zycie Literackie (Krakow), September 9, 1972.
9. Trybuna Ludu (Warsaw), February 8, 1971.
10. Neue Zurcher Zeitung (Zurich), May 15, 1973.
11. Stevan Zivanovic, despatch to the BBC from Belgrade.
12. Trybuna Ludu (Warsaw), December 21, 1970.
13. Krajowa Agencja Informacyjna (Warsaw), May 31, 1972.
14. Annual Register of World Events, (London), 1972.
15. Dan Van der Vat, despatch to the BBC from Bonn, March 12, 1975.
16. Suddeutsche Zeitung (Munich), June 11, 1976.
17. Trybuna Ludu (Warsaw), June 12, 1976.
18. Trybuna Ludu (Warsaw), June 21, 1973.
19. ADN from East Berlin, June 20, 1973; also Robert W. Dean, "Polish Visit to GDR: New Impetus," RFE Research Poland 12, (Munich), June 26, 1973.
20. Despatch to the BBC from Warsaw, May 31, 1972.
21. Noel Clark, Despatch to the BBC from Warsaw, June 1, 1972.
22. Baltimore Sun, October 14, 1974.
23. Trybuna Ludu (Warsaw), October 10, 1974.
24. Washington Post, October 14, 1974.
25. Polityka (Warsaw), April 8, 1972.
26. Jonathan Steele, The Guardian (London), June 17, 1975.
27. PAP from Warsaw, June 17-20, 1975.
28. PAP from Warsaw, October 15, 1976.
29. Stefan Olszowski in interview with Noel Clark in his despatch to the BBC from Warsaw, July 11, 1975.

30.   Interview given to the BBC Polish Section, December 14, 1976.
31.   Trybuna Ludu (Warsaw), May 30, 1974.
32.   Wojsko Ludowe (Warsaw), May 1972.
33.   The Times (London), April 1, 1977.
34.   The Times (London), June 16, 1977.

                              CHAPTER 6

1.   Financial Times (London), December 5, 1975.
2.   Hella Pick, The Guardian (London), December 10, 1975. Thomas E. Heneghan, "Poland on the Eve of the seventh Party Congress," RFE Research Background Report Poland 168 (Munich), December 3, 1975.
3.   Trybuna Ludu (Warsaw), December 9, 1975.
4.   Ibid, December 10, 1975.
5.   David Lascelles, "Comecon", Financial Times (London), 1976.
6.   Ibid.

                              CHAPTER 7

1.   Trybuna Ludu (Warsaw), December 20, 1975.
2.   Reuter from Warsaw, January 11, 1976; DPA from Warsaw, January 13, 1976.
3.   AFP and DPA from Warsaw, December 15, 1975.
4.   AFP from Warsaw, December 16, 1975.
5.   Reuter from Warsaw, December 19, 1975.
6.   Polish text from Episcopate's Press Office.
7.   AFP from Warsaw, April 18, 1976. Financial Times (London), April 22, 1976.
8.   Noel Clark, despatch to the BBC from Vienna, March 24, 1976.
9.   Richard Davy, The Times (London), May 5, 1976.
10.   Trybuna Ludu (Warsaw), April 29, 1976.
11.   Hansjakob Stehle, "The Independent Satellite," Pall Mall (London), 1965.
12.   Information Catholique Internationale (Paris), April 15, 1976.
13.   Polish Text from Episcopate's Press Office.

                              CHAPTER 8

1.   Trybuna Ludu (Warsaw), December 9, 1975.

CHAPTER 9

General sources:

Reuter, DPA, AFP, UPI, AP from Warsaw, June 24-30, 1976; Christopher Bobinski from Warsaw in the Financial Times (London); Peter Osmos, Herald Tribune (Paris); The Times (London); Manuel Lucbert, Le Monde (Paris); H. Bader in Frankfurter Allgemeine Zeitung from Warsaw; my own interviews in Poland

1.   Trybuna Ludu (Warsaw), June 25, 1976.
2.   PAP from Warsaw, June 24, 1976.
3.   Reuter from Warsaw, June 25, 1976.
4.   BBC Monitoring, June 26, 1976.
5.   Radio Warsaw, June 28, 1976.
6.   Trybuna Ludu (Warsaw), July 1, 1976.
7.   Zycie Partii (Warsaw), June 1976.
8.   Trybuna Ludu (Warsaw), July 6, 1976.
9.   "The Situation in Poland: A Special Study," European Trade Unions Confederation (Brussels), October 1976.
10. PAP from Warsaw, November 19, 1976.
11. ANSA (Rome), July 19, 1976.
12. UPI from Rome, July 20, 1976. l'Unita (Rome), July 22, 1976.
13. Radio Warsaw, September 4, 1976.
14. Trybuna Ludu (Warsaw), October 10, 1976.
15. Polish text from Episcopate's Press Office.
16. Polish text from the Primate's Press Office.
17. Trybuna Ludu (Warsaw), September 23, 1976.
18. Chris Cviic, "Poland: The Shape of Socialism," presented on Radio 4 in the series Analysis, December 16, 1976.
19. Alex Pravda, New Statesman (London), August 13, 1976.
20. Thomas E. Heneghan, "The Loyal Opposition: Party Programmes and Church Response in Poland", RFE Research (Munich) February 28, 1977.
21. Le Monde (Paris), October 13, 1976.
22. Trybuna Ludu (Warsaw), October 15, 1976.
23. RFE Research, Poland 40 (Munich), November 29, 1976.
24. Reuter and DPA from Warsaw, November 20, 1976.
25. Reuter from Warsaw, November 28, 1976.
26. Reuter from Warsaw, December 4, 1976.
27. Trybuna Ludu (Warsaw), December 13, 1976.
28. Thomas E. Heneghan. "Civil Rights Dissent Spreads in Eastern Europe", RFE Research (Munich), January 28, 1977.
29. Reuter from Warsaw, January 6 & 30, 1977.
30. Reuter from Warsaw, January 16, 1977.
31. Trybuna Ludu (Warsaw), February 4, 1977.

CHAPTER 10

1. David Lascelles, Financial Times (London), June 29, 1976.
2. Thomas E. Heneghan, "The Summer Storm in Poland," RFE Research Background Report 176 (Munich), August 16, 1976.
3. Nowe Drogi (Warsaw), January 1975.
4. Trybuna Ludu March 29, 1976 and April 9, 1976.
5. International Herald Tribune (Paris), July 2, 1976.
6. David Lascelles, "Comecon," Financial Times (London), 1976.
7. PAP from Warsaw, February 28, 1975.

CHAPTER 12

1. The Times (London), editorial, July 17, 1976.
2. The Times (London), November 26, 1976.

CHAPTER 13

1. Trybuna Ludu (Warsaw), November 18, 1976.
2. Ibid., January 20, 1977.
3. Manuel Lucbert, Le Monde January 27, 1977.

CHAPTER 14

1. Richard Davy, The Times (London), November 26, 1977.
2. Neal Asherson, The Observer (London), June 27, 1976.
3. The Economist (London), January 15, 1977.

CHAPTER 15

1. Trybuna Ludu (Warsaw), April 15, 1977. DPA from Warsaw, April 15, 1977.
2. Ibid., April 26, 1977.
3. Zycie Warszawy (Warsaw), May 5, 1977.
4. Le Point (Paris), May 31, 1977.
5. Reuter and DPA from Warsaw, April 25, 1977.
6. Reuter from Warsaw, March 18, 1977.

7.   BBC Survey of World Broadcasts, SWB EE 5516/B/1, September 20, 1977.
8.   Sztandar Mlodych (Warsaw), April 20, 1977.
9.   Zycie Warszawy (Warsaw), April 18, 1977.
10. Adam Michnik, "The New Evolutionism", Survey (London), 1977.
11. David Sells, BBC filmed "Newsday" report, May 25, 1977.
12. Reuter and DPA from Warsaw, May 4, 1977.
13. Reuter from Warsaw, May 17, 1977.
14. AP from Warsaw, May 19, 1977.
15. H. Bader from Warsaw, Frankfurter Allgemeine Zeitung, May 7, 1977.
16. Polish text from Episcopate's Press Office.
17. Neal Asherson, The Observer, August 7, 1977. Michael Dobbs, The New York Sunday Times, September 25, 1977.
18. Washington Post, June 10, 1977.
19. Trybuna Ludu (Warsaw), July 1, 1977.
20. Reuter & DPA from Warsaw, July 25, 1977.
21. Vatican Radio in English, July 18-19, 1977.
22. SWB BBC EE/5627/B/3, September 29, 1977.
23. Trybuna Ludu (Warsaw), September 22, 1977.
24. SWB BBC EE/5528/C/1, June 2, 1977.
25. Trybuna Ludu (Warsaw), June 8-9, 1977.
26. SWB BBC EE/5644/B/4, October 19, 1977.
27. PAP from Warsaw, August 8, 1977.
28. SWB BBC EE/5664/B/3, November 11, 1977.
29. Trybuna Ludu (Warsaw), October 8, 1977.
30. Trybuna Ludu (Warsaw), January 17, 1977.
31. SWB BBC EE/5653/1 and EE/5653/C/3, October 29, 1977.
32. Trybuna Ludu (Warsaw), May 31, 1977.
33. SWB BBC EE/5616/AL/1, September 16, 1977.
34. A. Werblan & Prof. Z Rybicki, "Historical Place of Socialist Democracy," Ideologia i Polityka (Warsaw) September 4, 1977.
35. PAP from Warsaw, October 29, 1977. Warsaw Radio & TV, September 29-30, 1977.
36. Reuter from Warsaw, November 7, 1977.
37. Polish text from Episcopate's Press Office.
38. Vatican Radio, February 5, 1978.
39. William F. Robinson, "Whither Dissent in Poland," RFE Research Background Report 101 (Munich), May 26, 1978.
40. Polish text, issue no. 1, October 1977.
41. KSS/KOR Polish text (Warsaw), October 10, 1978.
42. Jacek Kuron, "Reflections on a Programme of Action," Polish text.
43. ZDF West German second TV channel, August 31, 1978.
44. Christopher Bobinski, despatch to the BBC from Warsaw, January 11, 1978. Trybuna Ludu (Warsaw), January 9-11, 1978.

45. SWB BBC EE/5926/B/2, September 26, 1978; PAP in English, September 22, 1978.
46. Trybuna Ludu (Warsaw), December 14, 1978.
47. Christopher Bobinski, despatch to the BBC from Warsaw, April 10, 1978; my interview in Krakow, November 1978.
48. Polish text from Episcopate's Press Office.

CHAPTER 16

1. For full biography see this author's John Paul II: A Man from Krakow (London: Weidenfeld and Nicholson, 1979); see also The Pope in Poland (Munich: Radio Free Europe Research, 1979).
2. PAP from Warsaw, October 17, 1978. SWB BBC EE/5946/A1/a, October 19, 1978.
3. Trybuna Ludu (Warsaw), October 20, 1978; SWB BBC EE/5948/A1/5, October 21, 1978.
4. Vatican Radio, October 23, 1978. SWB BBC EE/5951/A1/1, October 25, 1978.
5. SWB BBC EE/5977/1, November 24, 1978.
6. Reuter and UPI from Warsaw December 20, 1978 and Polish text.
7. SWB BBC EE/5949/1, October 23, 1978.
8. Richard Davy, The Times (London), November 2, 1978.
9. Radio Warsaw, January 24, 1979.
10. Reuter from Warsaw, February 2, 1979.
11. Tygodnik Powszechny, Krakow, February 12, 1978.

CHAPTER 17

1. Richard Davy, The Times (London), April 1, 1977.
2. Ibid.
3. J.F. Brown, "Hungary and Poland Twenty Years Ago; Thoughts in Retrospect," RFE Research Background Report 207 (Munich), April 1, 1977.
4. Edward Crankshaw, The Observer (London), November 13, 1977.
5. Elliot R. Goodman, "Reflections on the Shifting East-West Balance of Forces", Survey (London), Summer-Autumn 1976.
6. Zbigniew Brzezinski "Comments on East-West Relations" Survey (London), Summer-Autumn 1976.
7. Arrigo Levi, "Eurocommunism and East-West Relations," Survey (London), Summer-Autumn 1976.
8. Robert F. Byrnes, "Soviet American Academic Exchange," Survey (London), Summer Autumn 1976.
9. Edward Crankshaw, The Observer (London), June 19, 1977.

Selected
Bibliography

Annual Register of World Events, Vols. 1969 - 1978. Ivison Macadam and then H.V. Hodson eds., London: Longmans.

Aspects of Contemporary World History. London: 1966.

Association of Polish Students and Graduates in Exile. Dissent in Poland 1976-1977, Reports and Documents in translation. London: Polish Students Association, 1977.

Barnett, Clifford R. et al. Poland, Its People, Its Society, Its Culture. New Haven, Conn.: Hraf Press, 1958.

Barton, Paul. Misere et Revolte de l'Ouvrier Polonais. Paris: Confederation Force Ouvriere, 1971.

Bethell, Nicholas. Gomulka, His Poland and His Communism. Longmans, London: 1969.

Blazynski, George. John Paul II - A Man from Krakow. London: Weidenfeld and Nicholson, 1979.

Bozyk, Pawel. Rozmowy o polityce spoleczno-gospod arczej PRL. Warsaw: Ksiazka i Wiedza, 1973.

_____. Poland's Foreign Trade and Economic Development in the Years 1961-1975 Warsaw: Foreign Trade Research Institute, 1973.

Bromke, Adam. Poland's Politics: Idealism vs. Realism. Cambridge, Mass.: Harvard University Press, 1967.

_____., and Strong, John W., eds. Gierek's Poland, New York: Praeger, 1973.

Bronska Pampuch, Wanda. Polen zwischen Hoffnung und Verzweiflung. Koln: Verlag fur Politik un Wirtschaft, 1958.

Brown,   J.F.   The New Eastern Europe: The Khrushchev Era
and After. New York: Praeger, 1966.

Brus,   Wlodzimierz.   The Economics and Politics of Socialism.
London and Boston: Routledge and Keegan Paul, 1973.

Brzezinski, Zbigniew.   The Soviet Bloc.   Cambridge, Mass.:
Harvard University Press, 1960.

Chrypinski,   Vincent.   The Movement of Progressive Catholics
in Poland. Ann Arbor: University of Michigan Press, 1958.

Davies, Norman.   White Eagle, Red Star.   London: Macdonald,
1972.

Djilas, Milovan.   Conversations with Stalin.   Edited by Rupert
Hart-Davis.   New York: Harcourt-Brace Jovanovich, 1962.

Dziewanowski,   M.K. The   Communist   Party   in   Poland.
Cambridge, Mass.: Harvard University Press, 1959.

Fontaine,   Andre.   History of the Cold War.   London: Secker
and Warburg, 1965.

Gibney, Frank.   The Frozen Revolution.   New York: Farrar,
Strauss and Cudahy, 1959.

Gomulka,   Wladyslaw.   Przemowienia   1956-1959.   Warsaw:
Ksiazka i Wiedza, 1960.

Hiscocks,   Richard.   Poland: Bridge for the Abyss.   Oxford:
Oxford University Press, 1963.

Hotchkiss,   Christina.   Home to Poland Forever.   New   York:
Farrar, Strauss and Cudahy, 1958.

Karski, Jan.   Story of a Secret State.   London: Hodder and
Stoughton, 1945.

King,   Robert   R.   and Dean, Robert W., eds. East European
Perspectives on European Security and Cooperation New York:
Praeger, 1974.

Kolakowski, Leszek.   Der Mensch ohne Alternative.   Munich:
R. Piper and Co., 1960.

Komorowski, Bor T. The Secret Army London: Gollancz, 1950.

Korbonski, Stefan.   Warsaw in Chains London: Allen and
Unwin, 1959.

Lane,   Arthur   Bliss.   I Saw Poland Betrayed.   Indianapolis:
Bobbs-Merrill, 1948.

Lascelles, David.   Comecon London: Financial Times, 1976.

Lewis, Flora.   The   Polish   Volcano.   London: Secker and
Warburg, 1959.

Marsch, Renate. "Bleibende Starke trotz Kommunismus." Herder Korrespondenz. January 1977.

Michnik, Adam. Kosciol, Lewica, Dialog. Paris: Instytut Literacki, 1977.

Mikolajczyk, Stanislaw The Pattern of Soviet Domination. London: Sampson, Low, Marston, 1948.

Montias, John Michael. Central Planning in Poland, New Haven, Conn.: Yale University Press, 1962.

Newman, Bernard. Portrait of Poland. London: Robert Hale, 1959.

Perzanowski, Lucjan, and Kuczmierzcyk, Antoni. Niema chleba bez wolnosci. London: Polonia, 1971.

Poland - a Handbook. Warsaw: Interpress Publishers, 1974.

Polish Problem No. 1 [Polski Problem No. 1] Warsaw: Panstwowy Instytut Wydawniczy (PIW), 1972.

Raina, Peter. Political Opposition in Poland 1954-1977. London: Poets and Painters Press, 1978.

_____. Gomulka. London: Polonia, 1969.

Rakowski, Mieczyslaw F.; Maziarski, J.; Szeliga, Z.; and Zdanowski, H. The Polish Upswing 1971-1975 Warsaw: Interpress Publishers, 1975.

Remington, Alison Robin. The Warsaw Pact. Cambridge, Mass.: Massachusetts Institute of Technology Press, 1971.

Schoepflin, George, ed. The Soviet Union and Eastern Europe. New York: Praeger, 1970.

Secomski, Kazimierz. Premises of the Five Year Plan in Poland, 1956-60. Warsaw: Polonia, 1958.

Sharp, Samuel L. Poland: White Eagle on a Red Field. Cambridge, Mass.: Harvard University Press, 1953.

Skilling, Gordon H. The Governments of Communist Eastern Europe. New York: T. Y. Crowell, 1966.

Steele, Jonathan. Eastern Europe since Stalin. London and Vancouver: David and Charles Newton Abbot, 1974.

Stehle, Hansjakob. The Independent Satellite. London: Pall Mall, 1965.

Stomma, Stanislaw. Mysli o polityce i kulturze Krakow: Znak, 1960.

Syrop, Konrad. Spring in October. London: Weidenfeld and Nicholson, 1957.

_____ . Poland between the Hammer and the Anvil.   London: Robert Hale, 1968.

Szczepanski, Jan. Polish Society. New York: Random House,
1970.

Wacowska, Ewa. Rewolta Szczecinska i jej znaczenie.   Paris:
Instytut Literacki, 1971.

Woods, William. Poland - Eagle in the East. London: Andre
Deutsch, 1969.

Wyszynski, Stefan. A Strong Man Armed   London: Geoffrey
Chapman, 1966.

Zinner,   Paul.   National Communism and Popular Revolt in
Eastern Europe. New York: Columbia University Press, 1956.

Index

Baluta, Jan (Chairman, Strike
  Committee Szczecin shipyards
  January 1971), 45
Baranczak, Stanislaw (poet and
  critic), CDW, on, 277
"new wave" in literature, 154
Barcikowski, Kazimierz
  (Deputy PB member, former
  Minister of Agriculture), 26-
  7
"Citizens Tribune", on, 161
Barecki, Jozef (editor-in-chief,
  Trybuna Ludu),
paper's objective, 163
Beck, Jozef (prewar Polish
  Foreign Minister, died 1944),
  330
Belveder Palace, xv-xvi
Benefits and allowances:
 farmers' benefits, 189-90,
  332-3
increases, 7, 257-8, 286
Berliet, 197
Berlinguer, Enrico (First Sec-
  retary CC Italian Communist
  Party), 237, 269
Bernard, Henri, Colonel (or-
  ganizer of resistance groups
  in Belgium during the war,
  professor of military history
  at the Belgian Military
  Academy):
Gierek in Belgium, 79-80
Bienkowski, Wladyslaw (former
  Minister of Education):
constitutional reforms, on,
  245
June 1976, 280-81
Bierezin, Jacek (young poet),
  155-156
Bierut, Boleslaw (former Pres-
  ident of Poland, PB member,
  CC general secretary, died
  1956), xv
Gierek on, 351
"Bloody Thursday," 15-18
Bonarski (young writer), 152
Brandt, Willy (Chairman of
  SDP West Germany), 220-
  21, 334,

Brezhnev, Leonid (General
  Secretary CC Soviet Com-
  munist Party, President of
  U.S.S.R), xviii, 21
Gierek, relations with, 216-
  17
British-American-Soviet
  Alliance, xii
British-Polish Relations, 232-33
Brother (unofficial opposition
  paper), 342-43
Bukowski, Jerzy (professor,
  Warsaw Polytechnic), 144
Bulhak, Jan (prewar Polish
  photographer), 153-54
Bundestag, 220, 222-23

C.C. (Central Committee):
administrative reforms, 130-31
changes in, 154, 311
constitution amendments, 245
economic plans 1976-80, 125
economy, 4-5
first TV and radio report on
  plenum, 53
8th plenum October 1956, xv-
  xvi
6th plenum 1970, 8-9
7th plenum 1970, 22
8th plenum February 1971,
  52
plenum September 1971, 7
plenum December 1976, 124-
  125
plenum October 1977, 332
plenum December 1978, 348-49
C.C.T.U. (Central Council of
  Trade Unions), 135-141
C.D.W. (Committee for the
  Defence of Workers), 275-
  80, 317
arrests, 322-325
formation of, 274-75
harassment, 322
C.D.U., 223
C.I.C. (Catholic Intelligentsia
  Club), 288
C.S.C.E. (Conference on
  Security and Cooperation in
  Europe), 238-39

About the
Author

George Blazynski, diplomat, writer, political commentator, and broadcaster, was born in Poland. Except for the period 1952-1955, when as senior editor in the Polish desk of Radio Free Europe, he was responsible for all political commentaries and reporting on international conferences, he has been working, since 1950, for the BBC, writing and broadcasting on Polish and world communist affairs and chairing regular discussions with British, American, French, German, Italian, and Belgian journalists on topical international events.

He was for some years in charge of Polish programs transmitted to Poland and then became assistant head of the Central European Service, supervising broadcasts to Czechoslovakia, Hungary, Poland, and Finland. Retired from the BBC in 1976, Mr. Blazynski is the author of the first British biography of the new pope, John Paul II - A Man from Krakow, and a regular contributor to the Annual Register of World Events. Some of his broadcast comments were reprinted in the British, German, French, Austrian, and Japanese press.

Pergamon Policy Studies